MW00465995

Glen Canyon
and the
San Juan Country

Gary Topping

University of Idaho Press
Moscow, Idaho
1997

Copyright © 1997 The University of Idaho Press
Published by the University of Idaho Press
Moscow, Idaho 83844-1107
Printed in the United States of America
All rights reserved

97 98 99 00 01   1 2 3 4 5

Library in Congress Cataloging-in-Publication Data

Topping, Gary, 1941–
    Glen Canyon and the San Juan country / Gary Topping.
      p.   cm.
    Includes bibliographical references (p.   ) and index.
    ISBN 0-89301-204-1 (alk. paper)
    1. Glen Canyon Region (Utah and Ariz.)—History.
    2. San Juan River Valley (Colo.–Utah)—History.   I. Title.
    F832.G5T67   1997
    979.2'59—dc21   96-50298
                                        CIP

Jacket photos by Gus Scott.

Printed on recycled paper using soy based inks.

For Dick Sprang

Contents

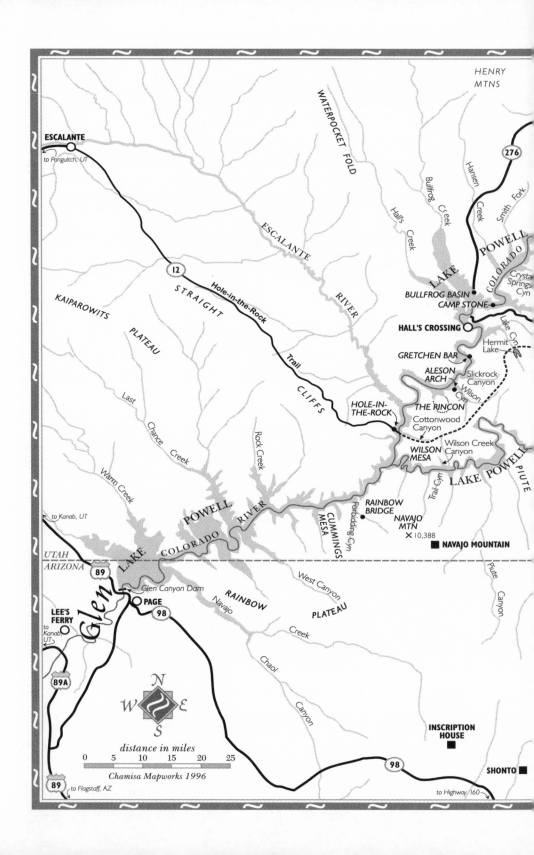

HENRY
MTNS

ESCALANTE
to Panguitch, UT

276

WATERPOCKET FOLD

Bullfrog Creek

Hansen Creek

Smith Fork

ESCALANTE RIVER

Hall's Creek

12

Hole-in-the-Rock

STRAIGHT

KAIPAROWITS

PLATEAU

Trail

CLIFFS

LAKE

COLORADO

Crystal
Springs
Cyn

BULLFROG BASIN

CAMP STONE

HALL'S CROSSING

Lake Cyn

Hermit
Lake

GRETCHEN BAR

ALESON
ARCH

Slickrock
Canyon

Wilson
Cyn

THE RINCON

HOLE-IN-
THE-ROCK

Cottonwood
Canyon

Wilson Creek
Canyon

Last

Chance

Creek

Rock Creek

WILSON
MESA

Trail Cyn

LAKE POWELL

PIUTE

Warm Creek

to Kanab, UT

POWELL

LAKE

COLORADO

RIVER

CUMMINGS
MESA

Forbidding Cyn

RAINBOW
BRIDGE

NAVAJO
MTN

✕ 10,388

■ NAVAJO MOUNTAIN

Piute

Canyon

UTAH
ARIZONA

89

Glen Canyon Dam

RAINBOW

West Canyon

LEE'S
FERRY
to Kanab, UT

Glen

PAGE

98

Navajo

PLATEAU

Creek

89A

Chaol

Canyon

INSCRIPTION
HOUSE ■

N
W E
S

distance in miles

0   5   10   15   20   25

Chamisa Mapworks 1996

89
to Flagstaff, AZ

98

SHONTO ■

to Highway 160

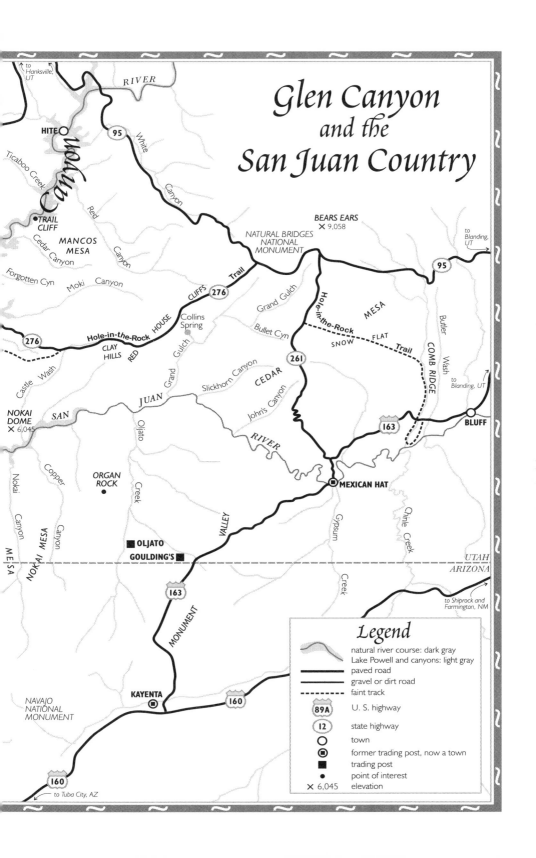

Acknowledgments

Only another author can understand the number and variety of debts one incurs during a project such as this, and also the frustration one experiences in trying to corral them where they can be acknowledged. I am keenly aware that the following list falls far short of exhaustiveness, and I can only hope that those deserving people whose names I have omitted will forgive the frailties of my memory and accept my thanks under a blanket acknowledgment.

My interest in the history of Glen Canyon and the San Juan country developed while exploring the country itself, and during the course of my research and writing, I embraced the happy obligation to corroborate my archival research by field investigations. While many of those explorations were solitary trips of as much as a week at a time, on others I enjoyed the company of my son Danny and various friends whose canyon country expertise and savoir faire in outdoor living greatly enriched my knowledge and enjoyment. Whether wandering down Moki Canyon with Harvey Leake or Stan Jones, drifting down the river with Gus and Sandra Scott, four-wheeling out in the Lost Cowboy country with Dick Sprang, or trotting over Mancos Mesa to the joyful jangling of Eric Bayles's packhorse bells, our conversations ranged widely and freely, but they always returned to our common passion for the history of that region, and I was an eager student.

It was originally planned that the name of Harvey Leake would share the title page with mine, and some of Harvey's prose in fact appears in the chapter on Charles L. Bernheimer. Harvey's heritage as a great-grandson of John and Louisa Wetherill gave me immediate access to sources and traditions I would otherwise have missed. But the pressures of other obligations soon forced him to step back into the role of research assistant. In addition to sharing his exhaustive bibliographic knowledge and offering critiques of chapter drafts, Harvey assumed the responsibility of researching the massive Otis

Marston collection at the Huntington Library. Harvey's brother Stanley Leake rendered vitally important assistance in procuring copies of Herbert E. Gregory's field notes and correspondence from the United States Geological Survey records in Denver and at the Bernice Bishop Museum in Honolulu. Betty Anderson helped me with research in the papers of Charles L. Bernheimer and Richard Wetherill at the American Museum of Natural History in New York City, and Nancy Warner pursued some of my interests during her research on Alice Eastwood at the California Academy of Sciences.

Doris Valle, an immensely talented writer and Indian trader in Mexican Hat, Utah (now retired in Albuquerque), extended an open invitation to me to share her home and her favorite canyons, which I happily accepted on countless occasions. On my winter pack trips with Eric Bayles, we enjoyed the company of Wayne Black and Navajo cowboys Julian and Henry Wilson and Leonard Begay.

I would like to thank the reference staffs at the various libraries, museums, and archives cited in the bibliography whose materials I have used. They are far too numerous to list individually even if I had remembered to record all their names. Having worked at the reference desk at the Utah State Historical Society for a good portion of my twelve years' employment there, I have a vivid idea of the difficulties of their work, and I commend them for serving me for the most part with cheerfulness and competence.

My longtime friend and editor at the University of Idaho Press, Peggy Pace, continued to believe in me and to solicit something she could publish. I was happy at last to be able to offer this manuscript to her, and I thank her and her production staff for their competence and cooperation.

Harvey Leake read at least one draft of every chapter and saved me from several factual errors. Three other historians of the canyon country read late drafts and made valuable suggestions, most of which I have incorporated. I owe a great debt to them: Professor James Aton of Southern Utah University; retired (but not inactive!) Professor Charles S. Peterson of Utah State University; and my boss for many years, Dr. Melvin T. Smith, former director of the Utah State Historical Society. My colleague Marianna A. Hopkins generously shared her canyon country expertise and in her role as a poet and writing teacher encouraged my occasional lapses into the English language.

A portion of Chapter 10 appeared in *Canyon Legacy* 24 (Summer 1995). Earlier drafts of Chapters 12 and 13 appeared in *Utah Historical Quarterly* 55 (Spring 1987).

I have tried to discharge a very small part of my incalculable debt to Dick Sprang on the dedication page. During the years we spent down in the big canyons it was "morning all day long," as he put it. I wrote this book for him.

Introduction

National interest in Glen Canyon emerged during the 1950s as a result of the debate over water storage projects in the upper Colorado River basin, and decisions from that debate led to the flooding of the canyon under the waters of what was later named Lake Powell. Glen Canyon was lost through a choice by the Sierra Club and other conservation organizations to put their efforts into saving Echo Park, which they regarded as savable, from a similar dam and to ignore (and thus sacrifice) Glen Canyon, which they thought they could not effectively defend. As Mark W. T. Harvey points out, there was never an explicit agreement between the Sierra Club and the Bureau of Reclamation to trade Glen Canyon for Echo Park, but the result was the same as if there had been: Defeated at Echo Park, the water engineers turned their eyes to an alternative site that the conservationists had chosen not to defend.[1] The sacrifice of Glen Canyon in other words was a sin of omission by conservationists rather than a sin of commission by the Bureau of Reclamation.

But it was a sin to conservationists nevertheless, as the Sierra Club admitted in 1963 when it published its first book, Eliot Porter's *The Place No One Knew: Glen Canyon on the Colorado*.[2] There was a grim solipsism in the title, as historian C. Gregory Crampton, himself the author of no less than six books on Glen Canyon by that time, pointed out in an interview just before his death. "It may have been the place the *Sierra Club* didn't know," he chuckled, but that did not mean it was unknown.[3] As scholars from a variety of disciplines mounted a massive study of the region during the 1950s anticipating creation of the dam, they learned to their astonishment, as archaeologists Jesse D. Jennings and Floyd W. Sharrock reported, "that *anyone* could and has lived in this hostile country."[4] In fact, the Sierra Club did know the place, or at least many individual members did, even if the club itself chose not to acknowledge the canyon. Prominent Sierra Clubbers like Randall Henderson, Francis Farquhar, and Wallace Stegner, along with many less celebrated members, had enjoyed river trips, horseback rides, and hikes in the Glen Canyon region during the 1930s and 1940s. And there were thousands of others who enjoyed the same experiences, either on their own or as members of professionally guided river or pack trips.

In the larger perspective of history the list can be extended even further. The home of ancient inhabitants for perhaps 11,000 years or more, Glen Canyon was first viewed by white men when the Franciscan missionaries Dominguez and Escalante arrived at the later site of Lee's Ferry in the fall of 1776. There is evidence that fur trappers visited the area during the early 1800s, and by the middle of that century an ever-increasing stream of scientists, adventurers, prospectors, Indian traders, cattlemen, and recreationists had begun to flow in.

As the number of visitors increased, the literature of the canyon grew. To the mysterious rock paintings and carvings of the prehistoric peoples (not literature, but a form of communication) were added travel journals, scientific reports, memoirs, and business records. Paintings, photographs, and movies made vain attempts to express the visual drama of the canyon. Nor did the literary flow cease after the flooding of the canyon, for scientific studies, reminiscences, and other sources have continued to appear. As a result, the modern historian of "the place no one knew" finds himself presented with such a bewildering array of material that he almost despairs of mastering it all.

Perhaps it is the vastness of that literature that has prevented previous scholars from attempting a comprehensive synthesis of Glen Canyon history. Although there are numerous biographies of people important in the region, and detailed histories of various expeditions and themes, only the redoubtable C. Gregory Crampton attempted before this study to grasp that history as a whole. At the beginning and conclusion of his federally funded preinundation survey of historical sites in Glen Canyon and the lower San Juan River, Crampton published brief syntheses of his knowledge. His *Outline History of the Glen Canyon Region, 1776–1922* (1959) sketched the larger historical context within which the specific sites he proposed to study could be interpreted; and his *Standing Up Country: The Canyon Lands of Utah and Arizona* (1964) offered a thoroughly researched text and dozens of vivid photographs summarizing his knowledge for a popular audience.[5] While neither volume accomplished what I have attempted here, they were trailblazing enterprises that have been my inspiration.

The reader needs to understand the geographical and chronological scope of my research and the principles I have followed in choosing what to include and to emphasize. Draw an isosceles triangle beginning with a line from Hite, Utah, to Mexican Hat and form the other two sides by following the Colorado and San Juan Rivers from those two points southwestward to their confluence. The area within that triangle is my central interest. It includes most of the land flooded by Lake Powell and a vast unsettled backcountry in between. Historian P. T. Reilly, reflecting its popular image, calls that backcountry "the unknown triangle." Although I think this book shows that triangle to be no more unknown than Glen Canyon proper, it is a happy term, for while much of it falls within the Glen Canyon National Recreation Area and some of it is at this writing under study for wilderness designation, it is one of the most rarely visited parts of the Colorado Plateau. Compared with places like Arches or Canyonlands National Parks, it is indeed a blank place on the map in most people's minds.

Realizing that the history of that triangle is integrally related to much of the adjacent region, my scope includes the northern Navajo country south of the San Juan to Kayenta, Arizona, and west through the mighty Tsegi canyons to Rainbow Bridge. To a much lesser degree, I have tried to include some of the country to the north of Glen Canyon, at least the Escalante River and Kaiparowits Plateau. Although these geographic limits are admittedly somewhat idiosyncratic, I nevertheless believe they define a historically integral region.

Because there is no comprehensive term denoting the entire area (the National Park Service uses the term "Glen Canyon National Recreation Area" even though it includes the northern drainage of the lower San Juan River) I have used the terms "Glen Canyon" and "the San Juan country" almost interchangeably to designate not only specific canyons but the entire region as well. I hope the context will make my meaning clear in all cases.

Chronological limits are somewhat more definite and logical. The narrative proper begins with a brief summary of the original inhabitants, the date of whose arrival is necessarily indefinite, but perhaps extends well before the Christian era. While I sketch some post–Lake Powell developments, the effective terminal date is March 13, 1963, when workers closed off the bypass tunnels at the Glen Canyon Dam, causing the reservoir to begin to fill. The old rivers continue even today to flow within their channels for considerable distances before being deadened by the slack waters of Lake Powell, but the history that centered on those rivers effectively ended on that day.

In addition to those geographical and chronological boundaries, this study exists within certain intellectual ones as well. The history of this region contains extraordinarily rich material for examining one of the primary human circumstances: the place of Man in Nature. Man acts upon Nature, and Nature in turn acts upon Man. I have sought evidence documenting both of those forces. Rich in economic opportunity, scientific interest, and scenic beauty, Glen Canyon invited human activity, and the San Juan canyon only slightly less so. But not everyone who was lured to the region responded positively. While Harry Aleson told his tourist clients that Glen Canyon is a friendly canyon, and John Wetherill said, "the desert will take care of you," others came to gloomier assessments. P. T. Reilly has calculated that of the fifty documented fatalities on the Colorado River from Cataract Canyon through the Grand Canyon from 1869 to 1969, no less than fifteen occurred in Glen Canyon and at Lee's Ferry.[6] Charles Kelly, as seen in chapter 13, apparently hated and feared Glen Canyon and applauded its flooding. So the relationship between Man and Nature in this region was as varied and complex as human personality itself, and I believe its history opens a wide window upon the human condition and the world we mysterious humans inhabit.

This book is both a synthesis and an original contribution to knowledge. Where sound studies of relevant themes and people exist, I have based my narrative on them. Those studies are often much more lengthy and detailed than my narrative, so my footnotes and bibliography not only happily acknowledge my debt to my predecessors but also guide future students seeking additional detail and knowledge. My debt to other scholars is particularly acute at the points where I trespass into fields remote from my own, such as geology and anthropology, where I am at some pains to disclaim having attempted any original contributions. On the other hand, there are vast areas in the history of this region that have never felt the bite of the scholar's spade, and I have joyfully pressed out onto those frontiers.

NOTES

1. Mark W. T. Harvey, "Echo Park, Glen Canyon, and the Postwar Wilderness Movement," *Pacific Historical Review* 60 (February 1991): 43–67. This point is also one of the minor theses of his *A Symbol of Wilderness: Echo Park and the American Conservation Movement* (Albuquerque: University of New Mexico Press, 1994).

2. San Francisco: Sierra Club, 1963.

3. C. Gregory Crampton, interview with Jay M. Haymond, November 15–17, 1994, 58, Utah State Historical Society.

4. Jesse D. Jennings and Floyd W. Sharrock, "The Glen Canyon: A Multi-discipline Project," *Utah Historical Quarterly* 33 (Winter 1965): 39.

5. Crampton, *Outline History of the Glen Canyon Region, 1776–1922*, University of Utah Anthropological Paper No. 42 (Salt Lake City: University of Utah Press, 1959); *Standing Up Country: The Canyon Lands of Utah and Arizona* (New York: Alfred A. Knopf, 1964).

6. P. T. Reilly, "How Deadly Is Big Red?" *Utah Historical Quarterly* 37 (Spring 1969): 259. Reilly failed to tabulate the 1932 death of prospector Sam Gates at Hite, which brings the Glen Canyon–Lee's Ferry total to sixteen—equal to the number of Grand Canyon deaths for the period. See Chapter 13 below. Also, the reader should note that Reilly himself has never maintained that Glen Canyon was a gloomy or unfriendly place. I am pointing out simply that those who died or suffered other misfortunes there substantiate a darker view of the canyon, and Reilly's statistics call attention to the fact that travel through Glen Canyon posed considerable risk.

The Nature of the Country

"A lot of rocks, a lot of sand, more rocks, more sand, and wind to blow it away."[1] Scientific reports before and since 1938 have added a good deal of sophisticated nomenclature to this cowboy's description of the rugged country west of the Clay Hills recorded by geologist Herbert E. Gregory in that year, but it remains, in its vigorous directness, a valid characterization of much of Glen Canyon and the San Juan country.

The topography of that region is similar to the rest of the Colorado Plateau province, of which it is a part, with the patterns of flora and fauna that go with a desert environment. It is a desert not from simple lack of water, but rather from a colossal maldistribution of water, for two mighty rivers—the Colorado and the San Juan—flow through it. The larger of the two rivers is the Colorado, which made its gentle course through Glen Canyon, an area of legendary beauty and majesty. The San Juan is much smaller in volume, but more turbulent in its course, as its gradient is steeper than the Colorado River through the Grand Canyon. Whereas Glen Canyon had few rapids worthy of the name, the San Juan had a half dozen, with many smaller riffles. Both rivers would swell immensely in the spring, as highland snowmelt augmented their volume and turned them a silty brown—"too thick to drink, too thin to plow," as the old proverb has it, or "liquid mud," as Gregory called the discharge of the San Juan River during dry years.[2] Much of both rivers is now lost to view, however, as they flow silently in the depths of their own watery grave formed by the Lake Powell reservoir. They reappear only occasionally, in low-water years when the reservoir partly recedes, and during spring runoff, when the silty discharge of the old river marks the Colorado's course beneath the clear reservoir water as far downstream as the Hite, Utah, marina.

Away from the rivers it is a dry country. There are infrequent springs, generally in the tributary canyons of the rivers. Where such water exists, and along the rivers, the canyon floors are often unforgettably beautiful, shaded with spreading cottonwood trees and decorated by the blossoms of datura and monkey flowers. Otherwise, on the plateau tops, Gregory's sand, rock, and wind description usually holds true, with vegetation dominated by sagebrush, small cacti, and other small desert brushes and grasses. Yet, even there, springtime often brings mallows, columbine, Indian paintbrush, and other wildflowers to punctuate the sandy expanses.

There is considerable faunal variety, though numbers are limited, and one commonly encounters only small birds like cliff swallows and doves, and small lizards. Vultures are common, too, as are ravens and various raptors, and bats almost always whiz above one's evening campfire. Larger mammals are present but rarely seen. Coyotes are sometimes audible at night, and deer will occasionally startle the unobservant hiker by bolting from a cover of underbrush. Much more rarely, one can see a bighorn sheep, evidently vastly reduced in number since the coming of the white man, for depictions of them dominate prehistoric petroglyph panels. Beaver were once common, too, until the reservoir drowned so much of their habitat that they have had to move up into the side canyons. Even at that, they still flourish in localized areas like lower Moki Canyon just above the reservoir headwaters, where a succession of immense dams provides a serious obstacle to hikers and horsemen. Cha Canyon, a southern tributary of the San Juan River, means "Beaver Canyon" in the Navajo language, and the Glen Canyon tributary today known as Crystal Springs Canyon was first named Beaver Canyon for the many dams along its course.

The major geological differences between the San Juan country and the rest of the Colorado Plateau are that the former presents only a limited portion of the spectrum of geological strata that occur throughout the province, and that it is, to a considerable degree, rougher country. Roughness—and beauty—are recurring themes among the first impressions recorded by visitors to the San Juan country. Gregory again, on the topography of the area west of the Clay Hills: "It is a region of bare rock towers, alcoves, arches, and deep vertical-walled grooves—the roughest country seen in the plateau province." And Hugh D. Miser, on the area around the mouth of Grand Gulch, which "presents some of the wildest scenery along the San Juan. It is a dark narrow canyon, with vertical red walls several hundred feet in height, at whose base lie heaps of huge boulders and great piles of driftwood."[3]

Rough, but beautiful, and not at all forbidding. There is, to be sure, a Forbidding Canyon west of Navajo Mountain, but it acquired that ominous name only when the 1921 Charles L. Bernheimer party found that drop-offs in its watercourse blocked horseback access to Rainbow Bridge; previously it was known blandly as West Canyon.[4]

No, Glen Canyon was a friendly canyon, as river guide Harry Aleson used to stress when introducing the place to his customers. It is a theme eloquently elaborated by his off-season river partner Dick Sprang:

> . . . to seek secluded communion with nature's wonders, and finding there untouched and unspoiled by man a warm and intimate scenery where humans could feel at home with their primitive origins—indeed where prehistoric Indians had lived for century upon century, and you sense why they had lived there. For the river in Glen Canyon is serene. You feel at home among the sunny bars, the green willows, caves and ferny glens, protected by magnificent yet broadly separated walls of orange and buff sandstone below which in the Pioneer [mining claim] area the grey-green and purple Chinle formation form[s] folded hills near the river, with Navajo sandstone domes rising above far in the distance.[5]

It is not that the country is devoid of perils; far from it. Almost one-third of all river fatalities calculated by P. T. Reilly (fifteen out of fifty) during the first one hundred years of boat travel on the Colorado River (1869–1969) occurred on the placid waters of Glen Canyon. "I ain't afraid of the river, and I hope you ain't, but man, I respect it!" the old riverman Art Greene emphasized. "You gotta respect it or the goddamn son of a bitch will GET YA!" Sprang, who spent over a decade running Glen Canyon in the fall, knew the river's other face as well:

> Now there's been a lot of malarky written about the river in Glen Canyon being such a placid stream that you could turn your kids loose at Hite and they'd wind up at Lee's Ferry perfectly safe. Well, don't believe it. . . . The current on the Col-

orado River is never a gentle thing. It's very deceptive. On a placid stretch of river, it looks like Sunday afternoon on a park pond. Well, it's not. It can be difficult and it can be very, very strong. The Colorado in Glen always found a channel through the broad areas of the river where many underwater sandbars existed. You really had to be on your toes and a darn good water reader in low water stages to find the channel through that morass of barely-below-the-surface sand bars, and when you did find that channel the river was swift in there and extremely powerful.[6]

Even in the fall, when the river lost its silty opacity and reflected the deep blue of the sky, it was never clear enough to see underwater obstacles dangerously close to the surface, and the boatman had to watch for the swell of a rock that could snag his boat while the on-rushing river capsized it. And neophyte boatmen soon learned, when facing the shore as they drifted along, to keep their downstream oar out of the water. If that oar became lodged in a shallow invisible sandbar, a heavily loaded boat could ride up over the top and break it. Thus the advisability of an extra oar or two. The San Juan River, with its much swifter current and bigger rapids, offers even greater perils to the poorly prepared, and overland travel likewise: a failed fuel pump, a broken spring, a punctured radiator can spell disaster. But backcountry living anywhere in the world offers certain risks that require proper preparation, and those of the San Juan country, while different in nature from other types of terrain, are not necessarily different in degree.

In fact, for the properly prepared traveler it is the very perils of the desert that make possible its keen pleasures. Deftly navigating through a rapid or executing a graceful landing where all one's boat-handling skills come together harmoniously brings a unique delight. For the motorist equipped with four-wheel drive, extra food, fuel, water, and camping gear, and skilled in the use of shovel and jack, even the inevitable bogging down in loose sand or mud can be seen as an opportunity for joyful triumph over adversity.

Nowhere is this kind of experience described more memorably than in historian Frank McNitt's narrative of his 1961 automotive replication of the route of Col. John M. Washington's Navajo country reconnaissance in 1849. Driving a heavily laden Land Rover nicknamed the Beast for its rough ride, McNitt and the trader John Arrington encountered an immense rainstorm between Mexican Water and Dinnehotso that turned what had been a road into "a darkening and deepening plain of water and gluey adobe." Not surprisingly, they became stuck:

> Not far above Many Farms—the headlights on, the windshield muddied and visibility about ten feet—the road dropped away beneath us, and we fell into a branch of the Chinle Wash. For two hundred yards, perhaps, The Beast, now lost and beaten, followed the wash and then, with a sucking sound, sank. We sank to the floorboards in red, oozy clay which could have been quicksand, but happily was more like liquid cement.

The pair pulled out their camping gear and waded to higher ground. In the dim light of soggy morning, Arrington discovered a tarantula excavating a burrow beneath the spot where he had thrown down his bedroll. Some Navajos happened along soon and helped them dismantle an abandoned hogan. After four hours' hard labor they fashioned an escape route for the Beast out of timbers and rocks. "I do not believe," McNitt related, "that Colonel Washington's artillerymen, at any point of crossing Washington Pass, opened their palms with larger blisters." (Gloves ought to be a part of one's emergency outfit!) Eventually the camaraderie of shared adversity brought them to a happy ending. Hosteen Harrison, one of the helpful Navajos, lived some six miles to the south, and McNitt and Arrington gladly accompanied him to his hogan. "Here we left him," McNitt reminisced, "surrounded by small children and several dogs, he speeding us on our way with the gift of two melons and a newspaper bundle of meat-filled corncakes, each wrapped in corn husks."[7]

Like the rest of the Colorado Plateau, the geology of the San Juan country is almost exclusively sedimentary, with sandstones and shales predominating, and limestone playing a lesser role. The most common formations range from the Cedar Mesa, (of Permian age) conspicuously exposed in the Hite area, White Canyon, and Grand Gulch, to the much younger Navajo (of Jurassic age), which exists almost continuously throughout the area, perhaps most conspicuously in the Navajo Mountain region, where it has formed the most celebrated feature of the canyon country, Rainbow Bridge. Both older and younger formations are locally exposed, but it is this middle range of strata that gives the country its main character.

As Gregory conceived the geologic history of the Colorado Plateau, much of it at one time contained the full range of geologic systems, from Carboniferous to Tertiary, though not every formation, of course, was everywhere present. During the eons since that original deposition, erosion has been insistently active, so that some geologic series have been completely washed away in some localities (if they ever in fact existed there), and others cut into deeply. This process has left, in the San Juan country, a series of large plateaus with an average elevation of about 5,500 feet above sea level. The uneven effects of erosion have left many mesas and buttes extending above that level, while watercourses have cut deep canyons far below it.

The varied topography of the region, Gregory pointed out, is impossible to grasp from any single vantage point. Standing atop the Kaiparowits Plateau and looking along its surface, for example, one can only see the rims of the canyons that drain the mesa, and they appear only as "insignificant breaks in a horizontal sky line," concealing both their number and size. "Even Glen Canyon," he continues, "appears from a distance as a narrow groove in a broad expanse of flat land." Try to traverse that apparently flat expanse, however, and its true ruggedness quickly becomes apparent. In the vicinity of Canaan Peak on the Kaiparowits, he reported, "the heads of 14 canyons were crossed in a distance of about 3 miles."[8] Nor can that ruggedness be totally grasped from within the canyons. The famous meanders called the Goosenecks of the San Juan are so remarkable that the State of Utah has established a state park on their north rim, from which vantage point their famous convolutions have been captured on innumerable snapshots and picture postcards. Yet when one is on the river—even the fast-flowing San Juan—one is scarcely aware of the radical changes of direction in the river's course. Finally, the vast scale of the region taken as a whole tends to obscure its lesser dramas so that, as Gregory puts it once again, "features in the landscape unnoticed here would be prominent and picturesque landmarks in other surroundings."[9] This, then, is the basic structure of the San Juan country.

There is no point in duplicating the geological treatises of Gregory and Miser here,[10] except to call attention to significant features of specific formations that affect human life in the area. In the Cedar

Mesa sandstone, for example, one finds a scenically spectacular off-white rock covered with black tapestry streaks and containing immense arches like the Natural Bridges in the White Canyon system, which have drawn droves of visitors since their discovery in the late nineteenth century. Perhaps equally important, though, is the fact that the Cedar Mesa sandstone erodes into horizontal "biscuits," as Gregory called them, providing in some places several levels of terraces ideal for human shelter. Those abundant shelters in White Canyon and Grand Gulch, the two most extensive canyons in the Cedar Mesa, attracted large, though dispersed, populations during the entire Anasazi era, from Basketmaker to Pueblo.

Above the Cedar Mesa and below the Glen Canyon group, one finds mainly dark red or varicolored beds of Permian and Triassic shales and conglomerates that contrast dramatically with the bright Cedar Mesa sandstone. These strata are important in human terms for several reasons. For one thing, they are visually appealing, from the fluted columns of the Organ Rock member, to the rippled walls of the Moencopi, to the kaleidoscopic colors of the Chinle memorably exposed at Clay Hills Pass in hues of purple, green, yellow, and red. For another, these formations can present formidable barriers to travel in wet weather, at which time they become masses of slick clay. Although Clay Hills Pass presented the only practical way of descending the Red Rock Plateau for the Hole-in-the-Rock party of Mormon pioneers in 1880, building a road through the gooey Chinle shale in midwinter was no small chore, and even the modern paved highway through the pass tends toward sliding off into the canyon. Lastly, some of those formations contain valuable metals like copper and uranium, and the now dilapidated roads carved through that country during the uranium rush of the early 1950s offer in many places the only access for motorized vehicles.

The Glen Canyon group of Jurassic sandstone formations—the Wingate, the Kayenta, and the Navajo—are visible virtually everywhere in the San Juan country. The somber Wingate, whose dark red rock erodes into steep cliffs sometimes hundreds of feet high, provides some of the country's most majestic scenery, especially where the underlying Chinle is exposed below it in long, multicolored slopes. It is also the region's most implacable barrier to travel, with its sheer drop-offs that ordinarily have to be bypassed. The rare trails through the Wingate depend on fortuitous cracks through which one can clamber, or huge sand slopes that bridge the drop from canyon rim to floor.

The Kayenta is generally a thinner layer than the Navajo and Wingate between which it occurs. Also dark, with a maroon-gray cast, the Kayenta is harder than either Navajo or Wingate, and thus more resistant to erosion; many a Wingate cliff is maintained in its precipitous state by its Kayenta cap. The historic importance of the Kayenta is its erosional form, which gives way to narrow benches. Those benches rarely provided shelter for human habitation, but they frequently were useful for trails; the trails in both Wilson Creek and Bridge Canyons, on a historic tourist route from Blanding, Utah, to Rainbow Bridge, depend heavily in places on the Kayenta bench.

The buff-colored Navajo sandstone, which sits atop much of the San Juan country, erodes to natural arches like Rainbow Bridge, and to large, gently sloping domes. Its scenic beauty accounts for some of the most memorable vistas in the region, and its deep canyons with their domed rims also feature caves that the Anasazi found hospitable. Travel over and around the Navajo domes is arduous, but often possible by avoiding the steeper pitches and seeking sandy flats with which they are occasionally interspersed. Some stretches of the Navajo, however, like Nasja Mesa northwest of Navajo Mountain, are rugged slickrock jumbles that repel the hardiest traveler.

Although sandstones and shales dominate the San Juan country geology, other types of rock are worth mentioning. Limestone plays a role, for example, in the composition of some types of shale, adding its gray hues, for example, to the Chinle kaleidoscope. Lenses of limestone occur in the Cedar Mesa and other sandstones. Where those lenses appear on the surface, cowboys learn to avoid them, particularly in wet weather or while running their horses, for the limestone is considerably harder than sandstone, and even the hard metal beads welded onto their horseshoes for traction will not penetrate it, and ugly spills can result.

Igneous rock plays a minor but dramatic role in the San Juan country. There is no extrusive igneous rock—lava fields where volcanic eruptions have reached the surface and cooled—in the San Juan country as there is in other parts of the Colorado Plateau, most significantly, perhaps, as the caps of the Hopi Mesas. In the San Juan country the igneous rock is intrusive: lava that boiled up beneath overlying sandstone strata without breaking through the surface. These intrusive deposits take two basic forms. One is volcanic necks like Agathla Peak north of Kayenta, where a dramatic black spire remains after erosion has removed the sandstone that once surrounded it, or long vertical veins of lava like the Porras dikes northeast of Kayenta, similarly formed. These necks and dikes, like Shiprock in New Mexico, form famous landmarks often visible at a great distance.

The other form of intrusive lava is the laccolith, where igneous rock has been forced beneath overlying sandstone strata to form a dome. All the mountains in or visible from the San Juan country are of this type of formation: Navajo Mountain, Carrizo Mountain, the Abajos, the Henrys.[11]

Legends of precious metals have played a role in the history of the San Juan country, though the legends have run considerably in advance of extractable quantities. The prospectors Mitchell and Merrick supposedly ventured too close to the Navajos' wealthy Pish-la-kai silver deposit and paid for it with their lives near the buttes that bear their names in Monument Valley. Rumors of Rocky Mountain gold trapped in the sandy bottoms of "nature's sluice box"—placid Glen Canyon and the San Juan River—were more substantial, and brought successive waves of miners in the decades around the turn of the century. The gold was there, but in such finely ground form that its extraction eluded technology, as engineer Robert Brewster Stanton and his backers learned expensively in the Hoskaninni Mining Company venture of 1898–1901. More successful were individual miners like Cass Hite, who worked placer deposits in the banks of tributaries like Ticaboo Creek, which were much shorter drainages than the Colorado and San Juan Rivers and thus did not grind the gold so finely. For years Hite derived his income from what he punningly called the Bank of Ticaboo, withdrawing gold as his meager expenses necessitated.[12]

Much of the interest of the San Juan country comes not from the geological regularity of its sedimentary sequences, but rather from the great traumas past and present that add variety, drama, and in some cases, danger. Primary among those traumas is the great upheaval at the end of the Cretaceous era that introduced the flexing and folding that often causes the broken ends of strata to point skyward. Passing across such folds—known as monoclines, anticlines, or synclines, depending on the direction of the fold—one feels as though the world were standing on end. Comb Ridge, the Nokai Dome, the Waterpocket Fold—some of the region's most dramatic features—are all results of this flexing.

The extreme temperature range of the region, which reaches well over one hundred degrees Fahrenheit and plunges below zero, lends a drama of its own. In the summer dryness, the traveler's attention is never far diverted from the location of the next water source. The old trails followed watercourses or passed by the infrequent springs. "Off the trail is away from water," Gregory warned.[13]

In the winter, both the San Juan and Colorado Rivers have been known to freeze over completely, making travel across them an easy matter. More commonly, the rivers continue to run, but become choked with ice floes. It is an unforgettably eerie sensation to stand alone beside the San Juan on a still, cold winter day and listen to the hiss of the ice floes sliding past one another. There are stories of them building up around an obstruction like a log jam, then suddenly breaking free. River travel at such times was dangerous and grueling, and thus rarely attempted.[14]

In spite of their extreme temperatures, the harsh seasons of winter and summer have their unique beauty. It is during the intervening seasons of spring and fall, however, that the canyon country is at its friendliest. Spring weather is least dependable of any season, for strong winds and sudden thunderstorms can bring an end to brief stretches of pleasant weather. There are compensations to spring's risks, though, in the plentiful fresh cold water in the canyons as spring runoff subsides, and in the bright green of the new cottonwood leaves that shimmer in the breeze as happy harbingers of summer. For many canyon aficionados, however, fall is the greatest time of year. Mid-October nights can have one shifting to the warmth of a winter bedroll, whereas the daytime sun can require shedding of jackets and sweaters. The autumnal beauties of the canyons would be the despair of even a Monet or a Cezanne, as the russet willow and squawbrush leaves blend with the golden cottonwoods and the livid red perils of the poison oak. And all through the quiet canyons there is a sense of bittersweet endings, of the transitoriness of all things beautiful.

The main dramatic interest in spring and fall is the thunderstorms that build quickly, drop a torrent of rain, then vanish as quickly, often giving way to clear, placid evenings. During the rain, waterfalls appear suddenly in hundreds of places atop the cliffs, often with a dramatic roar. When they subside, they have left over eons of time bold tapestry streaks from minerals carried down from above and leached out of the rock itself. Tapestry Wall in Glen Canyon is the most famous instance of this, where dark streaks plummet hundreds of feet to the riverbank. But such streaks are ubiquitous. In Grand Gulch their blackness contrasts utterly with the white canyon walls, suggesting a demon roofer, while covering the surrounding plateaus, allowed his tar to leak over the edge.

Sudden, heavy thunderstorms on a largely nonporous surface like sandstone spell flash floods. The largest of these have occurred since white habitation, with the overgrazing of soil-holding vegetation by livestock. The carrying power of such floods, which increases by the sixth power of the water's velocity, is astounding: Even small streams can propel rocks the size of bowling balls down their courses, and larger drainages can carry room-size boulders. Long and heavily eroded canyons like Grand Gulch at one time bore the best evidence of flash flood power. The driftwood jam at the mouth of the canyon observed by Hugh Miser was echoed at the narrow slot just below the mouth of Collins Canyon, where a pile of logs extended at least one hundred yards, and logs were jammed into the slot at a depth of twice a man's height. Travelers in such canyons on stormy days are well advised to heed Dick Sprang's warning and keep an ear out for the rumble of "an eight-foot wall of brown foam laced with cotton-wood logs plunging toward you from upcanyon."[15]

Quicksand is a converse phenomenon, where water is unable to drain from a deep bed of sand. The surface is sometimes dry, and tempts the unwitting traveler to step upon it. When he does, he instantly hits bottom or sinks to a level where he "floats" on the thick emulsion. Quicksand in the San Juan country rarely if ever presents the kind of hazard featured in matinee Westerns, where one sinks completely out of sight. "Like the Venus flytrap," Neil Judd's melo-dramatic prose has it, ". . . whose sticky leaves fold down upon the fluttering wings of a careless insect, the quicksands of Moki Canyon patiently wait to embrace the blind or heedless passer-by."[16] Animals, it is true, can die in quicksand as their struggles embed them more and more deeply and starvation or predators kill them. Humans generally find little difficulty in pulling themselves out, and experience nothing more serious than soaked feet and legs. A more serious possibility exists in the forward momentum of a fast stride pulling a muscle or breaking a bone in an entrapped leg.

Rainwater and snowmelt, which swell the Colorado and San Juan Rivers regularly in the spring and intermittently after storms, can cause sandwaves, a unique phenomenon in the silty southwestern rivers. Sandwaves are formed when the silt content of the water exceeds the saturation point and the silt precipitates to form underwater dunes that force the water above them into waves. The waves move slowly upstream in series and often break upstream at their crests like ocean waves. Herbert E. Gregory, a powerful swimmer, once swam through a series of sandwaves to test their depth and relationship to the river bottom. He found that at the crest of the waves, with his head well above the surface, he could touch bottom, but in the troughs, the surface was several feet over his head.[17]

It takes a swift current and a heavy silt content to generate sandwaves, and they were rare in Glen Canyon above the mouth of the San Juan. Below that point, however, where the Colorado picks up the silt of the San Juan, they could occur. The San Juan itself, though, was and still is the primary place for sandwaves, even since the construction of the Navajo Dam in New Mexico during the 1950s, which seriously limits the ferocity and volume of spring runoff.

River runners past and present have flocked to the San Juan in the spring seeking the sandwaves, which give an exhilarating ride. The flexibility of modern inflatable boats enables boatmen to run sandwaves almost any way they choose, but in the old hard-hull boats, the preferred technique was to run them sideways, or beam to. The steep slopes of the waves could capsize a rigid boat if approached bow first, while their relatively rounded crests enable the beam of the boat to slip over them ordinarily without shipping water.[18]

No description of the salient features of the San Juan country would be complete without mention of the winds, which are almost as ubiquitous as the sandstone itself. Winds are particularly insistent during the transitional seasons of spring and fall, when they can blow upcanyon in the afternoon with enough velocity to propel a boat upstream. Sails, in fact, were sometimes used for upriver travel in Glen Canyon, though the winding course of the river and the high cliff walls rendered the winds erratic.

Like other features of the unpredictable climatology of this country, wind can come up unexpectedly. Indian trader Frank H. Hyde perhaps described it best:

> Very often you will pitch camp, hobble your horses out on grass, and go get your supper, put your tarp down and go to bed, perfectly calm, nice weather. There will come up a sand storm, this red sand, it drifts right along the ground, the same as a snowstorm; it might blow all that night, maybe quit before morning; you get up, and the sand is probably an inch deep on your tarp, and the grass you hobbled your horses out on might be buried in it; the next day it might reverse and come the other way, and uncover that grass.[19]

The basic nature of the San Juan country, then, is not radically different from the rest of the Colorado Plateau. The main differences are to be found in the limited range of geological strata, which happen to be those that most observers find to be among the most striking, and the existence of no less than two of the province's mightiest rivers. The contrast between the rivers—the swift San Juan with its sandwaves and rapids and often narrow canyon, and the broad, relatively placid Colorado in Glen Canyon with its majestic walls, its friendly sandbars, and inviting side canyons—offer a wide range of opportunities for explorers, exploiters, and recreationists. And the surrounding plateaus and canyons add their own mixture of prehistoric sites, economic resources, and scenic beauty. Equally challenging, though far less well known than other parts of the Colorado Plateau, the San Juan country disappointed few of the infrequent visitors who chose to make its acquaintance, and there is good reason to expand to the entire region Gregory's tribute to the Kaiparowits Plateau: "For variety and interest of topographic forms no part of the plateau province offers more attractions. Distant and near-by views amply repay the necessary hardships of travel."[20]

NOTES

1. Herbert E. Gregory, *The San Juan Country: A Geographic and Geologic Reconnaissance of Southeastern Utah*, USGS Professional Paper No. 188 (Washington, D.C.: Government Printing Office, 1938), 21.

2. Herbert E. Gregory and Raymond C. Moore, *The Kaiparowits Region: A Geo-*

graphic and Geologic Reconnaissance of Parts of Utah and Arizona, USGS Professional Paper No. 164 (Washington, D.C.: Government Printing Office, 1931), 13. Page 2 makes it clear that this is Gregory's phrase, not Moore's.

3. Ibid., 14; Hugh D. Miser, *The San Juan Canyon, Southeastern Utah: A Geographic and Hydrographic Reconnaissance*, USGS Water Supply Paper No. 538 (Washington, D.C.: Government Printing Office, 1924), 10.

4. Charles L. Bernheimer, *Rainbow Bridge: Circling Navajo Mountain and Explorations in the "Bad Lands" of Southern Utah and Northern Arizona* (Garden City, N.Y.: Doubleday, Page & Co., 1924), 96.

5. "Comments by Richard W. Sprang RE *Chaffin vs. U.S.*," (1965), 3, Milton R. Oman Papers, Utah State Historical Society.

6. P. T. Reilly, "How Deadly Is Big Red?" *Utah Historical Quarterly* 37 (Spring 1969): 250–52; Elizabeth Sprang, *Good-bye River* (Reseda, Calif.: Mojave Books, 1979), 1; Dick Sprang, transcription of recorded statement on Hite, Utah, July 1984, Utah State Historical Society, 40.

7. Frank McNitt, ed., *Navaho Expedition: Journal of a Military Reconnaissance from Santa Fe, New Mexico, to the Navaho Country, Made in 1849 by Lieutenant James H. Simpson* (Norman: University of Oklahoma Press, 1964), xi–xii.

8. Gregory and Moore, *The Kaiparowits Region*, 13.

9. Ibid., 12.

10. Herbert E. Gregory, *The San Juan Country*, and Hugh D. Miser, *The San Juan Canyon*, previously cited, plus Gregory's USGS Water Supply Paper No. 380 and USGS Professional Paper No. 93, all of which are cited and discussed fully in later chapters.

11. On the structure and distribution of igneous rock, see Herbert E. Gregory, *Geology of the Navajo Country*, 83–108. The laccolithic structure of mountains on the Colorado Plateau was the discovery of the great Powell survey geologist, Grove Karl Gilbert, as developed in his *Report on the Geology of the Henry Mountains* (Washington, D.C.: Government Printing Office, 1880). Gilbert's description of the formation of various types of dikes on pp. 28–29 is well illustrated.

12. C. Gregory Crampton, *Standing Up Country: The Canyon Lands of Utah and Arizona* (New York: Alfred A. Knopf, 1964), 120–47, sketches the various mining ventures in Glen Canyon and the San Juan.

13. Gregory, *The San Juan Country*, 4.

14. John Wetherill and Patrick Flattum's upriver trip from Lee's Ferry to Rainbow Bridge in January 1931 was a rare exception, and the joint diary kept by them dramatically illustrates the hazards and discomforts. Even they could not get the redoubtable Wetherill down, though, for his January 15 entry observes that "the hardships we went through only add value to a wonderful experience." [C. Gregory Crampton, ed.], "Early Trip up the Colorado from Lee's Ferry to Rainbow Bridge, January 1931." *Plateau* 34 (October 1961): 33–49.

15. Joseph Wood Krutch, "Lightning Water." In Alan Ternes, ed., *Ants, Indians, and Little Dinosaurs* (New York: Charles Scribner's Sons, 1975), 288–91. Dick Sprang to Gary Topping, January 27, 1983, in possession of the author.

16. Neil M. Judd, "Beyond the Clay Hills," *National Geographic* (March 1924): 294.

17. Hugh D. Miser, *The San Juan Canyon*, 52–55, discusses the formation of sandwaves and reports Gregory's experiment.

18. A good photograph of the celebrated river runner Norman D. Nevills employing this technique is in Alfred M. Bailey, "Desert River Through Navajo Land," *National Geographic* (August 1947): 151. For an account of running sandwaves on the Colorado below the mouth of the San Juan, see Charles Kelly, "Sand Waves," *Arizona Highways* (April 1944): 36–39.

19. Frank H. Hyde testimony, Colorado River Case, Utah State Historical Society.

20. Gregory and Moore, *The Kaiparowits Region*, 14.

Indians of the San Juan Country

The American Indian inhabitants of the San Juan country, which consist of a variety of prehistoric cultures plus the Utes, Paiutes, and Navajos of the historic era, occupy a uniquely important place in the region's history. Not only did all three groups far antedate white occupation of the region, but also their persistence in the area after arrival of the whites contributed an element of cultural diversity that accounts for a large part of its historical interest. Perhaps most important, though, is the fact that the Indians have been almost the only people to occupy the region as permanent inhabitants with a complete sociopolitical structure. Only in rare and isolated instances have Anglos occupied the San Juan country with families and permanent dwellings. With the exception of some few Indian traders and even fewer missionaries, and of tiny, temporary, isolated communities like Hite and White Canyon Cities, the Anglo presence in the region has consisted almost exclusively of transient explorers, scientists, miners, and recreationists—all small, mostly male groups—who arrived, accomplished their business, and left. Even the cowboys who, of the Anglo occupants of the region, had the most long-lasting engagement with the country, lived in sporadically occupied camps and left their families in towns like Bluff and Blanding, on the periphery of the San Juan country. It was the Indians who found in the San Juan country a home. It was a friendly place to them, a place where they could make a life as well as a living. They brought their families, they built permanent dwelling places, and they developed a complete society, demonstrating that the San Juan country was a place to live, not just to visit.

Archaeologists have identified human inhabitants of the American Southwest as early as 10,000 B.C., and some assume a much earlier arrival date, perhaps 30,000 to 40,000 B.C.. Several evolutionary stages are identifiable among these early people: Lithic, whose economy was based entirely on the pursuit of big game like mammoths and bison with stone-tipped spears; Archaic, sometimes called Desert Culture, whose economy included both hunting and gathering wild plants; and the Southwest Formative, which saw the beginning of agriculture.[1] Although sites of these early cultures are present in the San Juan country, the region's archaeological significance comes from its great abundance of sites affiliated with the succeeding culture that developed during the first thirteen centuries of the Christian era: the Anasazi (Navajo: "Ancient Ones" or "Ancient Enemies").

The Anasazi culture developed in two primary stages: Basketmaker, which began well before the Christian era and lasted until about A.D. 750, and Pueblo, from about A.D. 750 to 1300. Each stage is further subdividable into perhaps three additional stages, depending upon which of several popular classification schemes one chooses to follow, and some schemes add a Pueblo IV and V, which follow the culture through its decline and abandonment of the San Juan basin to its present centers on the Hopi Mesas, Zuni, and the Rio Grande.[2] To complicate things further, the Pueblo stage is manifested in at least three geographic phases as well: the Chaco, centered at Chaco Canyon, New Mexico; the northern San Juan, centered at Mesa Verde, Colorado; and Kayenta, centered in the Marsh Pass–Tsegi area of Arizona.[3] The San Juan country exhibits a fairly continuous occupation (though not in all areas) through the entire Anasazi period, but it contains evidence of only the Kayenta and Mesa Verde geographic phases; although Chaco Canyon has emerged in recent research as a cultural center for a vast region of Anasazi settlements, its influence seems not to have significantly reached the San Juan country. More important than any Chacoan influence was a Mesoamerican influence that filtered northward through the contemporaneous Hohokam and Mogollan cultures of Arizona.[4]

Anasazi remains in the San Juan country are almost as ubiquitous as the sandstone itself. Very few indeed are the canyons whose cliffs contain no masonry dwellings, whose walls feature no pictographs, and whose streambeds do not frequently turn up potsherds. Therefore, almost any canyon could serve as a microcosm of Anasazi culture. This chapter, however, focuses on three: Grand Gulch, the homeland of the Basketmakers; the Tsegi, whose immense and prolific ruins were the womb of the Kayenta phase during the Pueblo period; and Glen Canyon, which was a transitional zone between the

Kayenta and the Mesa Verde phases and the related Fremont culture, which flourished north of the Colorado River.[5]

Richard Wetherill's epoch-making Grand Gulch expeditions of 1893–94 and 1897 will be covered in a later chapter, so it will suffice here merely to note that their primary achievement was the discovery of an earlier culture than the cliff dwellers (Pueblo). In a series of breathless letters to his sponsor, Talbot Hyde, and his friend from his Mesa Verde excavations, Gustaf Nordenskiold, Wetherill announced that "we have *discovered a new race to history much older than the cliff dwellers*." The remains were located "under the ruins, three feet below any cliff dweller sign. . . . They had feather cloth and baskets, no pottery—" and ominously, "six of the bodies had stone spear heads in them."[6]

The term "Basketmakers" is somewhat unfortunate, since many cultures make baskets (it was coined by Talbot Hyde simply to distinguish the earlier culture from the Pueblos, who made pottery). The primary cultural features that distinguish the Basketmakers from their predecessors are, in the chronological order of their development, corn, architecture, and finally, experiments with pottery.[7] Cultivation of corn gave the Indians, for the first time in their history, control over a highly nutritious food source and changed them into a largely sedentary culture. With a sedentary economy, permanent habitations became desirable. The Basketmakers developed a semi-subterranean pit house in which a hole in the ground was covered by a system of rafters and a brush and adobe roof, which was extended several feet above the surface of the ground by upright forked poles.[8] The pit house, which evolved from earlier slab-lined subterranean storage cists, evolved in turn to the kiva, the ceremonial chamber of the Pueblo, and thus facilitated both social and religious development. Finally, toward the end of the Basketmaker era, pottery emerged. Although late Basketmaker pottery is crude, it signaled the development of a much more permanent (though fragile) and esthetically expressive artistic medium than had been afforded by either basketry or rock art.[9]

Although Anasazi culture continued to develop in Grand Gulch through the Pueblo stage—it was, after all, the Pueblo cliff houses that had lured Richard Wetherill to the canyon where he went on to discover the Basketmakers—the most significant level of Pueblo development in the San Juan country took place in the Tsegi (Navajo:

"Canyon"), the network of canyons draining the Shonto Plateau into Laguna Creek on the south. While Pueblo remains throughout the San Juan country ordinarily consist of individual, isolated structures like granaries, or small dwelling places designed to house one or at the most a few families, the Tsegi contains the region's only genuine urban developments, large cliff cities rivaled only by Mesa Verde, Canyon de Chelly, and Chaco Canyon.[10] The great ruins of Betatakin, Keet Seel, and, in a tributary of neighboring Navajo Canyon, Inscription House, are the primary features of what is now Navajo National Monument, and represent the heartland of the Kayenta phase of the Pueblo.

Although Navajo National Monument contains evidence of Anasazi occupation as early as the late Basketmaker era, all the great ruins date from the Pueblo III period, roughly the twelfth and thirteenth centuries A.D. Like Mesa Verde and Chaco Canyon, the Kayenta culture of the Tsegi was not an isolated phenomenon, but instead formed the center of a vast cultural network extending as far east as Canyon de Chelly and as far north as Forgotten Canyon on the Colorado River.

Diagnostic features of the Kayenta phase include distinctive masonry and pottery styles. Of the three primary Anasazi masonry styles—Kayenta, Mesa Verde, and Chaco—the Kayenta is physically the weakest and esthetically perhaps the least pleasing to the modern eye. The Chaco style, which consists of rubble-filled double walls faced with carefully chosen and fitted pieces of thin stone, is the strongest and is generally regarded as the most beautiful of the three. The Mesa Verde, however, is a close second on both counts. It consists of thick walls of carefully fitted stones generally thicker than the Chaco style, held together with adobe mortar, and is capable of sustaining great weight and height, as in Mesa Verde's Square Tower and Cliff Palace ruins, both of which have towers several stories high. The Kayenta, by contrast, consists of sloppily fitted stones of irregular size and shape, anchored rather insecurely by copious quantities of mortar. The imperfections of Kayenta masonry are often disguised by a covering of adobe stucco. Even with its imperfections, Kayenta masonry sustains structures of more than one story at each of the primary ruins in Navajo National Monument.[11]

Whatever the shortcomings of Kayenta masonry, they are compensated for dramatically by Kayenta ceramics. Although the corrugated coil and the black-on-white decorative styles of other Pueblo regions are also found in the Kayenta area, the characteristic Kayenta pottery is a striking polychrome, often black on red or black on orange. Although the Mesa Verde, and especially the Chaco black-on-white styles have their devotees, the spectacular color and delicate lines of the Kayenta somewhat suggest the complex and colorful motifs of the popular and expensive ceramics of the modern Rio Grande pueblos.

Writing in 1959 during the Glen Canyon salvage project, archaeologist William Y. Adams observed that in spite of repeated expeditions during the ninety years following the first John Wesley Powell exploration, Glen Canyon remained the most poorly understood archaeological district in the canyon country.[12] Adams pointed out that the lack of systematic and cumulative results from those parties had been attributed to the canyon's vastness and remoteness. Though one must agree with Adams that those obstacles should have spurred scientists into a heightened resolve to do whatever they could intensively rather than superficially exploiting myriad previously worked sites, one can nevertheless appreciate the magnitude of the problem. Both Grand Gulch and the Tsegi offer problems enough for the archaeologist, but they are models of geographic compactness when compared with Glen Canyon, with its 170 miles of river and countless miles of side canyons, most of which were utilized by the Anasazis. One might observe further that even in spite of the voluminous reports compiled by the Glen Canyon survey, Glen Canyon will always remain largely unknown, for the constraints of time and funds—always the great frustrations of American archaeology— placed severe limits on the thoroughness and extensiveness of investigation. Making a virtue of necessity, Jesse D. Jennings reported that the Glen Canyon project forced the development of new excavation techniques in which the camel's hair brush and the trowel yielded much of the time to the garden spade and wheelbarrow.[13]

Glen Canyon archaeologists agree that the region was a cultural transition zone during the Pueblo era. Basketmaker sites, with the exceptions of Moki Canyon and one site in a tributary of Navajo Canyon, were nonexistent. Instead, during the demographic and cultural development of the Pueblo period, Glen Canyon became a sort of Anasazi frontier in which colonization from both Kayenta and Mesa Verde regions occurred. Pottery and masonry styles from both areas occur in Glen Canyon, but the dividing line between spheres of influence was drawn somewhere between Moki and Forgotten Canyons. In that context, Forgotten is of considerable archaeological interest: Its ruins, including Defiance House, are constructed in the Kayenta style, but the pottery is heavily Mesa Verde.[14]

If done circumspectly, some conclusions can be made regarding Anasazi culture by observing that of their descendants, the modern Pueblo Indians. The necessity for circumspection is worth emphasizing, both because anthropologists are uncertain exactly which modern Pueblos are descended from which Anasazi, and also because the approximately 200 elapsed years between the abandonment of the Anasazi country and the first white contact no doubt saw considerable cultural change: During 200 years, Anasazi culture developed from Pueblo I to Pueblo III, for example.

Nevertheless it seems reasonable to deduce, as does Jennings, that the Anasazi of the region of this study were remarkably adaptable and creative exploiters of very slim natural resources.[15] Besides introducing their domesticated corn and squash whose cobs and rinds litter many of their dwellings to this day, the Anasazi apparently domesticated the prickly pear cactus, harvested many other wild plants, and supplemented their vegetarian diet with occasional kills of rabbits, bighorn sheep, and deer. Their domestic turkeys, whose bulbous shape and footprints are depicted in many pictographs, were evidently not used for food, as the first Spanish explorers who visited the Rio Grande pueblos observed to their amazement. Besides weaving turkey feathers into warm robes, the Anasazis fashioned religious devices from them, and the resulting sacredness of the birds was poignantly exhibited in the spectacle of Pueblo Indians fleeing Spanish attacks with turkeys in their arms—their most indispensable possession.[16]

Like their modern descendants, the people themselves were organized into "sober, egalitarian societies, built upon principles of harmony among themselves and with the spirits of their universe," whose intensely group-centered ethos alternated between field work and "ceaseless rounds of inherited ceremonials to propitiate [those] ruling spirits." The kiva, an ordinarily round but sometimes square subterranean chamber found in most Anasazi villages of any size, was the center of male social, religious, and political life. Community leaders had primarily religious functions, eschewing secular affairs so painstakingly that the culture was quite vulnerable to the schismatic effects of internal dissension. Although generally peace loving, the society could mobilize an effective citizen militia against external threats, and recent research has increased our awareness of the disturbing frequency and violent nature of such conflicts, which may even have included cannibalism.[17]

What happened to the Anasazis? It is the most vexed question of southwestern archaeology. The two most popular answers have been conflict with later arrivals like the Utes, Paiutes, and perhaps even the Navajos, who historically have been more aggressive than the Pueblo peoples, and prolonged drought, which destroyed their agricultural economy. While later invaders may have preyed upon some of the small, isolated pueblos, they were, as explained below, too few in number and impoverished at the time the Anasazis abandoned the San Juan country to have been a significant agent in that movement.

Drought is currently the favored explanation. Paleoecological studies have demonstrated a prolonged and severe drought from A.D. 1130 to 1190 throughout the entire San Juan basin. Although the hoarding of nonperishable food sources like corn against the inevitable drought years was a primary enterprise of Anasazi agriculture, as demonstrated by the widespread presence of tiny granaries on little rock ledges in almost every canyon, such supplies were necessarily limited. Sixty years—an entire lifetime—of inadequate rainfall to sustain the level of agricultural production necessary to support the by then large Anasazi population would have been more than enough to require drastic measures. Accordingly, archaeologists believe the Anasazis undertook long-distance migrations to areas in the south and east where fresh starts could be made. Those in the San Juan country and as far east as Canyon de Chelly moved to the Hopi Mesas of northern Arizona, while those at Mesa Verde and Chaco Canyon went to the Rio Grande in northern New Mexico.[18]

The history of the American Indian during the nineteenth and twentieth centuries is a tragic tale of encroachment, conflict, and cultural destruction. No aspect of that history is more tragic than that of the San Juan Paiutes, for whom constant conflict with the Hopis, the Navajos, the Southern Utes, and the white cattlemen, miners, and settlers led to population decline, dispossession, and eventual reservation confinement. In the mid-nineteenth century, the San Juan country was Paiute country; by the mid-twentieth century, the

Paiutes were virtually extinct south of the San Juan River, while a remnant of the tribe maintained a precarious existence on the White Mesa Ute Reservation, a tiny fraction of the territory over which they had once roamed.

There are several Southern Paiute tribal communities that enjoy widely varying levels of internal cohesion and federal recognition. Some Southern Paiute bands, like the Moapas, Las Vegas, and Chemehuevis of southern Nevada and southeastern California, live on large reservations and have a well-organized tribal structure. Others, like the so-called five bands in southwestern Utah, have been artificially reconstituted as the Paiute Tribe of Utah after having been individually "terminated" as tribal entities by the federal government during the 1950s. The San Juan Paiutes, whose traditional homeland ranged from Monument Valley west to the Little Colorado, and from the San Juan River on the north to Black Mesa and the Moencopi Plateau on the south, now live outside the boundaries of the area of this study, as noted above, on a reservation created in 1923 in the Allen Canyon-White Mesa area west and south of Blanding, Utah. The so-called White Mesa Utes, of which they are a part, are not a tribe, but rather a polyglot group of San Juan Paiutes. They include Southern Utes, who historically refused to live on the Southern Ute Reservation in southwestern Colorado, and some few Navajos who have chosen, for whatever reasons, to live with them.[19]

The origin of the Paiutes and other Numic-speaking cultures is a controversial topic among anthropologists. There is some agreement that the Numic-speakers evolved from earlier cultures in the Mojave Desert, spreading eastward and northward from there, but the chronology of this development is still being debated, with dates as early as 10,000 years ago and as recent as 3,000 years ago.[20] Either date would allow us to assume, with a reasonable expansion rate, that the Paiutes probably arrived in the San Juan country at some time during the Anasazi occupation and coexisted with the earlier occupants until the Anasazis left.

At the time of earliest white contact in the late eighteenth century, there appear to have been two major bands of San Juan Paiutes. One lived in the Willow Spring area near Moencopi and modern Tuba City, and the other in the Navajo Mountain area, particularly Piute Canyon (this older spelling persists in geographic names). From these bases, the Indians ranged widely, as far as House Rock Valley and the San Francisco Peaks to the northwest and southwest, and Elk Ridge and the Abajo Mountains on the northeast and Ute Mountain on the east. By the late nineteenth century, retreating from encroachment and conflict with the Hopis and Navajos, the locus of tribal life shifted to the area of Douglas Mesa, Oljato, and Monument Valley in the east. In addition, a significant number of Paiutes began spending most of their time north of the San Juan, where they could hunt (both wild game and white men's cattle) in the Abajos and on Elk Ridge in the summer, and live off the largesse of Mormon settlers at Bluff and Montezuma Creek (and later Blanding and Monticello) during the winter. Disgruntled Utes and occasionally Navajos gradually and erratically left reservation life to join the Paiutes in the mountains north of the San Juan River.

The traditional sociopolitical structure of the Southern Paiutes was highly informal, personal, and temporary—characteristics conspicuously observable during the historical period. Society was egalitarian, rather than hierarchical, and the basic social unit was the family; most larger social ties were based on the extended family. Tribal government was extremely limited and simple, consisting of a council of elders composed of adult members of the tribe, both men and women, and an informally selected leader whose tenure was often lengthy, but whose authority was very limited, primarily moral rather than coercive. Government was thus not a conspicuous part of Paiute daily existence, and tended rather to emerge periodically during moments of crisis.[21]

The Paiute economy changed significantly during the historical period. Traditionally, the people were hunters and collectors who followed deer, antelope, and bighorn sheep while gathering various wild plants. Farming was practiced, but only occasionally and inefficiently to supplement temporarily meager supplies of wild foods. By the beginning of the twentieth century, farming became the fundamental economic base of the Paiutes as wild game disappeared in response to Navajo overhunting and competition from Navajo livestock. Complex irrigation works at Willow Spring and Piute Canyon attest to this change. Later, the Paiutes learned grazing from the Navajos as farmland diminished through encroachment by Navajos south of the San Juan and whites north of the river.

Although there were conflicts with the Hopis in the Moencopi area, the greatest destructive force on Paiute culture was encroach-

ment by Navajos and whites. Navajo-Paiute contact was minimal before the mid-nineteenth century, but members of the two tribes
were thrown together during Kit Carson's Navajo campaign in the
1860s. A significant number of Navajos under the leadership of
Hoskininni fled the marauding white army to Navajo Mountain, correctly assuming the soldiers would not regard it worth the trouble
and risk to ferret them out of the tangled canyons of the Rainbow
Plateau.[22] During the Bosque Redondo incarceration of the Navajo
majority, 1864–68, Hoskininni's Navajos settled in with the Paiutes,
and although they moved out after the return of the rest of the tribe
from exile, many Navajos moved into the area south and west of
Navajo Mountain, preferring independence in that wild region to life
on the new reservation.

The postexile demographic and economic recovery of the Navajos
was dramatic: During the last half of the nineteenth century, the
tribe's population doubled to 20,000, and it has continued with few
setbacks to its late-twentieth-century level of well over 150,000,
making them by far the largest American Indian tribe. Although
Paiute oral recollections are definite that by 1900 no Navajos had yet
moved into the Navajo Mountain area, encroachment proceeded
rapidly after that date. By the late 1930s, the population of Navajos at
Navajo Mountain had grown from zero to 135, while the Paiute population had remained stable at 42, and the Navajo herds numbered
twice as many as those of the Paiutes. For the Paiutes, the Navajos
were burdensome neighbors whose flocks, as mentioned above, destroyed the wild game grazing areas and cut off access to the Shonto
Plateau, where the Paiutes had seasonally moved their livestock. To
make desperate matters even worse, around the turn of the century a
significant number of Willow Spring Paiutes moved to Navajo
Mountain, overtaxing the agricultural productivity of the area and
forcing many of the resident Paiutes eastward to Oljato and Douglas
Mesa. Even there they were not to find peace. A vivid illustration of
the degree of Navajo encroachment as early as 1906 is found in the
story of the establishment that year of the Wetherill-Colville trading
post at Oljato. Although Oljato was squarely in the midst of traditional Paiute country, it was the Navajo headmen Hoskininni and his
son Hoskininni-begay who at first resisted the traders, then finally allowed them to settle.[23]

The arrival of white settlers north of the San Juan in the area of

McElmo and Montezuma Creeks in 1878 and 1880 offered a new opportunity for the Paiutes, but new perils as well. The opportunity existed in the missionary orientation of the Mormons (the expedition was officially called the San Juan mission), which prompted them to feed the hungry Indians in spite of their own meager food supply and in the fact that the whites had cattle which the Indians could surreptitiously butcher. The settlers had different ideas of land use from those of the Indians, a conflict as old as Indian-white contact itself. The whites practiced intensive land use in farms and livestock, whereas the Indians practiced extensive use, ranging far and wide to harvest wild plants and animals.

There was a fundamental tension in the San Juan Mormons' expectations of the Indians that led eventually to tragedy. The Mormons felt a missionary obligation to feed and convert the Indians, but conversion and coexistence depended on the Indians' willingness to adopt the Mormon way of life, and the Indians generally refused to do so. This Mormon assumption that coexistence depended upon civilizing the Indian came out in the testimonies of two Mormons during the debate over possible removal of the Indians from San Juan County in 1908. One was Albert R. Lyman:

> I think it would be a great benefit to the stockmen to have [the Indians] removed, but the Indians have always been here and belong here. Within the last two years many of them have become workers. I think a school should be established in this county for their children. I believe if a school was established at or near Bluff the Indian children could be induced to attend it.

And the other was J. P. Nielsen:

> In some respects they are an advantage, in others a disadvantage. They are a roving band with no fixed place of residence and accumulate no property. They work for the whites in building ditches, etc. and the women do washing and cleaning. On the whole I think it would be better if they could be put on the reservation and their children be kept in school and taught something of civilization.[24]

The Mormons were increasingly frustrated at the Indians' refusal to become what the Mormons wanted them to be and at their persistence in begging, thievery, and other petty harassment.

The Mormons were not the only frustrated whites. Large non-Mormon cattle outfits had preceded the Mormon settlers in grazing their herds in the Abajo Mountains and on Elk Ridge, as well as in the area from Montezuma Creek eastward into Colorado, and the Paiutes in all of these regions often stole their animals. The non-Mormon cowboys had none of the missionary impulse of their Mormon neighbors, and did not shrink from retaliation. Perhaps the most celebrated instance of such retaliation began at Montezuma Creek in 1884 when a Paiute tried to steal a cowboy's horse, whereupon a skirmish broke out that left two cowboys wounded, two Indians dead, and precipitated a general wave of horse thievery by the remaining Indians. A motley Colorado posse consisting of soldiers from Fort Lewis and outraged cattlemen pursued the Indians west as far as White Canyon. At the site known today as Soldier Crossing, gunfire from the Indians pinned down the posse and killed two of its members, "one named Wormington who was a packer and Scout and a cattle man named James Higgins from Bromleys on the Mancos."[25]

Trouble with the Paiutes and their occasional Ute collaborators became so violent by 1888 that the federal government passed a law providing for the white abandonment of virtually the entirety of San Juan County north of the San Juan River to create an immense tract of individual land allotments for the Southern Utes and Paiutes. This act was passed in response to three impulses. One was the new Dawes Act of 1887, which encouraged elimination of reservations in favor of such individual allotments. Another was a request, which many later suspected of having been extorted, from the Indians for such a tract in Utah. Finally, many whites in southern Colorado believed that moving the Indians into San Juan County and settling the claims of the few non-Mormon cattlemen there would be much less costly than continuing the increasingly frequent and costly altercations between the Indians and the growing white population in Colorado.[26]

Colorado cattlemen and Mormon settlers joined forces in supporting the measure, the former hoping to get rid of the Indians, and the latter hoping to get rid of the troublesome Gentile cattlemen in Utah.[27] Glen Canyon gold miners, however, protested the action because the proposed reservation included the left bank of the Colorado River where many of them had potentially profitable mining claims that they had developed at considerable trouble and expense in equipment.[28]

Although Congress had passed the measure, protests against it were compelling enough that it was never put into effect. In 1895 it was rescinded, primarily because the Mormon settlers reversed themselves after having received permission from church authorities to move out of the unproductive Bluff area and onto White Mesa. Instead, the Paiute problem was resolved, or so it was hoped, by enrolling them and the other renegades at the Southern Ute Agency in Colorado, where they could receive government support.[29]

Enrolling them there and keeping them there were two different matters. For one thing, living in Utah was better than life on the reservation, for the Indians were free to roam as they pleased, and the generosity of the Mormons, whether freely proffered or unintentionally given in the form of untended cattle, suited the Indians' taste better than the government provisions. As noted, this was appealing even to some of the reservation Utes, who periodically joined the Paiutes in Utah. Also, the Paiutes generally did not get along well with the reservation Utes and were not welcome there. In spite of the government provisions, life on the reservation was rough, and the Utes were not enthusiastic about sharing its meager resources with their distant cousins, the Paiutes. "I do not want to live on the reservation," reported Paiute John Benow from his Montezuma Creek home in 1908, "because the Indians there are stingy of their grass and water and for the farther [*sic*] reason that the medicine men make bad medicine. I am afraid they will kill me."[30]

So friction between the whites and the Paiutes continued, and the history of San Juan County is a story of sporadic encounters and harassments until two major episodes in 1915 and 1923 forced a definite resolution. In February 1915, one of the renegade Indians[31] named Tse-ne-gat (Anglicized as Everett Hatch) allegedly killed a Mexican sheepherder named Juan Chacon. Local authorities attempted to arrest him, but found the band of Indians too strong and unwilling to submit one of their number to white man's justice.[32] A U.S. marshal at Salt Lake City, Aquila Nebeker, was summoned for assistance, but he, too, proved unable, in spite of a pitched battle near Bluff, to subdue the Indians and make an arrest. The Paiutes wisely retreated to Navajo Mountain, where they knew the whites would deem it impossible, or at least too costly, to chase them out of the maze of tangled canyons on the Rainbow Plateau. Things had quickly reached desperate proportions.

Having exhausted their local resources, Utah authorities, in their frustration and embarrassment, turned to the U.S. Army, and summoned Gen. Hugh Lenox Scott from Fort Myer, Virginia. It was a fortunate turn of events for both sides. Although a military man, Scott had a reputation for skill in peaceful mediation in Indian-white hostilities, a reputation that was fresh in San Juan country memories after his defusing of a potential Navajo war at Beautiful Mountain, an eastern peak of the Lukachukai Mountains in western New Mexico in the fall of 1913. There Scott had narrowly avoided a bloody conflict between federal troops and a large Navajo force under a medicine man named Bi-joshii by skillful diplomacy and trust built between himself and Bi-joshii.[33]

Scott quickly received approval for the venture, and with two subordinates boarded a train for Utah. Before doing so, however, he wired the Navajo agent at Shiprock to ask Bi-joshii to meet him at Bluff in order to vouch for his trustworthiness to the Paiutes. As things turned out, Bi-joshii was less help than the traders John and Louisa Wetherill, who had been living and trading in Paiute country for almost a decade and had built the knowledge and trust of the Paiutes that Scott needed.[34]

John Wetherill met Scott at Bluff, Utah, and informed him that he and Louisa and another trader, Arthur H. Spencer of Mexican Hat, were trying to find a Paiute to take a message out to Navajo Mountain, inviting the Indians to meet Scott at Spencer's trading post. After several days the Wetherills succeeded, and Scott was able to persuade Tse-ne-gat and three other Paiutes to submit to arrest and trial at Denver. The soldiers and Indians journeyed to Salt Lake City together by automobile, where they were greeted enthusiastically by various civic groups, and the Indians went on to Denver. Louisa Wetherill, firmly convinced of Tse-ne-gat's innocence, rounded up various witnesses in his behalf, and even journeyed to Denver to testify at the trial. As things turned out, the case against Tse-ne-gat was flimsy enough that acquittal came easily.

The apparent peace that resulted from Tse-ne-gat's acquittal turned out to be shaky, and in fact sowed more ill will than good among the white settlers in San Juan County. Most felt, for one thing, frustration in their opinion that justice had not been done by the Denver jury. Tse-ne-gat was a handsome and charismatic person whose journey to Salt Lake City and Denver had been almost a triumphal tour, and many San Juan settlers suspected that he had duped both press and jury with a "noble Indian" image. And support of Tse-ne-gat by the Indian Rights Association, whom many San Juan residents regarded as outside meddlers, fanned the flames of their hard feelings even further. Historian Charles Kelly, though no friend of the Mormons, captured their frustration well in observing that Tse-ne-gat "became the object of so much attention from sob sisters lamenting the plight of the poor Indian that he considered himself a hero."[35]

The Mormons furthermore were stung by Scott's facile success where they had failed so completely. Contemptuous of "swivel-chair men from Washington" who presumed to be able to settle affairs in remote San Juan County, they told M. K. Sniffen of the Indian Rights Association that they were ready to wager a thousand dollars on Scott's failure, and made Scott the butt of much behind-the-back mirth. When Scott eventually brought off his amazing feat of negotiation (with the help of the non-Mormon Indian traders), the joke suddenly was on them.[36]

Eight years of fermented frustration, punctuated by another shooting scrape in 1921, explain the ugliness of the Mormon reaction when the Posey War broke out in 1923. In March of that year, two Utes were arrested and brought to trial in Blanding for robbing a sheep camp and burning a bridge. Found guilty, they escaped with the help of Posey, a Paiute leader, during the obligatory recess between the trial and sentencing. Faced with renewed allegations of bungling law enforcement (Sheriff William Oliver's revolver had misfired twice, thus permitting the escape), the San Juan Mormons were determined not to allow what promised to be a repeat of the 1915 conflict. Building on the interest aroused by the 1915 episode, the 1923 incident was being closely followed by the press. When news of the violent escape reached General Scott, he offered to intervene once again to try to bring about another peaceful resolution, but this time the Mormons were determined to handle it themselves. Some members of the posse that formed to pursue Posey "had blood in their eyes and were ready to die if they had to in order to bring [the Indians] to justice." Sheriff Oliver gave full rein to their emotions by informing the posse that "every man here is deputized to shoot. I want you to shoot everything that looks like an Indian."[37]

As one would expect, the Paiutes recognized as in 1915 that their best strategy lay in flight to Navajo Mountain, but the posse formed quickly enough to cut them off at Comb Ridge. One of the Indians, Joe Bishop's Boy, was killed outright, and Posey himself suffered a leg wound from which he later died in a lone refuge in one of Comb Wash's myriad tributary canyons. A macabre coda ended the Posey War: San Juan County authorities refused to accept the word of Indian messengers that Posey was dead, and the body had to be exhumed no less than three times before all parties were satisfied and the emotional underpinnings of the episode could finally be released.

In the mythology of San Juan County, the Posey War occupies a place equal to the Hole-in-the-Rock expedition, and virtually every old-timer in Blanding has some kind of recollection of the incident and will talk about it enthusiastically. But it seems a curious point of pride, rooted as it was in a mounting sense of failure of the San Juan mission and embarrassment at the success of Gentiles and outsiders in the face of Mormon failure in 1915. In fact, as Robert S. McPherson points out, the incident was much more of a white uprising than an Indian one.

In the end, the Mormon "victory" in the Posey War was not the final resolution of the Indian-white conflict in San Juan County. That resolution was effected, once again, by the federal government in the creation of the White Mesa Reservation in 1923. The Posey War was evidence that contact between free-roaming renegade Indians and white settlers would continue to produce violence, but federal Indian administrators knew the renegades could not successfully be settled on the Southern Ute Reservation, for that attempt had failed since 1895. Accordingly, they created a separate reservation for them based at first on allotments in Allen Canyon under the Dawes Act of 1887, then on an auxiliary settlement at White Mesa south of Blanding during the 1940s. The expanded reservation provides adequate scope both for seasonal grazing and agriculture, and peace between Indians and whites has been the result.[38]

The Paiutes south of the San Juan River fared much less happily at the hands of the government. Subject to pressures from the expanding Navajo population, from white miners who wished to be allowed to explore for oil, and a declining population that was particularly devastated by the influenza epidemic of 1918, the Paiutes fought a hopeless delaying action whose end was expropriation and extinction.[39]

During the years 1884–1933, the Paiute Strip between the San

Juan River and the Arizona border experienced a checkered history of withdrawal from and return to the public domain: In 1884 it was withdrawn, in 1892 it was returned, in 1907 it was withdrawn again, in 1922 it was returned, and finally in 1933 it was added to the Navajo Reservation. The final destruction of the Paiute Strip in 1933 was accomplished over the protests of a number of advocates of Paiute rights, including John and Louisa Wetherill and Charles L. Bernheimer, a New York mediation expert, but the declining Paiute population and Navajo pressure doomed the protest.⁴⁰

Some Paiutes lingered in the Navajo Mountain area until well past the midcentury mark. In 1960 there were still eighteen Paiutes there—five men, five women, and eight children—figures that indicate a continuing demographic decline. All of them, according to a recent study of the community, were "Navajoized on the surface." Some had married Navajos and been absorbed into the clan society of that tribe, while others maintained a Paiute identity. All, however, were listed as Navajos in the census, and all possessed full political rights in the Navajo community.⁴¹

The Navajo Reservation, unlike many of those set aside for other tribes, has expanded, sometimes in great leaps, since its establishment in 1868. Nevertheless, its boundaries only approximately resemble those of what the Navajos call the *Dinetah*, their traditional homeland. This discrepancy is a result of several factors, one of which is, as skeptics would suspect, the ignorance and insensitivity of a distant and bloated federal bureaucracy. Other factors include the fact that the Navajos, in spite of their adoption of agriculture, have never entirely abandoned their prehistoric nomadism. Though hunting is no longer a major part of the Navajo economy, sheep raising is, and Navajo herdsmen follow their flocks over vast expanses of territory. Therefore, the Navajos utilize much more land than they occupy at a given time, thus blurring the precise boundaries dear to white culture and especially to white bureaucrats, and making occasional adjustments in those boundaries necessary. Further, the Navajo population has grown steadily and often dramatically with almost no setbacks since well before establishment of the reservation, thus making extension of the reservation from time to time a demographic and economic necessity. Finally, the locus of Navajo population has shifted westward since prehistoric times, and away from the original *Dinetah*.⁴²

It is easier to explain where the Navajos came from than to tell when. Linguistic evidence links them definitely with other Athabascan-speaking tribes in Canada. From Canada, at least two southward migration routes brought the Umpquas and Hupas along the Pacific Coast to Oregon and California, and the Navajo along probably the eastern slope of the Rocky Mountains to the Southwest.[43]

If Anasazi archaeology has its mysteries, Navajo archaeology is so imprecise as to be almost futile. The difference is in the permanence of Anasazi sites, which are often located in dry caves where remains are preserved for centuries, whereas the Navajo have always tended to live in the open and in ephemeral structures that rarely last more than a few years after abandonment. Tree-ring dating is about the only tool of the archaeologist that is applicable to Navajo sites, for the typical prehistoric Navajo dwelling was the forked-pole conical "male" hogan; the poles of the very rare extant hogans constructed in that manner can sometimes be approximately dated. Although the earliest date obtainable by that method is A.D. 1540, speculative dates for other sites suggest a date of arrival of Athabascans in the Southwest around A.D. 1000. That early date is corroborated by Navajo oral traditions that place them in the Chaco Canyon area while the great Anasazi pueblos were being constructed.[44]

Navajo mythology and tradition define the *Dinetah* as a rough parallelogram bounded at the corners by the four sacred mountains: the La Plata Mountains and Sierra Blanca in Colorado, Mount Taylor in New Mexico, and the San Francisco Peaks in Arizona; and the four sacred rivers: the Rio Puerco of the South, the Little Colorado, the Colorado, and the San Juan.[45] Thus the original locus of Navajo occupation was far from the area of this study, and although expansion westward over the centuries brought the San Juan country increasingly into the Navajo orbit, it was always peripheral, a frontier into which the Navajos could escape in time of peril, but an area sparsely settled and lightly utilized, and largely immune to the cultural and technological change that swept the rest of the reservation. This peripheral area included the entirety of the San Juan country as defined in the present study. The Navajos ranged not only onto the Rainbow Plateau when the need arose but also north of the San Juan River: White Canyon hogan remains yield tree-ring dates as early as 1620, with subsequent dates in the eighteenth, nineteenth, and twentieth centuries. Oral traditions point to Elk Ridge as a well-known "place of refuge in time of war," and an important Navajo headman in the lower San Juan region, K'aayelli, left his name on his Elk Ridge birthplace, Kigalia Spring.[46]

Navajo migration into the Southwest did not occur at once, in a massive *volkwanderung*. Rather, the Athabascans straggled southward in small, impoverished family groups. Their encounter with the Pueblo peoples, who had lived in the Southwest for centuries, was full of potential for the Navajos. It was not a matter, as some writers have had it, of a fierce, aggressive army of nomads swooping in to ravage the peace-loving Cliff Dwellers who then fled for refuge to their Hopi Mesas to the south. The Navajos at the time were in fact far inferior in numbers, technology, and cultural sophistication to the Pueblo peoples. In the face of that older civilization, the Navajo had nothing to teach and everything to learn, and they went to school immediately. From the descendants of the Ancient Ones, the Navajos learned agriculture, weaving, and the vast body of mythology and ritual that even today make the Pueblo peoples the spiritual gurus of the Southwest.[47]

The future, of course, belonged to the Navajos, though no one could see it at the time. As erosion and drought doomed the agricultural economy of the great pueblos and drove the Anasazis south and east to the Hopi Mesas and the Rio Grande, the greater mobility in the Navajo's nomadic heritage enabled them to continue, not only establishing themselves in the *Dinetah*, but expanding throughout the present Navajo country. By the time the whites encountered them—first the Spanish and Mexicans during the sixteenth to early nineteenth centuries, then the American soldiers, settlers, and traders—the Navajos were numerous, well established, and would not be easily dominated.

As indicated above, the Navajos on the northwestern frontier— the San Juan country of the present study—developed a frontier psychology that distinguished them from those in the more populous parts of the reservation. While the others would feel the white man's lead and steel, while they would see their cornfields and peach orchards in flames, while they would know the *Naahondzond*—the Fearing Time—the Long Walk, and the Bosque Redondo, the Navajos of the San Juan country would fight a long guerrilla resistance to Spaniards, Mexicans, and Anglos. They would know an exile of their own in the big canyons of the Rainbow Plateau and the San Juan Triangle, but it was an exile of independence that they chose over the subjugation, poverty, and cultural destruction of the Rope Thrower (Kit Carson) and his soldiers. Even today, their descendants on the Rainbow Plateau live largely untouched by the laws and bureaucracy of both whites and Indians. They are a minor but notable enclave of anachronism as the twentieth century sweeps through the Navajo country.

The architect of this psychology, if one person can claim that distinction, was the great headman of the western Navajos, Hoskininni.[48] Born near Kayenta in the 1820s, Hoskininni would not have had a personal memory of his people's flight from Jose Antonio Vizcarra's Mexican soldiers in 1823, but their bitter recollection would have shaped his famed skepticism of the white man. When news of the Rope Thrower's campaign of total-war destruction reached him in 1863, he hastily gathered a small group of seventeen family members and fled to Navajo Mountain. The speed of their departure and the necessity of traveling light limited them to only three horses, twenty sheep, and one ancient muzzle-loading rifle. When, in time, he returned with two others to salvage whatever he could from the ravages of the soldiers and their Ute collaborators, Hoskininni fought a bloody skirmish with some Utes, but recovered some horses and a few other Navajo survivors and returned to the mountain.

For five years, until the treaty of 1868 and the Navajos' return from the Bosque Redondo exile, Hoskininni and his rebel band ranged across the Rainbow Plateau and even north of the San Juan River, a region that was also familiar to him, for he had used White Canyon during his youth as a range for his horses. During that period, the Navajo population in the San Juan Triangle seems to have been greater than at any other time, for Hoskininni and his people encountered other rebels there under K'aayelli and several other headmen. Exile in that wild country, and knowledge of the depredations of their enemies in their old homeland, were enough to create an indelible skepticism of the white man, a skepticism that the 1868 treaty did nothing to erase, and a skepticism passed down to Hoskininni's son, Hoskininni-begay, and even to later generations.

Hostility to whites had actually begun even before the flight of Hoskininni's band. In November 1860, a bloody encounter occurred between a party of Mormon explorers on the Kaibito Plateau under Jacob Hamblin, who were looking for a route by which missionaries

could reach the Hopi Mesas, and a group of Navajos who were fleeing white depredations in the east. The hapless Mormons became
the innocent targets of the Navajos' wrath, and young George A.
Smith, Jr., eighteen-year-old son of the Mormon apostle, was murdered while trying to recover his stray horse. (Several inscriptions in
the Navajo Canyon system, including the long-disputed one that
gives Inscription House its name, document the passage through
that canyon the following spring by the Mormon party sent to recover young Smith's remains. It was the first recorded visit of whites
to Navajo Canyon.)[49]

Well aware of the Smith incident, the Mormon church nevertheless sent another party through the San Juan country in the spring of
1879. This group of thirty-six men, women, and children, a dozen
wagons, eighty horses, and perhaps 200 cattle, was the exploratory
expedition for the San Juan mission. Along their route from Lee's
Ferry to Moencopi through Marsh Pass to a crossing of the San Juan
River and on to Montezuma Creek, the Mormons experienced a
mixed reception by both Navajos and Paiutes. On the one hand, the
Indians were grateful for the new wells dug along the route for the
Mormon livestock and for occasional handouts of food, but they re-
sented the Mormons' use of existing water sources, and a band of
Navajos claiming to be the ones who had murdered Smith threat-
ened the explorers with similar treatment. That Indian hostility, plus
the difficulty of the dry drive through Indian country, caused the
Mormons to reject that route to their new settlement and to develop
the Hole-in-the-Rock route instead.[50]

Henry L. Mitchell, the Gentile rancher and farmer who had preceded the Mormons to the San Juan River, became a focal point of
contention between Indians and whites in the area, and a source of
considerable frustration to the Mormons. A trickle of complaints to
Indian authorities about Utes, Paiutes, and Navajos became a stream
early in 1880 when word of the murder of his son, Ernest, and a partner named James Merritt (often given as Merrick in the literature) in
Monument Valley reached him. The two young men had represented their venture across the San Juan as an exploration for a place
to graze livestock, but Merritt confided to one of the Mormon explorers that the two were really looking for the legendary Pish-la-kai
silver mine, whose ore was reputed to assay at 90 percent.

In February 1880, four mules belonging to the prospectors turned up in a Paiute camp, and a search of their route led to discovery of their murdered bodies. Mitchell retrieved the bodies, and threatened Navajo agent Galen Eastman with a general war between whites and Indians if the murderers were not punished. Although investigation eventually revealed that some Ute or Paiute renegades living north of the San Juan River had committed the crime, Mitchell's inflammatory rhetoric did nothing to alleviate the skepticism of all Indians in the area, including the Navajos, regarding the proclaimed goodwill of the whites.[51]

Ernest Mitchell and James Merritt were only the first to seek the Pish-la-kai mine. According to Hoskininni-begay, the year after the Mitchell-Merritt murders Cass Hite, a lone prospector, rode into a Navajo encampment in Monument Valley and announced that he was looking for the silver mine. The Indians were on the verge of killing him when he began to give them presents, and his obvious goodwill not only saved his life but also even penetrated the thick skepticism of Hoskininni, who befriended the miner. The Indians took Hite through the area and showed him other metal deposits, but not the Pish-la-kai mine. Hite returned the following summer with the same result. Although Hite continued to explore on his own in the Navajo Mountain area, Hoskininni showed him what came to be known as the Dandy Crossing of the Colorado River and advised him to look for gold in that area. The placer deposits he discovered at Ticaboo were rich enough that Hite respected the wishes of the old Navajo and generally stayed north of the river.[52]

The next prospectors in Monument Valley were not so fortunate. In 1884 Samuel Walcott of Baltimore, Maryland, and a young partner, James McNally of Illinois, outfitted themselves at Mitchell's trading post at McElmo Creek and headed into Monument Valley to look for the Pish-la-kai mine. Like Hite, they encountered Hoskininni's Navajos, but they were unable to win the Indians' friendship. When trade negotiations broke down, Hoskininni-begay, according to a Navajo who was present, decided to kill the white men. "The reason I want to kill the Americans," he argued, "is because they killed some of my people away back when I was a small boy." While McNally went after their horses, the Navajos killed Walcott, then murdered McNally when he returned.

Navajo agent John Bowman recovered the bodies and attempted to arrest Hoskininni-begay, but neither he nor a cavalry force from

Fort Wingate was able to bring the wily Navajo to trial. His father, Hoskininni, and two other Navajos from his band, turned themselves in and spent seven months in jail at Fort Defiance and St. Johns, Arizona, as well as forfeiting several hundred dollars' worth of jewelry and other possessions, but Hoskininni-begay was never arrested.[53]

Hoskininni died in 1909 and leadership passed to Hoskininni-begay, his only son. Before his passing, however, the beginnings of an accommodation with the whites had been accomplished. The agents of that accommodation were John and Louisa Wetherill and Clyde Colville, whom Hoskininni had allowed to establish the first trading post in his area at Oljato in 1906. Louisa Wetherill, who had become a remarkable expert on Navajo culture and spoke the language like a native, was particularly beloved of Hoskininni, who even adopted her and appointed her the executrix of his estate before his death.[54] Oljato was only the beginning; later, similar posts were established at Kayenta, Shonto, Goulding's, Inscription House, Piute Mesa, and Navajo Mountain, and the Navajos settled down to a peaceful relationship with traders at those far-flung outposts.

In time, missionaries followed the traders, but they made only minor inroads into the Navajo community, particularly the most conservative ones at Navajo Mountain. At that place, there is a small fundamentalist Protestant congregation of about twenty-five, a monthly Episcopal mass celebrated by a priest from St. Christopher's Mission east of Bluff, and sporadic Mormon missionary activity.[55]

Otherwise, the Navajo Mountain Navajos are standard-bearers of Navajo conservatism among whom white culture has made only the most limited inroads. Traditional Navajo dress and social practices like polygamy are still prevalent. When Mary Shepardson and Blodwen Hammond studied the community in the 1960s, not a single member of the community was registered to vote, either because of illiteracy, apathy, or the sixty-mile journey to the polls at Tonalea. Neither white nor Navajo laws hold any particular reverence for the Navajo Mountain community. Compulsory education and laws against overgrazing and polygamy are regularly ignored, as are any court rulings unacceptable to the local chapter (a local representative body in Navajo government). "The community," Shepardson and Hammond conclude, "has successfully ignored things that threaten the old order."[56]

NOTES

1. Jesse D. Jennings, *Glen Canyon: A Summary*, University of Utah Anthropological Paper No. 81 (Salt Lake City: University of Utah Press, 1966), 32–33; Robert H. and Florence C. Lister, *Chaco Canyon: Archaeology and Archaeologists* (Albuquerque: University of New Mexico Press, 1981), 184–88.

2. Lister and Lister, *Chaco Canyon*, 208–9, n. 1, is a handy sketch of the various classification schemes with supportive literature, but see also Jennings, *Glen Canyon: A Summary*, 33–34.

3. Jennings, *Glen Canyon: A Summary*, 33, lists Canyon de Chelly (Arizona) as another geographic phase of Anasazi culture, but Campbell Grant, *Canyon de Chelly: Its People and Rock Art* (Tucson: University of Arizona Press, 1978) finds pottery and masonry styles—the primary diagnostic features of these geographic phases—from all three of the other areas and treats the canyon as a "peripheral region" dominated by its "powerful neighbors" (52).

4. David Grant Noble, ed., *New Light on Chaco Canyon* (Santa Fe: School of American Research Press, 1984); Robert H. and Florence C. Lister, *Those Who Came Before: Southwestern Archeology in the National Park System* (Tucson: Southwest Parks and Monuments Association, 1993 [rev. ed., 1994]), 18–38; Fred Plog, "Prehistory: Western Anasazi." In Alfonso Ortiz, ed., *Southwest*, Vol. 9 of William C. Sturtevant, ed., *Handbook of North American Indians* (Washington, D.C.: Smithsonian Institution, 1979), 108–16.

5. Jesse D. Jennings and Floyd W. Sharrock, "The Glen Canyon: A Multi-discipline Project," *Utah Historical Quarterly* 33 (Winter 1965): 39–40.

6. Richard Wetherill to Gustaf Nordenskiold, February 6, 1894, reproduced in Olof Arrhenius, *Stones Speak and Waters Sing: The Life and Works of Gustaf Nordenskiold* (Mesa Verde National Park: Mesa Verde Museum Association, nd), 83 (emphasis is Wetherill's); Wetherill to Talbot Hyde, December 1893, quoted in Frank McNitt, *Richard Wetherill: Anasazi* (Albuquerque: University of New Mexico Press, 1957), 65.

7. Charles Avery Amsden, *Prehistoric Southwesterners from Basketmaker to Pueblo* (Los Angeles: Southwest Museum, 1949); M. Edward Moseley, "The Discovery and Definition of Basketmaker: 1890 to 1914," *Masterkey* (October-December 1966): 140–54.

8. Amsden, *Prehistoric Southwesterners*, 49, 52, illustrates pit house construction.

9. Ibid., 116–17; Robert H. and Florence C. Lister, *Anasazi Pottery* (Albuquerque: University of New Mexico Press, 1978): 8–21.

10. Hal K. Rothman, *Navajo National Monument: A Place and Its People, An Administrative History*, Southwest Cultural Resources Center Professional Paper No. 40 (Santa Fe: Southwest Cultural Resources Center, 1991).

11. Each of the masonry styles are effectively described and illustrated in Grant, *Canyon de Chelly*, 56–63.

12. William Y. Adams, *Ninety Years of Glen Canyon Archaeology, 1869–1959*, Museum of Northern Arizona Bulletin 33 (Flagstaff: Northern Arizona Society of Science and Art, Inc., 1960), 19.

13. Jennings, *Glen Canyon: A Summary*, 6–7.

14. Ibid., 37 contains a map showing the various culture influence areas. W. B. Lipe, et al., *1959 Excavations, Glen Canyon Area*, University of Utah Anthropological Paper No. 49 (Salt Lake City: University of Utah Press, 1960), 102–21. While trade could account for the cross-cultural nature of the remains in Forgotten Canyon, its first explorer, Dick Sprang, speculates that marriages between Kayenta men (masonry builders) and Mesa Verde women (potters) could also account for it. Dick Sprang to Stan Jones, May 9, 1985, copy in possession of author.

15. Jennings, *Glen Canyon: A Summary*, 30.

16. Elizabeth A. H. John, *Storms Brewed in Other Men's Worlds* (College Station: Texas A&M University Press, 1975), 49.

17. Ibid., 4–5; Winston B. Hurst and Christy G. Turner II, "Rediscovering the 'Great Discovery': [Richard] Wetherill's First Cave 7 and Its Record of Basketmaker Violence," in Victoria M. Atkins, ed., *Anasazi Basketmaker: Papers from the 1990 Wetherill–Grand Gulch Symposium* (Salt Lake City: Bureau of Land Management, 1993), 143–91.

18. Lister and Lister, *Chaco Canyon*, 203–5, discusses the drought and migration patterns, while Grant, *Canyon de Chelly*, 67, contains a map showing the migrations.

19. In addition to the primary sources cited below, this account of the San Juan Paiutes is based on Pamela A. Bunte and Robert J. Franklin, *From the Sands to the Mountain: Change and Persistence in a Southern Paiute Community* (Lincoln: University of Nebraska Press, 1987); and Floyd A. O'Neil and Gregory C. Thompson, "White Mesa Ute Project," prepared in 1980 as part of the White Mesa Ute Collection at the Utah State Historical Society.

20. A recent review of the debate, indicating an inclination to favor the earlier date,

is Margaret M. Lyneis, "Prehistory in the Southern Great Basin." In David B. Madsen and James F. O'Connell, eds., *Man and Environment in the Great Basin* (Washington, D.C.: Society for American Archaeology, 1982), 172–85. Grant, *Canyon de Chelly*, 54, contains a map showing the Numic migrations.

21. Isabel T. Kelly and Catherine S. Fowler, "Southern Paiute." In William C. Sturtevant, ed., *Handbook of the North American Indian* (Washington, D.C.: Smithsonian Institution, 1966), Vol. 11, 368–97; and Robert C. Euler, *Southern Paiute Ethnohistory*, University of Utah Anthropological Paper No. 78 (Salt Lake City: University of Utah Press, 1966).

22. Clifford E. Trafzer, *The Kit Carson Campaign: The Last Great Navajo War* (Norman: University of Oklahoma Press, 1982) is the standard account of the campaign, but fails to mention the band that fled to Navajo Mountain. That aspect is recounted by Charles Kelly, "Chief Hoskaninni [sic]," *Utah Historical Quarterly* 21 (July 1953): 219–26; and J. Lee Correll, "Navajo Frontiers in Utah and Troublous Times in Monument Valley," *Utah Historical Quarterly* 39 (Spring 1971): 145–61. For general material on Navajo history and culture, see Garrick Bailey and Roberta Glenn Bailey, *A History of the Navajos: The Reservation Years* (Santa Fe: School of American Research Press, 1986), Chapters 1 and 2; Raymond Friday Locke, *The Book of the Navajo* (Los Angeles: Mankind Publishing Co., 1976); David M. Brugge, "Navajo Prehistory and History to 1850," and Robert Roessel, "Navajo History, 1850–1923," both in Alfonso Ortiz, *Southwest*, William C. Sturtevant, ed., *Handbook of North American Indians*, Vol. 10 (Washington, D.C.: Smithsonian Institution, 1983), 489–501, 506–23; and Clyde Kluckhohn and Dorothea Leighton, *The Navaho* (Cambridge: Harvard University Press, 1946; 1974).

23. Frances Gillmor and Louisa Wade Wetherill, *Traders to the Navajos: The Story of the Wetherills of Kayenta* (Boston: Houghton Mifflin Co., 1934), 71–74; Mary Apolline Comfort, *Rainbow to Yesterday: The John and Louisa Wetherill Story* (New York: Vantage Press, 1980), 39–40.

24. Albert R. Lyman and J. P. Nielsen, 1908 depositions, White Mesa Ute Collection.

25. H. L. Mitchell to Warren Patten, Southern Ute Agency, July 8, 1884; Maj. R. H. Hall to Patten, July 20, 1884, and "Smith," Durango, Colorado, to Patten, July 23, 1884, all in the White Mesa Ute Collection.

26. C. F. Stollsteimer, Southern Ute Agency, to commissioner of Indian Affairs, February 6, 1888; *Report of the Commissioner of Indian Affairs, 1889*, 76–77.

27. Bennett Bishop deposition, January 23, 1890; F. A. Hammond, "Additional

Notes with Map in support of House Bill No. 156, to ratify and confirm agreement with the Southern Ute Indians," n.d., both in White Mesa Ute Collection.

28. Fourteen miners to Southern Ute Indian Commission, December 19, 1888; L.H. Hite to John H. Oberly, commissioner of Indian Affairs, January 8, 1889, both in White Mesa Ute Collection. The former letter includes a map of the proposed reservation.

29. Petition from San Juan County residents, July 22, 1893; 28 *Stat* 677 (1895); *Report of Commissioner of Indian Affairs, 1896*.

30. John Benow, 1908 testimony, White Mesa Ute Collection. See also Joseph O. Smith, Southern Ute agent, to commissioner of Indian Affairs, March 21, 1901, same collection.

31. Although the whites considered Tse-ne-gat a Paiute, he himself claimed to be a Southern Ute, offering in evidence the fact that he was not afraid of the dark, as Paiutes were. He probably was indeed a Ute, but he was a member of the renegade band principally composed of Paiutes. *Denver Post*, April 10, 1922, 2.

32. The story of what is often presumptuously called "the last Indian war" is one of the legends of San Juan County history and has been recounted many times in both published and unpublished narratives. Although biased and inaccurate in places, Charles Kelly's "The Poke and Posey Wars," *Desert Magazine*, (May 1965): 18–19, is a concise summary of the episodes. The Mormon point of view is told by Albert R. Lyman in *Indians and Outlaws: Settling the San Juan Frontier* (Salt Lake City: Bookcraft, Inc., 1962) and *The Outlaw of Navajo Mountain* (Salt Lake City: Deseret Book Co., 1963); and in Perkins, Nielsen, and Jones, *Saga of San Juan* ([Monticello, Utah]: San Juan County Daughters of Utah Pioneers, 1957), 244–55. An accurate and perceptive recent account is Robert S. McPherson, "Paiute Posey and the Last White Uprising," *Utah Historical Quarterly* 53 (Summer 1985): 248–67.

33. Frank McNitt, *The Indian Traders* (Norman: University of Oklahoma Press, 1962), 347–58.

34. The following account is based on Hugh Lenox Scott, *Some Memories of a Soldier* (New York: The Century Co., 1928), 533–41; the Louisa Wetherill diary, June 26–July 8, 1915, and other Wetherill papers in the Museum of Northern Arizona.

35. Kelly, "The Poke and Posey Wars," 18.

36. Scott, *Some Memories of a Soldier*, 538.

37. McPherson, "Paiute Posey and the Last White Uprising," 258. To be fair to the

Mormons, McPherson cites other posse members who had serious reservations about the hysteria and bloodshed, but their cautious voices were not to prevail in this instance. Hugh Lenox Scott to commissioner of Indian Affairs, March 21, 1923; Charles H. Burke, commissioner of Indian Affairs, to Scott, March 22, 1923, White Mesa Ute Collection.

38. O'Neil and Thompson, "White Mesa Ute History Project," provides a concise account of the band's history since 1923.

39. It was the Paiutes' great misfortune that their population during the 1918 influenza epidemic contained a high proportion of people in the vulnerable age range of twenty to thirty. Although the Navajos, by comparison, were often just as isolated as the Paiutes from medical assistance, they suffered less because of a higher proportion of their population outside the vulnerable age range. One of the most lamented Paiute casualties, incidentally, was the celebrated Nasja Begay, who had been instrumental in guiding the first white visitors to Rainbow Bridge in 1909. He and four children died while trying to reach medical help in Blanding. Bunte and Franklin, *From the Sands to the Mountain*, 127–28.

40. Bunte and Franklin, *From the Sands to the Mountain*, passim and 174–94; Charles L. Bernheimer Field Notes, May 22, 1929, copies at Utah State Historical Society and Museum of Northern Arizona.

41. Mary Shepardson and Blodwen Hammond, *The Navajo Mountain Community: Social Organization and Kinship Terminology* (Berkeley: University of California Press, 1970), 37.

42. James M. Goodman, *The Navajo Atlas* (Norman: University of Oklahoma Press, 1982), 55–56, shows prehistoric migration patterns and the history of expansion of the reservation, while the table on p. 61 shows the growth of the Navajo population through admittedly imprecise and irregular census figures. Grant, *Canyon de Chelly*, 120–21, shows the Navajo demographic shift over time, as does the unpaginated map toward the beginning of Clyde Kluckhohn and Dorothea Leighton, *The Navaho*.

43. Grant, *Canyon de Chelly*, 74.

44. Kluckhohn and Leighton, *The Navaho*, 33–34; Raymond Friday Locke, *The Book of the Navajo*, 8; Correll, "Navajo Frontiers in Utah," 147, shows the remains of a forked-pole hogan from San Juan County, Utah, occupied during the 1860s.

45. Goodman, *Navajo Atlas*, 55; Herbert E. Gregory, *Geology of the Navajo Country* (Washington, D.C.: Government Printing Office, 1917), 11.

46. Correll, "Navajo Frontiers in Utah," 146–49; evidence of a Navajo presence north of the San Juan River is also presented in the account of George B. Hobbs, one of the scouts for the Mormon Hole-in-the-Rock expedition of 1879–80, who says that for much of their route from Castle Wash to Grand Gulch, and again at Comb Ridge, the scouts were following what he calls a "Cliff Dwellers trail." This trail obviously had been made by livestock of modern Indians, since the Anasazis had been gone for some 600 years, and had had no beasts of burden that could have made such a trail. David E. Miller, *Hole-in-the-Rock: An Epic in the Colonization of the Great American West* (Salt Lake City: University of Utah Press, 1959), 87, 89.

47. Kluckhohn and Leighton, *The Navaho*, 34–35; Locke, *The Book of the Navajo*, 9, 12; Richard I. Ford, "Inter-Indian Exchange in the Southwest." In Alfonso Ortiz, *Southwest*, in Sturtevant, *Handbook of the North American Indian*, Vol. 10, 711–15; and Elizabeth A. H. John, *Storms Brewed in Other Men's Worlds*, 114–17.

48. Correll, "Navajo Frontiers in Utah," uses the better phonetic spelling, Hashkeneinii, but I have elected to stay with the more familiar Anglicization. The following section is based primarily on Correll's article.

49. Albert E. Ward, *Inscription House: Two Research Reports* (Flagstaff: Northern Arizona Society of Science and Art, 1975), 10–17.

50. Miller, *Hole-in-the-Rock*, 17–33.

51. Robert S. McPherson, "Navajos, Mormons, and Henry L. Mitchell: Cauldron of Conflict on the San Juan," *Utah Historical Quarterly* 55 (Winter 1987): 50–65; Correll, "Navajo Frontiers in Utah," 145–61; Kelly, "Chief Hoskaninni [*sic*]," 223, says Hoskininni-begay told him that Mitchell and Merritt found the mine, but were killed by Utes for failing to give them tobacco.

52. Charles Kelly, "Lost Silver of Pish-la-ki [*sic*]," *Desert Magazine*, (December 1940), 5–8.

53. Correll, "Navajo Frontiers in Utah," 151–61.

54. Ibid., 160–61.

55. Shepardson and Hammond, *The Navajo Mountain Community*, Part One.

56. Ibid., 22.

Precursors

There are few better examples of the American penchant for romance over reality than the deathless legends of Spanish presence in the canyon country. To those with historical stars in their eyes, the entire region was crisscrossed with Spanish trails; the Henry Mountains, for example, supposedly produced so much gold from their bounteous Spanish mines that the sharp observer can still discern grooves cut in the rock by the sharp hooves of gold-laden Spanish burros. Some of the legends are completely bizarre, such as the reputed golden statue of Jesus secreted in a side canyon of the Colorado River and awaiting some lucky discoverer. The mysterious Spaniards have become focal points of all the larger-than-life thinking encouraged by a larger-than-life landscape—superhuman deeds must have been done there by superhuman adventurers who made (and always lost) superhuman fortunes. Moreover, the Spaniards have served as a historical catch-all explanation for the rationally inexplicable. With an insight borne of many years' study of the canyon country, historian C. Gregory Crampton describes the phenomenon perfectly:

> When you find something in the Southwest that cannot otherwise be explained, it is common practice to call it Spanish in origin. The better lost mines, for example, were lost by Spanish discoverers. You hit upon the remains of an old trail. Who made it? The ubiquitous Spanish.[1]

Unfortunately for the purveyors of romance, the record of Spanish, or even Mexican, *entradas* into the San Juan country is so thin as to be almost nonexistent. Although there were undoubtedly some unrecorded ventures into the area—by slave traders, not miners—the documented expeditions before the area passed into American hands in 1848 can be numbered easily on the fingers of one hand.

The Spanish borderlands, including the province of Nuevo Mexico, of which the San Juan country would have been considered a part, was always an imperfectly explored, loosely held, and inefficiently governed part of New Spain. The problem was not, as some have thought, that Spain cared little about the northern frontier, for the region was important in two ways: as a source of Indians to convert; and as a buffer that shielded the richer "silver provinces" to the south from other European colonial powers and the Americans, and from unsubdued Indian tribes like the Commanches, the Apaches, and the Navajos. No, the relatively light Spanish presence in the north resulted not from apathy but rather from the immense expense of governing a vast, remote, and war-plagued region, particularly because it held almost no economic resources to offset that expense.[2]

The Navajo country in the remote northern reaches of the Spanish empire did hold one economic resource that the Spanish exploited as well as they could: Indian slaves. Although slavery in the New World began among the Indians long before European discovery and continued in the American Southwest through the Spanish, Mexican, and American occupation until passage of the Thirteenth Amendment in 1865, its nature and importance, particularly during the Spanish and Mexican periods, is a vexed question of continuing and even increasing interest. Since slavery was a well-established institution among both Indians and Europeans, replacement of Aztec by Spanish rule in Mexico in the sixteenth century had little effect on the practice except to exchange one set of masters for another. Though the Spaniards did not, of course, practice human sacrifice and cannibalism, the harshness of their rule paralleled that of the Aztecs in torture, exploitation, and murder. When the inconsistency of such practices with Christianity insistently forced itself upon the attention of the Spanish king (and Holy Roman emperor) Charles V, the eventual result was the Law of 1573. The law outlawed slavery, but allowed continuance of peaceful conversion and exploitation in the form of forced labor under the institutions of *encomienda* and *repartimiento*.[3]

For the Indians, the consequences of the law were mixed. Although the law was very shoddily enforced and de facto slavery continued, slavery became much less immovably entrenched in New Spain than it was to become, by comparison, in the southern United

States. The condition of slavery, for one thing, was not inheritable: The children of Indian slaves were born free. Also, slavery tended to be a temporary condition that ended with conversion to Christianity or marriage to a free Indian. Finally, the racism that lay at the base of American Negro slavery was much less conspicuous and rigid in the Spanish attitude toward the Indians. The Spanish not only converted the Indians but also intermarried with them and integrated them into their larger colonization program.[4]

Other scholars point out that slavery is slavery, and that attempting to disguise the fact under the argument that it had the salubrious effect of opening the door for barbarous Indians to enter into Christianity and civilization is nothing more than "euphemistic deceit." Regardless of the true nature of Spanish slavery—and the debate cannot be resolved here—there is no question that the quest for slaves was an important Spanish enterprise on the northern frontier. Whether one accepts the thesis of Frank McNitt that Spanish slave raids and retaliatory reprisals by the Navajos were the sole mechanism of Spanish-Navajo relations, for the San Juan country of this study, slave raiding and the conflicts resulting from it were only one aspect, though an important one, in Indian-white relations.[5]

Although the first Spaniards had viewed the canyon country as far back as 1540 when Coronado's men peered awestruck into the Grand Canyon, the upper reaches of the Colorado River remained unknown to them for another 200 years. It was not until 1765 that Juan Maria de Rivera led two expeditions north of Santa Fe, visiting some of the Anasazi ruins at Hovenweep and Mesa Verde, and evidently reaching the Colorado River near modern-day Moab, Utah, on the second trip.[6] Eleven years later the first European *entrada* of the San Juan country of the present study occurred when the Dominguez-Escalante expedition discovered Glen Canyon and made the famous Crossing of the Fathers at the mouth of Padre Creek.

The motives of the Franciscan Fathers who led the 1776 expedition were religious and geographic. Aware of the existence of unconverted Indian tribes outside the area of Spanish settlement, the two priests wished to visit, study, and preach to them, and to lay the groundwork for permanent missions among them. Conversion of Indians had been a primary goal of the Spanish since the time of Columbus, but Dominguez and Escalante were further motivated by the geographic goal that had driven Spanish explorers since Balboa's discovery of the Pacific Ocean: the search for a convenient route linking the two oceans across the American continent. This latter motive became increasingly insistent during the eighteenth century as Father Junípero Serra and other Franciscans had established the now-famous chain of missions northward along the California coast, which, during 1769–76, had been extended all the way from San Diego to San Francisco. New Mexico during the eighteenth century closely resembled California. As the California missions were narrowly strung out along the coast, New Mexico consisted of a precarious string of missions and Indian pueblos huddled along the Rio Grande from El Paso to Taos.[7] Linking these two narrow northern spear-thrusts of Spanish civilization would have obvious military, commercial, and administrative value.

Although both leaders of the 1776 expedition were young—Francisco Silvestre Vélez de Escalante was about twenty-six and his religious superior Francisco Atanasio Dominguez was about thirty-six—both were seasoned New Mexican missionaries with unflinching commitment to the goals of converting Indians and linking the two northernmost provinces of New Spain.[8] Although they failed in both of their primary goals and crossed the area of the present study only for a few miles, they produced the first narrative of exploration in the area (including the maps drawn by artist and sculptor Bernardo Miera y Pacheco, who accompanied the party).

Because the Spanish had met with consistently unfriendly reception by the Hopis and Apaches, the explorers decided to avoid a westward route in favor of a northerly loop through the territory of the more cooperative Utes. On July 29, 1776, the party, which averaged about thirteen men with Indian guides who came and went, left Santa Fe attempting to follow Rivera's route to the north. Although they eventually lost Rivera's trail, they found their own way through western Colorado to a crossing of the Green River near present Ouray, Utah, and through the Wasatch Mountains to Utah Valley via Spanish Fork Canyon. There they turned in a more southerly direction but were unable to find a way into California before the lateness of the season overtook them. Somewhere near modern Cedar City, Utah, in a famous lot-casting episode designed to impress the secular-minded expedition members eager to taste the fleshpots of California with the fairness of the Fathers, they decided to seek a southeasterly route back to Santa Fe. This route led them through

House Rock Valley and along the Vermilion Cliffs to the Colorado River at what later became Lee's Ferry.

Although the walls of Glen Canyon dip low enough at that point to permit access to the river on both banks, the crossing itself is a dangerous one, for the river is deep, the current strong, and the rapids of Marble Canyon not far downstream.[9] The Spaniards made two unsuccessful attempts to cross the river. Two of the men swam across in the icy water but lost their clothes, which they had bundled on their heads, in midstream. Escalante himself then built a driftwood raft, but failed to get it out into the main current because of contrary wind-whipped waves and the depth of the water, which exceeded the length of the poles he and his men were using to propel the craft. Both attempts seethed with risks that were fully comprehensible only by much more savvy rivermen than the Spaniards, and they made a fortunate decision after the second attempt to seek a better crossing.

Although the party had no Indian guides at that point, Indians had told them of a possible crossing upstream, and they set out to find it. Traveling a few miles up Paria Creek, they discovered a steep access to the Paria Plateau on the east and crossed from there to Wahweap Creek. Heading south from there, they attempted another crossing to the mouth of Navajo Canyon, but the difficulty of river access and an inexplicably unfavorable report of a scout who explored the lower reaches of the canyon led them to continue upstream along the north rim of Glen Canyon. Eventually they came to a promising ford at the mouth of Padre Creek. Although they had to cut steps down the steepest part of the cliff to reach the river, they found the river bottom solid and the water shallow, and made a successful crossing. After so much difficulty in finding a route through such rough country during often inclement weather, the Spaniards staged an understandable celebration on the south bank of the river, "praising God our Lord and firing off some muskets in demonstration of the great joy we all felt in having overcome so great a problem, one which had caused us so much labor and delay."[10]

The celebration was slightly premature, for crossing the river did not mean their troubles were over. The party proceeded south for a distance along the rim of Navajo Canyon, then attempted unsuccessfully to go directly eastward across the Rainbow Plateau. Some Indians advised them of an access point to the floor of Navajo Canyon and suggested that they follow it up to its confluence with Kaibito Canyon, where they would find a way to ascend the Kaibito Plateau and go from there to the Hopi Mesas where Escalante had been before, and would know the route back to Santa Fe.

Although both Dominguez and Escalante were assigned to other projects upon their return, and thus never followed up on their geographical reconnaissance or their proposed missions, other Spaniards found their exploration useful. In time, various portions of the Dominguez-Escalante route became what was called the Old Spanish Trail, which linked Santa Fe with Los Angeles. By the time that trail was developed in the 1820s, however, revolution had separated Mexico from Spain, and the Spanish Trail was used instead by Mexicans and by American fur trappers and traders. None of the variations of the old Spanish Trail were used often. The most popular one followed the Dominguez-Escalante route fairly closely to the point where they cast lots in southern Utah, then continued to the southwest, crossing the southern California desert to reach Los Angeles.

Another route, of which we have record of a traverse in 1829–30 by a party of sixty traders under Antonio Armijo, proceeded west from Abiquiu, northwest of Santa Fe, and followed a route approximating the Dominguez-Escalante trail back to the Crossing of the Fathers. Finding the ascent of the north wall of Glen Canyon even more difficult than the padres had found the descent, the Armijo party spent December 8 improving the trail: "We stopped the train and repaired the upgrade of the canyon, the same one which had been worked by the padres."[11]

Other Mexican *entradas* into the San Juan country were not so peaceful. One was a military expedition in 1823 led by the New Mexico governor Jose Antonio Vizcarra. The immediate cause of the expedition was conflict between Navajos and Mexican settlers who had moved into the Cebolleta area east of Mount Taylor in the eighteenth century. It was a hotly disputed region in which ancient Navajo usage was contested by Mexican stockmen, and the bloody history of the region was heightened by Spanish and Mexican slave raids. Vizcarra, who was the only effective governor of New Mexico during the Mexican period, took an army of 1,500 deep into the San Juan country in 1823 to try to defeat the Navajo headmen Juanico and Segundo and protect the Cebolleta settlers.[12]

The Navajos led him on a merry chase west from Santa Fe past

Chaco Canyon, Canyon de Chelly, and the Hopi Mesas. There he learned that the enemy was at Chellecito ("Little Canyon," referring to the Segi-ot-sosi) "near a mesa that has only one ascent, which they use in time of trouble"—undoubtedly Hoskininni Mesa. By the time he was able to get his large force ready to move, Vizcarra headed instead northwest toward Moencopi, evidently having heard the Indians had moved in that direction. From there, however, he turned back through Tonalea and on to Skeleton Mesa, where the two forces fought a pitched battle. The Navajos utilized what had by then become their most effective strategy against the whites: retreat and dispersion, relying on their superior knowledge of the rough country. In the end, the results were inconclusive. Although the Indians had lost some thirty-two men (not counting five Paiutes mistakenly murdered by the Mexicans) and considerable livestock, their will to fight was diminished little if at all in spite of the Mexicans' demonstrated determination to pursue them almost to the limits of their territory. As David M. Brugge points out, the Cebolleta controversy was the beginning of almost continuous hostility between the two races until the defeat and exile of the Navajos in 1864.

Even the Navajos of the San Juan country, remote as they were from the political capital of New Mexico at Santa Fe, were not immune to the strife, as the Vizcarra campaign demonstrates. Also, as Hoskininni-begay recalled many years later, the Navajos were constantly having to fight Mexican raiders, and reciprocated by attacking Mexican settlements in the east:

> In those days (1840–60) we were always fighting with the Noki
> (meaning black, or Mexicans). They would come into our coun-
> try to steal women, horses, and sheep. Then we would go into
> their country to steal, but we did not steal Noki women. Some-
> times the Mexicans would raid as far north as Chinle, then re-
> turn, gathering up stock as they went.

The last of the raids the old headman knew about took place about 1848, when a raiding party chased the Navajos and their stock up through Monument Valley and down Copper Canyon to the San Juan River. After rounding up a large number of Navajo sheep, the Mexicans turned back, but the Indians followed them, sniping and harassing them in their camps. Five Mexicans were killed at Agathla Peak, and a pitched battle took place at Teec-nos-pas, where others lost their lives. With that, the remainder of the Mexicans fled and the Indians recovered their stock. It was a violent environment, and Hoskininni-begay remembered that both sides were about equally responsible: "All this trouble was caused by stealing, and we were about as bad as the Mexicans. Most of our trouble with the white men was caused by stealing."[13]

New Spain lasted for more than three centuries. The Mexican hold on the Borderlands was much less secure; they drove the Spanish out in 1821, but lost Texas as soon as 1836, then the rest of the Borderlands—the present states of California, Arizona, New Mexico, Nevada, and Utah—in 1848 to the Americans. To the Americans, the Southwest, like the Rocky Mountains and much of the Oregon country, was a blank page, and they spent the last half of the nineteenth century taking measure of their new acquisitions.

Before the Civil War, various emigrants' trail guides, the popular reports of the charismatic John C. Fremont, and the multiple volumes of the Pacific Railroad survey of 1853 made available a rich store of knowledge of the interior of the continent. After the war, government funding for exploration, both military and civilian, again became available. Modeled upon the California survey of the 1860s and staffed in large part by well-trained scientific specialists, the Great Surveys of Clarence King, George Montague Wheeler, Ferdinand V. Hayden, and John Wesley Powell made great inroads into the terra incognita of the American interior. From 1869 until their termination with the founding of the United States Geological Survey in 1879, the Wheeler, Hayden, and Powell surveys at various times circled around the San Juan country, but still left the area a geographic blank.

Of the three surveys, Wheeler's was least significant for this area. Wheeler's interest in the Colorado River country was largely confined to retracing Lt. Joseph Christmas Ives's 1857 upriver expedition, and some exploration in 1873 north of Glen Canyon. The latter expedition was led by Lt. R. L. Hoxie. Little came of Hoxie's presence in Glen Canyon beyond a couple of place names—Hoxie Creek (Hall's Creek) and Pine Alcove Creek (Bullfrog Creek)—which were replaced by later explorers and miners.[14]

The concurrent survey of Hayden spent much more time in the canyon country than Wheeler, but nevertheless skirted the area of this study. Hayden's greater interest in the canyon country can be explained in terms of the divergent goals of the Wheeler and Hayden surveys. Wheeler, an army officer, was something of an anachronism in the 1870s, a throwback to the great military surveys of the 1850s whose purpose was military reconnaissance, and for whom science was a mere adjunct to the central mission. Hayden's goals were my-opic in their own way, but they saw more in the San Juan country than Wheeler cared about. Hayden was, in William H. Goetzmann's characterization, a "Gilded Age explorer," a "businessman's geologist" in whose view economic resources loomed largest.[15] Those resources included tourism, however, and the canyon country obviously contained much to feed that interest. Through the romanticized landscape paintings of W. H. Holmes and the immense glass plate negatives of photographer William H. Jackson who accompanied various Hayden expeditions, the awe-inspiring beauties of what are now Yellowstone and Mesa Verde National Parks first dazzled the eyes of the American public—and of fund-appropriating congressmen.[16]

It was a detachment of the Hayden survey of 1875 that came closest to the area of this study. Impressed by Jackson's photographs of some of the Mesa Verde ruins in 1874, Hayden sent him the next year to investigate the extent of such ruins in the San Juan River drainage. Accompanied by a reporter, E. A. Barber of the *New York Herald*, a guide (Harry Lee), two packers (Bob Mitchell and Bill Whan), and a cook (Bill Shaw), Jackson departed from Parrot City, Colorado, on the La Plata River to explore for six weeks down the San Juan to Chinle Wash, then up to Canyon de Chelly, the Hopi Mesas, then back, exploring Montezuma Creek on the return journey. Although the party discovered a number of ruins, the ones that merited specific mention in Hayden's annual report included Casa del Eco, the now-famous tourist attraction accessible by the footbridge near St. Christopher's Mission, and Poncho House in Chinle Wash.[17]

The only one of the Great Surveys actually to enter the San Juan country was that of Maj. John Wesley Powell, who passed through Glen Canyon twice, in 1869 and 1871. Although the two main Powell parties were responsible for some permanent place names such as the Dirty Devil River, Music Temple, and the Henry Mountains to the north, other names did not endure, such as Mount Seneca Howland (Navajo Mountain) and his original names for the canyon itself: Mound Canyon, from the Dirty Devil River to the San Juan, and

Monument Canyon, from the San Juan to the Paria. His eventual name, Glen Canyon, which appeared in his 1875 report, of course stuck as well.[18]

Nor did the two main parties do much exploration in the canyon. Low on food and exhausted from the rigors of Cataract Canyon, the Powell parties enjoyed drifting through the beautiful scenery, but never ventured far from the riverbank. Powell recognized the scientific potential of Glen Canyon, however, with its interesting landforms and prehistoric sites, and on the second expedition made arrangements for a more extensive investigation of the canyon by a detachment from his main party in 1872 after the reconnaissance of the previous year had been completed. Accordingly, one of his boats, the *Canonita*, was cached near the mouth of the Dirty Devil to be used for the later survey.[19]

The four men chosen for the *Canonita* survey of June-July, 1872 were photographer James Fennemore, an English immigrant Powell had found in Salt Lake City; his assistant John K. Hillers, a German immigrant who became one of the most famous photographers of the canyon country; Frederick S. Dellenbaugh, a young artist related by marriage to Powell; and William Derby Johnson, Jr., a Mormon schoolteacher from Kanab hired by Powell at Pipe Spring the previous March.[20]

Accompanied by other members of the Powell party, the men journeyed overland from Kanab, discovering on the way the river later named the Escalante, which they temporarily mistook for the Dirty Devil. Although the Escalante runs through a mighty canyon and drains a vast area, its flow is modest except during the spring, and the two previous Powell river expeditions had failed to identify it as a river. Traveling down North Wash (Lost Creek, as explored by Powell and Stephen Vandiver Jones the previous year, and known later as Crescent Creek) they reached the Dirty Devil at last, where they found that although they had cached the *Canonita* as far from spring flood danger as possible, one of the oars had washed away. Also, the sand they had shoveled into the boat to anchor it had dried out its planking considerably, so recaulking was necessary. Dellenbaugh took advantage of the delay to paint the boat's name in bright red letters on the stern, a red star right and left on the bow, and stripes around the sides. "It did not leak much," Johnson reported when they tested the resplendent craft in the water.[21]

On Wednesday, June 26, they began their journey. "I ask the Lord to bless us and take us safe through," the pious Johnson wrote, but that day's run contained few perils, for they stopped to explore the famous Moqui Fort, an Anasazi ruin high on the left bank near the mouth of White Canyon, and camped there for the night.

In the absence of modern place names and accurate mileages, it is impossible to follow the party exactly, but it is clear that by July 1 they were in the California Bar area. Johnson describes a climb to the top of a spectacular cliff on the right bank (Tapestry Wall), which gave an excellent view of the Henry Mountains, and the downriver side canyon systems of Smith Fork and Hansen Creek on the right, and Forgotten and Crystal Springs on the left. He also mentions "some hieroglyphics . . . on the vertical wall of the creek," which were probably the immense petroglyph panel below Smith Fork. It was some of the most scenic and interesting country in Glen Canyon, rich in Anasazi remains, and the explorers were in no hurry to move on. July 4 brought them to Hall's Crossing, where they celebrated by firing a salute and enjoying a lemon cake and peach pie baked by Dellenbaugh in two frying pans.

They did little exploring for the next few miles, noting only the scenery, the verdant vegetation along the cliffs, and the rapids at Lake Canyon. In the vicinity of the Rincon they found their provisions were getting low, but stopped to explore the Escalante River, which previous parties had missed. Hillers observed that it was flowing only eight or ten inches deep, "while on the mountain [where they had mistaken it for the Dirty Devil] it just boomed," and speculated that "the sandstone drinks it all."

The next day they passed the San Juan River, which Dellenbaugh said "was running a very large amount of water," though Johnson estimated it as only one-third more than the Virgin. They camped at Music Temple, a fortunate site, because it began raining and forced them to lay over the next day, enjoying "the large and small cataracts falling from the top of the cliffs into the river, some . . . five hundred feet, some few one thousand feet. Many lost themselves in spray before reaching the ground or river." (Johnson)

Food shortage forced fairly rapid progress when the rain let up, and the explorers had to forgo most side canyon ventures in the lower canyon. They found the Crossing of the Fathers and Sentinel Rock, but rushed on to the Paria River, which they reached the morning of July 13. Although it was the end of their journey, it contained the greatest danger they had faced, because Rachel Lee, wife of John D. Lee, the Mormon fugitive for his role in the Mountain Meadows Massacre, met them with a gun; the Lees could not afford to make any assumptions about strangers! Fortunately, "Brother Lee" recognized Johnson, and they were safe.

Were the Powell parties the first white men to explore the entirety of Glen Canyon? A tantalizing inscription on the right bank opposite Lake Canyon at Mile 113.2 suggests that a French explorer may have preceded Powell by over thirty years. Although faint and somewhat vandalized when C. Gregory Crampton recorded it during the preinundation survey of historic sites, the inscription appeared to read "Ce Jan.—1837," which could mean, "This January, 1837." Crampton's speculation is reasonable, that this might have been Denis Julien, a fur trapper whose presence at about that time is well documented by similar inscriptions in Labyrinth and Cataract Canyons, as well as other sites both certain and contested. Glen Canyon's abundance of beavers, both in the river itself and in side canyons, would have been attractive to Julien. In this case and the others where his name appears, the lack of fuller documentation for Julien's career leaves a regrettable gap in history.[22]

It was the Mormons of the San Juan mission (or, as it is more popularly known, the Hole-in-the-Rock mission) of 1879–80 who first seriously explored the San Juan country, both north and south of the San Juan River. Although the Mormon settlements on the San Juan were initially at Bluff and Montezuma Creek, and later at northern communities like Blanding and Monticello, and thus outside the area of this study, the Mormon explorations and emigrant parties were the first whites to explore the area in some detail, to get to know its terrain and its Indians intimately, and, through grazing cattle in the so-called Lake Country north of the river, to exploit the region economically.[23]

Mormon colonization was something different in western history. As a product of the revivalistic and utopian frenzy of upstate New York's "burned-over district" in the early nineteenth century, the Church of Jesus Christ of Latter-day Saints featured a communitarian ethos that uniquely suited it for settling in harsh western conditions, but that set it apart, nevertheless, from the individualism that otherwise characterized Anglo pioneers. Mormons did things as a group, and although the isolated Mormon pioneer or family is not unheard of, most of the great advances of Mormon civilization into the West were accomplished by means of colonies deliberately appointed and instructed by the central church. Every attempt was made to balance the personnel of the colony among necessary professions, trades, and skills so the community had a good chance to become largely self-sufficient. Mormon colonies, furthermore, were composed of families rather than the single men who constituted most non-Mormon settlements.

Several motives lay beneath the San Juan mission. For one thing, during the 1870s the Mormon Church was beginning to find itself under pressure to conform to mainstream American culture, in particular to abandon its peculiar institutions of authoritarian government and polygamy. The Mormons had come to Utah in the first place to find an isolated haven where they could establish such institutions, but had found themselves almost from the beginning sucked back into the vortex of American culture. Annexation of the region from Mexico in 1848 had been followed by the Gold Rush, then the building of the transcontinental railroad, all of which defeated the isolation and self-sufficiency sought by Brigham Young. Thus, whatever freedom of scope remained for development of Mormon institutions needed to be protected by Mormon expansion to the natural frontiers of Utah, and the San Juan country was one of those unclaimed frontiers.

The Mormons also desired to bring civilization to an area that was becoming known as a home for some of the wilder elements of frontier society. Miners and cattlemen were already moving into southwestern Colorado and southeastern Utah, and the Mormons hoped to counter their lawless ways by establishing civilized communities among them.

Finally, and primarily, the San Juan mission was a mission to the Indians. Mormons hold the anthropologically bizarre idea that American Indians are a decadent branch of one of the Lost Tribes of Israel whose past transgressions may nevertheless be redeemed (and their skin color lightened!) through acceptance of Christianity. Thus preaching to the Indians has always been a centrally important Mormon enterprise.

Most of the members of the San Juan mission were chosen from among the Mormon communities in southwestern Utah, which was geographically the closest pool from which such settlers could be chosen. During the last week of December 1878, at Parowan, Utah, the first group of missionaries were "called" (selected for the venture by church authorities). Since the country into which they were being asked to go was known to be extraordinarily rough and remote, the call was optional, and in fact not all of those selected actually went.

How to get there? Mormons had some knowledge of northern Arizona, for they had recently begun colonizing along the Little Colorado River and had established a road there via Lee's Ferry, so it was natural that they should first attempt to utilize as much of that route as possible. The mixed success of the exploring expedition that reached the San Juan River at Montezuma Creek by that route has already been recounted. The likelihood of conflict with Indians and the infrequent water sources led the church to seek a better route north of the San Juan.

There were other routes. One, which was already well known, followed the old Spanish Trail eastward to a crossing of the Colorado River at the present site of Moab, Utah, then south roughly along the route of Highway 191 to the San Juan River. This route, which had been used by the Mormon Elk mountain mission that briefly settled at Moab in 1855, was entirely practical but was deemed to be too long to enable the San Juan settlers to get themselves established before winter. (Mormon colonies were typically sent out in the fall with enough food to last through the winter, so crops could be put in during early spring while roads and trails were still impassable.)

Shorter routes were also available, though they were as yet unknown and would have to be discovered by exploration. Both were later employed as major roads to the San Juan. One proceeded west from Escalante to a crossing of the Escalante River via Harris Wash, then across the Waterpocket Fold and down Hall's Creek to a good ferry site at Hall's Crossing. This route included two of the major obstacles of the Hole-in-the-Rock road—Clay Hills Pass and San Juan Hill—but it avoided the other bad places like the Hole itself, the "little" Hole-in-the-Rock, Shoot-the-Chute Canyon, and the fearsome descent from Grey Mesa to the head of Wilson Canyon. Another route crossed the Waterpocket Fold at Capitol Gorge in present-day Capitol Reef National Park, then turned south at present-day Hanksville and along the eastern slope of the Henry Mountains to what Cass Hite called the Dandy Crossing of the Colorado River (Hite, Utah), joining the Hole-in-the-Rock road south of White Canyon near present-day Natural Bridges National Monument. This route retained the major obstacle of San Juan Hill, but avoided all the others.

Why, then, with easier routes available to them, either already known or easily discoverable (both the Hall's Crossing route and the Dandy Crossing were in operation within a few years of the Hole-in-the-Rock trek), did the San Juan mission choose to pioneer the most unpromising route across some of the roughest country in the United States? The answer is to be found in a combination of egregiously poor scouting by Escalante residents Charles Hall, Andrew Schow, and Reuben Collett, who recommended the route, and unquestioning obedience of church leadership by the members of the party. There is no question that the resulting expedition was, in the words of its best historian, David E. Miller, "an epic in the colonization of the great American west," but there is also no question that it was one of the most unnecessary and ill-advised epics in American history.

Escalante, Utah, the farthest settlement along the proposed route, was to be the jumping-off point for members of the expedition, who were to proceed southeastward along the massive escarpment of the Kaiparowits Plateau (locally known as the Fifty Mile Mountain) to a rendezvous point at Forty Mile Spring near Dance Hall Rock. Late in October 1879, the first of what would eventually total perhaps 250 members purchased the last of their supplies at what they considered extortionist prices in Escalante, and turned their wagons out along the new trail.

The expedition members' first sight of the Hole and the rough country through which they must pass on the other side of the river was not encouraging, nor did a scouting party through some miles of that country turn up reason for optimism. Nevertheless, Silas S. Smith, leader of the expedition, decided to go ahead with it. In December four scouts were sent ahead on horseback to lay out the road all the way to Montezuma Creek while the rest of the group blasted sandstone and built up a roadway through the Hole. Both ventures took six weeks, finishing toward the end of January 1880. The entire trip from Escalante to Montezuma Creek was to have taken no longer than that.

After ferrying the river, the party proceeded up Cottonwood Valley and reached its rim by means of a road almost as steep as the one they had just descended across the river; in fact, Miller named this one Little Hole-in-the-Rock. This gave access to a small meadow where a brief recuperation was possible. At that point a resupply party arrived from Panguitch bringing pork, cheese, and other food. The cheese, for some mysterious reason, was auctioned off instead of freely distributed, and the excitement of the auction led to naming the site the Cheese Camp. From there, one more fearsome ascent remained before easy going could be reached. This was the crossing of Syncline Canyon or, as it is still locally known, Shoot-the-Chute Canyon, a steep slickrock incline leading to the summit of Grey Mesa.

Grey Mesa is a flat plateau offering easy passage and the most spectacular view along the route. The Mormon road passed directly above the bight of the Great Bend of the San Juan, from which a complete circle of scenery was available: the Nokai Dome ahead, with Monument Valley and Navajo Mountain, the Kaiparowits Plateau, and the Henry Mountains visible in a clockwise sequence.

Getting off Grey Mesa presented a challenge equal to getting onto it. George B. Hobbs, one of the four scouts sent ahead to lay out the road, credited a bighorn sheep (which he called a llama) with revealing a trail to him. While he attempted to lasso the animal, it plunged down a slickrock slope that offered the potential for a trail. Part of the descent from Grey Mesa rivals in steepness even the Hole itself, and steps had to be cut to provide footing for the animals.

Bypassing the head of Wilson (now known as Iceberg) and Slickrock (sometimes called Colorado) Canyons, the route led to a crossing of Lake Canyon at Hermit Lake, where the party found ample pasturage and fresh water and remained for several days to rest their weary animals. Hermit Lake had long been used by Navajos for livestock grazing, and was to become an important center of the Mormon cattle business as well, as a later chapter will recount.

From Hermit Lake, the scouts had followed an Indian trail to the northeast across what cowboys today call the Lost Cowboy country to Castle Wash and Clay Hills Pass. The pass lies entirely in the Chinle shale, and presents some serious road-building problems. The Utah Department of Transportation has learned that the Chinle provides a shifty foundation for a highway even under the best of conditions, for the modern road tends to slide off into the canyon below. In the midwinter conditions encountered by the Mormon pioneers, the Chinle was a treacherous mass of slippery clay that stuck to feet and wagon wheels, but it offered the only practical access to Grand Flat below, and after a week of mud digging, the wagons were brought down.

Here a significant detour was required, because the apparent easy going across Grand Flat to the east was blocked by Grand Gulch, whose tortuous fifty-mile course presented no possible crossing for wagons. Consequently, the route turned toward the Bear's Ears in the northeast and rounded the head of Grand Gulch under the foot of Elk Ridge before turning to the southeast at Snow Flat and gaining the floor of Comb Wash via the Twist (a crooked descent into Road Canyon).

Comb Ridge was the last formidable barrier on the route. It is one of the most dramatic features in the canyon country. Extending all the way from Black Mesa in northern Arizona to the Abajo Mountains in Utah, the immense monocline is a jagged cliff thrown up in the face of would-be travelers. Modern state highways 95 and 163 have been heroically blasted through cracks in its facade, but in 1880 the pioneers saw nothing but a barrier several hundred feet high and extending, it seemed, infinitely into the distance both north and south.

There were, in fact, several crossings of Comb Ridge available to them, none of which was very appealing. One would have been to ascend Elk Ridge as a later road did from Blanding to the Natural Bridges, passing between the Bear's Ears and along the slope of the Abajo Mountains around the north end of Comb Ridge. Another was through a narrow crack in the facade at Navajo Hill where Highway 163 crosses today. Finally, there was a steep ascent of the ridge at San Juan Hill on the north bank of the San Juan River where the river broke through the ridge. It was this last route that the pioneers chose.

San Juan Hill today appears much less forbidding than it proved to be to the pioneers. As far back as Grand Flat, the once unified party had become spread out as weaker teams found it impossible to keep up, and wagons were being abandoned. Consequently, San Juan Hill, a minor ascent compared with others they had previously negotiated, became one of the greatest tribulations, and its upper reaches were bloodied by the skinned knees of stumbling animals. It is no wonder that a nameless member of the party chiseled "We Thank Thee, O God" into the cliff face near the top of the trail.

The Hole-in-the-Rock party never finished its trek. The pitiful struggles of the overtaxed animals ascending San Juan Hill, and the weariness of the people themselves who found what they anticipated to be a six-week trek had turned into an almost six-month journey, convinced them to end their pilgrimage at what they thought were fertile bottomlands almost twenty miles short of their goal of Montezuma Creek. There, on April 6, 1880, most of the party had gathered, and the decision was made to locate their mission at what they would call Bluff City.

It was the end of the first real reconnaissance of the San Juan Country. The Spanish had raided through parts of the area, and the Dominguez-Escalante party had even mapped some of it. The Great Surveys of the 1870s had skirted it and brought to public knowledge something of the nature of the terrain that continued beyond their studies into the mysterious canyons of the San Juan. But the Hole-in-the-Rockers had crossed it again and again as their scouts plotted a roadway and guided the large wagon train slowly through its labyrinthine geography. It was a scenically spectacular but also forbidding region, and a more detailed knowledge of it would come slowly and in piecemeal ways as cowboys, miners, scientists, and others gradually ventured into it.

NOTES

1. C. Gregory Crampton, *Standing Up Country: The Canyon Lands of Utah and Arizona* (New York: Alfred A. Knopf, 1964), 48.

2. John Francis Bannon, *The Spanish Borderlands Frontier, 1513–1821* (New York: Holt Rinehart & Winston, 1970), 188–89.

3. J. H. Parry, *The Age of Reconnaissance* (Cleveland: World Publishing Co., 1963), 320–37; Elizabeth A. H. John, *Storms Brewed in Other Men's Worlds* (College Station: Texas A&M University Press, 1975), Chapter 1.

4. Bannon, *The Spanish Borderlands Frontier*, 6; although highly skeptical of arguments based on the supposed lightness of Spanish slavery, Frank McNitt, *Navajo Wars* (Albuquerque: University of New Mexico Press, 1972), 12–13, presents those of Fray Angelico Chavez.

5. McNitt, *Navajo Wars*, 12: "A central thesis of the present book is that a direct link existed between continuing slaving forays and prolonged Navajo warfare upon the settlements; that in proportion to captives lost to the raiders, Navajo attacks on pueblos and white settlements increased or diminished."

6. Austin N. Leiby, "Borderland Pathfinders: The 1765 Diaries of Juan Maria Antonio de Rivera," (Ph.D. dissertation, Northern Arizona University, 1984); G. Clell Jacobs, "The Phantom Pathfinder: Juan Maria Antonio de Rivera and His Expedition," *Utah Historical Quarterly* 60 (Summer 1992): 200–23.

7. See maps in Bannon, *Spanish Borderlands Frontier*, 31 and 165.

8. In addition to the brief account of the expedition in Crampton, *Standing Up Country*, 43–48, see David E. Miller, "Discovery of Glen Canyon, 1776," *Utah Historical Quarterly* 26 (July 1958): 220–37; and Fray Angelico Chavez and Ted J. Warner, *The Dominguez-Escalante Journal: Their Expedition Through Colorado, Utah, Arizona, and New Mexico, in 1776* (Provo, Utah: Brigham Young University Press, 1976).

9. Until P. T. Reilly's massive history of Lee's Ferry is published, the best available account is C. Gregory Crampton and W. L. Rusho, *Desert River Crossing: Lee's Ferry on the Colorado River* (Layton, Utah: Peregrine Smith, 1975).

10. Chavez and Warner, *The Dominguez-Escalante Journal*, 100 (November 7, 1776).

11. LeRoy R. Hafen, ed., "Amijo's Journal of 1829–30; the Beginning of Trade Between New Mexico and California," *Colorado Magazine* 27 (April 1950): 120–31.

12. The account that follows is based on McNitt, *Navajo Wars*, 52–65, and David M. Brugge, "Vizcarra's Navajo Campaign," *Arizona and the West* 6 (Autumn 1964): 223–44.

13. Charles Kelly, "Chief Hoskaninni [*sic*]," *Utah Historical Quarterly* 21 (July 1953): 224.

14. C. Gregory Crampton, *Historical Sites in Glen Canyon: Mouth of Hansen Creek to Mouth of San Juan River*, University of Utah Anthropological Paper No. 61 (Salt Lake City: University of Utah Press, 1962), 49, 58.

15. William H. Goetzmann, *Exploration and Empire* (New York: Random House, 1966), 489–529, especially 498.

16. Ibid., 499–500, 503–4; Mike Foster, *Strange Career: The Life of Ferdinand Vandeveer Hayden* (Niwot, Colo.: Roberts Rinehart Publishers, 1994); William Henry Jackson, *Time Exposure* (New York: G. P. Putnam's Sons, 1940).

17. F. V. Hayden, *Ninth Annual Report of the United States Geological and Geographical Survey of the Territories . . . For the Year 1875* (Washington, D.C.: Government Printing Office, 1877), 12–17; Jackson, *Time Exposure*, 236–38.

18. Most of the sources for the Powell expeditions are published in *Utah Historical Quarterly*, Vols. 15–17 (1947–49). See also J. W. Powell, *The Exploration of the Colorado River and Its Canyons* (Meadville, Pa.: Flood & Vincent, 1895 [reprinted in 1961 by Dover Books]). For Glen Canyon, a useful primary source, though written much later, is Frederick S. Dellenbaugh, *A Canyon Voyage: The Narrative of the Second Powell Expedition* (New York: G. P. Putnam's Sons, 1908). Pending publication of Donald Worster's biography of Powell, in progress at this time, two useful studies are William Culp Darrah, *Powell of the Colorado* (Princeton: Princeton University Press, 1951), and Wallace Stegner, *Beyond the Hundredth Meridian: John Wesley Powell and the Second Opening of the West* (Boston: Houghton Mifflin, 1954).

19. Dellenbaugh, *A Canyon Voyage*, 135–36.

20. Biographies of each member of the *Canonita* survey are in *Utah Historical Quarterly*, 16–17 (1948–49): 492–503. Johnson, Hillers, and Dellenbaugh kept diaries of the trip, which have been compiled by Otis R. Marston. A copy is available in the Harry L. Aleson Papers, Utah State Historical Society.

21. Dellenbaugh, *A Canyon Voyage*, 209, and his diary describe the paint job, but only Johnson mentions the longitudinal stripes. All quotations in the following passage come either from Dellenbaugh's book or the diaries.

22. Crampton, *Historical Sites in Glen Canyon: Mouth of Hansen Creek to Mouth of San Juan River*, 44–45 (Historical Site 101).

23. By far the best of several accounts of the San Juan mission is David E. Miller, *Hole-in-the-Rock: An Epic in the Colonization of the Great American West* (Salt Lake City: University of Utah Press, 1959), which ably interprets, though with a Mormon bias, the meager primary sources, and even includes transcripts of the most important ones in appendices. This narrative is largely based on Miller's book.

The Search for the Anasazis

The world has many beautiful places, and although the canyon country of the Colorado Plateau offers brilliant colors, dramatic topography, and scenic attractions to rival anything on the planet, perhaps its most enduring appeal to casual tourists as well as seasoned explorers has been the ubiquitous presence of Anasazi remains. The Spanish were too preoccupied with their quest for the wealth of the supposed Seven Cities of Cibola or with the search for converts or, more darkly, with their quest for slaves, to comment at much length on the Anasazi sites they encountered. But to the Americans, from the soldiers under Colonel Washington who first saw Chaco Canyon in 1849, to the government surveys of the 1870s, to backpackers over one hundred years later, the Anasazis have exerted an undiminished appeal.

Why? For scientists, the opportunity to study the remains of a primitive culture that occupied the canyon country for over a millennium offers obvious potential for adding to the story of the development of mankind. But why have the Anasazis captivated the rest of us so completely, from the casual hiker poking around in a cliff house and pondering a pictograph, to the collectors who provide a consistent and lucrative market for the thieveries of pothunting vandals? It is a problem for the psychologist rather than the historian, but perhaps Nathaniel Hawthorne pointed toward its solution in the preface to *The House of Seven Gables*, when he observed that America is "a country where there is no shadow, no antiquity, no mystery, no picturesque and gloomy wrong, nor anything but a commonplace prosperity, in broad and simple daylight." Can it be that the Anasazis provide those shadows, that antiquity, those mysteries for which we hunger?

The Wetherills' discovery of the great ruins of the Mesa Verde and the Tsegi and their excavation of those in Grand Gulch and Chaco

Canyon produced a significant increase in both scientific and popular interest in the Anasazis. During the decades around the turn of the twentieth century, others followed in their footsteps, often, in fact, accompanied by the Wetherills or guided by their advice, to study the Anasazis and collect their artifacts. A complete enumeration of those tourists, pothunters, or even the scientists who followed the Wetherills into the San Juan country is impossible here, but the stories of several important groups and individuals will indicate something of the varied nature of those who found themselves under the spell of the Anasazis.

Pothunting—the collecting of Anasazi pots, baskets, mummies, and other artifacts for sale—was already a common practice in the canyon country by the time the Wetherills began making their dramatic discoveries. The Wetherills themselves often sold artifacts, though scientific understanding rather than financial gain was always their primary value, and they tried wherever possible to keep their collections together and to place them in public museums. Others were much less scrupulous, and the earliest scientific expeditions into the San Juan country contain the earliest complaints against vandalism and mercenary excavation.

Among the most successful of the pothunters were two friends of the Wetherills from Durango, Colorado, Charles Cary Graham and Charles McLoyd. With other friends like Graham's brother Howard, Lee Patrick, and the Wetherills' brother-in-law, Charles Mason, they became interested in the casual excavation of Anasazi sites. In 1890 Graham and McLoyd went looking for a ranch in western Colorado and traveled into Utah as far as Bluff, seeking Indian artifacts as well. It was perhaps there that some of the Mormon settlers must have told them of Grand Gulch, and they spent the first four months of 1891 excavating in that fertile field of Anasazi remains. It was the first of several trips into the area, which led them eventually into White Canyon and as far west as Lake Canyon on the Colorado River. The artifacts they brought back to Colorado, literally by the wagonload, not only proved to be lucrative for them but also piqued the scientific interest of the Wetherills, and led to their great expeditions of 1893–94 and 1897 during which the Basketmakers were discovered.

Graham kept a diary of some of their explorations and excavations in Grand Gulch, and it is a revealing glimpse into the modus operandi of a pothunter. Most pothunters, of course, kept no record at all of their ravages, but although Graham is an exception, his diary is of little or no scientific value, consisting as it does of little more than mileages traversed and an inventory of artifacts excavated. During the first week of January 1891, the pair reached what they called Graham Canyon (now known as Bullet Canyon) and began building a trail over which they could take their pack animals. From there they exploited ruins not only in Graham Canyon but also in main Grand Gulch, which they traveled upcanyon to its head and downcanyon all the way to the San Juan River. Their activities are clearly revealed in a random excerpt from Graham's diary, chosen here from the first few days in March:

> 1. Sunday. We went up the main canon about a mile, 7 sandals, 10 arrow points, 1 knife blade, 1 spinner, 1 sample of fur cloth, 2 bone awls, strings.

> 2. We were making trail up the canon about 8 miles. 1 arrow point.

> 3. I went up Graham canon after the horses. Mc went to foot of trail to get some groceries we left there. 1 sandal with designs on bottom, 1 bunch of hair, 1 horn impl. may have been used to make arrow points.

> 4. We moved up the main canon about 8 miles to Salt Cave. 1 flint knife, 1 horn vessel, 1 mummy with feather cloth and part of the reed matting. 1 board—some cotton.

Although the motives of Graham and McLoyd were purely commercial, some of their artifacts found their way to museums. According to Graham's account, the material from their first trip went to a Rev. C. H. Green, pastor of the Baptist church in Durango, who exhibited them for a time. Artifacts from later trips went to "the man who owned the land on which the Aztec Ruins are on," an unspecified "eastern museum," and the Denver Museum.[1]

Of those who followed in the Wetherills' footsteps, perhaps the most ambitious and yet the least known was a group sent to the San Juan country in the summer of 1892 by *The Illustrated American*, a New York weekly magazine similar to *Life* in its attractively illustrated news and feature articles. Piqued by reports of prehistoric Indian ruins from government surveys by Powell, Hayden, and James H.

Simpson, the editors noted that those surveys had been more interested in geology and geography than anthropology, and had thus done
little more than note the existence of such ruins. Thus they proposed
to send a party of young, well-trained, and well-equipped scientists
along the San Juan River, where prehistoric sites were known to be
concentrated, to try to learn more about the Anasazis.[2]

Although none of the members of the expedition had had any experience in the Southwest, and ultimately found themselves defeated by the harsh environment of the San Juan country, the party
was about as well chosen and equipped as one could expect. Most
members of the party were from Ohio, and were qualified for such
a venture as this by their previous work in studying the Mound
Builders, prehistoric Indians in the Ohio and Mississippi River valleys. The leader of the expedition was Warren K. Moorehead,
twenty-six years old, an archaeologist of some experience, who had
been engaged in studying the Mound Builders since 1889. That experience, plus, no doubt, his work on the *Illustrated American* expedition, led to a distinguished archaeological reputation. Moorehead
eventually became editor of *The Archaeologist* magazine, where he
published some of Richard Wetherill's Anasazi research. He became
curator of the Department of Archaeology at Ohio State University,
and even worked for a few weeks in 1897 alongside Richard Wetherill and Claude Pepper at Chaco Canyon.[3]

Joining Moorehead was Lewis W. Gunckel, who, as a son of an ex-
congressman from Ohio, might have been seen as a political ap-
pointee (and his role in that capacity may have been significant),
except for the fact that he was an 1891 graduate of Yale's Sheffield
Scientific School, perhaps the best center for the study of the natural
sciences available at the time. Other members included Remington
Lane, a German-trained art instructor at the Cincinnati Art School;
Clinton Cowen, thirty-one years old and also of Cincinnati, a topog-
rapher and surveyor who had worked with Moorehead on the
Mound Builder excavations; and a Mr. Rowley, an entomologist provided by the American Museum of Natural History in New York
City, who was to collect mammals and birds along the San Juan. Finally, Dr. C. H. Manly of Denver, who wished to study the crania of
any prehistoric skeletons discovered, joined the expedition as its
physician; and William W. Ralston, another Moorehead associate,
was employed as assistant to the others.

The organizers of the expedition did an impressive job of raising support (here one suspects Gunckel's political connections may have played a role), both among scientific institutions and private businesses. Among the former were the American Museum of Natural History, the Smithsonian Institution, and the Peabody Museum of Boston, each of which had been promised exhibits of any artifacts brought back by the explorers (an exhibit was also planned for the World's Columbian Exposition in Chicago in 1893). Donations in kind were provided by two railroads, who provided transportation from New York City to Durango, Colorado; the Armour and American Biscuit Companies, who provided food; the National Cordage Company, who provided rope; Colgate, who provided soap; and the Winchester and Colt Arms Companies, who donated rifles and pistols. Supplies were carried in two horse-drawn covered wagons, one of which was a Charles Goodnight-type chuckwagon, and on pack burros.

The expedition set out with what modern scientific hindsight might regard as interesting, not to say comical, preconceptions. For one thing, unprotected lowland sites were thought to be erected by a peace-loving culture who anticipated no need for protection, while the less accessible cave and cliff sites must, by implication, have been occupied by a more warlike people who needed fortresses. The prehistoric structures themselves were thought to be mysteriously perfect squares or circles. Part of this romantic conception made a special place for the towers, like those at Hovenweep, and the circular kivas, for it was thought that they "had a religious origin, and that the eternal fire, which appears to have been an essential of their worship, was kept in such enclosures, the circles symbolizing the Sun, who was the deity worshipped by the people who constructed them."[4] In the light of the expedition's ultimate findings, a certain amount of this initial anthropological silliness is easy to overlook, for Moorehead and Gunckel, the two primary scientists in the party, were no fools. They ended up asking the right questions about the Anasazis, questions that helped set much of the intellectual agenda for early southwestern archaeology. They wanted to know, for one thing, what the relationship of the Anasazis was to the Mound Builders and the Aztecs, the other two prehistoric American cultures of which anthropologists of the time were aware, and what their relationship was to the modern southwestern Indians: the Utes, Navajos, and Apaches. They were aware of cranial deformities in some, though not all, Anasazi skeletons, a feature that would become one of the diagnostic differences between Basketmaker and Pueblo phases. They wanted to know why the Anasazis had abandoned the San Juan country, and sought an answer in the aridity of the environment. Finally, they devoted considerable attention to the rock art of the Anasazis and concluded, as modern archaeologists have continued to believe, that it is symbolic rather than linguistic. The next generation of archaeologists would solve some of those problems, but others would continue to puzzle scientists to the present. All in all, it was not a bad summer's work, especially for a bunch of complete dudes who had never seen the Southwest before.

The party left New York City on February 29 for Durango, Colorado, their supply and departure point. Durango was a fortunate choice, not only for its proximity to the San Juan country, but also because of the nearby availability of the Wetherills and Charles McLoyd, who knew more than anyone about the Anasazis and the location of their ruins. Several times in their articles, the *Illustrated American* explorers acknowledge advice from the Wetherills, and Moorehead, acting as an agent of the American Museum of Natural History, even purchased McLoyd's Colorado River artifacts.

The planned itinerary was to work their way from Durango down the La Plata and Animas Rivers to the San Juan, then follow it as far as possible to the west. Success came almost immediately, and the May 7 issue contained Cowen's map of the La Plata Valley with many ruins plotted on mesas above the river, and his floor plan of the great ruins at Aztec, New Mexico, the study of which would become the life work of Earl H. Morris. "Work for the archaeologist, you ask?" Moorehead concluded his article. "Why, there is work for the scientist for years, right in this valley. We used to call ourselves fortunate when we obtained permission to open one mound in Ohio. Here we have thousands of them."

The initial optimism soon received a sobering setback. Directing the main party to proceed overland to Noland's trading post on the San Juan at the Four Corners, Moorehead took Cowen and a guide named Smith on a side trip down the Animas in a homemade boat from Aztec, intending to reach the San Juan and float down to a rendezvous at Noland's. It was a nearly disastrous decision, for the boat, constructed of heavy two-inch planking and navigated by a twenty-foot sweep in the stern and two poles, proved to be completely at the mercy of the swollen spring currents. One-half mile from the San Juan the party wisely decided to abandon the boat and make their way overland to Noland's. They arrived at the rendezvous safely, but shaken, and impressed with some of the difficulties of travel in the Southwest. That lesson would soon be reinforced.

Following a suggestion from the Wetherills, the group established a base camp at the mouth of McElmo Canyon and explored up-canyon in its various branches, reaching the now famous ruins at Hovenweep. Returning to the San Juan River, they began what turned out to be an almost completely demoralizing leg of the journey in which they struggled to get their heavy wagons over the sandy road to Bluff, Utah. "For my part, I would rather walk five miles on an Ohio pike than one mile on any of the 'roads' in Southern Utah or Northern New Mexico," the author of the July 16 article complained: "You cast your eyes about you to see something of beauty, but you see nothing save great frowning sandstone cliffs, an occasional crow, a coyote, or a sand crane. You sigh for the green fields and shady woods of the East." The laborious trek was enough to end the *joie de vivre* with which the trip had begun:

> At night the members of the survey retire early. There is not much story telling as there was during the first month. Everyone comes in tired and hungry. The main desire on the part of everyone is to get through as rapidly as possible and return to the delights of the East.[5]

For what was to be the last of the San Juan tributaries explored by the party, they decided to leave the wagons in a base camp established slightly west of Bluff, and to proceed with pack animals. They rode west to Comb Ridge, then turned up Butler Wash, which, in its western tributaries from short canyons draining Comb Ridge, is one of the greatest concentrations of Anasazi sites in the Southwest. In spite of their weariness and homesickness, the party found renewed interest in their venture as they rode up into one canyon after another and found impressive ruins. Their discoveries included sites such as Cold Spring Cave, Giant's Cave, and Monarch's Cave, each of which they named and often carved a record of their visit on the cliff wall. They followed Butler Wash upcanyon until they could cross over into Cottonwood Wash, which they then followed back to their base camp.

Although the *Illustrated American* group was mistaken in some of their conclusions, for example, that pictographic depictions of sheep indicate their domestication by the Anasazis, most of their conclusions were sound and helped advance scientific understanding of the prehistoric Southwest. They determined, for one thing, that there were no similarities between the Anasazis and the Mound Builders or the Aztecs, and that instead they closely resembled, in their architecture and burial practices, the Zunis and other Pueblo cultures. They observed that the Anasazis were an agricultural people, from the presence of irrigation works, permanent dwellings, and grain-grinding implements. Finally, they observed that the Anasazis were unrelated to the modern southwestern Indians, and even proposed an evolutionary conception of their culture that anticipated the views of later scientists like T. Mitchell Prudden and Herbert E. Gregory. As Moorehead put it, the Anasazis avoided and were different from the Utes, Navajos, and Apaches, "the cruel, vindictive, inhuman races surrounding them on all sides. We find them more human than their neighbors, more like the early races of Europe. . . . we accord them a higher place than that occupied by other American tribes of pre-Columbian times." Sadly, the explorers also noted the ravages of pothunters, "roving bands of Ute and Navajo Indians [who] have gutted nearly all these ruins. The post traders pay the Indians for such pottery, axes, and arrow-heads as they bring in, hence the vandalism is encouraged." Unfortunate as well is the fact that Moorehead, who was making it possible for the American Museum of Natural History to purchase the Charles McLoyd collection, was unable to include McLoyd, one of the greediest of all pothunters, among his villains, and instead characterizes him as a collector "of judgment and discrimination," and a gentleman "who has done scientific work of great value in the Colorado River Valley."[6]

Though they were friends of McLoyd and were often accused of being pothunters themselves, the Wetherill brothers were the most indefatigable explorers of the San Juan country who made, as we have seen, fundamental geographic and archaeologic discoveries. Blessed with acute natural curiosity and scientific temperaments, none of them, nevertheless, had the benefits of much formal education, and although most of them could express themselves clearly and even wittily, reporting their research in scientific and popular publications proved beyond their capability. Thus most of their work was revealed to the world through the writings of others like Gustaf Nordenskiold, Byron Cummings, and Charles L. Bernheimer. One of their most important publicists was T. Mitchell Prudden, an annual Alamo Ranch guest and partner in many taxing desert tramps and cave excavations throughout the San Juan watershed. In a series of articles in *Harper's* and *American Anthropologist* and in a popular book, *On the Great American Plateau*, Prudden announced to scientific and popular audiences the Wetherills' discovery of the Basketmakers. Aided by the Wetherills, Prudden went on to make his own contributions to southwestern archaeology through studies of the developmental Pueblo stage (Pueblo I and II), and through his book, a genuine contribution to American literature, to reveal to the general public something of the character of life on the Colorado Plateau.[7]

Theophil Mitchell Prudden (1849–1924) descended from a long line of Congregational clergymen dating back to Rev. Peter Prudden, who was one of the Puritan founders of the New Haven and Milford, Connecticut, colonies in the seventeenth century. Although Prudden resigned his church membership as a young man because of its skepticism of modern science—particularly Darwinian evolution—he retained a puritanical high seriousness about life and work, which led him through a distinguished academic career.

Prudden never married, and embraced his work with a monkish single-mindedness. After an undergraduate degree at Yale's Sheffield Scientific School (which trained such other distinguished Western scientists as Clarence King and Herbert E. Gregory), Prudden went on to earn the M.D. at Yale Medical School. A highlight of his Yale years, incidentally, was an 1873 trip to the Uinta Mountains with Professor Othniel C. Marsh, whose western expeditions contributed major paleontological evidence in support of Darwinian evolution.[8] Although Prudden taught for a time at his alma mater and worked in public health in New York, his medical career consisted primarily of a professorship in pathology at Columbia University Medical School, 1892–1909. Prudden was well known in the medical profession as the author of standard textbooks in histology and pathology (with Francis Delafield), the latter of which went through twelve editions during his lifetime.

To his students, his puritanical intensity and high standards could be intimidating, though his cold demeanor and infamous sarcasm seem primarily to have been employed in deflating overblown egos. The young Alfred Vincent Kidder, at the beginning of a career that would make him one of the most revered of southwestern archaeologists, approached Prudden humbly for advice on the San Juan country and found him not only congenial but also generous both in advice and financial support. Clayton Wetherill remembered how Prudden's stony glare could silence a Navajo packer's flippance and overfamiliarity, but the Wetherills valued his companionship above almost all other easterners. "All of us considered it a privilege to be able to accompany him on any of his trips through the Southwest," Al Wetherill asserted, and in his letters to the brothers, Prudden naturally fell into an imitation of their colloquial style and droll cowboy wit. When news of Richard's murder reached John and Clayton, they were at Marsh Pass assisting in one of Prudden's excavations, and Prudden immediately abandoned the project to ride with the brothers to Pueblo Bonito where, in white-hot anger, he penned a demand for an investigation into the role of inept and hostile Indian agents as a factor in the incident. "I feel that there is nothing I can do that will begin to pay him for what he has done for my brothers and myself," John Wetherill wrote to Prudden's sister upon learning of the doctor's death; "He was always to be found when we needed him the most."[9]

In a posthumous tribute to Prudden, Kidder observed that "although archaeology was an avocation with Dr. Prudden, he brought to it the resources of a mind naturally adapted to and specially trained for scientific endeavor." That, during the formative years of southwestern archaeology, was more than enough to support major contributions to the field. Prudden first appeared at the Alamo Ranch in 1895, the year after Richard Wetherill's epoch-making discovery of the Basketmakers in Grand Gulch. At the ranch, and during a protracted pack trip with the brothers to the Hopi Mesas that summer, Prudden recognized the scientific significance of the discovery. During successive visits, Prudden placed at the brothers' disposal his literary abilities and access to popular and scientific journals in the East. In *Harper's New Monthly Magazine* for June 1897, Prudden published his first article on the Anasazis, "An Elder Brother to the Cliff Dwellers," in which he reported the evidence supporting Richard Wetherill's theory of the Basketmakers. It was the first announcement to the scientific community and to the general public of the existence of the earlier culture.[10]

But the Anasazis had captivated Prudden on their own. Not content just to report the investigations of others, Prudden set out to make his own contribution to anthropology. On the one hand, he noted, were the Cliff Dwellers, whose immense stone cities were conspicuous at places like Mesa Verde, Chaco Canyon, and the Tsegi. On the other hand were the Basketmakers, whose antiquity was either inconspicuously exhibited in pictograph panels or storage cists, or completely hidden, sometimes many feet beneath the Cliff Dwellers' ruins. How were the two cultures connected?

As a Darwinian, Prudden suspected there was an evolutionary relationship between the two cultures, which represented two basic phases in a larger cultural continuum. To investigate the thesis, he chose to study the more modest ruins in the San Juan watershed that might represent a transitional phase from Basketmaker to Pueblo. These structures he called the "unit type" of Pueblo. Characteristically, these consisted of three elements: a small kiva, partially surrounded by a three-sided open rectangle of one-story rooms communally occupied by, at most, a few families, and a burial mound. As the size of the community expanded, additional rooms would be attached on any or all sides and perhaps additional stories added.[11] Architecturally, this phase of Anasazi development came to be known as the Developmental Pueblo, or Pueblos I and II in the Pecos classification, and preceded the immense cities of the Mesa Verde, Chaco Canyon, and the Tsegi, which characterize the Great Pueblo, or Pueblo III phase.

Prudden's definition of this phase was the subject of several articles in the *American Anthropologist* from 1903 to 1918. Accompanied by Prudden's hand-drawn maps, which were the first accurate plottings of prehistoric sites in the San Juan country, the articles were, as Kidder asserted, models of archaeological reconnaissance that "laid the foundation for all subsequent research on the developmental side of Southwestern civilization."[12]

Prudden was one of the Wetherill brothers' favorite traveling companions, not only because of what they found to be his personable company but also because of his uncomplaining endurance—a rare quality, no doubt, among their eastern guests who regularly spent little time in the saddle. "We had made other trips with him and knew his habits," Al Wetherill wrote of Prudden:

> There were many days through desert sands or mountain forests when we were often short on food; many a dry camp

with trail-tired horses; days of blistering sunshine or frosty nights in the high country—but never a complaint from the Doctor.[13]

Although many of Prudden's trips with the Wetherills were research journeys among Anasazi sites, he had come, as he put it, "under the spell of the Grand Canyon," and their most memorable trip together was an 1897 visit to both the north and the south rim of the Grand Canyon. The trip included Prudden, Al and Clayton Wetherill, and a Navajo packer. It was their longest and most arduous journey together, and both Prudden and Al Wetherill left lengthy accounts of it.[14]

Beginning at the Alamo Ranch, their route was to have been along the San Juan to Comb Wash, then toward the Bear's Ears, through Clay Hills Pass to Hall's Crossing, Escalante, Panguitch, and Kanab to the north rim of the Grand Canyon. They would then cross the Colorado at Lee's Ferry, visit the south rim, and return via the northern Navajo country. Since much of the route would have taken them through Mormon settlements in southern Utah, the Wetherills thought it wise to procure letters of introduction from Mormon friends in Mancos to facilitate acquisition of supplies along the way. Al reported that other friends, hearing of those letters, jibed, "Ha Ha? so you had to get pass ports did you?" But Mormon clannishness fortunately proved to be no obstacle at all, and the letters were never necessary, "for we found the people the best ever whenever we passed through a Mormon town."[15]

A revision of the itinerary became necessary when they learned there was no boat available at Hall's Crossing, so they decided to cross the Colorado River at Hite instead. It became the great adventure of the trip, and is recounted in detail by both Al Wetherill and Prudden. Upon reaching the Dandy Crossing, they learned there was no boat available there, either, and that they would have to go upstream, evidently to the site of the Harshberger ferry, where there was a skiff they could use. Unfortunately, there was only one elderly woman at the Harshberger site, and she protested that she lacked the strength to get the boat across.

Al Wetherill was elected to attempt the crossing to get the boat. Swimming a horse across seemed to be an obvious strategy, but, as Al learned, the horses were poor swimmers: "I nearly drowned two horses before deciding that they knew less about water than we did."

Desperation led to employing a largely water-soaked log as a flotation device, "not because I was afraid," Al protested, "but one has more confidence in their [*sic*] ability if there is something to buoy them up." At last, "I put in my best licks at swimming and managed to get through the roaring current and crawl out on the bank." No doubt to his considerable chagrin, he found Prudden waiting for him when he landed; the woman had gotten up her courage and brought the boat across while Al was making his heroic plunge.[16] By ferrying their gear in the boat and towing the frightened horses, the party at last wound up on the north bank.

The rest of the trip was relatively uneventful except for difficulties on the homeward leg caused by food and water shortages, which forced them to replace some of the animals. One amusing development occurred at the Grand Canyon, where Prudden was amazed at the nonchalance of their Navajo companion, who was obviously much less "under the spell" of the scenery than Prudden:

> We came suddenly to the brink at a great promontory looming far out over the profound deeps. He walked forward to the edge exclaiming, "A-la-ha-ni!" which, as one of my comrades suggested, would be fairly interpreted, "Well, I will be darned!" Then he at once turned his back to the canyon, sat down, rolled and smoked a cigarette, and fell asleep. From that time during all the days which we spent skirting the chasm he paid, so far as I could see, not the slightest attention to the outlooks.[17]

Prudden distilled his travel experiences with the Wetherills and his research on the Anasazis into a thoughtful and engaging book, which, if it were better known, would be ranked equal to similar classics of desert literature like John Van Dyke's *The Desert* and Ross Calvin's *Sky Determines*. Prudden's *On the Great American Plateau: Wanderings Among Canyons and Buttes, in the Land of the Cliff-Dweller, and the Indian of Today* appeared in one 1907 printing and sold well, but for some reason has never been reprinted.

Not the least of the book's virtues is Prudden's "sketch map," a fold-out sheet included between the last page of text and the index. Although based on Prudden's personal noninstrument reconnaissance methods, and small in scale (its 10½ by 6½ inches dimensions include an area from eastern California to western Texas, and from central Utah to southern Arizona and New Mexico), it is the

first accurate map of the Colorado Plateau, showing in their proper
relationships the major landforms and river courses with a particular
emphasis on modern Indian pueblos and Anasazi areas. But his verbal description of the Colorado Plateau is equally vivid:

> If one takes a map of the United States drawn on such a scale
> that it is about seven inches from New York to San Francisco,
> and puts a silver quarter of a dollar upon it so that the head of
> the alleged bird of freedom, looking toward the west, lies just
> over these four corners [where Utah, Colorado, New Mexico,
> and Arizona meet], he will have covered a tract considerably
> larger than New England, almost as dry as Sahara, and as rich in
> the relics of a vanished race as any classic country of them all.[18]

The Colorado Plateau, as he sees it, is a region that civilization bypassed, and it thus appears today in its relatively pristine and primitive form. Prudden points out that the great tide of white emigration
to the West took two major routes: the Great Salt Lake Trail and the
Santa Fe Trail. "Thus a vast, wild region behind the mountains which
makes up the larger part of the Great Plateau lay long undisturbed
between the two active routes of far western travel."[19]

Elaborating on the nature and significance of the plateau, Prudden adopted a position of "hard" cultural primitivism, in which the
largely uninhabited backcountry of the Southwest is placed in favorable comparison with the overcivilized urban East:

> [The Colorado Plateau] is so lavish in stories of the world's fash-
> ioning, so rich in fading glimpses of strange old barbarians who
> are gone, so quaintly peopled with kindly children of the earth
> and the sun who bid one welcome to homes and firesides where
> for centuries they have foregathered; a land withal so alluring
> for its absolute freedom from fret and fume, where you and you
> alone are owner of the day, that when once you have broken the
> link which bound you to the rails and head off into the dreamy,
> shimmering mazes which lure you on and on, it will be strange
> indeed if you do not for some lucid hours care least of all things
> whether the fortunes of the way are ever to lead you back.
>
> Nothing matters much so long as you can find a little water
> for yourself and your faithful beasts, and a few stray sticks to
> cook your simple fare. . . . Such are the sufficient aims of days

and weeks of wandering on the Great Plateau when once you have forgotten that the twentieth century has just begun, and have drifted back into the simple days and ways before the Spaniards came.[20]

It is, in his view, the rigors of southwestern life that impart its special virtue to its visitors and inhabitants: "Here is elemental life, here is genuine freedom; but those exalted states are not to be won without strict conformity to the inexorable requirements of the land."

> Altogether the wanderer who does not mind the wholesome sunburn upon the skin, and has a good supply of water, is as free and comfortable and happy as good mortals deserve to be. How far away the great city seems! And for the thousand unnecessary things which we gather about us in our winter thralldom and dote upon, how pitiful are they, if we deign to recall them! This is living. We get down to sheer manhood, face to face with the bare, relentless, fascinating old earth. And ever above is the marvellous sky and ever a nameless witchery of the air, making far things strange and beautiful, and more than all else luring the wanderer back to these hot wastes year after year.[21]

As a devoted Darwinist, Prudden's views of the Indians were similar to those of Lewis Henry Morgan, whose *Ancient Society* (1877) proposed an evolutionary anthropology in which man advanced through three stages: savagery, barbarism, and civilization. The American Indian, in Prudden's view, consisted of "masses of dusky people, from one seaboard to the other, [who] lived out their simple lives face to face with nature, won their way slowly through savagery to barbarism, and even here and there began to press eagerly through the portals which open toward civilization." This evolutionary process was interrupted by the coming of the Europeans, whose appearance represented a considerable misfortune for the Indian. With the coming of the whites, "the native advance was stayed, and soon the doors were closed forever upon a genuine American barbarism just shaping itself into a crude civilisation in favored corners of the land."[22]

The Pueblo Indians represented an exception to this general experience of Indians. In their culture, "the wreckage of the abortive experiment in primitive man-culture in America, still survive. . . .

Some of them present to-day a significant transition phase in the advance of a people from savagery toward civilisation. . . ." Consequently, the Pueblos offered a rare and precarious opportunity for anthropologists, who must record their transient stage of evolution while the opportunity still exists, for

> . . . when such people get on cotton shirts, need coffee and sugar, want rum, and begin to name their sons after the Presidents, they will not continue long to send messages to the gods by rattlesnakes, nor propitiate the elements by feathers and songs.[23]

Although the Navajos, in Prudden's view, were not as advanced as the Pueblo cultures and thus did not represent as fortunate a research opportunity as the Pueblos' transitional phase from barbarism to civilization, they were still well worth studying as classic examples, in their pastoralism, of Native American barbarism:

> Altogether they are among the most interesting of the aborigines who live in the old fashion, hold to the old deities, and maintain a degree of self-respect and independence in the face of the blighting influences of civilisation which is noteworthy and admirable.[24]

Finally, Prudden saw that a great deal of the research potential of the Anasazis was being wasted by pothunters who ignored science in the interest of economic gain. Undoubtedly well aware of contemporary attacks on his friends the Wetherills for alleged hurried excavations of ruins, inadequate records, and sale of artifacts, Prudden included an impassioned denunciation of pothunting, vindicating, by implication, his associates the Wetherills:

> Most of the prehistoric ruins of the south-west are given over to-day to unbridled vandalism. A pot or a skull is worth a few dimes to the trader and a few dollars to the tourist, and so has been evolved the holiday and the professional pot-hunter. Everywhere the ruins are ravaged. More is destroyed in the search than is saved. No records are kept. But worse than this the Indian, in whose domain are many of the most interesting ruins, has learned his lesson from the white brother, and has learned it well.[25]

With the advent of cultural relativism, which was already coming into favor when Prudden's book appeared, in the work of Franz Boas and his students at the Johns Hopkins University, Prudden's evolutionary view has become antiquated. Whatever he wished to make of southwestern Indian culture, though, his research into the Anasazis and his keen interest in and friendship with the Navajos and the Pueblos enable his book to wear well in the late twentieth century while other condescending treatises, like Morgan's, have become museum pieces. On the other hand, his admiration of the Wetherill brothers as capable desert dwellers and, within the context of their times, capable scientists, has been increasingly confirmed by subsequent research that has objectively transcended the animosities and jealousies that dominated in Prudden's day.

While Prudden was no more than an avocational archaeologist, his systematic research and analytical mind enabled him to make sounder and more profound contributions to the study of the Anasazis than some professional archaeologists. Although the archaeological activities of Byron Cummings (1861–1954) were in fact as avocational in nature as those of Prudden, Cummings, as a student of ancient culture and professor of classics at the University of Utah and later the University of Arizona, considered archaeology to be something of a professional interest, yet he made less impressive contributions to the field than did Prudden.

Cummings was a New Yorker, born in Westville and trained at Oswego Normal School and Syracuse High School. In 1889 he received an A.B. degree from Rutgers College, and an M.A. from the same institution in 1892. Although Rutgers made him an honorary doctor of science in 1924, the M.A. was his highest earned degree, and with it he began a teaching career in Latin and Greek at the University of Utah in 1893. Cummings rose through the academic ranks, and became the university's first dean of the College of Arts and Sciences in 1906. He resigned from that institution in 1915 along with several others in protest against President Joseph T. Kingsbury's dismissal of four non-Mormon faculty members for their support of progressive political measures and, so rumors had it, because of their hostility to the Latter-day Saints Church. Cummings accepted a similar deanship at the University of Arizona, where he remained until his retirement in 1938.

Although the frail physique of "the Dean," as his students affectionately called him, did not suggest a hardy desert explorer, Cummings impressed everyone who knew him with his energy. Like the Greeks whose culture Cummings knew so well, he admired physical skills as complementary to the life of the mind, and was an avid promoter of the athletics programs at the University of Utah. On remote canyon trails, Cummings became a famous Dutch oven cook and wrangled recalcitrant mules alongside the packers and guides. A final badge of his character is that he became one of John Wetherill's favorite companions and joined that great canyon explorer in his discoveries of Rainbow Bridge and the cliff city of Betatakin.[26]

Cummings's major achievements as explorer and archaeologist came in the three field seasons of 1907 to 1909, during which he took groups of university students into the San Juan country for direct experience with prehistoric sites. The impulse for these trips came from Cummings's acquaintance with Edgar L. Hewett and the formation of a Utah chapter of Hewett's American Society of Archaeology. This affiliation put Cummings in touch with the world of professional archaeology and with soon-to-be famous archaeologists like Alfred Kidder, who joined the 1908 expedition.

A brief trip to Nine Mile Canyon in eastern Utah in 1906 gave Cummings his first taste of prehistoric Utah. In 1907 he organized a major expedition to see the Natural Bridges in White Canyon and to survey the archaeological potential of the area. The Natural Bridges were discovered in 1883 by the miner Cass Hite, but their existence was not widely publicized until visits in 1903 and 1905 that resulted in articles in national publications, so the Cummings expedition had a opportunity for original work. Proceeding by way of Bluff over portions of the Hole-in-the-Rock road to Grand Gulch, where they investigated some ruins in its tributaries, the party continued into White Canyon, where they identified numerous ruins for later excavation.[27]

The 1908 expedition, accompanied by Hewett and Kidder, focused on Alkali Ridge in the Montezuma Creek drainage west of Blanding, where Cummings and his students actually engaged in their first excavations. An important event of that season was Cummings's meeting with John Wetherill at Bluff, with whom he and the students toured the Segi-ot-sosi and Segi Canyons. At Oljato, Louisa Wetherill told Cummings of the existence of an immense sandstone arch near Navajo Mountain, and the Dean began making plans for a trip there in 1909.

During his most famous field season, 1909, Cummings accomplished excavations in both the Segi-ot-sosi and the Segi before setting out with the party of William Boone Douglass on the route that led to the discovery of Rainbow Bridge. Before returning to Salt Lake City, the Cummings party explored upper Navajo Canyon.

Although Cummings was an indefatigable explorer and collector of Anasazi artifacts, his scientific contributions were minimal. For one thing, Cummings's field notes show that he approached his excavations with no focused scientific problems in mind. They contain sketch maps of canyons showing the locations of ruins, floor plans of some of the ruins investigated, and copies of rock art at each site. Beyond that, there is a general description of the site's features, such as the number of buildings and stories, general masonry characteristics, and types of pottery. Then there is an inventory of artifacts removed. His records are, in short, no real advancement over the Wetherills' primitive Grand Gulch records almost two decades previous. As a result, Cummings developed no theories about the Anasazis, nor have subsequent archaeologists been able to use his records as contributory data to their own investigations.[28]

Another reason for the limited archaeological contribution of Cummings's expeditions is that Cummings regarded himself primarily as a teacher, and therefore a popularizer, rather than a scientist. As his student Neil M. Judd put it, Cummings "sought to popularize his subject; to explain it in words all could understand." Cummings thought his best service toward promoting popular understanding of and respect for the Anasazis would be to assemble a comprehensive collection of artifacts to be placed on public display at the University of Utah. The Utah chapter of the American Society of Archaeology, Cummings stated in 1908,

> feels that there should be in the possession of the state and accessible to all a museum collection which will adequately set forth the history of the inhabitants of its territory, both historic and prehistoric. The intelligence, education and general culture of the people demand a museum of art, archaeology and history. . . . Both ancient and modern Indians present an excellent field for research and study; accurate and complete date regarding their traditions, their life and their customs must be collected and preserved. And surely Utah will take pride in a museum

that will furnish an adequate history of her people from earliest times.[29]

The Anasazis, then, had begun to provide a powerful lure to the San Juan country that had brought a diverse group to study, enjoy, and often exploit their remains by the time the United States entered World War I. The following decades would see that interest grow, and the diversity of the visitors increase. To the pothunter whose crude and hastily dug pits appeared in sites all over the region, was added the wide-eyed tourist like Charles L. Bernheimer, motivated equally by the romance of Zane Grey and the science of Herbert E. Gregory, and finally the ever-increasing sophistication of archaeologists like Neil Judd and Earl Morris.

NOTES

1. Helen Sloan Daniels, *Adventures with the Anasazi of Falls Creek* (Durango, Colo.: Occasional Papers of the Center of Southwest Studies, Fort Lewis College, 1976), 13, 15. This publication includes the entirety of Graham's diary. During the late 1980s a privately funded venture called the "Wetherill-Grand Gulch Research Project" studied the Graham-McLoyd and other early Grand Gulch expeditions. Records of their project, which must be regarded as the definitive study of the area, are at the Edge of the Cedars Museum in Blanding, Utah.

2. The account of *The Illustrated American* expedition that follows is documented in weekly issues of the magazine from April 2 to August 27, 1892. The members, sponsors, and goals of the expedition are given in the April 2 issue.

3. Frank McNitt, *Richard Wetherill: Anasazi* (Albuquerque: University of New Mexico Press, 1957), 36, 178.

4. *The Illustrated American*, April 2, 1892, 307.

5. Ibid., July 23, 1892, 400.

6. Ibid., May 28, 1892, 88; July 9, 1892, 361–65; August 20, 1892, 23.

7. A complete bibliography of Prudden's writings is in [Lillian E. Prudden, ed.], *Biographical Sketches and Letters of T. Mitchell Prudden, M.D.* (New Haven, Conn.: Yale University Press, 1927), 293–300. See also McNitt, *Richard Wetherill*, passim; Prudden, *On the Great American Plateau* (New York: G. P. Putnam's Sons, 1907); and Maurine S. Fletcher, ed., *The Wetherills of the Mesa Verde: Autobiography of Benjamin Alfred Wetherill* (Rutherford, N. J.: Fairleigh Dickinson University Press, 1977), 233–45. The Prudden Papers are at Yale University.

8. Prudden, *On the Great American Plateau*, 79–80; William H. Goetzmann, *Exploration and Empire: The Explorer and the Scientist in the Winning of the American West* (New York: Alfred A. Knopf, 1966), 425–29.

9. [Prudden], *Biographical Sketches and Letters*, 155, 149; Fletcher, *The Wetherills of the Mesa Verde*, 233; McNitt, *Richard Wetherill*, 295–96.

10. McNitt, *Richard Wetherill*, 85–94; [Prudden,] *Biographical Sketches and Letters*, 177–78.

11. Prudden, *On the Great American Plateau*, 145–55, summarizes his "unit house" paradigm, and includes a floor plan of a typical one on p. 148.

12. [Prudden], *Biographical Sketches and Letters*, 178; see the photographs of models of unit dwellings constructed by Prudden for the American Museum of Natural History opposite p. 176; McNitt, *Richard Wetherill*, 87.

13. Fletcher, *The Wetherills of the Mesa Verde*, 233–35.

14. Prudden, *On the Great American Plateau*, 36–71; Fletcher, *The Wetherills of the Mesa Verde*, 235–44. See Fletcher's map on p. 234.

15. Al Wetherill journal, Museum of Northern Arizona; Fletcher, *The Wetherills of the Mesa Verde*, 239.

16. Al Wetherill journal; Fletcher, *The Wetherills of the Mesa Verde*, 238–39.

17. [Prudden], *Biographical Sketches and Letters*, 142.

18. Prudden, *On the Great American Plateau*, 93–94.

19. Ibid., 180–81.

20. Ibid., 7–8; Arthur O. Lovejoy, et al., *A Documentary History of Primitivism and Related Ideas* Vol. 1: *Primitivism and Related Ideas in Antiquity* (Baltimore: Johns Hopkins University Press, 1935), 7–11.

21. Prudden, *On the Great American Plateau*, 10–12.

22. Ibid., 25.

23. Ibid., 25–26.

24. Ibid., 31–32.

25. Ibid., 172–75.

26. Biographical data on Cummings is found in the Ralph Vary Chamberlin Papers at the Utah State Historical Society and in Chamberlin's history *The University of Utah* (Salt Lake City: University of Utah Press, 1960), 587; and in Erik K. Reed and

Dale S. King, eds., *For the Dean: Essays in Anthropology in Honor of Byron Cummings on His Eighty-ninth Birthday, Sept. 20, 1950* (Tucson and Santa Fe: Hohokam Museums Association and Southwestern Monuments Association, 1950). Important collections of Cummings Papers are at the University of Arizona and the Arizona Historical Society.

27. Neil M. Judd, "Pioneering in Southwestern Archaeology." In Reed and King, eds., *For the Dean*, 11–27.

28. These generalizations are based upon perusal of Cummings's field notebooks at the Arizona State Museum, particularly those for 1909 transcribed by James H. Knipmeyer in 1987.

29. Cummings, "Cummings Describes Natural Wonders and Scientific Treasures of San Juan Region," *Salt Lake Herald*, November 1, 1908.

The Wetherills: Explorers-Archaeologists

There are other names that resound through the history of this country, both families and individuals: Hite, Chaffin, Gregory. But one name recurs throughout every corner of the country, as a skilled Navajo weaver works her birds, her crosses, her serrated lines as motifs across the expanse of a fine rug. The name is Wetherill. As cattlemen and miners, as explorers, as archaeologists, as Indian traders and peacemakers, as tourist guides, the Wetherills wrote their names again and again in the annals of the San Juan country so that there is simply no understanding of the history of this country without a major focus on them.

All of the five brothers—Richard, Al, John, Clayton, and Winslow—whose birth dates range from 1858 to 1871, made their contribution to the history of the San Juan country, but the two most important ones by far were Richard and John, and it is upon them that this chapter focuses.[1] If they could read this, Richard and John would object to being singled out from their siblings, for the brothers were the tightest knit of families; although their wives disagreed and even sometimes feuded with one another, the sources contain not even the slightest hint of conflict among the brothers themselves. Though in time each married and broke off to pursue his own enterprises, anything the brothers did together was always a group effort, with the hardships, the profits, and the glories all shared alike. Historical understanding, nevertheless, requires recognition of the unique achievements of Richard, as the oldest brother and the acknowledged leader of their group endeavors, and John, after he took up residence at Oljato in 1906 and began to explore the San Juan country on his own.

As the full story of all five brothers cannot be told here, neither can the full range of activities of even Richard and John be given. Their roles as Indian traders and guides appear in later chapters.

Here the focus is upon their achievements as explorers and archaeologists on the Mesa Verde, in Grand Gulch, in the area now included in Navajo National Monument, and at Rainbow Bridge.

The Wetherill family can be traced back to England, where some of its early members became inoculated by the Quaker faith and emigrated to Pennsylvania, a refuge for their persecuted coreligionists. The Quaker religion is a vitally important fact in the family history, for although none of the later Wetherills were churchgoers nor religious in any formal sense, the Quaker peace ethic and the quiet moral integrity that has characterized Quakers from the beginning were fundamental Wetherill attributes. There was a profound courage and resolve about the brothers that was clearly rooted in their residual Quakerism, a belief in cosmic order and the ultimate triumph of truth that sustained them in poverty, hardship, and attacks by jealous contemporaries. If those attacks have been almost entirely refuted, they have been refuted by later scholars looking impartially at the record, never by the Wetherills themselves, who simply assumed that truth would prevail.

Benjamin Kite Wetherill, the father of the five brothers, was born in Pennsylvania in 1831. The Quakers have become proverbial in American history for prosperity resulting from the Benjamin Franklin virtues of hard work and thrift, coupled with a vigorous dose of shrewdness. But B. K. Wetherill had a wanderlust that led him west, turning his back on the farm and the counting house. Settling for a time in Fort Leavenworth, Kansas, where his Quaker wife, Marion Tompkins, kept house and looked after their growing family, Wetherill found work as a government Indian agent along the Chisholm Trail. The government had long since discovered that the Quakers made good Indian agents, because their inner fortitude gave them a quiet courage and diplomatic firmness, while their lack of racism and materialism contrasted vividly with the typical arrogant and exploitive white settler and cattleman. B. K. Wetherill was a small man, but those Quaker qualities made both cowboy and Indian respect him, and he was able to defuse many a dangerous conflict.

The Fort Leavenworth years were important in developing both a family closeness and a tradition that Richard, the oldest brother, was their leader in any cooperative enterprise. With B. K. Wetherill often away from home, Richard naturally became the man of the house in his absence. Health problems also began to plague his father, and

Richard found himself thrust into an ever greater role in running the family affairs as his father weakened.

A Colorado mining boom led the family even farther west in the 1870s, but the rich strikes eluded them. Nor did farming at first work out, when they attempted to cultivate the river bottoms of the treacherous San Juan above Bluff. Eventually they migrated back to Colorado, where in 1882 they established the Alamo Ranch on a bend of the Mancos River near the northeastern escarpment of the great Mesa Verde.

Settling in southwestern Colorado at that time was a perilous undertaking, because the rapid incursions of white miners and settlers had created friction with the powerful Ute Indians who were already there. Blood had been spilled, and most white men were carrying guns. The Wetherills were unique in being undaunted by the dangers of the place, and began building living quarters and outbuildings, cultivating the rich soil, and building a herd of cattle. By the early 1890s, the Wetherills owned 1,000 acres of land, 300 of which were under cultivation, and were counted among the area's prosperous residents.[2]

The Wetherills' developing relations with the Utes were of profound significance for their future. Unlike most of their white neighbors, the Wetherills neither feared nor distrusted the Indians, and exhibited their goodwill by refusing on most occasions to go about armed beyond the normal saddle guns carried by all cattlemen. There were positive overtures, too: In hard times the Indians learned that the Wetherills would feed them, and that they would doctor them when ill. The Indians reciprocated by allowing the Wetherills, alone among the Mancos settlers, to graze their cattle in the canyons of the Mesa Verde, which the Utes otherwise fiercely guarded as their private territory. It was while grazing cattle there that Richard and his brother-in-law, Charles Mason, made the discovery that changed the family's destiny forever. Although the great Anasazi cities of the Mesa Verde lie far outside the geographic scope of this book, it is impossible to understand the later history of the Wetherill brothers without recounting their discovery of those cities and the effects of their explorations there upon the brothers' destiny.

The existence of prehistoric ruins in the canyons of the Mesa Verde was anything but a secret; not only had the Indians told the Wetherills about them, but inscriptions, newspaper articles, and even government reports from the 1874 Hayden survey documented sightings of such ruins by white settlers and explorers.[3] But the Indians had long guarded the mesa jealously, and none of the previous white visitors had developed an accurate idea of the size and extent of the ruins. The Wetherill brothers, with Mason and a few other friends who occasionally joined them, were the first whites to have the permission, the time, and the curiosity to explore the area. "In the course of time," Al Wetherill later recalled, "the younger children were able to do housework and field work and we elder ones began to scout around to find out just what sort of a land we had tied onto."[4] The base for their explorations was a camp near the mouth of Johnson Canyon that they established in 1884 or 1885.

It was Mason's discovery of Balcony House and Al's excavations of Sandal House that established the existence of large ruins full of significant artifacts and spurred the brothers' interest. Given that ripening interest, Al reminisced, "it seems strange that it should have taken us so long to explore the canons until we found the ruin that has ever been our pride and joy—Cliff Palace."[5] A controversy later emerged among outside observers (never among the Wetherills themselves) about the identity of the actual discoverer of Mesa Verde's most celebrated ruin. Al claimed to have sighted it from the floor of the canyon while on foot, but found himself too tired to make the climb into the cave where it is situated. It was like the Viking discovery of America—a great but sterile event for not having been followed up.

The Cliff Palace sighting that did "take" occurred on a December day in 1888 when Richard Wetherill and Charles Mason, following some of their half-wild cattle over the mesa top, came suddenly upon a view of the great ruin from across the canyon. The great writer Willa Cather, while slightly altering history for her fictional purpose, captured the moment in "Tom Outland's Story" better than any historian:

> I wish I could tell you what I saw there, just *as* I saw it, on that
> first morning, through a veil of lightly falling snow. Far up above
> me, a thousand feet or so, set in a great cavern in the face of a
> cliff, I saw a little city of stone, asleep.[6]

Nor was Cliff Palace the only discovery of the day, for on their way back to camp, the pair discovered Spruce Tree House and Square Tower Ruin. It had been, to say the least, a fine day's work.

But it was a day's work that changed the family history profoundly, leading eventually to poverty, controversy ending in government intervention in the form of the Antiquities Act of 1906, and ultimately Richard Wetherill's murder at Chaco Canyon in 1910 by a Navajo spurred by jealous whites who wished to dispossess and evict the Wetherills. The significance of the brothers' great discoveries was not lost upon Al Wetherill:

> Thus began an eighteen-year self-imposed assignment of excavation and research among the ruins of the Mesa Verde. Ranching, unfortunately, took a secondary place in our interests and we gave time, material, and labor we could ill afford to cleaning out the ruins and giving the necessary care to the artifacts that we excavated in order to preserve them.

The underlying motive for their "self-imposed assignment," as Al remembered it, was an almost mystical sense of identification with the Anasazis, which seemed to obligate the brothers to become the curators of their culture:

> To know that you are the first to set foot in homes that had been deserted for centuries is a strange feeling. It is as though unseen eyes watched, wondering what aliens were invading their sanctuaries and why. . . . We could not shake off the feeling that we were possibly predestined for the job [of preserving the Anasazi culture], knowing what depredations had been committed by transients who neither revered nor cared for the ruins as symbols of the past.[7]

Persecution and tragedy remained in the future, but poverty made an immediate appearance as the brothers neglected ranching for archaeology. They lived on such simple fare as baking powder bread browned in a frying pan, and beans and meat steeped overnight in a buried Dutch oven. The brothers learned to compensate for their lack of warm bedding by sleeping in shallow trenches on the leeward side of a campfire. Castoff tents became canvas overalls, and three-cornered sections of old gunnysacks were fashioned into sneakers, a big improvement on their heavy boots for clambering around in cliff houses. "Any hardships were our own responsibility," Al admitted, but quickly added that in spite of it all, "everybody was in the same position, so all that made little difference to us.

Everyone just took things as they came and no one was ever far from happiness."[8]

Fame came soon enough, as word of the discoveries got out and visitors from farther and farther away came to view the informal museum that grew up at the Alamo Ranch and to seek out the brothers as guides to the ruins themselves. The most significant of the visitors was a young Swedish scientist named Gustaf Nordenskiold who arrived at Mancos in 1891. After impressing the Wetherills with his expertise, he gained permission to work alongside them and to remove a collection of artifacts to publicize the scientific value of their discoveries. Based on only four months' work, Nordenskiold wrote *Cliff Dwellers of the Mesa Verde*, which appeared in 1893. Soon translated from Swedish into English, it became the classic account of the Mesa Verde Anasazis and drew the world's attention to the Wetherills and their work.[9]

But fortune did not follow fame, and as the Wetherills continued to fail as ranchers, they sought support from various scientific organizations, mostly to no avail. Benjamin Wetherill, for example, wrote to the Smithsonian in an attempt to convince them of the scientific value of Mesa Verde and the need for support, but the prestigious institution was too lacking in funds at the time to help.[10] Local agencies could do little better. The brothers put together a traveling exhibit in 1889 that they hoped to sell to a worthy museum to finance further work. After shows in Durango, Pueblo, and eventually Denver, the Colorado Historical Society scraped together $3,000, largely in promissory notes instead of cash, to purchase the artifacts. Although the frugal Wetherills could work for a long time on such a sum, permanent institutional funding was not forthcoming, and the brothers found themselves trying to piece together a consistent income out of dude ranch fees at Alamo Ranch, guide fees to Mesa Verde, and sporadic sales of artifacts. In all, they assembled four large exhibits of Mesa Verde artifacts, the most famous of which appeared at the Chicago World's Columbian Exposition in 1893, but in spite of the fame gained by the exhibits and by the books of Nordenskiold, T. Mitchell Prudden, and Frederick H. Chapin,[11] the brothers entered the 1890s in a very poor economic condition.[12]

The struggle to remain financially solvent would plague Richard Wetherill to the end of his life, often bringing him to the brink of desperation. But the interest generated in the Anasazis by his exhibit at the Chicago exposition brought him the closest thing he would ever know to consistent financial support in the persons of Fred and Talbot Hyde, heirs to a soap manufacturer. It was not his first meeting with the Hydes, but it was the one that cemented the brothers' interest in southwestern prehistory and convinced them to support the collection of Anasazi artifacts that they could place at the American Museum of Natural History in New York City. That support from what became known as the Hyde Exploring Expedition enabled Richard Wetherill to undertake two of his most ambitious projects: the search for the Basketmakers of Grand Gulch, and the excavation of Pueblo Bonito in Chaco Canyon.

It was the Grand Gulch expeditions of 1893–94 and 1897 that established Richard Wetherill as the preeminent southwestern archaeologist of his day, although that reputation has not gone without challenge either in his day or ours. It would take a better psychologist than the present author to explain adequately why the Wetherill brothers—quiet, gentle, humble, and supremely competent—have been repeatedly accused with no foundation whatsoever of being, on the one hand, greedy pothunters who carelessly destroyed ruins to get at artifacts that they could turn into cash, and on the other hand of claiming credit for discovery of natural and prehistoric sites that supposedly had been long known to others. The issue of the originality of some of their discoveries will be addressed, but their explorations and excavations in Grand Gulch offer an opportunity here to examine the quality of their archaeological work.

Richard Wetherill's biographer, Frank McNitt, observed that "it has been his misfortune that certain scientists have been severe in their criticism of him, if a gentle term may be used, because he failed to employ [archaeological] techniques which were not devised until a generation after his death."[13] Again, the reasons for that mistreatment are problematic, but the Grand Gulch expeditions clearly indicate their injustice. From the time of their earliest excavation of Mesa Verde, the Wetherills had kept the best records they could devise regarding the provenance of each artifact removed. They supplemented those records with photographs (Richard had become interested and competent in the complicated wet plate photographic process during the excavation of Mesa Verde). On the eve of his first trip into Grand Gulch, however, Richard devised an improved system of record keeping in which a standard form was used for each ruin. Eight categories of information were to be recorded in boxes ruled off for the purpose. In addition,

> Each article to be numbered with India ink and fine pen or with tube paints white, red or black.

> Plan of all houses and sections to be made on paper or book, to be ruled both *ways*.

> Drawings of article to be made on paper with numbers and name. Photograph each house before touched, then each room or section and every important article in position as found.

> I think you will find this will meet all the requirements of the most scientific but if you have any suggestions whatever I will act upon them. This whole subject or rather the subject of it is in its infancy and the work we do must stand the most rigid inspection and we do not want to do it in such a manner that anyone in the future can pick flaws in it.[14]

It was, by modern archaeological standards, an inadequate system, but as McNitt pointed out, southwestern archaeology was virtually nonexistent in 1893. Those anthropologists who were studying prehistoric sites at all, like Adolph Bandelier, were content to examine and measure exposed features with no excavation, and most of the others were ethnographers studying living cultures. Such excavation was undertaken by pothunters who recovered artifacts for tourist sales, who not only kept no records but also attempted no scientific interpretation of their finds. In that embryonic scientific environment, Richard Wetherill was on the cutting edge.[15]

Grand Gulch had come to Richard Wetherill's attention through Charles McLoyd and Charles Graham, his Mancos friends from Mesa Verde days, and through his brother John, who had accompanied McLoyd and Graham on one of their recent trips.[16] Although Graham kept a diary of his expeditions, it was not a scientific record, and he and McLoyd were simply pothunters. Nevertheless, they were interested enough in the culture they were excavating to observe, as Richard had at Mesa Verde, that there actually appeared to be two cultures represented in Grand Gulch. The remains of one could be recovered on the surface and through shallow excavations, while the other appeared only through deeper digging under the floors of the ruins and under the midden heaps, or trash dumps, on the slopes below.

Other than the depth of the artifacts, the primary cultural feature distinguishing the two groups, as observed by McLoyd and Graham, was an undeformed occipital bone at the rear of the skull in those found at the deeper level. Those at the upper levels were flattened in the manner of modern Indians who strap babies to cradle boards while the skull is still relatively soft. But other differences were apparent, too: Atlatls, or spear launchers that augmented the power of a thrust by lengthening the throwing arm, were found in lieu of bows and arrows; baskets were plentiful, whereas such pottery as appeared was crudely fashioned; and the fiber sandals at the lower sites were square-toed, lacking the indentation for the little toe found at the upper levels.

The 1893–94 Hyde Exploring Expedition was a relatively modest affair. Richard, Al, and John left Mancos on November 29 with three others, and were joined in Bluff, Utah, by two more. During the four months the party was in the field, they made a tremendous collection of 1,216 artifacts including 96 skeletons, not only from Grand Gulch but also from Cottonwood Wash and what came to be known as Poncho House in Chinle Wash south of the San Juan River, all of which were carefully documented in fifty-two pages of field notes.

The significance of the expedition was that the Wetherills had deepened the scientific data on the artifacts they excavated significantly beyond that of McLoyd and Graham, enabling them to draw conclusions about the Anasazis that had eluded the earlier explorers. Their primary achievement was to develop the principle of stratigraphy, which had not been previously applied to southwestern sites, and which Richard Wetherill apparently discovered independently. Stratigraphy is the idea that the age of an artifact is directly proportional to its depth in an undisturbed site, and that the artifacts McLoyd and Graham and the Wetherills had found at the deeper levels represented an earlier culture.[17]

Two problems were suggested by this discovery: what to call the two cultures to distinguish them from one another, and what was the relationship between them? The first was relatively insignificant. Richard Wetherill chose to focus on the predominant presence of baskets instead of pottery in the earlier culture and call them Basket

People to distinguish them from the later Cliff Dwellers (a term already used during the Mesa Verde excavations), but he deferred to Talbot Hyde, who financed the expedition, and called them Basketmakers instead.[18]

The relationship between the two cultures was much more difficult to solve, and persisted as a problem until the mid-twentieth century. Evidence of violence was conspicuous in some of the Grand Gulch sites, suggesting that the Cliff Dwellers were invaders who had dispossessed the Basketmakers, though Richard Wetherill himself never explicitly advocated that theory. It was not until the 1940s that continuity was established between the two cultures, who are now regarded as two phases of Anasazi civilization.[19]

The Wetherills returned to the Basketmaker sites of Grand Gulch in 1897 in a much more handsomely funded expedition than the previous one. Alarmed by rumors that the Field Columbian Museum of Chicago was sending a scientific party to Grand Gulch, Richard Wetherill approached the Hydes for funding to complete his work there. Although Richard was primarily occupied by the archaeological promise of Pueblo Bonito, where he would spend the rest of his life, the scientific opportunities of Grand Gulch were still tempting enough to divert his attention. The Hydes, however, were unable to help.

Although the Field Museum changed its focus to other San Juan canyons, Richard nevertheless found an unexpected chance to return to Grand Gulch when a wealthy Harvard undergraduate, George Bowles, appeared in Mancos with his tutor, C. E. Whitmore, seeking an archaeological adventure. The resulting party, which set out for Grand Gulch in January 1897, consisted of thirteen men and one woman (Richard's nineteen-year-old bride, Marietta, who gamely chose to celebrate their honeymoon in the canyon) and over forty horses—an expedition probably second in size in the history of the San Juan only to the 1929 Charles L. Bernheimer party.

In contrast with the balmy winter weather of 1893–94, the January weather of 1897 was inhumanly cold, with intermittent snow and threats of blizzards that forced Richard to drive his workers hard lest a storm trap them in the canyon before they could finish their work. As it was, they stayed in the canyon only a month but collected some 550 artifacts and compiled an impressive, if erratic, photographic and documentary record. Upon completing their work, bad weather forced the large party to split up into smaller groups, thus covering a larger region but lessening the need for the entire group to endure trips to the more remote sites. Accordingly, Richard sent his brother Clayton and two others to explore Moki Canyon on the Colorado River, while Charles Mason and two others journeyed to Mysterious Canyon near Navajo Mountain. Leaving Marietta with friends in Bluff, he took the remainder of the party up Chinle Wash to work some more in Poncho House.[20] All were to rendezvous after a time at Marsh Pass.

Misfortune struck the united group after the rendezvous; Indians kidnapped Bowles and Whitmore and held them for ransom. None of the rest of the party had enough ready cash to meet the ransom, and Richard had to send someone to Bluff to borrow the money. It took several days, but Richard's credit was good, and the two easterners were released, shaken and cold, but alive.[21]

The 1897 Grand Gulch expedition returned to Mancos with a treasure trove of almost 2,000 artifacts from the various sites it had excavated. Busy now under Hyde funding at Pueblo Bonito, Richard Wetherill had no opportunity to dispose of the material until the following October. Bowles and Whitmore had offered him half the proceeds from its sale and, pressed by debts on the Alamo Ranch, Richard offered it to the Hydes for $5,500, but had to settle for $3,000.

In the interval between the two Grand Gulch expeditions, the restless Richard Wetherill had undertaken a freelance trip of his own, unsupported by financial backers. He went into the Tsegi Canyon system and discovered the second of the three major strains of Anasazi culture—Mesa Verde, Kayenta, and Chacoan. Although the Alamo Ranch was deeply in debt in the winter of 1894–95 and Richard had been unable to convince the Hydes to lend him money, he determined that sitting around the ranch fretting about money during the slow winter months would accomplish nothing. In January he, Al Wetherill, and Charles Mason set off to spend several months searching for Anasazi ruins in the Marsh Pass–Tsegi area through which they had briefly passed in 1893.[22]

After spending some time in some small ruins in Marsh Pass, the trio set off up into the Tsegi. As the mighty lower canyon began to divide into several tributary fingers, it was a matter of guesswork to select one to explore. Richard's choice of one of the central branches appeared for a time to have been a mistake. Although the steep walls of the gorge gave way to well-watered grassy plains, there was no sign of human habitation. At last, a small ruin appeared in a high alcove, and the tired explorers stopped for the night.

In one of history's fortuitous accidents, during the night Richard's mule, Neephi, broke its hobbles and wandered on up the canyon. The next morning while pursuing the animal, Richard suddenly came upon one of the most immense ruins on the Colorado Plateau. He called it Long House for the huge cave through which it spread, but the thousands of discarded potsherds that littered the ground below it led eventually to the name Keet Seel—"broken pottery," in Navajo.

The party spent several days exploring and excavating some of the 115 rooms they counted at Keet Seel. During the process, they observed several interesting features. One was that the original inhabitants were members of a significantly different cultural strain from those at Mesa Verde. Whereas black-on-white pottery similar to that at Mesa Verde was found, much of the pottery was black-on-red polychrome—one of the characteristic features of the Kayenta Anasazi. Further, although the explorers found several round kivas similar to those at Mesa Verde, they lacked the roof support pillars and the peripheral stone benches. Other kiva-like structures missing at Mesa Verde consisted of regular rectangular rooms with kiva-style fireplaces with stone air deflectors and benches around the perimeter. Finally, they found evidence of deliberate, orderly abandonment: Rooms had been carefully sealed, after being packed with pottery vessels too large to be conveniently carried. The residents of Keet Seel had not been driven out by violent invaders, but had made the choice voluntarily, and probably after a period of careful deliberation.[23]

In the fall of 1895 Richard Wetherill made a lengthy visit to Chaco Canyon with his future wife and her family. The immense archaeological potential of the place, particularly Pueblo Bonito, seized his imagination. Although he was lured back into Grand Gulch and the Tsegi in 1897 by fear of preemption by the Field Museum party and the promise of the sumptuous Bowles-Whitmore funding, Richard's heart remained in Chaco Canyon. Thereafter, the initiative in Wetherill explorations in the lower San Juan country passed to his younger brother John.

Even in a family of indefatigable explorers, John Wetherill (1866–1944) was a standout. Though the youngest of the three older brothers, he had been a major participant in their archaeological enterprises since the earliest days on the Mesa Verde. His skill with pack animals had moved his brothers to assign him the responsibility of getting the fragile artifacts down the precipitous mountain trails to the Alamo Ranch. He had been the first of the brothers to see Grand Gulch when he joined the second McLoyd-Graham expedition, and was a member of the 1893–94 expedition. In time the Navajos came to respect John Wetherill's wisdom, fairness, integrity, and intrepid abilities in the backcountry so much that they referred to him as Hosteen John—their sign of highest respect.[24] In 1896 he married Louisa Wade, a member of another pioneer Mancos family, and a young woman who would distinguish herself in her own ways as his partner in remote trading posts and as a celebrated authority on Navajo culture.

The years around the turn of the century were a time in which the Wetherill brothers were all shifting their primary focus from the nuclear family at Alamo Ranch, getting married, and striking off on their own enterprises. In 1900 John and Louisa took over the Hydes' trading post at Ojo Alamo, north of Chaco Canyon, where they were joined by an impoverished young Kansan named Clyde Colville, who became an excellent businessman and cemented a lifelong partnership with the Wetherills. In 1906 the trio struck out on their own, tempted by the trading opportunities in the untapped remoteness of the northwestern Navajo Reservation, and established a new trading post at Oljato, Utah. Although it proved to be a less-than-ideal location for a trading post, Oljato became the base for some of the most remarkable discoveries made by any of the Wetherills: Inscription House, Betatakin, and the mighty Rainbow Bridge.

All three discoveries were made within two months—July and August 1909. During the previous year, Byron Cummings had brought the first of his summer student archaeological groups to Oljato, and had begun forming the bond with the Wetherills that would last a lifetime. Out of their discussions that year, Cummings had decided to enlist John Wetherill as a guide to the ruins in the Tsegi. It was a natural choice because John had been exploring the area on his own and had found numerous promising sites for excavation. It became even more so the following spring when realization of the importance of Keet Seel had led the government to create a new Navajo National Monument around it on March 20, 1909, and John Wetherill was appointed its first custodian.[25]

The Cummings party set up their headquarters at Keet Seel, where they worked until July. On July 13, John and Louisa Wetherill took their children Ben and Ida, with Cummings and his son Malcolm and Stuart Young, one of Cummings's students, into Nitsin Canyon, a branch of Navajo Canyon, where a Navajo named Pinieten told them of a large ruin nearby. It was a major discovery, and the group lingered to survey its archaeological potential. Malcolm Cummings and Ida Wetherill, playing in one of the rooms, discovered some writing on the wall. To the adults, indecipherable fragments of words accompanied a date, which appeared to read 1661. Although later research has demonstrated convincingly that the date is actually 1861, and was left there by a Mormon scouting party of that year who hid in the ruin while beleaguered by hostile Navajos, the distinctive writings led to the naming of the ruin Inscription House.[26]

It was an exciting discovery, but the day was not yet finished. Attempting to reach Oljato by night, the Wetherills stopped briefly in the Tsegi to rest themselves and their footsore horses at the hogan of one of Louisa's friends, Nedi Cloey. Upon learning that the party had been looking for Anasazi ruins, Mrs. Cloey informed them of a large one only two miles up the canyon from her hogan. Although the closeness of the ruin tempted the party, the animals were too sore to attempt a visit, and they continued to Oljato. But memories of it lingered, and on August 9, John Wetherill hired Mrs. Cloey's son-in-law, Clatsozen Benully, to take him and a party consisting of Cummings and his son and students Neil Judd, Donald Beauregard, and Stuart Young to the ruin. After thirty minutes they reached what came to be known as Betatakin, Hillside House, the third and last of the major ruins that today comprise Navajo National Monument.[27]

The tangled story of the discovery of Rainbow Bridge can only be recounted briefly here.[28] By the time John and Louisa Wetherill had moved to Oljato, Louisa, realizing that the remainder of her life would likely be spent in proximity to the Navajos, had set out to learn as much of their language and culture as possible. Her interest was not, as she explained later, based on anything inherent to the Navajos; rather, it was simply a desire to feel at home in her environment.

"I'd have studied the customs of any people in any place where I lived," she wrote. "Otherwise it wouldn't be home."[29] In time, her facility with the Navajo language and knowledge of Navajo culture became legendary, both among Indians and whites. Her Navajo friends would tell her of Anasazi sites and other features of the country in which the Wetherills were interested.

One of the things they told her about was the existence of a huge natural bridge near Navajo Mountain, in a labyrinth of canyons that repelled all but the hardiest humans. It is even possible, though undocumented, that Sharkie, the one-eyed Navajo living near Shonto who told Louisa of the bridge's existence, may have shown Hosteen John the bridge from the summit of Navajo Mountain, and, less probably, even have taken him there before 1909. "I never heard my father ever say he had been to the natural bridge prior to 1909 when Nasja Begay took them in there," said Ben Wetherill, John and Louisa's son. "He could have been. It was my father's way to keep quiet, doing no talking at all, once he took people to some place he hired them to."[30]

At any rate, in 1909 John Wetherill proposed, with the assistance of Paiute guides who claimed to know the way, to take Cummings's student group to the bridge. Competition and strife entered the story at the beginning, for William Douglass, U.S. examiner of surveys, working for the General Land Office, had been following Cummings around in the White Canyon area since 1908, attempting to gather evidence on the unscientific nature of Cummings's excavations that would enable him to revoke Cummings's permits. Through one of the Paiutes with whom John Wetherill was negotiating for guide services, Douglass learned of the bridge, and began planning his own expedition. As rivalry between Cummings and Douglass mounted, Wetherill's Quaker diplomacy was put to the test, but in the end a decision was made to mount a joint expedition.

The Wetherill Trail, as it came to be known, from Oljato to Piute Canyon was over a well-established Indian trade route linking the Navajo Mountain area with Monument Valley. The country beyond Navajo Mountain, however, was some of the roughest and least traveled terrain in the world, known only sketchily even by the handful of Indian stock herders who sometimes ventured there. Although Mike's Boy, a Paiute who had attached himself to Douglass's party, claimed to know the way, Wetherill had more confidence in Nasja

Begay, another Paiute living with his father, Nasja, in Piute Canyon. However, when the party stopped to talk to Nasja Begay, his father informed them that he was away with some sheep, and promised to send him after them when he returned. Temporarily depending upon Mike's Boy and Wetherill's knowledge of the way, the party continued.

The roughness of the route followed by the party around the north and west of Navajo Mountain was later made famous in the writings of Zane Grey, Theodore Roosevelt, Charles L. Bernheimer, and other wealthy and articulate clients who hired Wetherill to take them to the bridge. The precarious slickrock domes of the Glass Mountains gave way in time to the faint steps cut down the walls of Nasja Canyon by Hoskininni during his flight from Kit Carson in the 1860s, and eventually the verdant freshness of Surprise Valley. While in camp there, threatened mutiny by the Paiutes and some of the whites was averted by Wetherill's scorn, and perhaps more important by the arrival of Nasja Begay late in the evening of August 13.

The final dash to the bridge occurred the next day, August 14, 1909, as the party climbed over the divide into Oak Canyon, then over another, which put them into Bridge Canyon. The upper chord of the arch can be seen a ways up the canyon, then it passes out of view again momentarily as the canyon bends. Cummings claimed to have been the first white man to have sighted the arch, but the rivalry between him and Douglass to have been the first to ride beneath the structure was resolved by John Wetherill, who spurred his horse ahead of the party and beat them all to it.[31]

Rainbow Bridge figured often in John Wetherill's later career, and some of his more significant expeditions will be recounted in later chapters. One of his last major ventures, though, the Wetherill-Flattum upriver expedition from Lee's Ferry to Rainbow Bridge during the frigid January of 1931, especially reveals the character of Hosteen John in the face of hardship and danger.

Rainbow Bridge had been made a national monument in 1910, and John Wetherill was appointed custodian. But some visitors to the bridge and the surrounding country thought the monument ought to upgraded to a national park, and the area increased vastly to include Monument Valley and Glen Canyon. In order to publicize the idea, two California businessmen, Frederic A. Stearns and Patrick M. Flattum, enlisted Hosteen John as guide on an upriver trip in a steel boat of their design. Both still photographs and a movie were to be made to advertise the project. There was room for only two people, and Flattum was selected to join Wetherill. It turned out to be even more of an adventure than either had anticipated.[32]

The outboard motor was untested but seemed, with modifications to keep ice out of the cooling system, to be adequate. Calculating the likely gas mileage while bucking the powerful current and dodging ice floes, however, was "like figuring how far a frog would jump by the way he sits or looks," as Flattum put it. The stress was exacerbated, too, when the partners decided to tow an abandoned wooden boat to carry some of their gear.

Tests and calculations completed, they started off on January 4. They learned almost immediately that the steel boat would have to be abandoned because the castaway vessel proved much lighter and efficient under the trying conditions. So the *Chisler*, the Stearns-Flattum steel craft, lasted only one day. The ice, however, threatened the wooden boat, and they found themselves taking turns lining the boat through icy stretches (pulling it by a bowline from shore or while wading in the ice water) and fending off the icebergs while seated in the boat.

Disaster nearly struck on January 7, when an ice floe wrenched the boat, with Flattum aboard, free from Hosteen John's grasp and carried it far downstream. Flattum eventually got the motor started and fought his way back to where Wetherill was sitting on a rock, puffing on his pipe and seemingly unconcerned that all his camp gear and food were nearly lost.

Both spent almost as much time in the ice water as in the boat. "It seems like I am booked for two to four ice baths a day," Flattum wrote on January 11. "Building a fire and wringing out wet clothes and putting them back on, and going back to work in those channels—that should be sport for kings but not for John and I."

On the 13th, tragedy finally caught up with them. An iceberg coming down through a long rapid tore loose their food bag, and they were barely able to save the boat. With three to six days left to Rainbow Bridge and the nearest supplies another day's hike beyond at Rainbow Lodge on the south side of Navajo Mountain, things seemed pretty grim. Flattum's courage was bolstered, though, by the realization that his companion was, after all, the great John Wetherill, "with that never fading smile on his face, that signifies patience and great courage; in his presence one feels that there is something more in life than just mere joy of living, something more eternal." For his part, Hosteen John noted that they had salvaged their tea and sugar from the accident, and things were far from desperate: On the 14th, he wrote that "our breakfast was tea and sugar. We dined on tea and we suppered on tea." The following day they made great time, and reached Bridge Canyon in the afternoon. "That shows what tea will do for a fellow," he observed.

Eventually they reached Rainbow Bridge, found food at Echo Cave, where Bill Wilson had cached supplies for his tourist trips, re-supplied at Rainbow Lodge, and continued on upriver as far as Hole-in-the-Rock before turning the bow downstream beside the ice floes. They returned to Lee's Ferry on January 22.

One cannot fail to be impressed in the Wetherill-Flattum diaries with their uncomplaining acceptance of nature's imperatives, and their determination to appreciate the beauties of the experience re-gardless of suffering and deprivation. "This has been a grand trip," Flattum's last entry reads, "and to have been with an old pioneer like John Wetherill is certainly a privilege few travelers can ever enjoy, as he is a real Western scout who knows no defeat." Hosteen John recorded his own evaluation of the trip while in camp at Echo Cave: "Had a wonderful trip through a country of much grandeur and beauty. I doubt if it can be surpassed anywhere else in the world. The hardships we went through only add value to a wonderful experience."

"The desert will take care of you," Hosteen John observed after a long life of desert exploration. "At first it's all big and beautiful, but you're afraid of it. Then you begin to see its dangers, and you hate it. Then you learn how to overcome its dangers. And the desert is home."[33] To no one was the desert more of a home than the Wetherills.

NOTES

1. The literature on the Wetherills is extensive, but diffuse and generally inade-quate. The only adequate biography of any of the five brothers is Frank McNitt, *Richard Wetherill: Anasazi* (Albuquerque: University of New Mexico Press, 1957). Though roundly criticized for its lack of documentation (a mistake McNitt did not repeat in his later books), the volume is nevertheless a classic in canyon country lit-erature, and functions almost as a group biography of the brothers until shortly be-fore Richard's murder in 1910. In spite of her combative tone, Maurine S. Fletcher

served Al well by editing *The Wetherills of the Mesa Verde: Autobiography of Benjamin Alfred Wetherill* (Cranbury, N. J.: Associated University Presses, 1977). The literature on the other brothers is less successful. Two group biographies of John and Louisa Wade Wetherill, Frances Gillmor, and Louisa Wade Wetherill, *Traders to the Navajos: The Story of the Wetherills of Kayenta* (Boston: Houghton Mifflin, 1934) and Mary Apolline Comfort, *Rainbow to Yesterday: The John and Louisa Wetherill Story* (New York: Vantage Press, 1980) are useful, but superficial and prone to errors. Clayton Wetherill died young, and appears in the historical record mostly through his role as guide to T. Mitchell Prudden, whose *On the Great American Plateau* (New York: G. P. Putnam's Sons, 1907) recounts their expeditions. [Lillian E. Prudden, ed.], *Biographical Sketches and Letters of T. Mitchell Prudden, M.D.* (New Haven, Conn.: Yale University Press, 1927), contains some of Clayton's letters. Winslow's career as an Indian trader is given pseudonymously as the character "Ken" in his wife's reminiscences: Hilda Faunce, *Desert Wife* (Boston: Little, Brown, 1934).

2. McNitt, *Richard Wetherill*, 16–17. The material presented here on the early family history and the exploration of Mesa Verde is based on this volume and Benjamin Alfred Wetherill, *The Wetherills of the Mesa Verde*.

3. Duane A. Smith, *Mesa Verde National Park: Shadows of the Centuries* (Lawrence: University Press of Kansas, 1988), 7–18, sketches the history of early white visits to Mesa Verde and early reports of sightings of cliff dwellings.

4. Wetherill, *The Wetherills of the Mesa Verde*, 89.

5. Ibid., 108.

6. Willa Cather, "Tom Outland's Story." In *Five Stories* (New York: Vintage Books, 1956), 32. The story appeared originally as an interlude in her 1925 novel, *The Professor's House*.

7. Wetherill, *The Wetherills of the Mesa Verde*, 104, 111. McNitt, *Richard Wetherill* recounts the full story of that brother's conflict with the government and tragic end.

8. Benjamin Alfred Wetherill, *The Wetherills of the Mesa Verde*, 96, 104, 108.

9. Nordenskiold suffered from tuberculosis and died at age twenty-six, making his Mesa Verde book his only outstanding scientific achievement. Olof W. Arrhenius, *Stones Speak and Waters Sing: The Life and Works of Gustaf Nordenskiold* (Mesa Verde National Park: Mesa Verde Museum Association, [1984]) includes a brief biography and a translation of his Mesa Verde field notes. Wetherill, *The Wetherills of*

the Mesa Verde, 214–32, includes a narrative of a trip Al Wetherill and Nordenskiold made through the Navajo country to the Grand Canyon.

10. David Harrell, "'We Contacted Smithsonian': The Wetherills at Mesa Verde," *New Mexico Historical Review* 62 (July 1987): 229–48.

11. Frederick H. Chapin, *The Land of the Cliff-Dwellers* (Boston: W. B. Clark, 1892).

12. Smith, *Mesa Verde National Park*, 22–41, and McNitt, *Richard Wetherill*, 30–33, sketch the Wetherills' increasing fame and poverty.

13. McNitt, *Richard Wetherill*, 33.

14. Richard Wetherill to Talbot Hyde, "No date but early 1893," according to a type-written transcription supplied by the American Museum of Natural History. See Frank McNitt's discussion of this letter in *Richard Wetherill*, 62–63.

15. McNitt, *Richard Wetherill*, 37–38.

16. On the early exploration of Grand Gulch, including the Wetherill expeditions, see Ann Phillips, "Archaeological Expeditions into Southeastern Utah and Southwestern Colorado between 1888–1898 and the Dispersal of the Collections," in Victoria M. Atkins, ed., *Anasazi Basketmaker: Papers from the 1990 Wetherill–Grand Gulch Symposium*, Cultural Resource Series No. 24, (Salt Lake City: Bureau of Land Management, 1993), 103–18.

17. M. Edward Moseley, "The Discovery and Definition of Basketmaker: 1890 to 1914," *Masterkey* 40 (October-December 1966): 140–54, points out that McLoyd and Graham deserve much more credit for the observations that led to Richard Wetherill's definition of the Basketmakers than they have previously received. Nevertheless, although the name Basketmaker came from Talbot Hyde, who financed the Wetherill expedition, the principle of stratigraphy upon which the differentiation of the two peoples are based is Richard Wetherill's.

18. Richard Wetherill to Talbot Hyde, February 4 and March 28, 1894, typescripts provided by the American Museum of Natural History. See McNitt's discussion of this issue, *Richard Wetherill*, 64–66.

19. Moseley, "The Discovery and Definition of Basketmaker," 153.

20. The identity of this canyon is somewhat debatable, but the reader should not confuse it with Mystery Canyon, at Mile 73.8 in Glen Canyon. In his report on the 1897 expedition, Richard Wetherill said Mysterious Canyon was reputed to contain

"cliff houses ¼ of a mile long each." He added that "Mysterious Canon drains all the country south of Navajo Mountain in the West Canon, thence to the Colorado River." It seems unlikely that he meant Tsagieto (Segi-to) Canyon, which drains the immediate southern slope of Navajo Mountain and flows into Forbidding Canyon, once known as West Canyon, a tributary of the Colorado River. Rather, the size of the ruins more strongly suggests Nitsin Canyon, a branch of the Navajo Canyon, known as West Canyon in the 1880s, which drains the Rainbow Plateau to the south and flows into the Colorado River. Nitsin Canyon contains Inscription House, an immense ruin (though not nearly one-quarter mile long), which was known to Mormon pioneers as early as 1861. Richard could have learned of it from Mormons or from Indians in the Tsegi, where he had discovered Keet Seel in 1895. [Richard Wetherill], "The Expedition of 1896 and 1897 Grand Gulch," 2, typescript copy furnished by the American Museum of Natural History. C. Gregory Crampton, *Historical Sites in Glen Canyon: Mouth of San Juan River to Lee's Ferry*, University of Utah Anthropological Paper No. 46 (Salt Lake City: University of Utah Press, 1960), 32. Albert E. Ward, *Inscription House: Two Research Reports*, Museum of Northern Arizona Technical Series No. 16 (Flagstaff: Northern Arizona Society of Science and Art, 1975).

21. McNitt, *Richard Wetherill*, 162. Note that this story is at variance with two versions originating with Marietta, who claimed that it was she and "Ben" (not Bowles), the Harvard student, who were kidnapped, and that the episode occurred in Grand Gulch, not at Marsh Pass. There are numerous other discrepancies. Richard Wetherill does not mention the episode at all in his report on the expedition, and in the absence of documentation in McNitt's book, it is difficult to identify his source. Marietta Wetherill (as told to Mabel C. Wright), "Prisoners of the Paiutes," *Desert Magazine* (April 1952): 17–20; Kathryn Gabriel, ed., *Marietta Wetherill: Reflections on Life with the Navajos in Chaco Canyon* (Boulder, Colo.: Johnson Books, 1992), 77–84.

22. The story of the discovery of the various ruins that comprise modern Navajo National Monument is based primarily on McNitt, *Richard Wetherill*, 77–84; Hal K. Rothman, *Navajo National Monument: A Place and Its People, An Administrative History*, Southwest Cultural Resources Center Professional Paper No. 40 (Santa Fe: Southwest Cultural Resources Center, 1991), 14–26; and Albert E. Ward, *Inscription House*.

23. Tree-ring dating later disclosed that Keet Seel flourished during the Tsegi phase of the Pueblo III period, roughly A.D. 1116–1286. A period of drought beginning in 1276 added to the decline of agriculture produced by stream erosion and made it

impossible to feed Keet Seel's increasing population. McNitt, *Richard Wetherill*, 83; Rothman, *Navajo National Monument*, 4–5.

24. Although the term is ordinarily translated "mister," that common English word conveys little of the weight that the original carries in Navajo. "Monsignor," as a title of extraordinary respect conferred upon the Catholic clergy, or "sir," the form of address for English knights, are perhaps closer to the meaning of Hosteen for a Navajo.

25. Rothman, *Navajo National Monument*, 20.

26. Ibid., 21–22. Research establishing the text and origin of the inscription at Inscription House was accomplished by archaeologist Albert E. Ward, *Inscription House*, 5–17.

27. Rothman, *Navajo National Monument*, 23; John Wetherill, "BETATA KIN," MS at Navajo National Monument Headquarters, June 1934.

28. The only satisfactory attempt to reconcile, or at least to compare, the conflicting sources on the topic is Stephen C. Jett, "The Great 'Race' to 'Discover' Rainbow Natural Bridge in 1909," *Kiva* 58 (1992): 3–66. My narrative here is based on Jett's article.

29. Gillmor and Wetherill, *Traders to the Navajos*, 256.

30. Quoted in Jett, "The Great 'Race,'" 41. Although I consistently reject the other after-the-fact recollections and speculations with which the literature of the Rainbow Bridge discovery is replete, this one has at least marginal plausibility in accounting for John Wetherill's vigorous leadership of the discovery party during the absence or confusion of the Paiute guides who were supposed to know the way. After a confusing conference with Nasja in Piute Canyon, for example, W. B. Douglass's Paiute guide, Mike's Boy, who was supposed to know the way, was reluctant to continue with no better information than that supplied by Nasja. John Wetherill, however, was eager to set out. "If Mike's Boy hesitated to proceed on the basis of Nasja's presumably inadequate instructions," Jett observes, "one must wonder why Wetherill continued onward with apparent confidence" (19–20). Again, when some of Douglass's white packers and his two Paiutes, Mike's Boy and Dogeye Begay, threatened mutiny, Jett quotes Neil Judd to the effect that "Wetherill laughed them to shame and forced their continued, though unwilling, cooperation under threat of telling all the Indians who visited his post that these two had failed under hardship and displayed less stamina than white men" (22). Both of these caustic portrayals of Douglass's Paiute guides, one must note, are tainted by coming from members of Cummings's party.

31. The discovery of Rainbow Bridge, perhaps the greatest scenic wonder in the American West, spawned a jealousy that has produced a veritable literary industry of claims of sightings of Rainbow Bridge prior to 1909, all of which, according to the canons of evidence acceptable to the historical profession, must be disregarded until corroborated by uncontrovertible firsthand sources like those that support the 1909 visit. The depositions of James Black, for example, copies of which are available at the Navajo National Monument headquarters, claim that he visited the bridge during the 1890s while prospecting for gold, and reports visits by others prior to him. Weldon F. Heald, "Who Discovered Rainbow Bridge?" *Sierra Club Bulletin* 40 (October 1955): 24–28, discusses the claim of William Franklyn Williams and his father to have visited the bridge as early as 1884. Finally, trader and author Gladwell "Toney" Richardson, whose family were rivals of the Wetherills in both the trading and tourist guide businesses, claimed that "scores of men" had seen the bridge before 1909, and that many of their names had been incised upon the bridge and its environs before the Wetherill party arrived. Anticipating the inevitable question of why those early visitors had not reported the bridge's existence during the twenty-five years before 1909, he says, "They did, in fact, talk about it to others who were about to enter that far country. Then consider that there are a thousand square miles of southern Utah and northern Arizona containing natural bridges galore. Of what special interest to them was one more, when they were a dime a dozen?" Gladwell Richardson, *Navajo Trader* (Tucson: University of Arizona Press, 1986), 61–62. The last word, it seems belongs to John Wetherill, who himself disavowed discovery of the bridge. "The Indians found it long before the white man came," he said. Quoted in Jett, "The Great 'Race,'" 42.

32. C. Gregory Crampton, ed., "Early Trip Up the Colorado from Lee's Ferry to Rainbow Bridge, January 1931," *Plateau* 34 (October 1961): 33–49.

33. Gillmor and Wetherill, *Traders to the Navajos*, 256.

The Bank of Ticaboo—And Its Branches

When Cass Hite first came to the canyon country in 1881, he was thirty-seven years old and a man of many contradictions. He was a tall, handsome ladies' man but he never married. Although he was approachable and made friends easily, he served time in the penitentiary for killing a man in an Old West-style gunfight. A gregarious con man, he spent most of the last decade of his life as a hermit in Glen Canyon. Although he made his living from the Colorado River, he never owned a boat, and may actually have been afraid of the river. One thing, though, emerges unambiguously in Hite's career: He was a miner, and no one's shadow falls longer across the mining history of the San Juan country than his. But even in that there is an irony, for he was very much a man of the nineteenth century, whose mining interests moved from copper to silver to gold, and who never became caught up in the twentieth century's obsession with oil, on the one hand and uranium on the other. The internal combustion engine, which devours petroleum products—the San Juan country's most enduring extractable resource—and nuclear war, which is based on uranium—the region's most lucrative resource—touched Hite's life little in the first instance and not at all in the second.

The young Cass Hite cut a striking figure. About six feet tall, he kept his prematurely balding, dark hair cut close to his scalp, but grew a luxuriant mustache, which he waxed in the fashion of the day, and a thin, Buffalo Bill Cody-style goatee. A good man with a violin, he was also a good man with a gun, and the lonely sound of his music lingered in the minds of his Glen Canyon visitors with stories of his marksmanship. He was limited in formal education but he had a quick mind. Even during his hermit days he liked to keep up on world affairs, which he enjoyed discussing with his nearest neighbor, Bert Loper, during occasional get-togethers (Loper's left-wing ideas clashed with his conservatism, though, and led to an eventual falling-out).[1]

Cass was born on an Illinois farm in 1845, and lived in Salem from 1855 to 1859.² Lewis Hite, his father, became a forty-niner, and both his gold fever and his wanderlust seem to have affected Cass and two of his brothers, John P. and Ben R., who eventually joined Cass in Glen Canyon.

After the Civil War, the family moved to Missouri, where an unsubstantiated rumor began that Cass had ridden with Quantrill's guerrillas. What did happen was that the young man wandered throughout the Rocky Mountains, doing some prospecting in Colorado and Idaho, but found the cold winters distasteful and returned home. While in Colorado he had heard of the legendary Pish-la-kai mine of the Navajos (the term is a corruption of Spanish and Navajo words meaning the "silver peso" mine) from which the Indians supposedly acquired the abundant silver used in their jewelry. Although Ernest Mitchell and James Merritt had recently been killed by Indians in Monument Valley during their search for the mine, Cass determined to search for it himself.

That he was able to form a quick and close friendship with the Monument Valley Navajos says something important about his personality. Made wary of the white man by vast cultural differences and unhappy historical experience, the Navajos were naturally skeptical of any whites who entered their country. This was especially the case in Monument Valley, where the headman, Hoskininni, had led his people into the wilds of the Navajo Mountain and San Juan Triangle regions to avoid incarceration during the 1860s. The Mitchell-Merritt murders, though they may have been committed by Paiutes rather than Navajos, were poignant evidence nevertheless of the still raw hostilities between the cultures. Hite, who was a member of the party that buried the bodies of the two prospectors, was well aware of the perils when he and several others crossed the San Juan River in 1881.

Hite and Hoskininni formed a fast friendship "as intimate friends as it is possible for an Indian and Whiteman to be," that lasted until the old chieftain's death, and for the next two years the prospectors roamed widely throughout the northwestern part of the reservation, openly trying to find the fabled silver mine. Cass's persistence in his search for silver during this time led the Navajos to nickname him Hosteen Pish-la-kai, or Mr. Silver. Hite and his men did find copper, in the area of Hoskininni Mesa and Copper Canyon, but no precious metals, though they ranged as far as Navajo Mountain. Aware that other Indians were less enthusiastic about the prospectors than he, Hoskininni thought it wise to divert Cass's mining interests to a less dangerous environment, and suggested he investigate gold in the Colorado River near a site that he would show him. In the fall of 1883, the old Indian took Hite down White Canyon to a crossing of the Colorado near its mouth. (It was evidently on that trip that Cass became the first white man to view the three great arches that now are enclosed by Natural Bridges National Monument.[3]) Although his horse had to swim part of the way, Cass pronounced it a "dandy crossing," and he was even more impressed by the gold the Indian pointed out in the sand and gravel of the river and its tributaries. He inscribed his name and the date, September 19, 1883, on a nearby canyon wall and set out to create the great Glen Canyon gold rush.[4]

Hite had an entrepreneurial eye, and the potential of the Dandy Crossing struck him immediately. Although there were other river crossings in Glen Canyon, the nearest one with the kind of practicality offered by the Dandy Crossing was Lee's Ferry, over 162 miles downstream. The wide river bottom in the area could be reached from Green River or Hanksville and the Mormon communities of Wayne County by means of Crescent Creek (later North Wash) five miles upstream, or from Monument Valley and the Mormon communities of San Juan County by means of the Clay Hills or Chinle Creek crossings, the Hole-in-the-Rock road, and White Canyon. If neither route was exactly a beckoning highroad of commerce, both were immediately usable on horseback and improvable for wagons and eventually even automobiles, after the San Juan was bridged at Goodridge (Mexican Hat) and a ferry constructed across the Colorado.

Cass and others began staking out mining claims along the riverbanks, which were traversable on foot for a considerable distance downstream. They formed mining companies and mining districts to govern themselves, and began selling stock and advertising the area's potential. Cass's brothers, John and Ben, and his nephew, Homer, joined him in 1888 and began developing the small community of Hite at the mouth of Trachyte Creek on the right bank just downstream from the Dandy Crossing. Homer became the first postmaster there in 1889, serving twenty to twenty-five men (this number would grow by over four times by the turn of the century).[5] In later years, particularly during the long residency of Arthur Chaffin, Hite became locally famous for its comfortable, shady environment and the prodigious fruit and melon crops produced by the fertile alluvial soil of Trachyte Creek.[6]

Cass himself moved downstream to Ticaboo Creek, where he began mining both there and downstream at Good Hope Bar with his brothers. For Glen Canyon in the late 1880s, the Hites' mining operations were big business. Both pumped river water to wash sand and gravel from the riverbanks in sluice boxes where the gold was separated out. At Good Hope, they used a huge water wheel to raise river water 40 feet into a 300-foot flume, and at Ticaboo, they installed a 10,000-pound boiler that powered two 1,000-pound pumps. The latter machinery was hauled from Green River by mule team to Hite, then down to Ticaboo on a barge.[7]

Ticaboo is a Ute word meaning "friendly," and Cass's residence was a friendly place indeed. In later years, long after Cass's death, it remained a favorite stopping place for river travelers who enjoyed its shade trees and pure water, and who marveled over the still productive grape vines that Cass had planted and irrigated with the creek water.

During his early years in Glen Canyon, though, Hite was little inclined to sit back and enjoy its friendly environment. Instead, he wanted to exploit its economic potential by attracting other miners, particularly those willing to invest in his own operation or in others for which he acted as broker. To this end, he journeyed regularly to outside locations where he published articles promoting opportunities in Glen Canyon and the San Juan country, and collecting investment capital.[8] His persuasive manner and engaging personality led to considerable success in attracting both people and money; in fact, as Dwight L. Smith and C. Gregory Crampton pointed out, Cass "probably mined as much gold out of other people's pockets as he did out of the diggings."[9] During his early years, Cass may have transcended the bounds of ethics in his zest for separating fools from their money. Charles Kelly reports a story of his accepting $1,600 from members of the party surveying the Utah-Arizona border for shares in the ephemeral Pish-la-kai mine, which Cass himself never found.[10] Although his business methods seem to have moved to a higher plane later, miners found extraction of the river gold difficult enough that one frustrated investor at the height of the gold rush in 1893 is said to have written on a rock at Navajo Spring in Comb

Wash, "One hundred dollars reward for the d_____d fool who started the gold boom."[11]

Others who came brought more than just verbal complaints.[12] Adolph F. Kohler was a Utah stockman who decided in 1889 to seek his fortune in Glen Canyon gold. He established a claim on the Schock Bar on the right bank of the river between the mouth of North Wash and Hite. Evidently Kohler came to the same conclusion Hite had arrived at—he could mine investors more profitably than gold, but he had to reckon with the fact that Cass's prior tenure and entrepreneurial skill presented tough competition. Rather than face that competition directly, Kohler resorted to trickery: He named his company so it would be easily confused with Hite's, and diverted some of Hite's potential investors into his company. One might reasonably speculate that the location of his claim at a point more accessible to travelers than Hite's was a calculated decision as well, though the site undeniably contained gold, and had been mined before Kohler's arrival.

Whether Kohler's scheme was unsuccessful or his greed got the best of him cannot be determined, but in 1891 he decided to try to run Cass out of the canyon. While Cass was on a trip to Denver, Kohler announced that he intended to kill him upon his return.

The showdown occurred in Green River on September 9. John Hite met his brother at Grand Junction, Colorado, on September 6 and warned him of Kohler's threat. While Cass took the warning seriously, he assumed he would be able to avert trouble if he could talk to Kohler. On September 8 they arrived in Green River and met Kohler at the Crescent Saloon where, with a number of other men, they drank together. But things were tense, and Cass determined that a private meeting with Kohler would be necessary. The next day he went over to Gammage's boardinghouse, where Kohler was staying. Kohler met him with a Winchester in his hand. Cass tried to keep things cool, spoke to Kohler "in a friendly way," and sat down.[13] Kohler remained standing, and according to witnesses was in an agitated mood. According to one account, Cass pointed out to Kohler that he had done him no harm, and asked him what he was going to do with the rifle. Kohler replied, "Shoot you, you s__ of a b____!" and fired two shots, both of which, incredibly, missed. Cass then fired, killing Kohler almost instantly. Other witnesses said the initial verbal exchange was less friendly, each accusing the other of cowardice.

Cass was brought to trial in Provo, and although there were several witnesses who testified to his peaceable nature and pleaded for acquittal on grounds of self-defense, the jury found him guilty of murder in the second degree and he was sentenced on October 15, 1892, to twelve years in the Utah State Penitentiary. There was a widespread feeling that the sentence was overly harsh, and in September and October 1893 a series of petitions for clemency, one of which was signed by eight members of the jury, reached Gov. Caleb W. West. Governor West pardoned Hite on November 29, 1893, and ordered his immediate release.[14]

Court Stewart, a friend of Cass's, brought him from Green River to Hanksville, and remembered that he was so ill, perhaps from tuberculosis, he was unable to stand (possibly a consideration in his pardon). The total ordeal changed his life drastically. Although he returned to the river, he became despondent. A drinker since he was fifteen, he began drinking more heavily.[15] Eventually he came out of his malaise, stopped drinking altogether, and returned to soliciting mining investors; Polk's city directories for Salt Lake City indicate that he was living at the Walker House from 1898 to 1900, and list him as either a broker or a miner.

Around the turn of the century, though, Cass moved back to Ticaboo. Although he sometimes visited friends at Hite or Hanksville, bursitis became a problem, and he traveled less and less frequently. Glen Canyon had not brought him or anyone else the bonanza he had hoped for. The individuals and small mining companies he had lured to the river in the 1890s began to depart, and after the failure of the immense mechanized operation of the Hoskaninni Mining Company (discussed below), gold mining in Glen Canyon dwindled to a few stalwart holdouts like Cass, Bert Loper, and Alonzo Turner. But they had learned that anyone content with a modest living could find it in Glen Canyon gold. Cass punningly called his claim the Bank of Ticaboo, for in the bank of Ticaboo Creek there were deposits he could withdraw whenever he needed.

It was an easy life in a friendly setting—perhaps the greatest riches of Glen Canyon, after all. Arthur Chaffin, John Hite, or one of the other miners would walk up to Hite each week and bring Cass's mail to him. There were card games and other visits from the few remaining miners. On February 22, 1914, Lon Turner stopped by for one of those visits and saw no sign of activity. He found Cass dead on the floor of his cabin, apparently from a heart attack; the last entry in his diary was February 15. "If anything ever happens to me," he had told his friends, "bury me just in front of the cabin door—I've always liked the place and I'm willing to stay." On February 23, a group of his old friends did just that, and erected a fence around the plot.[16] In an ironic gesture of historical sensitivity, the National Park Service anchored a buoy to the grave so that when the site was destroyed by their Lake Powell, its location would still be marked for (and probably puzzled over by) recreational boaters, but a severe storm broke the buoy loose, and Cass has since slept undisturbed and largely unremembered beneath 300 feet of water.

During his promotion of mining in Glen Canyon, Cass Hite had also promoted the San Juan. "That is a good gold country," he wrote in 1893, "and the fact that I did not strike it rich in there is no reason in the world why others may not."[17] Cass was preaching to the converted, for already, by December 1892, prospectors were flooding into the San Juan country on their own. "Durango has gone wild," the *Salt Lake Tribune* reported on December 22, nearby towns have been "depopulated," and "every available means of transportation has headed for the diggings." By January 4, the paper reported an influx of 200 men per day, with no less than 2,000 being employed by the Gabel Company in the Clay Hills Crossing area.[18]

Both small groups and large companies worked the San Juan. Among the former was Walter Mendenhall, a Lake City, Colorado, miner who arrived in Bluff in the summer of 1893 with a partner named Alonzo Savage and a horse-drawn wagon. They purchased some lumber in Bluff and transported it to Comb Wash, where they built a boat and a raft and started off into the San Juan Canyon looking for a place to mine. Although Savage was "an old raftsman," he soon learned that getting such a craft through the San Juan rapids was a big order, and the raft smashed into a rock and broke up. It was no disaster, since they had no equipment aboard and intended the raft only as material from which to build a platform for their mining operation. They set up a "Chinese pump" (probably a manually operated water wheel to feed a sluice box) at a location evidently somewhere around the mouth of the canyon, but it washed away in a flood. They gave their boat to some other prospectors and returned home.[19]

Mendenhall returned in October with his father and brother and spent some time exploring the area on horseback looking for good mining sites. As winter approached, he left the others, probably at what is now called the Mendenhall Loop, where they built a cabin and awaited his return in the spring. In March 1894 he returned from Durango with a small machine he had invented for saving the fine San Juan gold, and they built some boats and explored downriver. During that year, he said, they took between $4,000 and $5,000 in gold from the San Juan River, a highly questionable claim, since no one else was having much success, and the Mendenhalls themselves quit the San Juan for Glen Canyon at the end of that season.[20]

Another small operation was the Honaker mine at Mile 96.5, just downstream from the Goosenecks. Augustus C. Honaker was a Colorado freighter operating between Cortez and Bluff in 1893 when the gold rush began. He established a company with several brothers and sisters and other investors, and in the spring of 1894 began work on a precipitous 1,500-foot trail to the river. Although the trail was eventually widened to permit passage of pack animals, it was at first a precarious passage. A young Bert Loper, who worked for the Honakers that year, recalled that

> two or three of us young fellows at that time carried the stuff down from ledge to ledge until we got to the last big ledge [which] was about one hundred and thirty or one hundred and forty feet, [where] we had to let the stuff over with ropes, and then when we got our stuff let over the cliff we would go out to the point where the trail now goes over and climb down a rope ladder.[21]

Loper remained with the Honakers from March 1895 to May 1895, and remembered it as a rough life in which he and the other younger men had to do most of the work. Although one member of the company had some kind of invention that was supposed to save the gold, "it went the way of all other placer machines I ever saw, didn't amount to anything, so we sluiced and we rocked and sent out for more money to buy more grub with." But it all came to nothing—or almost nothing—for Mrs. Hazel Lyman of Blanding, a granddaughter of Augustus Honaker, wears a ring that she says contains the total amount of gold removed from the Honaker mine.[22]

The larger companies fared little better, if at all. One of the earliest was the Gabel Company, which staked over one hundred claims from Clay Hills Crossing to Copper Canyon. One of the organizers, Indian trader J. P. Williams, operated a huge barge with a pumping mechanism, which seems to have ranged between Oljato Wash and Copper Canyon. The headquarters of the operation was Williamsburg, on Williams Bar about one mile above Copper Canyon. In spite of the heavy machinery, however, C. Gregory Crampton is no doubt correct in speculating that most of the mining here, as elsewhere along the San Juan, was done by individuals with sluice boxes, especially if the figure of 2,000 men working these few miles of riverbank is even approximately accurate.[23]

Mining at Zahn's Camp in the vicinity of Mile 42 on the left bank evidently went on longer than at any other San Juan location. First identified as Gabel Camp in 1892, the site was worked by several individual miners, including Zeke Johnson, until 1902 when they sold out to five Zahn brothers of Los Angeles, who were still involved with the property into the 1930s.[24] The Zahns, though, were not very serious miners, and seem to have run the operation more as a hobby than as a business enterprise. When Hector Zahn arranged for purchase of the location in 1902, the previous miners had already installed a boiler and other machinery, to which the Zahns added additional items from time to time. Otto Zahn listed the equipment as "two steam engines and two Henry R. Worthington pumps and two centrifugal pumps, one six inch pump, the other an eleven inch pump."

From the beginning, the Zahn operation was plagued with problems. Lack of wood for the boilers was one. They devised a temporary solution by stretching a cable across the river to catch driftwood, but the cable broke. Then the river went dry, depriving them of water for both boiler and sluice boxes. At one point, drinking water could only be developed by digging a hole in the wet riverbanks and allowing subsurface water to seep in. During low river flows, the Zahns actually diverted the entire river into their pumps in order to keep working. If too little water was a problem, so was too much: During the flood year of 1911, the San Juan River covered the entire camp, and silt completely buried the house and tool shed built by the previous miners. Finally, even when the pumps were working, their longevity was limited by the sharp sand grains in the water, which cut the packing in the pumps and caused them to leak and lose sucking power.

Charles H. Spencer, who, in Crampton's words, "was a canyon

country entrepreneur who undertook dramatically conceived mining operations on the San Juan River and at Lee's Ferry on the Colorado," ran a much more ambitious operation than the Zahns at his Spencer Camp at Mile 38.4 not far downstream from Zahn's camp, also on the left bank.[25] Spencer's plan was to recover the minute quantities of gold and silver from the Wingate sandstone in fragmented piles at the river's edge at that point. To do this, he brought in a gasoline-powered rock crusher to pulverize rock, which would then be washed over an amalgamator with river water. Steam pumps were used to bring water to the amalgamator, and the boiler powering them was heated with logs cut atop Piute Mesa and dropped over the cliff. Spencer operated the plant twice, in the summer and again in the winter of 1909, but the experiment failed because of the small amounts of precious metals in the sandstone. After the assays proved to be discouraging, Spencer shifted his attention to Lee's Ferry, where the Chinle shales at that point promised greater returns in gold and silver.

By far the most ambitious of Cass Hite's protégés, though, was Robert Stanton (1846–1922), a civil engineer whose far-reaching schemes for the canyon country represent the overweening optimism, not to say arrogance, of Gilded Age technology.[26] Stanton was born in Mississippi to a prominent Presbyterian minister whose career included pastorates in several churches and college and seminary presidencies. When his father became president of Miami University in Oxford, Ohio, in 1866, Stanton enrolled there and received a classical education, graduating in 1871. Stanton's interest, though, was in engineering, and because his financial circumstances would not permit graduate study in the field, he added field experience in surveying and construction to his formal training in mathematics. Although it was largely a homemade education, it was a sound one nevertheless, and Stanton's skill won him positions with several railway companies, including the Union Pacific.

Stanton came to the canyon country as chief engineer with the Denver, Colorado Canyon, and Pacific Railway. The company was a creation of Frank Mason Brown, a wealthy Denver real estate man, who had come under the influence of one S. S. Harper, a prospector who, with no real knowledge of the country, was promoting the idea of a railroad along the banks of the Colorado River from Grand Junction to the Gulf of California. The immediate goal of the company was to transport Colorado coal to southern California, where energy needs were great and coal supplies nonexistent. But it was assumed that other economic prospects would emerge as the railroad was surveyed: Tourism in the beautiful river canyons was a likely possibility, livestock-men needed transportation to markets, and mining opportunities were also likely.

A riverbank railroad from Colorado to California? The idea at first glance seems absurd to a nonengineering mind, especially one with modern environmental sensibilities. But to an engineer like Stanton, it was not at all impractical. Harper's insight was sound. Unlike previous east-west railroad lines that had ignored the lay of the land and simply muscled their way over the predominantly north-south mountain ranges by extensive blasting and tunneling, this one would go *with* the land, following the relative gentle grade of the river as it sought its natural course across the West. The river survey, which Stanton at first accompanied, then led, during 1889–90 showed that a riverbank route could in fact be constructed with generally less heroic efforts than a direct route across the mountains. Gentle Glen Canyon, paradoxically, presented the greatest engineering difficulties, with frequent stretches of precipitous cliffs falling directly into the river and requiring extensive tunneling. The expense of the estimated fifteen tunnels bothered Stanton's materialistic mind, but his Gilded Age unbounded belief in progress and technology balked not a bit at the environmental violence of "dropping the top of the cliffs into the river" to get the railroad built.[27]

Stanton passed through Glen Canyon twice during the railroad survey. The first time, to his considerable irritation, he was rushed along by the eagerness of President Brown, who led the party, to get the survey finished and keep a rendezvous in California with a group of potential investors. Brown's drowning in Marble Canyon on July 10, 1889, was caused by inadequate equipment and undue haste and led to a temporary abandonment of the survey. When Stanton returned in December, he had better boats and was in charge of the expedition. He entered the river at the mouth of North Wash and took a closer look at Glen Canyon.

Although Stanton completed his survey all the way to the Gulf and submitted an enthusiastic report on the railroad's potential, his investors were lured off by prospects of more immediate gain, and the line was never built. Stanton himself never lost his faith in the railroad, and drafted a proposal for a shorter line from the mouth of the Grand Canyon to San Diego, but it, too, failed to interest backers.[28] But even he had been somewhat diverted during his survey by another scheme, almost as ambitious: mechanized mining of gold in Glen Canyon.

As one would expect, gold mining was the constant subject of conversation among the miners Stanton and his men encountered in Glen Canyon, and all overestimated its profitability. At Hite he was given estimates of 25 million yards of gold-bearing gravel above the mouth of the San Juan, paying twenty-five cents per yard. Edward Meskin, a trapper and miner, praised the ores twenty miles west of Hall's Ferry and indicated that it was profitable to carry them to the river to be washed, as well as the rich mines in the Henry Mountains.

It was the smooth-talking Cass Hite himself, though, who really got the attention of both Brown and Stanton. The party arrived at Ticaboo just after noon on June 27, 1889, and decided to remain there to repair the damage their boats had sustained in Cataract Canyon. Both Brown's notebook (which Stanton recovered when it floated to the surface after Brown's fatal accident) and Stanton's notes record Cass's energetic promotion of Glen Canyon's rich gravel bars. He claimed, for example, that the estimate of gold content by the miners at Hite were far too low; his own placers at Ticaboo were paying fifty-five cents per ton. Brown verified this by panning a little himself, and found about a dozen grains of gold. Others he watched panned, in one instance, from 20 to 25 grains, and in another 300 to 400. A new enterprise had been born. For the rest of the trip, Brown and Stanton added gold claims of their own to their survey notes, and during the second trip Stanton made even more.[29]

Disappointed but undaunted by the failure of his railroad projects, in 1897 Stanton shifted his attention to raising money for a mining proposal in Glen Canyon. On an extensive trip throughout the country, he met with Cass Hite in Salt Lake City, with a group of Ohio investors including Julius F. Stone, who would make a famous river expedition of his own in 1909, and with the Bucyrus-Erie Company, manufacturers of heavy equipment. The heart of his scheme was a geological theory of Glen Canyon as what he called "nature's sluice box," in which gold is washed out of deposits by the river itself and its tributaries and carried by their rapid currents into the placid waters of Glen Canyon, where the current force is no longer sufficient to carry it forward, and the heavy gold sinks to the bottom.[30] Small groups of miners washing gravel in sluice boxes with steam pumps, like the Hite brothers, were producing gold; why not increase the scale through engineering know-how and really start making some money? This could be done, Stanton thought, by means of an immense floating dredge that could be moved up and down the river, transferring gold-bearing gravel from nature's sluice box to Stanton's, where it would be screened, then washed across a series of amalgamating tables that would catch the gold.

Armed with investments from his new Hoskaninni Mining Company, Stanton left Salt Lake City on September 11 for Glen Canyon.[31] While awaiting completion of the dredge, the first item of business was to file as many mining claims as possible, for the expense of the machine could not be justified unless a sufficient quantity of ore were available. To that end, Stanton traveled the entire length of the canyon, staking unclaimed properties and, as smaller operations became discouraged and left, taking over their claims as well. Eventually, Stanton had the entirety of Glen Canyon claimed for his operation.[32] In making these claims, incidentally, Stanton was aided by Cass Hite's brother, Ben, who evidently decided that water was thicker than blood (if it contained gold-bearing sand), and deliberately caused the brothers' Good Hope claims to fail so Stanton could buy them out.[33]

In June 1900 the dredge was shipped by railroad to Green River, then by wagon the rest of the way.[34] Stanton's men built a road down Wilson Creek (later Stanton) Canyon, which reached the river in the midst of the Hoskaninni claims at Mile 121.4, then taken up almost to Mile 123. Both the Wilson Creek road and another project of cutting steps down the steep gorge at Hole-in-the-Rock to allow machinery to be brought into the canyon are among Glen Canyon's most ambitious engineering projects. The Hole-in-the-Rock steps counted as assessment work, but they were never used to bring equipment into the canyon; the company went broke.

The dredge assembled, it went into operation about the beginning of 1901, but only operated until May. Stanton was a fine engineer, but he had not properly reckoned the difficulty of saving the minute particles of gold in the river bottom sand. Flour gold, it was called, and although its weight was greater than the other bottom material, it had been ground into such fine particles before reaching "nature's sluice box" that it would actually float on the surface tension of the water. After two cleanups of the amalgamating tables in April and May netted only a little over $30 worth of gold each time, Stanton was forced to realize that the project was a failure. Although he recommended to the company that much larger dredges could be profitable, they wisely decided they had spent enough, and the company went into receivership.

Stanton's dredge was not Glen Canyon's last large-scale mining operation. That honor belongs to Charles Spencer's attempt to exploit the Chinle shales at Lee's Ferry. As noted above, he had failed to recover paying quantities of gold from the Wingate sandstone at Spencer Camp on the San Juan in 1909, and he arrived at Lee's Ferry in May 1910.[35] He found the thick deposits of Chinle in the cliffs behind the Lee's Ferry Fort, but he had been led to believe there were deposits of coal as well that could be used to fire steam pumps to sluice the Chinle, and they appeared to be missing. Not willing to delay his operation, he brought in a boiler anyway, and fired it temporarily with driftwood until coal deposits could be located.

The initial results were disappointing. In the first place, while the Chinle does contain gold, it assays much lower than Spencer had been led to believe. A more serious problem, though, was that the mercury in his amalgamator, which was supposed to trap the gold, kept getting clogged with some unidentifiable substance and would shortly begin losing what little gold there was. While chemists worked on a solution to that problem, Spencer devoted his attention to developing a coal supply.

That supply existed in a branch of Warm Creek Canyon about twenty miles from the river. At first intending to pack the coal to the ferry on mules, Spencer dug and blasted the dramatic Spencer Trail up the Echo Cliffs behind the fort (timing the dynamite blasts and other furious activity to coincide, incidentally, with the visit of a group of investors). Eventually, though, Spencer decided that building a wagon road to get the coal to the mouth of the canyon about twenty-eight miles above the ferry, and floating it down the river made more sense. His first attempt at this, however, was a failure: He brought in a twenty-six-foot launch, the *Violet Louise*, to tow a barge between Warm Creek and the ferry, but the launch engine proved to be far too underpowered to do the job.

Spencer became convinced the solution was to build a steamboat to bring the coal down. Built in San Francisco in 1911, it was ninety-two feet in length, twenty-eight feet wide, and powered by a twelve-foot-wide stern wheel. With the single exception of the Stanton dredge, it was the largest craft ever seen in Glen Canyon. Although he later claimed that he only reluctantly supported the idea of the boat, Spencer allowed it to be christened the *Charles H. Spencer* when it was assembled at the mouth of Warm Creek after having been freighted in via wagons from Marysvale.

The captain of the boat was Pete Hanna, the only one of Spencer's men to have had any steamboating experience, and Hanna quickly learned what steamboat captains on the lower Colorado had known for a half century: The sandbars in the slower sections of the river would severely tax the skill of anyone who dared to pilot a large craft through them. Loaded with coal, the *Spencer* left Warm Creek and quickly ran aground. It was freed the next day, and Hanna cleverly developed a unique technique that oarsmen had only recently begun to use. He turned the boat around and backed it downstream so the engines were working against the current, giving the boat both maneuverability and speed control. In this way, they reached the ferry without further mishap.

But the *Spencer* proved to be a fuel hog when operated in that manner, and the crew learned that it was barely able to carry enough coal to get *itself* up and down the river, let alone have any left over for the mining operation. Spencer solved that problem by having the steamboat pull an empty barge up to Warm Creek which, when loaded, was drifted downriver to the ferry.

The unsolvable problem, though, was the chemistry of the Chinle. The problem turned out to be the presence of a rare element called rhenium, and although extraction of rhenium is a simple procedure, it was not discovered until long after Spencer gave up his mining enterprise.

Two footnotes: In the 1960s Spencer learned that rhenium itself is highly valuable to the electronics industry as a superconductor, and returned as an old man to the Paria area to mine that, rather than gold, but the operation was unsuccessful. Also, the *Charles H. Spencer*, no longer needed to transport coal, was tied up at Lee's Ferry and abandoned. A flood in 1915 sank the boat, and its remains become less and less visible in the riverbank mud as the years go by.

The Glen Canyon gold rush was over, and the might of human

technology had proved impotent against the gold deposits locked up in the inscrutable river and its canyon. In the end, the only ones who succeeded as miners were the little guys, the individuals unconsumed by greed, who loved the peaceful environs of Glen Canyon and were content to eke out a comfortable living from their small sluice boxes.

Cass Hite spent his last decade making small withdrawals from the Bank of Ticaboo. Bert Loper was another. Born in 1869, the year of Major Powell's first exploration of the river, he was orphaned at an early age and placed in a foster home, but he ran away to seek his fortune in the mines of Colorado. He migrated to Bluff and the San Juan gold fields in the 1890s, left to enlist in the army during the Spanish-American War, and returned to Colorado in 1900. He became involved in labor agitation there and was run out of the state.

Loper's Glen Canyon experience began as a result of an unhappy river-running experience with Charles Silver Russell and Edward Monett in 1907.[36] After successfully running Cataract Canyon, Loper stopped at Hite to send a camera out for repairs, promising to join his partners at Lee's Ferry later to continue through the Grand Canyon. But when he arrived at the ferry, they had gone on without him, and he decided to go back upriver and live in Glen Canyon. It was an epic journey, pulling his boat alone through rapids and over sandbars in January and February 1908. When he reached Ticaboo, Cass Hite convinced him to take up residence upriver on the left bank and the mouth of Red Canyon, where A. P. Adams had a small cabin. Loper worked out a lease arrangement for the cabin, but his biographer, Pearl Baker, doubts that any money ever actually changed hands, because Adams wanted a caretaker.

As Loper described it, the little place at Red Canyon had everything he wanted:

> On this low bar or bottom land was a little ranch, only about seven or eight acres, or nine acres, under cultivation, we had to raise horse feed, had a little orchard, little vineyard, chicken yard, wagon and mower, things like that. . . . The cabin is right in cottonwoods.[37]

And he did a little mining. Loper had an ore car that he would fill by means of a team and scraper and dump into a bin. He would fill a small sluice box from the bin and wash it with Red Canyon water.

The gold recovered was never much—his diary records a fall 1909 cleanup that netted only $87.70, and his biographer notes that he never recorded more than $200 in a cleanup—but it was enough to finance his simple needs, "a little flour, coffee, baking powder, soap, bacon, salt, sugar, and he wore only the heaviest and most serviceable work clothing, which he ordered from Sears Roebuck."[38] He augmented his mining proceeds by keeping an eye on some of Al Scorup's livestock, for which he received, two or three times a year, $10 to $25 or a quarter of beef.

For companionship he had the other Glen Canyon hermits: Cass Hite, whom he visited occasionally to discuss world affairs, and Lon Turner, who mined at California Bar. There was a companionship among such men that shared experience in a rough country brings. When reminded during his testimony in the Colorado River Case that Cass Hite, to whom Loper had referred as a neighbor, was actually located some miles away, Loper replied, "Yes, he was; he was a neighbor, just the same." The best companionship, though, was the river: "I lived with that river so much, it pretty near became a part of me; I would sit on the banks and watch it; I would boat it; I would do everything; about the only companion I had."[39]

Oil wells have been a much more enduring and profitable resource for the San Juan country than precious metals, but as a result of a few tentative explorations, oil men have found little in the area of this study to interest them. Most of the oil appears to be located along the San Juan River itself, in the area of Mexican Hat, and between Bluff and Aneth, where pumps and tanks are a common sight.

Emery Langdon Goodridge, an Ohioan who migrated to Colorado in search of gold, was the first to notice oil seeps along the San Juan during his 1882 boat trip to the mouth of the river (the first recorded boat trip to that point). Upon his return, he staked an oil claim at Mexican Hat, but lacked sufficient funds to exploit it until 1907. His investors were rewarded on March 4, 1908 with the sight of an immense gushing well that spouted seventy feet into the air.[40] At a later date, Goodridge built a road from present-day Mexican Hat across upper John's Canyon and down a steep grade to the mouth of Slickhorn Canyon to drill at the oil seeps he had found there. Unfortunately, after bringing his machinery 175 miles across the rough San Juan country, an accident occurred on that last grade, and his ma-

chinery fell down the canyon wall, where it is still visible on the right
bank of the river just upstream from the canyon mouth. After that, he
evidently confined his mining to the Mexican Hat area.[41]

Although Herbert E. Gregory's 1917 study of the geology of the
Navajo country reported that oil deposits evidently did not exist in
paying quantities outside the above-mentioned areas, that did not
discourage explorers from verifying his findings on their own. When
John Wetherill was guiding Neil Judd's 1923 expedition "beyond the
Clay Hills" and had to return to Kayenta for supplies via Clay Hills
Crossing, he found an oil exploration crew near Organ Rock and bor-
rowed their Model T Ford.[42]

Nor did oil explorers in Glen Canyon fare any better. Early river
explorers had noticed oil seeps on the right bank of the river in the
Rincon area at Mile 98.2, which became known as Oil Seep Bar.
In 1920–21 Frank Bennett, previously a Glen Canyon gold miner,
brought drilling machinery to the area and sank four shafts. Perhaps
because the deepest shaft only went down about 150 feet, Bennett's
Henry Mountains Oil Company found no exploitable quantity of oil.[43]

The most recent oil exploration failures took place west of the
Clay Hills, on the Nokai Dome and Mancos Mesa. In 1952 the Skelly
Oil Company built a road all the way from present Highway 95 paralleling or duplicating the old Hole-in-the-Rock road through Clay
Hills Pass and across Castle Wash, where it turned off to the south
and climbed to the top of the Nokai Dome. Such uplifts in the earth's
surface often signal subterranean oil deposits. Skelly was convinced
that that was the case, so they built a small settlement atop the dome,
complete with an airstrip. But the project was abandoned as quickly
as it arose, when no paying quantities of oil were found. The road,
however, remained a handy means of access to latter-day explorers
through the rough Lost Cowboy country, as has a road built to the
north of Castle Wash in 1971 by the Exxon Company for an equally
unsuccessful exploration of Mancos Mesa. The road enters Moki
Canyon via the sand slide at Red Cone Spring and exits the canyon to
the north via the dramatic cut at what has recently been called Harrison Canyon, which is four miles upcanyon.[44]

It is perhaps appropriate that the discovery of the first deposits of
radioactive material, which would become the most profitable of the
Colorado Plateau's mineral resources, was made by that greatest of
all canyon country discoverers, John Wetherill. In 1898, while guid-

ing an archaeological expedition in the Red Canyon area, Hosteen John began probing in the wall of a cave where the party had stopped for lunch, and discovered some yellowish matter embedded in petrified wood. Scientists in those days were only beginning to explore the nature and possible uses of radioactive materials, and Wetherill thus could have had little inkling of the significance of his find, but it looked interesting, so he wrote a mining claim and posted it in a rock cairn in the cave. He never bothered to record the claim, but in 1943 he remembered the site and the claim, and described its location to a young friend, Preston Redd, who returned to it and developed his own mine there. It became the Blue Lizard Mine, one of the richest strikes in Utah.[45]

Hosteen John did not live long enough to see the economic potential of radioactive materials achieve its peak. Early uses of radioactive material included only such things as X-rays and radiation treatment for cancer, and required only limited amounts of radium. Discovery of deposits of pitchblende in the Belgian Congo in the 1920s robbed even that limited economic potential of the available low-grade American ores. It was not until the development of nuclear weapons and the cold war that a market for domestic radioactive ores suddenly blossomed, and the discovery at about that time of high-grade deposits of uranium on the Colorado Plateau—particularly in southeastern Utah—caused a mining rush reminiscent of the gold rushes in California and Alaska during the previous century. In this case, the federal government was the sole customer, for Executive Order 9613 in 1945 had withdrawn all radioactive materials from the commercial market and reserved them for the government. Prices boomed nevertheless, and between 1946 and 1959 no less than 309,380 uranium claims were filed in four southeastern Utah counties.[46]

In the San Juan country, the most profitable uranium mine by far was the Happy Jack, an old copper mine in the mesa between White and Red Canyons that had been developed in the 1890s. In 1946 a Moab road contractor named Joe Cooper and his father-in-law, Fletcher Bronson, bought the Happy Jack for $500. The mine was unprofitable because the low-grade copper ore was too contaminated with uranium to be economically refinable. They were about to sell the mine for back taxes when the government announced its uranium-buying program. They immediately withdrew the mine from sale and began producing uranium. During its peak in the

1950s, the Happy Jack produced thirty tons of ore per day, and netted its owners over $25 million.[47]

Evidence of the uranium boom is conspicuous throughout southeastern Utah. Although prospectors like Joe Plosser at White Canyon used low-level airplane flights with a scintillometer to locate potential mines, many others operated from Jeeps, and built roads to the claims that are still visible and often still used by backcountry explorers. Most of the uranium exploration in the Glen Canyon area took place in the upper canyon between the mouth of the Dirty Devil and Good Hope Bar.[48]

Production at the Happy Jack and other mines in the area led to construction by the Vanadium Corporation of America of an ore-reduction mill at the mouth of White Canyon, which began operation in July 1949. From that time until mid-1954 when the mill shut down, a significant community existed around the mill, consisting of every type of dwelling from tents to "fairly substantial homes," and including a post office and a school with thirty pupils taught by the well-known historian of southeastern Utah, Pearl Baker. No less than forty people were employed at the mill, and 100 to 125 people received mail at the post office. It was, as Dick Sprang remembers, "one heck of a community, I'll tell you: every kind of expert and greenhorn prospector, and a full contingent of weirdos."[49]

Although the government has eventually begun to allow a limited commercial market for radioactive materials, its own stockpiles became large enough by the late 1950s that it became a less and less important customer, and prices dropped to a point where many low-grade deposits ceased to be profitable. Although uranium mining is still an important industry in southeastern Utah, the great fortunes made possible during the boom of the 1950s are a thing of the past.[50]

Nuclear weapons and power plants, X-rays, and radiation treatments all seem part of a vastly different world from the time when Cass Hite first spurred his horse into the Colorado River at Dandy Crossing. But surely he would have recognized the motives of a Joe Cooper, a Fletcher Bronson, or a Joe Plosser as much as he recognized those of a Bert Loper, a Charles Spencer, or an Arthur Chaffin—to make a living, and perhaps even strike it rich, in the harsh but dramatically beautiful environment of the San Juan country.

NOTES

1. [Frank Beckwith], "Knew Cass Hite," *Millard County Chronicle,* May 5, 1932; Pearl Baker, *Trail on the Water* (Boulder, Colo.: Pruett, 1969), 77.

2. Unless otherwise cited, the biographical information on Cass Hite comes from his autobiographical poem, "The Trail of Hosteen Pishlaki for Sixty Snows," and Martin Clark Powell, "A Study and Historical Analysis of the Document 'The Trail of Hosteen Pishlaki for Sixty Snows,'" (M.A. thesis, University of Redlands, 1963). Powell's thesis includes the poem and a collation of its variant versions. Also useful are P. T. Reilly's notes on Arthur Chaffin's reminiscences of Cass Hite, in possession of the author.

3. Byron Cummings, "The Great Natural Bridges of Utah," *University of Utah Bulletin,* Part 1, 3 (November 1910): 10–11.

4. Hite to Byron Cummings, May 11, 1911, Arizona Historical Society; C. Gregory Crampton, *Standing Up Country* (New York: Alfred A. Knopf, 1964), 121–26.

5. According to Louis Chaffin, over one hundred miners at Hansen Creek about 1895, tired of having to travel some thirty miles upstream to get their mail at Hite, petitioned the government (unsuccessfully) to establish a post office there. C. Gregory Crampton, *Historical Sites in Glen Canyon: Mouth of Hansen Creek to Mouth of San Juan River,* University of Utah Anthropological Paper No. 61 (Salt Lake City: University of Utah Press, 1962), 78.

6. Abundant testimony, both written and oral, exists about the nature of Hite. See especially the Hite oral history collection assembled for the Utah State Historical Society by Lisa Fisher.

7. Homer J. Hite testimony in the Colorado River Case, Utah State Historical Society.

8. Examples of his articles include "Colorado River Gold," *Beaver Utonian,* January 13, 1893, reprinted in *Utah Historical Quarterly* 7 (1939): 139–40; and *Salt Lake Tribune,* January 12, 1893.

9. Dwight L. Smith and C. Gregory Crampton, eds., *The Colorado River Survey: Robert B. Stanton and the Denver, Colorado Canyon & Pacific Railroad* (Salt Lake City: University of Utah Press, 1987), 47, n. 6.

10. Charles Kelly, "Lost Silver of Pish-la-ki [*sic*]," *Desert Magazine,* (December 1940), 5–8.

11. Crampton, *Standing Up Country*, 134.

12. The story of the Kohler incident that follows is based on news reports in the *Salt Lake Tribune* and the *Salt Lake Herald*, September 1891–March 1982, passim, and P. T. Reilly interviews with Arthur Chaffin.

13. *Denver Republic*, September 10, 1891, 1.

14. Records of Pardons, Utah State Archives.

15. Charles Kelly, notes on Cass Hite, Kelly Papers, Utah State Historical Society; Powell, "A Study and Historical Analysis," 33, n. 39; Julian Dana, "One Came Back," *True West*, (September-October 1962), 27.

16. Powell, "A Study and Historical Analysis," 36–38; [Beckwith], "Knew Cass Hite"; photographs of Cass's grave are in Powell, 41, and Kelly, "Lost Silver of Pish-la-ki [*sic*]," 6.

17. "Cass Hite on the San Juan," *Salt Lake Tribune*, January 12, 1893.

18. Quoted in C. Gregory Crampton, *The San Juan Canyon Historical Sites*, University of Utah Anthropological Paper No. 70 (Salt Lake City: University of Utah Press, 1964), 9. Pp. 6–11 give a summary of the San Juan gold boom and other mining activities, but, as Crampton points out, "practically all of the historical sites described below are related to one of these major areas of interest" (11).

19. Walter Everett Mendenhall testimony in the Colorado River Case, Utah State Historical Society.

20. Ibid.

21. Bert Loper testimony, Colorado River Case, Utah State Historical Society.

22. Ibid.; Crampton, *The San Juan Canyon Historical Sites*, 17–18; Doris Valle, *Looking Back Around the Hat: A History of Mexican Hat* (Mexican Hat, Utah: The Author, 1986), 5.

23. Crampton, *The San Juan Canyon Historical Sites*, 26–35, passim.

24. Ibid., 39–41; testimonies of Ezekiel Johnson, Hector and Otto Zahn, Colorado River Case, Utah State Historical Society.

25. Crampton, *The San Juan Canyon Historical Sites*, 42–44.

26. What follows on Stanton is based on Stanton's writings, Dwight L. Smith, ed., *Down the Colorado* (Norman: University of Oklahoma Press, 1965); Smith and

Crampton, eds., *The Colorado River Survey*; and Dwight L. Smith and C. Gregory Crampton, eds., *The Hoskaninni Papers: Mining in Glen Canyon, 1897–1902* (Salt Lake City: University of Utah Press, 1961).

27. Smith and Crampton, eds., *The Colorado River Survey*, 59.

28. Dwight L. Smith, "Robert B. Stanton's Plan for the Far Southwest," *Arizona and the West* 4 (Winter 1962): 369–80.

29. Smith and Crampton, eds., *The Hoskaninni Papers*, xi–xii. On the second trip, Stanton records negotiations with potential investors in the Good Hope claim, and refers to claims of his own on the first trip. Smith and Crampton, eds., *The Colorado River Survey*, 103.

30. Smith and Crampton, eds., *The Hoskaninni Papers*, 39, 73.

31. Although the name of the Navajo headman who led Cass Hite to the Dandy Crossing is spelled "Hoskininni," the name of the company is spelled as given here. Crampton, *Standing Up Country*, ix.

32. Ibid., 53.

33. Ibid., 18. Later, as Stanton was preparing for a trip to Salt Lake City, Ben advised him to tell Cass nothing of their transactions, though the reason he gave was the desirability of avoiding publicity, since Cass liked to trumpet everything to the newspapers (33).

34. C. Gregory Crampton, *Historical Sites in Glen Canyon: Mouth of Hansen Creek to Mouth of San Juan River*, University of Utah Anthropological Paper No. 61 (Salt Lake City: University of Utah Press, 1962), 62–71 is a convenient summary of the history of the Hoskaninni Mining Company.

35. The material on Spencer that follows comes from W. L. Rusho, "Charlie Spencer and His Wonderful Steamboat," *Arizona Highways* 38 (August 1962): 34–39; Rusho and C. Gregory Crampton, *Desert River Crossing: Historic Lee's Ferry on the Colorado River* (Layton, Utah: Peregrine Smith, 1975); and Crampton, *Historical Sites in Glen Canyon: Mouth of San Juan River to Lee's Ferry* University of Utah Anthropological Paper No. 46 (Salt Lake City: University of Utah Press, 1960).

36. The material on Bert Loper comes from Pearl Baker, *Trail on the Water* (Boulder, Colo.: Pruett, nd); Baker, "Man Against the River: 7,000 Miles of Rapids with Bert Loper," *Utah Humanities Review* 1 (April 1947): 113–21; Barbara Bingham, "Grand Old Man of the Colorado," *American West* 13 (March-April 1976): 26 f.;

Ronald L. Ives, "Bert Loper—The Last Chapter," *Journal of Arizona History* 17 (Spring 1976): 49–54; and Bert Loper testimony, Colorado River Case, Utah State Historical Society.

37. Loper testimony in the Colorado River Case, Utah State Historical Society.

38. Baker, *Trail on the Water*, 71.

39. Loper testimony, Colorado River Case, Utah State Historical Society.

40. E. G. Woodruff, *Geology of the San Juan Oil Field, Utah*, USGS Survey Bulletin 471 (Washington, D.C.: Government Printing Office, 1912), 98–99; Herbert E. Gregory, *The San Juan Country*, USGS Professional Paper No. 188 (Washington, D.C.: Government Printing Office, 1938), 111–13; Valle, *Looking Back Around the Hat*, 2.

41. Hugh D. Miser, *The San Juan Canyon, Southeastern Utah*, USGS Water Supply Paper No. 538 (Washington, D.C.: Government Printing Office, 1924), 28.

42. Herbert E. Gregory, *Geology of the Navajo Country*, USGS Professional Paper No. 93 (Washington, D.C.: Government Printing Office, 1917), 145; Neil M. Judd, "Beyond the Clay Hills," *National Geographic*, (March 1924), 285; the oil rig is mentioned in Judd's diary in the National Anthropological Archives, Smithsonian Institution.

43. Crampton, *Historical Sites in Glen Canyon: Mouth of Hansen Creek to Mouth of San Juan River*, 29–31.

44. Oral reminiscences of Dick Sprang, who spent a day at the Skelly camp on the Nokai Dome in 1952, and Eric Bayles, who has used the Exxon route to Mancos Mesa many times, both before and after construction of the road. A view of the Nokai Dome airstrip in operation is available in Harry Aleson's 1952 Glen Canyon movies, Harry L. Aleson Papers, Utah State Historical Society.

45. Gary Lee Shumway, "A History of the Uranium Industry on the Colorado Plateau," (Ph.D. dissertation, University of Southern California, 1970), 1–3.

46. Leonard J. Arrington, "Uranium Mining." In Howard R. Lamar, *The Reader's Encyclopedia of the American West* (New York: Thomas Y. Crowell, 1977), 1207–8.

47. Ibid.; Raye C. Ringholz, *Uranium Frenzy: Boom and Bust on the Colorado Plateau* (New York: W. W. Norton, 1989), 77.

48. Dick Sprang statement on Hite, Utah, 23–25; C. Gregory Crampton, *Historical Sites in Cataract and Narrow Canyons, and in Glen Canyon to California Bar*, Uni-

versity of Utah Anthropological Paper No. 72 (Salt Lake City: University of Utah Press, 1964), 31–32.

49. Crampton, *Historical Sites in Cataract and Narrow Canyons, and in Glen Canyon to California Bar*, 32; Sprang statement on Hite, 7–8, 25.

50. Arrington, "Uranium Mining," 1208.

Lake Country Cowboys

Lake Canyon begins inauspiciously in several jagged runoff gorges on the northeastern face of the craggy Nokai Dome, then flows for a half-dozen as-the-crow-flies miles to the northwest before changing direction in a great sweeping bend to the southwest several miles before it enters the Colorado River. From the human standpoint it is a fickle canyon, offering access only sporadically along its length. Some stretches, especially along the lower reaches of the east fork, are highly hospitable, with a perennial stream flowing through shady cottonwood bottoms whose leafy abundance contrasts dramatically with the domed walls of Navajo sandstone. In late autumn the east fork becomes one of the most memorable southwestern canyons as the cottonwoods and squawbrush turn a multitude of hues at once the delight and the frustration of artists and photographers. Farther down, the canyon becomes steeper and more restricted in its course: The bottoms are choked with brush, and even the domes along the rim seem to throw human intruders back. The last few miles, now under reservoir water, added high waterfalls to the hazards.

Nevertheless, Lake Canyon was a favorite haunt of prehistoric man. Wasp House, near the mouth of the canyon, was to river explorers Harry Aleson, Dick Sprang, and Dudy Thomas, "the perfect Moki house" in completely livable condition and offering the additional delight of decorative finger markings in its mortar. Such sites offer evidence against the theory popular among early archaeologists that the prehistoric inhabitants of Glen Canyon were mere transients who eked out a mean existence for a few lean years, then moved on, presumably to one of the big metropolitan centers like Mesa Verde or Chaco Canyon.[1] Better perhaps, to regard them as rebels like the later white men who took up residence in Glen Canyon out of distaste for urban congestion, preferring a life of solitude in a spectacular setting. Other ruins in Lake Canyon, though, offer hints that life there may have had its ugly aspects as well. Two limestone structures, one on a large dome extending into Hermit Lake, and another on the rim of the east fork overlooking a large open cove in the canyon, could have been lookouts at strategic vantage points, though the true purpose of neither has been definitely determined.[2]

The geography of Lake Canyon and its tributaries make possible an interesting geological phenomenon: a large natural lake in the midst of an arid slickrock canyon. The phenomenon occurs occasionally in the canyon country where there is a perennial stream in a main canyon and a tributary lengthy enough or steep enough to carry a great enough volume of debris during runoff to dam the main canyon. If the dam is solid enough, the stream in the main canyon builds a lake behind it. An excellent example of the process is observable today in Moki Canyon, Lake Canyon's nearest neighbor to the north, where the steep tributary named Camp Canyon by University of Utah archaeologists carries large enough quantities of sand into Moki to create a lake that is occasionally large enough to swim in, though it also frequently washes out almost completely, leaving a silty canyon bottom and a large field of cattails.[3]

In Lake Canyon two tributaries, known to cattlemen as Bobtail and East Lake or East Fork, once came together to enter Lake Canyon at the same point. Bobtail is a fairly substantial canyon, but East Lake is immense, well over five miles in total length and drains a vast amount of slickrock; during runoff periods the debris-carrying capacity of the system is very great. In prehistoric times the two tributaries created an immense dam in Lake Canyon, backing up a lake perhaps a mile in length. A recent measurement based on historic photographs that show the water level, and terrace remains at the lake bottom, shows the lake to have been sixty-four feet deep at its approximate midpoint.[4]

The past tense is appropriate here, for on November 1, 1915 an immense storm washed out the dam in what must have been a uniquely spectacular event even in a country famous for natural dramatics. So the lake, known variously during its brief recorded history as Red Lake, Black Lake, Lake Pagahrit, and Hermit Lake, is no more. Identifying its site is easy today even without historical photographs, for there is still a large silt flat where Bobtail and East Lake once came together (East Lake changed its course at a later date as the dam blocked its mouth and forced its outwash into the lake farther up on its shoreline), and the immense beds of black and white peatlike organic material many feet thick are conspicuous along its eastern shore.

Hermit Lake is largely known to us through the literary and photographic depictions of Albert R. Lyman, a Mormon cowboy who first saw it in May 1891, at the age of eleven in the company of his father, Platte D. Lyman, who used it as his range headquarters.[5] To young Lyman the lake was such a geographical oddity as to be rationally incomprehensible; accordingly, he added to Indian legends large doses of his own youthful Mormon imagination and left us, in his descriptions of the place, some of the more quaint contributions to Utah literature. He reports, for example, the existence of several floating islands "from ten to thirty feet long," evidently of tangled debris carried into the lake by its tributaries. "Covered with tall rushes as sails on a ship," he adds, "they sailed with every change of the wind from one side to the other of their little ocean. The water birds paddled along beside them, or rode as pirates on their own ship." By day the lake was an apparent mirage sufficient to drive thirsty desert travelers mad with temptation. At night, it was eerie as "the bittern calls from his floating island, and the distant answer of the coyote echoes itself to lingering death in the cliffs and caves."

The calls of the bittern and the coyote were not the only sounds to break the silence of Lake Pagahrit, for a horrible death lurked in its depths.

> There used to be a monster in this lake, so the story is told, and by day he hid in the green bowers at the bottom, but in the darkness he raised his head from the water and sang a shrill song of enchantment. Like the dreaded water sprites of old Europe he was a terrible thing, and the ancient savage hid and closed his ears at night, lest he be lured to the shore. In spite of this precaution, three Utes were charmed from camp in the silent hours of night, and no one saw them again. The story relates that a special pow-wow was held for the monster and he was killed by stratagem.

Maddening mirages, floating islands, the cries of the bittern and the coyote, and even a lake monster singing a "bedeviling song to lure men within its reach"—Lake Pagahrit was truly an enchanted place, and it is perhaps no wonder that Lyman recommended its re-creation as an additional resort attraction in the environs of Lake Powell.[6]

The Mormon scouts for the Hole-in-the-Rock mission who, in December 1879, were the first recorded white men to see the lake, were anything but maddened by the sight, and in fact were thankful to have found such a pleasant respite from the traumas of the trail. They were far from the last of their fellow Mormons to use the lake as a stopping place, and it may have been during the main party's halt there the following spring that Platte D. Lyman, de facto leader of the expedition, conceived the idea of using it as a base for a cattle business. From 1884 until the dam washed out in 1915, Mormon cattlemen camped in a huge cave in East Lake Canyon near the lake and grazed their cattle throughout the country they came to call the Lake Country. Since that time their successors have continued to find the range productive, and though they no longer camp there, the name for the entire range has persisted. This is the story of some of the men who have grazed cattle in the Lake Country and its neighboring regions: Mancos Mesa, Grey Mesa, and that almost trackless confusion of slickrock and sand between Lake and Moki Canyons known today from bitter experience as Lost Cowboy.

The Hole-in-the-Rock Mormons had come to the San Juan country to make a living, and although the primary economic vision of the colony was an agricultural one, the Mormon farmers were not ignorant of livestock and ranching, and the grazing possibilities of the big canyons they crossed on their journey would not have been lost upon them. The sources do not reveal how many of those canyons the scouts discovered. We know that they became painfully aware of Grand Gulch, for the scouts traveled along part of its rim on the westward trip, searching for a passage either through it or around its head (they chose the latter, though they traversed an indeterminable part of it inside the canyon on the return trip). Given the proximity to their route of Moki and White Canyons, they almost certainly found them as well. With fertile bottoms and generally adequate water supplies, the canyons offered natural corrals for cattle and their caves comfortable camps for the cowboys.

The first Mormon cattleman in the Lake Country was Platte DeAlton Lyman. Although Lyman had been officially only a counselor to Silas S. Smith, the president of the San Juan (Hole-in-the-Rock) mission, the field leadership was largely in Lyman's hands since Smith was required to spend most of his time in Salt Lake City trying to raise supplies for the beleaguered pioneers. The resulting arrangement was, in effect, "practically . . . two missions under two men," as Albert R. Lyman put it.[7] Platte Lyman was in some ways an unfortunate choice for that role (though his diplomatic and conciliatory personality, at least among his fellow Mormons, was a great asset), for his refined nature and lack of outdoor skills may have contributed to some of the party's difficulties. According to his son, Lyman was a man of some culture, with a "keen appreciation of learning, literature, music, [and] art," who was quite overwhelmed by the rough San Juan country. "How distressing the rawness and remoteness of this semi-savage country, its servile toil, its drudgery, its hardships and poverty," his son Albert R. observed.

> He loathed the stream of leanbrained outlaws racing like so many lice over the country; he recoiled from the degradation and filth of the natives with whom he had to deal every day. It was a hard world, loud with discord to the finer senses of his nature; yet the great loving Father had arranged his place in it that he might know heights and depths and extremes to amplify his perfection in worlds to come.[8]

Whatever Lyman's perfection in the worlds to come, it is certain that he went through the fires of hell in this one. Lyman's leadership of the colonization party may have shown a lack of felicity, but he did, after all, bring the party through some of the roughest country in North America with no loss of life, and for that he was rewarded in April 1882 with de jure as well as de facto leadership of the San Juan mission. Some in that position may have regarded it as a dubious honor, for he now had all the onerous responsibility of bringing civilization to what turned out to be an infamously recalcitrant country. But Lyman was ambitious for advancement in the Mormon Church, and if the path to glory was a rocky one, it was nevertheless the path to glory.

At first Lyman earned his living freighting railroad ties from the Colorado mountains, but it kept him from home and civic responsibilities for too long at a time, and from the beginning he began to build a small herd of cattle on the side that he hoped would free him from the freighting business. Although his diary does not record the placing of cattle at Hermit Lake before January 1884, his son says he had a herd out there even during his early freighting days, so it is uncertain just when the first herd grazed the Lake Country.[9]

What began as economic enterprise became home in exile. While Lyman was on a trip to the lake in September 1884, Mormon apostles Joseph F. Smith and Erastus Snow visited Bluff in response to a letter of complaint regarding Lyman's leadership and precipitously released (deposed) him. Lyman's journal reports the episode with a stoical matter-of-factness, but Albert can hardly be exaggerating when he indicates that the action was a crushing blow to his father. The cause of the letter, according to Albert, was the difficulty of agriculture along the treacherous San Juan River, a factor that Lyman obviously could not control, and he might have pointed out that the decision to settle at Bluff was originally accepted by the entire community. The mutiny was not unforeseen, but its summary resolution during Lyman's absence, with no opportunity for rebuttal, was a bitter pill that he swallowed with some difficulty. Thereafter the remoteness of the Lake Country became for Lyman a wilderness of exile in which he must have seen himself as an Old Testament holy man undergoing fourteen years of spiritual refining until he was finally restored to the good graces of his church and called on a mission to England in 1898.

The Lake Country, however, did not immediately figure in his exile. Upon hearing of his deposition, Lyman sold his cattle and moved his family back to Millard County where they had been living when he was called on the San Juan mission. But Lyman was at loose ends there economically, and within two years he was back in the Lake Country with another herd he had purchased in partnership with Bishop Thomas Yeates of Scipio. "If I were writing fiction," his son commented, "I would figure it rather a straining of the probabilities to make far-off San Juan this kind of a persistent attraction, but truth is stranger than fiction."[10]

When Lyman and Yeates pushed their herd across the Colorado River at Hall's Crossing in December 1886, they figured on a short stay, fattening the cattle on the fertile grazing of the Lake Country and selling them within the year at a considerable profit. It was not to be, for they had bought at a high price, and the market almost immediately took a plunge, thus requiring that they stay in the business long enough for prices to come back up, for their herd to increase in number, or sell at a loss. Yeates took the latter alternative and sold out to Lyman, but Lyman stayed on and engaged in a partnership with Joshua Stevens, who had cattle on Grand Flat, between Grand

Gulch and the Clay Hills. Albert Lyman recorded a premonitory dream his mother had about that time, in which Lyman and Yeates were both wrestling a lion. Yeates had the big cat by a front paw and was controlling it easily, but Lyman had it by the tail and struggled desperately with the enraged animal. "Pa has the lion by the tail," Mrs. Lyman told her children, "and no telling when he will be able to let go."[11]

With his family in Scipio and his cattle at Hermit Lake, Lyman's exile began in earnest. He was able to return home only about once a year and conducted his business instead once again in Bluff, the very seat of his humiliation. From January 1887 to November 1890 Lyman's diary is blank, but we have some idea of the suffering and tribulation of his lonely life in the Lake Country from his son, who joined him there in 1891 at the tender age of eleven to become a cowboy. Young Albert's presence was required by the withdrawal of Stevens from active partnership. (Lyman took Wayne Redd as a partner in 1892, thus relieving the boy of some of the heavy responsibility.) The boy had anticipated a paradise of green, but was met instead with the "wild contradiction" of

> a country of drifting sand and bald rocks, a country of dry desolation gashed deeply with crooked gulches. Its surface had been carved by the winds into knobs and pinnacles and figures of fantastic patterns. The hellish howl of coyotes echoed back and forth in the darkness of its nights, and long green lizards raced over its hot hills in the day. . . . It is significant that Pa should have fallen heir to that particular region to which he referred as "The abomination of desolation." With the country in general so distasteful to his feelings and ambitions, it is remarkable that he should have inherited the most rude corner of its whole extent.

Albert goes on for numerous pages detailing the raw winters and the thirsty summer drives to Elk Ridge, which left dying cattle in a ghastly trail all the way from Hermit Lake to the Bear's Ears.[12]

Lyman began with a herd of indeterminate size, but it is clear that his instinct for the grazing potential of the Lake Country was a good one, and his herd grew in spite of occasional setbacks from causes beyond his control. The Indians who had used the lake as a headquarters since prehistoric times, for example, saw Lyman's cattle as competitors with their horses for the grazing, and killed an estimated eleven head out of a herd of 225 in 1884. Dry years were another risk. Like his successors who still use the range in the same way, Lyman kept his cattle in the Lake Country during the winter, then drove them to Elk Ridge for the summer. On the way, he was dependent upon infrequent and uncertain water sources to sustain cattle and men, and often got into the desperate straits mentioned above. On one such drive, Albert calculated that they lost over half of the 600 head with which they had started.[13]

Lyman had an ambitious conception of the grazing capacity of the Lake Country. At one point he had between 700 and 800 head of cattle in the area, both his own and others entrusted to him by investors. For comparison, this is almost as much as the modern Lazy TY's entire grazing allotment from the confluence of the San Juan and Colorado to Mancos Mesa and Red Canyon. With such large herds, the risks were greater on the dry drives (the Lazy TY takes only 500 head to Elk Ridge each spring), and damaging effects on the country were beginning to show: With the depletion of vegetation, flash floods became more severe and the alluvial bottoms of canyons began to erode. Eric Bayles, who for many years was cow boss on the Lazy TY range, and who thus fought his own battles with the Bureau of Land Management for grazing allotments, admits that his predecessors had little conception of scientific range management, and mortgaged the future for quick returns in the present. If the BLM has become overcautious in its management of the range, it is at least partly because old-timers like Lyman were overambitious in what they attempted.[14]

During the exile of the 1890s, Lyman began working his way back into the favor of the leaders of his church. In 1891 he was appointed second counselor to President Francis M. Hammond of the San Juan stake, and he welcomed the call of church business as a respite from the lonely cattle country. Finally, in 1898 the church called him to preside over the European mission, and he jumped at the chance to leave the desolation of the San Juan. He left his son in charge of the cattle business, but the young man had no more taste for that life than his father, and the following year managed to get himself called to his father's mission, and sold out happily to a group of San Juan investors called the Bluff Pool.

Eric Bayles, who claims the right to make such an assessment by virtue of the fact that he is himself a Lyman on his mother's side, observes that the Lymans were poor cattlemen who hated the life and the country and persisted in them only from lack of alternatives.[15] It is hard to argue with that view, but it is also important to point out that they were successful pioneers in ways they never intended, in opening up the Lake Country's range and showing their successors how the business could be made to pay. Both the range and the economic scale of the operation would expand greatly during later phases, but it was the Lymans who showed the way.

The Mormon presence in the San Juan country was anything but uncontested during their early years, and in fact the Mormons often felt themselves to be a tiny beleaguered minority who were largely at the mercy of Indians, both Paiute and Navajo, and Gentile cowboys who were often outlaws and always unruly. The Lymans' selection of the Lake Country for their operation was thus not only a function of the area's fertility, but also of its remoteness from competition. Even at that, Indian harassment was always a possibility and sometimes a reality. Outlaws, too, began moving into the Lake Country at an early, though indeterminate, date. One was the elusive Alva Wilson, whose name and the date 1914 appear in a tributary of Cottonwood Canyon not far above its mouth, and who gave his name as well to Wilson Canyon (now called Iceberg Canyon on Lake Powell maps) and Wilson Creek Canyon. During World War I, a young, green Arizona cowboy named Kelly Dickison encountered Wilson when he was sent up from Flagstaff to check on a herd his employers had put somewhere in the area of the confluence of the San Juan and Colorado Rivers. Wilson, who was an old man by this time, offered to help Dickison find his cattle, but they searched the area fruitlessly, and Dickison had to report the herd missing. His employers told him he had been duped by Wilson, who was well known as a rustler.[16] There may actually have been more than one Wilson, for Herbert E. Gregory, who studied the area in 1927 for the U.S. Geological Survey, heard that Wilson was an outlaw who kept horses in the Lake Canyon area, but killed a Navajo and was forced to leave the country. He reportedly enlisted in the army and lost his life in World War I.[17]

So competition and harassment were among the reasons that the Lymans restricted their range to the Lake Country, Elk Ridge, and the corridor in between. It is fairly certain that they did not utilize the excellent grazing in such canyons as White Canyon and Grand Gulch, even though we know they utilized the water in some of their tributaries. Texas cattlemen, and later the Bluff Pool pretty much controlled White Canyon until the Scorup brothers squeezed them out in the 1890s. Explorers Charles Cary Graham, Charles McLoyd, and Richard Wetherill, who worked in Grand Gulch all during the 1890s, reported no evidence of cattle or cattlemen there.[18] It is also all but certain that cattlemen did not utilize Moki Canyon or Mancos Mesa, as the steep walls of Moki offer few points of access to either range. During the 1890s a new breed of Mormon cattleman entered the country, and they opened up all of the above-mentioned areas and others besides, so that by the early twentieth century virtually the entire country from Dark Canyon and Comb Ridge to the confluence of the Colorado and San Juan Rivers, plus a great deal more in adjacent areas, would be Mormon range.

When John Albert Scorup crossed the Colorado River at Dandy Crossing in 1891 at the age of nineteen and headed up into White Canyon in search of a small herd of longhorns he had been hired to watch, he bore little promise of becoming the dominant figure in the San Juan cattle business.[19] Although he reminisced in later years that he never wanted to be anything but a cowboy, and had gained an impressive reputation in his native Sevier County for his knack at handling cattle, when it came to the big, rough canyons and immense trackless mesas of the San Juan country, he was in a different league, and his greenness showed. He quickly ran through his meager grub supply, and though he sold a steer to some miners, he found Cass Hite's prices for supplies too high, and sought a job with a Texas outfit moving a herd over into Colorado to fatten his bankroll. Before he returned to White Canyon, he had established two relationships that were to mean much in later years. For one thing, he had met Franklin Jacob Adams, another tough Mormon cowboy who was to be Scorup's friend, partner, competitor, and successor over the years. Jacob Adams left his own large mark on the cattle business and even on the land, in the form of place names such as Jacob's Chair, Jacob's Rock, and Jacob's Spring, before his tragic death while foolishly trying to cross a flash flood in White Canyon.[20] Also, during a stopover in Bluff, Scorup had met Emma Bayles, who was to become his wife.

Upon his return to White Canyon, Scorup found his place had been preempted by a tough bunch of Texas cowboys and renegade Paiutes, all armed, who advised him to move on. He did, but only to return with another herd and his brother Jim. It was at that point that

Scorup devised the strategy that was to bring him a fortune: Push your cattle into country so rough that nobody else can handle it, live with the cattle in the canyons and become as tough as they are, and wait for the competition to go broke. Scorup knew the Texans would never last in that unfamiliar country, so he and his brother put their 300 head into the rough country on the right bank of White Canyon up behind the Woodenshoe Buttes and waited them out.

Rough country and rough competition made for an equally rough life for the Scorup boys for some years. When the Texans finally fell upon hard times, the Mormons in Bluff hastened them on their way by buying them out in 1893 through the Bluff Pool. For the Scorups, though, the departure of the Texans was a mixed blessing, since the pool drove their 1,300 cattle and 300 horses onto the very White Canyon range the Scorups were trying to use. The great advantage the Scorups had, though, was their constant presence in the canyons with the cattle; absentee ownership would not work in that country. Consequently, the brothers put in long days moving pool cattle away from the sparse grazing and water holes, and replacing them with Scorup cattle. By the spring of 1894, the pool had lost half its cattle and had to capitulate, hiring Al Scorup as their foreman. Even at that, returns were slow at first, and the Scorups sacrificed a great deal of personal comfort and monetary gain in order to buy more cattle or catch wild ones and extend the range. In 1898 the pool sold the White Canyon range to them, and the Scorup empire was on its way.

The Scorups, Jacob Adams, and especially another employee, later partner and son-in-law of Al, Harve Williams, were some of the most indefatigable explorers and backcountry experts ever to operate in the San Juan country, and they slowly and carefully extended their range by discovering reliable water sources, sheltered caves for line camps, and access points into canyons with verdant bottoms for grazing. Grand Gulch, which one might regard as a sister to White Canyon because of its proximity and identical geology, was one of the most important additions to the Scorup range. Its tortuous fifty miles offer some of the most spectacular scenery in the world, but more important for the cattlemen, it provided dependable springs and ample grazing for several hundred cattle. Eventually, before the establishment of the Grand Gulch Primitive Area in 1971 drove the cattlemen out altogether, Grand Gulch was used for their prime breeding stock.[21]

By the early twentieth century, the Scorups had acquired the Lake Country from the Bluff Pool as well, and set up headquarters for their Lazy TY range in the large cave near the mouth of the east fork where the Lymans had originally lived. (After the washout of Hermit Lake, the cowboys camped at the old Lyman cabin—now burned— at the former head of the lake in main Lake Canyon, and in another cave a mile or two upcanyon.) From that Lake Country base, the Scorups extended their grazing into other adjacent canyons like Castle Wash, Johnnie's Hole, and Butler Canyon (the western arm of the Rincon).[22]

Mancos Mesa was another range developed by the Scorups.[23] It was the most remote of all the Scorup ranges, and was reached by two dangerously steep trails that often left dead animals and injured cowboys. One access point was Trail Cliff, at the downstream end of the Little Rincon on the Colorado River, a boulder-strewn route over the Chinle shale at river level, then up a steep Wingate sandstone cliff. The cowboys reached this trail conveniently from either White or Red Canyons along the riverbank. The other access point was down the immense sand slide into Moki Canyon at Red Cone Spring (Red Tanks, the cowboys call it), then up a steep cut in the north wall of Moki at what is now called Harrison Canyon four miles to the east. This cut was widened in the early 1970s to allow motor vehicles, and the route changed somewhat, but in the days of Jacob Adams and the other old-time cowboys, it was a risky trail, especially when pushing a herd of half-wild cattle.

The main water supplies on Mancos Mesa are Jane's Tank (still the cowboys' headquarters) and Jacob's Spring in Cedar Canyon, and a couple of man-made watering places in Johnny Coldwater Canyon and Tater Hole. The old-time cowboys reached these remote areas with big pack trains that they put together at Green Water Spring just west of Clay Hills Pass. Before the road to Red Cone Spring was built, it was usually not possible to reach Jane's Tank in one day, and thus another hazard was added to the route, for the steep slickrock trail into the spring in Secret Canyon is enough to test the mettle of any horse.[24] At the end of the trail in Secret Canyon was a spartan campsite, which Eric Bayles calls a "Harve Williams camp: enough shelter for one man and to hell with everybody else." The trail is so steep that if it snowed while the cowboys were down in the canyon, they could not get their horses back out.

Development of the Mancos Mesa range forced the Scorups and their successors, Hardy Redd (1965–70), Kent Schmitt (1970–78), and Melvin K. Dalton (1978–present) to move the Lazy TY head-quarters first to Green Water Spring, then to Irish Green Spring in upper Castle Wash. Although the new camps were closer to town, the country itself still impressed the cowboys with its remoteness. An early inscription at Green Water Spring, now largely illegible, says, "This is the country where the coyotes bark at strangers," and another one in the big cave near Hermit Lake seems to read, "This is the damnedest country God ever put rocks in."

Like the Lymans, the Scorups found that their title to this far-flung range was never completely uncontested, for its remoteness meant that rustlers from across the San Juan or almost anywhere else could slip in and remove unguarded cattle with little risk of detection. Another inscription in the Hermit Lake cave attests to this constant nuisance: "Beware Ye Thieves, God Damn You."

In 1918 the Scorup business took a major new direction and added its final section of range to the empire. The brothers sold out their San Juan business to Jacob Adams and briefly retired to Salina, but Al had the San Juan country in his blood and joined with Bill and Andrew Somerville to form the Scorup-Somerville company and purchase David Goudelock's Indian Creek ranch, much of which today is in Canyonlands National Park. Al moved his headquarters to the Dugout ranch and spent the rest of his life in business there. After Jim's death in 1920, Al and the Somervilles joined Jacob Adams in partnership again, so that by 1921 their range included everything from Indian Creek to the confluence of the San Juan and Colorado, or almost 2 million acres.

The Scorup empire did not long survive Al's death in 1959, but cattle carrying the Lazy TY brand still crop grass in the Lake Country. Life on the modern range is perhaps best seen through the eyes of Eric Bayles, who worked there for the better part of twenty years (1969–89) as cowboy and later cow boss.[25] Eric was born in Moab in 1946 to Reed Bayles, a sheepman who grazed his flocks in Colorado ("He was everything they hated in Colorado: a Mormon and a sheep-man. But they learned to respect him"). Eric learned to ride, rope, pack, and handle animals at an early age. Like Al Scorup, he never wanted to be anything but a cowboy and never anywhere but on Scorup's old Lake Country range. A man of great excesses as well as great capabilities, he has lived a full life, but a rough and tragic one, marred by alcoholism, failed marriages, and periods of loneliness when the course of events led him away from the Lake Country from which he draws his complete identity. At one of those low points, he was working as a heavy-equipment operator on the Kaiparowits Plateau. "I looked over across the country there one day and saw the Bear's Ears," he recalls, "and I got so homesick I couldn't stand it."

During his years in the Lake Country, the Lazy TY owners drew most of their income from other parts of the old Scorup empire and regarded the TY as expendable. Accordingly, the TY got all the castoff equipment from the other ranges. That privation and the roughness of the country bred a toughness in the cowboys that Bayles points to with pride. "They used to send us all the horses that those Indian Creek cowboys couldn't ride," he remembers.

Although Navajos, who are often the only cowboys who can work for the wages the Lazy TY can pay, now comprise a high percentage of the TY workforce, in Bayles's youth the TY functioned as something of an employment agency for Blanding and other San Juan County communities. Most San Juan County youth with a taste for cowboying took a turn on the TY, though the life was rough enough and the isolation so great that few continued for more than a season or two. It was far from unskilled labor: TY cowboys had to be good riders and ropers, and they had to know how to pack and cook, which are almost vanished skills even in modern San Juan County. Large crews meant large pack strings, and each man had his part of the gear, which he was expected to pack and to care for. And civilized amenities were few. Until Melvin K. Dalton installed the mobile homes for the cowboys at Irish Green Spring (which still have no electricity, incidentally), their best year-round living accommodations consisted of the caves at Green Water Spring, Grey Mesa, and Jane's Tank; their worst could consist of nothing more than a tarpaulin bedroll on a snowy mesa top.

Though most young TY cowboys soon forsook the rough life of the Lake Country for a ranch or town job, for others it became an obsession. For Harve Williams, for example, sleeping in a cave all year and living on a monotonous diet of sourdough biscuits and beans was no hardship. One year when the company found itself in financial difficulties, he drew less than a dollar of the wages he had coming.[26] For Irwin Oliver, roping calves and jerking them down was life's greatest pleasure, and Bayles remembers seeing Oliver wear out a new set of Levi's in one afternoon roping cattle in Castle Wash with no chaps. Bayles himself relishes off-season wild bull hunts, when groups of top cowboys scour the remotest canyons at their own expense to find wild cattle that eluded roundups and to bring them in for sale.

The romantic life of the traditional cowboy is balanced on the modern TY range with a set of economic and political problems that recently drove even Eric Bayles to seek less frustrating employment. One challenge comes from the environmental movement, which has become increasingly strident in its demand for total removal of cattle—"these ugly, clumsy, stupid, bawling, stinking, fly-covered, shit-smeared, disease-spreading brutes," as Edward Abbey calls them—from public lands.[27] On the other hand, the cattlemen's case has been little helped by exploiters like the Lazy TY's Melvin K. Dalton, who professes no concern whatever for the consequences of overgrazing. Arbitrating between these extremes—the environmental Jacobins of the Southern Utah Wilderness Alliance and Gilded Age relics like Dalton—is the thankless mandate of the Bureau of Land Management, which consistently fails to please anyone.

Also, the existence of Lake Powell is a source of much bitterness among the cattlemen. Not only has it removed riverbank grazing and access to important trails like Trail Cliff for grazing on the mesa tops, but it has also introduced tourists who have little regard for the cattle.

The future of the Lake Country itself is uncertain, and the cattle business there is one of its least certain aspects. The economic profile of the Lazy TY is not consistently encouraging, and finding skilled cowboys willing to endure its physical and economic privations is increasingly difficult. If the cattle disappear from the Lake Country, it will be the end of a long tradition and part of a trend that is seeing the demise of similar ways of life from a time past all over the country. One would like to think that the shades of Platte D. Lyman, Al Scorup, and Jacob Adams ride with the TY cowboys on their lonely roundups, but whether they have the power from beyond the sunset to keep the old ways going in the modern world remains to be seen.

NOTES

1. Neil M. Judd was one who advanced the idea of temporary Anasazi occupation of Glen Canyon. See his "Beyond the Clay Hills," *National Geographic* (March 1924):

279. Wasp House and other sites, including Hermit Lake itself, in Lake Canyon are scientifically described and illustrated in Floyd W. Sharrock, et al., *1960 Excavations, Glen Canyon Area*, University of Utah Anthropological Paper No. 52 (Salt Lake City: University of Utah Press, 1961).

2. Referring to the Hermit Lake dome site, Sharrock, *1960 Excavations, Glen Canyon Area*, says "the position of the site and its shape suggest usage as some sort of defensive structure, although this is conjectural" (294).

3. The geography of Lake Canyon and Hermit Lake is described in Sharrock, *1960 Excavations, Glen Canyon Area*, 5–9; Herbert E. Gregory, *The San Juan Country: A Geographic and Geologic Reconnaissance of Southeastern Utah*, USGS Professional Paper No. 188 (Washington, D.C.: Government Printing Office, 1938), 14; and the writings of Albert R. Lyman cited below. The name "Camp Canyon" in Moki Canyon comes from Floyd W. Sharrock, et al., *1961 Excavations, Glen Canyon Area*, University of Utah Anthropological Paper No. 63 (Salt Lake City: University of Utah Press, 1963), though Sharrock does not refer to the periodic lake at its mouth.

4. The measurement was accomplished in October 1986, by Gary Topping and Dick Sprang.

5. Albert R. Lyman, "The Land of Pagahrit," *Improvement Era* (October 1909): 934–38; and "Memories of the Pagahrit," *Desert Magazine* (April 1963): 24–25. Both of these articles contain Lyman photographs of the lake, as do David E. Miller, *Hole-in-the-Rock: An Epic in the Colonization of the Great American West* (Salt Lake City: University of Utah Press, 1959); and Karl R. Lyman, *The Old Settler: A Biography of Albert R. Lyman* (Salt Lake City: Publishers Press, 1980), 7.

6. Lyman, "The Land of Pagahrit," 935; "Memories of the Pagahrit," 24–25.

7. Albert R. Lyman, "Platte DeAlton Lyman," unpublished manuscript at the Utah State Historical Society, 36.

8. Ibid., 36–37.

9. The account that follows is based on Albert R. Lyman's unpublished biography of his father cited above, and the unpublished diary of Platte DeAlton Lyman at the Utah State Historical Society.

10. Lyman, "Platte DeAlton Lyman," 46.

11. Ibid., 47.

12. Ibid., 65, 79–85.

13. Ibid., 76; Platte DeAlton Lyman diary, September 22, 1884. Those semiannual

drives between the Lake Country and "The Mountain," as the Lazy TY cowboys call Elk Ridge, still occur, even since the invention of cattle trucks. Heavy trucks can negotiate so little of the distance that they are not deemed worth the bother.

14. Platte DeAlton Lyman diary, sole entry for March 1892; oral communication with Eric Bayles.

15. Oral communication with Eric Bayles and Melvin K. Dalton.

16. This story comes from interviews with William E. "Gene" Ash and Dick Sprang, both of whom knew Dickison in later years in Sedona. The identity of Dickison's employers is uncertain. Both Ash and Sprang remember him saying it was the famous Babbitt family of Flagstaff, but an admittedly cursory search of the Babbitt archives at Northern Arizona University turned up no record of such a herd, and in a telephone conversation James Babbitt, historian of the family and its vast business enterprises, firmly denied that the company had ever grazed cattle east of the Little Colorado River.

17. Herbert E. Gregory, Traverse Book No. G VIII, May 27, 1927, USGS Field Records Library, Denver, Colorado.

18. Richard Wetherill's field notes are at the American Museum of Natural History in New York City; Helen Sloan Daniels, *Adventures with the Anasazi of Falls Creek* (Durango, Colo.: Center of Southwest Studies, 1976), 9–15, contains the diary of Charles Cary Graham.

19. The account that follows is based upon Neal Lambert, "Al Scorup: Cattleman of the Canyons," *Utah Historical Quarterly* 32 (Summer 1964): 301–20; David Lavender, *One Man's West* (Garden City, N. Y.: Doubleday, Doran & Co., 1944), 159–203; and Stena Scorup, *J. A. Scorup: A Utah Cattleman* (Privately published, nd).

20. Jacob Adams's drowning occurred in 1940 according to Lynn Lyman, "Exploring and Documenting the Hole-in-the-Rock Trail." In Allan Kent Powell, *San Juan County, Utah: People, Resources, and History* (Salt Lake City: Utah State Historical Society, 1983), 119. Lambert gives additional details in "Al Scorup," 308. Scorup himself, in memoirs dictated to his sister, gave the date as October 4, 1942. Scorup, *J. A. Scorup*, 75.

21. Oral communication with Eric Bayles.

22. C. Gregory Crampton, *Historical Sites in Glen Canyon: Mouth of Hansen Creek to Mouth of San Juan River*, University of Utah Anthropological Paper No. 61 (Salt Lake City: University of Utah Press, 1962), 25–26, describes the development of the Rincon by cattlemen before the building of the road in 1957–58.

23. The material on the geography and history of Mancos Mesa comes from the writers' personal experiences in the area and conversations with Eric Bayles, as does the material on Bayles's life and grazing experiences in the Lake Country.

24. In the bewildering confusion of place names in the San Juan country, this canyon appears on modern maps as North Gulch. North Gulch is the cowboys' name for Moki Canyon. The original usage appears on Herbert E. Gregory's map in *The San Juan Country*, where Secret Canyon is the canyon fed by Secret Spring.

25. A transcript of an extensive interview with Eric Bayles by Dick Sprang and Gary Topping is available at the Utah State Historical Society. Much of what follows is based on that interview, as well as information gleaned on winter rides with Bayles and other Lazy TY cowboys, and conversations with owner Melvin K. Dalton.

26. David Lavender, *One Man's West* (Garden City, N. Y.: Doubleday & Co., 1944), 202. Born in Missouri in 1886, Williams was a cowboy in New Mexico and Arizona before coming to the Blue Mountains in 1927. When he began competing with the Scorups in White Canyon, Al Scorup talked him into merging his cattle with Scorup's for a share in the company. Williams later became Scorup's son-in-law. Stena Scorup, *J. A. Scorup*, 77–79. From the company's viewpoint, Williams's spartan life was an asset; as the cowboys saw it, it was a nuisance. In later years, after he could afford to eat and live better, Williams kept to his old diet of moldy bacon and beans and insisted that his men live the same way, in the same primitive cave accommodations he had gotten used to as a young man. Conversations with Eric Bayles, 1987.

27. Edward Abbey, "Free Speech: The Cowboy and His Cow." In *One Life at a Time, Please* (New York: Henry Holt, 1988), 15. Inconsistent with this argument, Abbey recognizes elsewhere that the death of small family farms and ranches produces the ugly consequence of surrendering food production to corporatized, industrialized "agribusiness," and extols the appropriateness of "beef cows and antelope at home on the range over yonder." "Thus I Reply to Rene Dubos." In *Down the River* (New York: E. P. Dutton, 1982), 113.

Indian Traders

Bright letters nailed to the second-story roof proclaim the location of Valle's Trading Post in either direction from which a traveler approaches Mexican Hat, Utah. It is the most prosperous business in a small community clinging to the north bank of the San Juan River. Valle's inventory signals a diversity of clientele that old-time traders could never have imagined. Bags of flour and sugar and cans of coffee echo the three most lucrative commodities on the traditional trader's shelves, while display cases exhibit fine Navajo and Hopi silverwork, and a locked gate admits only serious browsers to a rug room usually containing several dozen Navajo rugs ranging widely in price. And out of sight in a back room is a shelf stuffed with brown paper bags containing pawned jewelry, reminders that even modern traders are financiers as well as storekeepers.

Otherwise, the shelves indicate a different customer and a different era. While the clerk behind the counter still needs to be conversant in "trading post Navajo"—the ability to count change in the language and to understand a few simple phrases—he is more likely to find himself selling beer to river runners (alcohol sales are a distinct advantage in this barely off-reservation location) or frozen dinners for the microwave ovens in the tourists' motor homes in the RV park out back. Typical features of modern trading posts missing at Valle's are gas pumps out front (other Mexican Hat outlets meet that need) and racks of video movies for rent (the fresh vegetable case—a perennial money loser—almost gave way to videos, but nevertheless remains at this writing). Even in a region where one can observe TV antennas and even solar cells on the roofs of hogans, perhaps no feature of life in the San Juan country today symbolizes the yeasty mixture of the old and the new more vividly than the modern trading post.

The advent of the traditional trading post can be dated precisely to 1868, when the main body of the Navajo tribe returned from its four-year exile in Bosque Redondo, New Mexico.[1] Defeated by the military and abandoned by the government to distant and often corrupt Indian agents, the Navajos relied upon the trader to help them—for better or for worse—find their way into the unstable equilibrium between the traditional and the modern that is reservation life. Sometimes accused of destroying the traditional Navajo culture by encouraging a taste for the alien food, clothing, and tools of the white man's civilization, the trader understood that the inherent restrictions of reservation life required economic and technological change, and he provided the wherewithal to make it possible. And he provided a market for the products of the reservation Indian: wool, piñon nuts, livestock, textiles, and jewelry.

In the process, the trader became much more than a storekeeper; he became the liaison between the traditional Navajo and the modern world. Kluckhohn and Leighton list, but do not by any means exhaust, the noneconomic functions of the trader:

> The trader's wife often dispenses simple medicines and gives first aid; the trader sometimes buries Navaho dead, mediates in quarrels, assists in settling estates, and translates and writes letters. This latter service became doubly important during the war years. In many ways the trader acts as a buffer against white society: he may help a Navaho get an automobile license or intercede with the police in his behalf. Navahos seek the opinions of trusted traders on governmental policies and programs and have acquired from them much useful information on animal husbandry, agriculture, and weaving.[2]

Although unscrupulous traders were not unknown in the Navajo country, they were remarkably rare and of brief tenure. Most traders formed a symbiotic relationship with their clients, linking their destinies inextricably. And, as William Y. Adams observed (in an otherwise frequently critical appraisal of the trader's role), after having provided for the Navajos the means for their necessary accommodation to reservation life, the trader generally was a conservative agent, encouraging the Indians to retain and even develop as much of their traditional culture as possible.[3]

In spite of the symbiotic relationship, the old-time trader had to be careful, for the trading posts were always remote from white settlements, the trader usually had no help beyond his family, and he possessed valuable goods that the Indians were sometimes tempted to steal. It was often the Indians' way to test the trader's mettle, to see if he was serious about protecting himself and his stock. Accordingly, the architecture of the trading post often resembled a small fortress. Upon first moving into an area, a trader often operated briefly out of a tent, but erecting a more substantial structure was an early concern. Constructed of stone, the buildings had heavy doors and barred windows. Inside, high, wide counters ran around three sides of the room with no access behind them from the "bull pen" they created in the center. In the more risky locales, a wire screen extended from the ceiling to within a few inches of the counter to prevent a customer from getting a rope over the trader's head. Guns were hidden at various handy places under the counter, never out of reach of the trader. The trade goods occupied shelves behind the counter, usually extending to the ceiling, from which also was hung various utensils, ropes, and harnesses, and all of which had to be requested individually by the customer. A ware room accessible from behind the counter or in an outbuilding contained the trader's surplus stock and the goods taken in trade.

As early as 1796, the federal government had asserted the right to regulate the Indian trade, and with the growth of the reservation system in the 1830s, federal regulations increased as well.[4] Most of the government regulations were reasonable, such as its prohibition against selling firearms and liquor, commodities whose dangerous potential was clear to Indian agent and trader alike. Other rules, such as the grace period for retaining expired pawn, were less universally agreed upon, for traders often had an immense amount of capital tied up in pawn. Regardless of the traders' attitude toward the government, they agreed that off-reservation sites were generally preferable to those on the reservation, in their relative freedom from regulation. The San Juan country included both on- and off-reservation trading posts, the latter ones located along the San Juan River and in Glen Canyon.

The Mormon pioneer John D. Lee was the first Indian trader in Glen Canyon, but he entered the role accidentally. By 1871 Lee had become a fugitive, hounded by the mounting public demand for justice for the victims of the infamous Mountain Meadows Massacre of 1857, and abandoned by the Mormon leadership who determined to protect the other perpetrators of that affair by making Lee a scapegoat. Moving surreptitiously from one isolated southern Utah settlement to another, Lee finally received instructions from Jacob Hamblin in the fall of 1871 that his hiding place was to be Lonely Dell, where the Paria River flows into the Colorado at the end of Glen Canyon.[5]

It was a lonely place indeed, and one can imagine the sense of exile and abandonment that Lee and his family must have felt in their new home. With the Ute Crossing some miles upstream, the area that became known as Lee's Ferry was one of only two possible crossings of lower Glen Canyon. As Father Escalante had learned in 1776, it was a treacherous crossing even at low water, and at flood stage it could be nearly impossible with primitive pioneer technology. Although Lee's original intention was simply to settle there and support himself by farming the Paria bottomland, he became both a ferryman and an Indian trader less than a month after his arrival.

On January 19, 1872, a group of fifteen Navajos hailed him from the south side of the river and asked to be ferried across in an old boat that Lee found moored on his side. Even though heavily outnumbered by the Indians, Lee and his family repaired the boat well enough for a crossing, and brought the Indians over. They stayed for three days, providing welcome manpower helping Lee build a stone corral, then traded him some blankets and clothing for two horses and a mule before they returned home.

Over the next two years the Indian trade and the ferry business both increased. Both Paiutes and Navajos came to Lee's Ferry as a means of access to Kanab and other southern Utah communities, and to trade with Lee himself. Both businesses increased dramatically after 1873, when the Mormon leadership decided to establish colonies along the Little Colorado River, to which Lee's Ferry provided the only practical access. Lee replaced the rowboat he had previously used with a ferry large enough to transport wagons. Although some Mormon emigrants complained of the facility's primitive character, both Mormons and Indians used it heavily.

After Lee's arrest in 1874 and execution in 1877, the ferry and the trading business continued, first under his wife, Emma, then from 1879 to 1896 under her assistant Warren Marshall Johnson, who continued after Emma Lee sold out to the Mormon Church. The Johnson family worked at the ferry until it finally closed when the Navajo Bridge across Marble Canyon opened to traffic in 1929.[6]

During the early years of the present century there were other traders in Glen Canyon. After the San Juan mission had created the Hole-in-the-Rock road, Indians began using it as a means of access to trading opportunities in Escalante. By 1900 the mining engineer Robert Brewster Stanton reported that both Navajos and Paiutes were using the crossing regularly. In the summer of that year, two traders, Henry Newell Cowles and Joseph T. Hall, blasted out a site on the north side of Hole-in-the-Rock Creek and built a one-room house and trading post to take advantage of that traffic. Although the Cowles and Hall trading post only lasted for two years, probably languishing because of its very remoteness and the difficulty of keeping it supplied, they did a good business during that time, with close to twenty-five or thirty Navajos and as many Paiutes camping there to trade at one time. Evelyn Cowles Carter, a daughter of Cowles, sketched the nature of the trade for historian C. Gregory Crampton:

> The Indians brought sheep and goat hides and wool to exchange for sugar, meat, tobacco, yardage, knives, hardware and livestock. The Navajos in addition brought hand-woven blankets, which found a ready sale in the Mormon settlements. The traders supplemented their menu with produce from a small garden up the creek a short distance from the post and on the opposite side. They used the creek water for irrigation.[7]

Another Glen Canyon trading post operated at Camp Stone on the right bank at Mile 122.85 for six or seven months in 1902–3. When the Hoskaninni Mining Company of Robert Brewster Stanton, financed mostly by Julius F. Stone, went broke in 1901, the gold dredge moored in the river at Camp Stone was bought by miner Frank Bennett. Bennett hired Arthur Chaffin, who had been mining in the canyon with his brothers, as caretaker, and Chaffin converted the buildings temporarily into a trading post to augment his income. In a 1966 interview with historian P. T. Reilly, Chaffin described the conversion:

> The dredge had had a boarding house there and they had a dining room in the back. There was two buildings: one was the kitchen, then the dining room where the men came in to eat. It had a big fireplace on one side, and then there was a door that led off into the kitchen. . . . There was a west end from the door, and I put my counter across from that door over to the wall.

Then I had my stock of goods in the back. To avoid maybe getting picked up with a lariat like sometimes the Indians used, I
put a screen wire across. It was up about eighteen inches above
the counter so they could work under it.[8]

Chaffin's Navajo customers, who once included Hoskininni himself, presumably crossed the San Juan from the Navajo Mountain
area at Trail Canyon and Wilson Creek (there being no trading posts
in that area of the reservation at that time) and rode across Gray
Mesa, arriving at Moki Canyon. There Chaffin built a trail for them
into Moki so they could reach the left bank of Glen Canyon and ride
down to Chaffin Bottom (New Year Bar), where he would ferry them
across to the trading post.

Upon their arrival at Camp Stone, Chaffin would provide food and
cooking utensils for them to prepare a meal. When that was over,
trading would begin. "The way you do to trade, or the way I done to
trade with them," Chaffin related,

> they'd come in with their blankets, throw them down on the
> counter, the one they wanted to sell, one at a time always. You'd
> look it over, you'd weigh it, and you'd lay amounts of silver what
> you'd give them for it. They'd look it over and usually try to get
> a little more, maybe start out at four bits more for the blanket,
> keep coming down, maybe a nickel, and if you wouldn't, I had
> the custom not to Jew with them, put down what I was going to
> pay them and let them take it or leave it. That way I saved a lot
> of time. If you'd start to Jew with one, why he'd Jew with you
> maybe for a half an hour over a dime. And so I didn't do that. I'd
> weigh it, if they didn't pick it up, I shove them back the blanket
> and come on with another one. I usually had no trouble. I was
> paying a little more for their blankets; I would give them a little
> better price than they could get over at Tuba City.[9]

Chaffin's business in Navajo textiles was unusual because it was
based entirely on cash transactions, both in the blankets and the supplies he sold to the Indians. He purchased the textiles at rates ranging from fifty cents to one dollar per pound, with only minor
consideration of design or color. He sold some of the blankets at re-
tail in various places between there and Denver, but most went at
wholesale to a supply house in Denver.[10]

There were off-reservation trading posts on the San Juan as well, but the first trader to operate there came to an unhappy end.[11] Although the San Juan mission of the Mormon Church, which created the arduous Hole-in-the-Rock road in 1879–80, intended to establish a stable agricultural community as a base for conversion of the Indians of the San Juan, there were members of the party who had more pecuniary ends in mind. One of those was Amasa Barton who, with Parley Butt, James Dunton, and another unnamed partner, drove a large herd of horses they hoped to sell at a considerable profit to the Navajos around Montezuma Creek, the intended site for the colony. A conflict with the main party at the Cheese Camp suggested a compromise in which the horse drivers proceeded on at a faster pace, thus leaving grass for the wagon teams. Once on the San Juan, and presumably having sold his horses as planned, Barton decided to continue trading, and with his father-in-law, William Hyde, established a post at Montezuma Creek.

The traders quickly learned the same lesson as the settlers, that the capricious San Juan River had a way of defeating human projects in its wild spring floods. Washed out at Montezuma Creek, in 1881 or 1882 Barton moved downstream to the Rincon, some nine miles below Bluff, where a solid rock ledge on the riverbank at least provided a firm foundation for a trading post, and a certain elevation above the river apparently offered protection from floods. The foundation held during the big flood of 1884 (and still remains at this writing), though the water reached the windows, but the water wheel he had erected to lift irrigation water to his field did not survive.

It was Barton's temper that led him to a violent end. In 1887 he caught a Navajo boy stealing wool from his storeroom by twisting it around the end of a frayed stick inserted through a crack in the wall. It was an insignificant enough transgression, but Barton's reaction was to beat the boy almost to death. When the boy made it back home, some of his relatives returned and shot Barton.[12]

After his murder, Barton's widow left both the trading post and the Mormon Church, remarried, and relocated eventually in Salt Lake City. The trading post itself, though, seems to have been out of business only briefly, if at all. C. L. Christensen, who lived in Bluff from 1890 to 1896, worked briefly in 1893 as a freighter hauling supplies from Bluff to the trading post at the Rincon, which he said was at that time a branch of the Bluff Co-op run by Lemuel H. Redd. In addition to the supplies Christensen took down in wagons, the trader would also use two ferry boats that he maintained to get his Navajo customers back and forth across the river, and to transport back to Bluff the wool, sheep and goatskins, and blankets that he procured from the Indians.[13] It is the last mention in the sources of the trading post, and the date and cause of its ultimate demise are unknown.

Two other locations farther down the San Juan River, both in the vicinity of modern Mexican Hat, proved to be good sites for trading posts. One is the site near the present bridge. There the canyon narrows and offers solid rock foundations on both sides of the river where various bridges have linked the Navajo country south of the river with the Mormon settlements to the north. The other is around Mexican Hat Rock, where both gold and oil prospecting have occurred since the 1880s.

The first trader of record at Mexican Hat was Emery Langdon Goodridge, a prospector originally from Ohio who reached the San Juan country as early as 1882.[14] Although the search for gold, and later oil, was Goodridge's primary concern, he also did a little trading for Navajo blankets, which he sold to his financial backer, Adrian C. Ellis, Jr., a Salt Lake City attorney. On April 25, 1901, Ellis wrote Goodridge to enclose a check for $100 and thank him for sending some blankets that Goodridge had selected. "I have no doubt whatever," he wrote, "about being pleased with your selections, & I desire to thank you very much indeed for your trouble in securing the blankets for me." He added that Goodridge should continue to seek "such others as [you] may find desirable."[15] Trading, however, appears to have been only an auxiliary interest to Goodridge's primary preoccupation of mining. Although he hit an oil gusher in 1908, his mining ventures eventually petered out, and trading was not enough to keep him in the area.

Others continued to see opportunity in Mexican Hat trading. One was the ubiquitous Ezekiel Johnson, whose name runs through so much of the history of the San Juan country. It may have been Johnson who bought out Goodridge, for Ben Wetherill recalled many years later that the "Mexican Hat trading post must have been established [in] 1907, or 1908. The old store was near the original [community of] Mexican Hat, about 1½ miles from the site of the present day post. Zeke Johnson was running it the first time I was ever there. I rather think Zeke was the one who put the first post in there."[16]

A trading post was operating near the bridge at least as early as 1917, when the trader there, Arthur Spencer, assisted John Wetherill in establishing peace during the Paiute conflict. Spencer's store was small, consisting of one room in the home he shared with his wife, Medora, and a daughter, Helen. Charles L. Bernheimer stopped there momentarily on a northbound trip in 1920, reported that there was "only one other little shack there comprising that outpost of civilization," and complained that the telephone was out of order. In 1923 two college students, Robert B. Aird and John Newell, nearing the end of an arduous pack trip that had ranged from Blanding to the Natural Bridges and south through Monument Valley to Oljato, spent an exhausting "rest day" at the Spencer establishment, helping him fill a water tank and pumping up flat tires as he repaired them. After setting out the next day, their tired Indian pony gave out completely, and they left him with Helen Spencer. Medora Spencer enjoyed a temporary bit of fame when the rough road down the hill on the north to the bridge was nicknamed Medora's Washboard. The Spencers sold out in 1928 to Cord and Gussie Bowen, who passed it along to Ray and Grace Hunt, who also ran the establishment at Mexican Hat Rock.[17]

The trading post at Mexican Hat Rock was run for a time by John Oliver, originally a resident of Bluff. According to Charles L. Bernheimer, who spent the night at the place in 1920, Oliver ran a very unimpressive operation. The buildings, he reported, were knocked together from lumber salvaged from the mining camp nearby after the mining boom collapsed. His food was not fresh and his housekeeping was unsanitary (Bernheimer's hypochondria made him perhaps a bit finicky about such things). His business was a shoestring affair, in Bernheimer's estimation: "Can you think of this man being sued for divorce and alimony by his wife? A couple of cheap Navajo horses, a dozen head of cattle, and $1,500 worth of goods in his trading store seems all the income producing value he possesses; besides he was lame." Although Oliver was the first Wilson Democrat Bernheimer had met in his travels (no compliment from Bernheimer, a lifelong Republican), he had a senatorial bearing, and sang beautifully in the moonlight after they had eaten.[18]

Ray, Emery, and Jim Hunt were three of the five children of Bluff pioneers John LaRay and Martha Hatch Hunt, and they dominated trading at both Mexican Hat locations from the late 1920s until

Emery sold out to Howard and Doris Valle in 1973. Ray and Grace Hunt supplemented their income from the trading post at the bridge by buying surplus sheep from the Navajos who were being forced during the 1930s to reduce their herds. But it was a meager income. During the latter part of World War II they leased it to John Johnson of Blanding, and Jim Hunt took it over after returning from military service. It was Jim Hunt and his wife, Myrtle, who made the business pay by building a large motel unit and starting a tourist guide business, Canyon Country Tours.[19]

Trading on the far northwestern corner of the reservation itself has been dominated largely by three great trading families: the Babbitts of Flagstaff, at places like Tuba City and Tonalea; the Richardsons, at places like Cameron, Kaibito, and Inscription House; and most important for the region of this study, the Wetherills, at Oljato, Kayenta, Shonto, Piute Mesa, and Navajo Mountain. Although there were other important traders, both during the Wetherills' time and since, John and Louisa Wetherill, their longtime partner, Clyde Colville, and their son Benjamin Wade Wetherill cast as long a shadow over trading in this region as Hosteen John did over its exploration.

John and Louisa Wetherill had entered the trading business in 1900 when they took over management of the Ojo Alamo trading post run by the Hydes north of Chaco Canyon. For the next six years they worked for the Hydes and then for Richard Wetherill at Ojo Alamo, Chavis, New Mexico, and at Pueblo Bonito. With that experience, a growing mastery of the Navajo language, a certain nest egg of capital, and a partnership dating from 1902 with Clyde Colville, a Kansan with a good business head, the Wetherills began looking for a place where they could get into the trading business on their own. Following their wanderlust perhaps as much as their business instinct, they chose Oljato, Utah, on the western edge of Monument Valley.[20] It was an extremely remote, and for whites, extremely dangerous part of the reservation. It was in the very heart of the territory of Hoskininni, the recalcitrant Navajo headman who had never surrendered to the U.S. Army in the 1860s, choosing instead to lead his people into the roughest part of the canyon country, around Navajo Mountain and across the river into the San Juan Triangle.

It was Jack Wade, Louisa's father, who got the Wetherills interested in Oljato. He had prospected there in 1892 and persuaded

John Wetherill to go back there with him at a later date. It was a beautiful country, which no doubt aroused Hosteen John's exploration urge, and there were no traders in that part of the reservation. In the cold spring of 1906, John Wetherill, his brother-in-law John Wade, and Clyde Colville set off from Pueblo Bonito with a stock of trade goods to set up business at Oljato.

One of the wagons broke down while crossing the San Juan River at Chinle Creek, but they got it as far as Moses Rock, where Colville remained with it while Wade and Wetherill pushed on to Oljato to unload their goods and return for him. They were immediately confronted by Hoskininni, who ordered them to leave. Drawing upon his Quaker diplomacy, Hosteen John suggested that the Indians and the traders collaborate in a rabbit feast before making a decision, the Indians providing the rabbits and the traders providing coffee, sugar, and bread. It was a shrewd move, for it introduced the Indians to the delights of the white man's cuisine, thus demonstrating some of the benefits of having a trading post in the area. Not only did Hoskininni allow them to stay, but he began a lifelong friendship with the Wetherills that was greatly deepened when Louisa, with her rapidly deepening interest in Navajo culture and almost preternatural command of the language, joined her husband on his next trip from Pueblo Bonito.

The first Oljato trading post was a tent with a board in front of it set on two boxes, as traders typically began business in a new area. Quickly, though, it grew into something much more impressive. Choosing a location under some large cottonwood trees on the west bank of Oljato Wash, the traders laid stone foundations and began fashioning a building of wood, stone, and adobe. An early photograph, probably from 1907, shows an already large, rambling building with a tent still in use to one side. It seems likely that construction never actually ceased during the four years the trading post was in operation, for none of the existing photographs can be entirely reconciled with the foundations, which are all that remain at the site.

It was at Oljato that the classic three-way partnership among the Wetherills and Clyde Colville matured, a partnership conspicuously in evidence during their greater success in later years at Kayenta, Arizona. It was Colville's primary responsibility to do the trading, keeping the shelves stocked and the bills paid. Louisa was the primary liaison with the Indians, and saw to the guest accommodations, which became increasingly popular. Scientific expeditions took advantage of Oljato's remote location and Hosteen John's expertise as a guide, which was his primary responsibility.

Oljato was the point of departure for some of John Wetherill's most celebrated expeditions. At Oljato he and Louisa made the rediscovery of Inscription House and Betatakin, and from there the Rainbow Bridge discovery party began its journey. Byron Cummings used Oljato as his supply point while excavating in the Tsegi, and Herbert E. Gregory's early scientific work in the Navajo country was based at Oljato. And Oljato was the first breach in the wall of resistance to the white man's culture by the most traditional of all Navajo bands, a breach through which, for better or worse, future traders, missionaries, and other agents of civilization would flow.

Eventually the Wetherills and Colville came to see that Oljato had its limitations, which primarily stemmed from its remoteness. Difficult to reach for supply wagons and those seeking guide services, the site was also limited in the social contacts the Wetherills deemed valuable for their children. Accordingly, in 1910 they decided to move south to Kayenta, Arizona, on the south bank of Laguna Wash, where a plentiful spring would make a substantial settlement possible and where visitors, both Indian and white, would have better access to them than at Oljato.

The original site, to digress briefly from the Wetherills, still possessed economic potential, however, even after the Wetherills left. Although the abandoned Wetherill building remained standing as late as 1923, when the Aird-Newell party camped there and made evidently the last photographs of it before it was dismantled at some later date, trader Joseph Hefferman decided to construct his own building when he began business at Oljato in the early 1920s. Hefferman was a New Yorker who moved to Colorado in 1876 and had gained some trading experience when he bought Noland's Four Corners trading post in 1908. Choosing a location farther down Oljato Wash, but almost in sight of the Wetherill buildings, Hefferman did business out of a tent for a time, then built the adobe building that is the basis for the present trading post. After his death in 1926, the business passed into the hands of John Taylor, then Jim Pearson, then to Reuben Heflin, a member of the family of O. J. "Stokes" Carson, a famous trader in New Mexico and later at Inscription House, and the business has remained in the Carson family since. A traditional bull pen design, Oljato nevertheless features a nontraditional museum of Navajo crafts. Although its business volume is so small that its suppliers, at this writing, leave Oljato's orders at nearby Goulding's, thus saving themselves an unprofitable drive of several miles, Oljato nevertheless fills an economic need and remains a rare modern example of a genuine old-time trading post.[21]

The Wetherill trading post at Kayenta became one of the most famous institutions on the reservation. Although many visitors commented on its status as the most remote post office in the United States, it was a much more accessible location for tourists than Oljato.[22] In fact, hundreds of them braved the heat and the sandy roads each year to enjoy the Wetherills' comfortable accommodations and friendly reception. While hardy vacationers and explorers had occasionally used the old-time trading posts as resupply points, the main business of those posts was the Indian trade. Kayenta, on the other hand, was one of the first modern trading posts in that it came to depend heavily upon the tourist trade made possible by improvements in the automobile after World War I. The availability of reasonably dependable and inexpensive automobiles like the Model T Ford, together with the surplus income and increased leisure time enjoyed by many families during the prosperous 1920s, led Americans out onto the road. One of their favorite destinations was the colorful rock formations, the mysterious prehistoric ruins, and the picturesque modern Indians of Navajo land, and Kayenta offered a civilized oasis from which it could be explored.

The phenomenal rise of Kayenta as a tourist destination during the Roaring Twenties is documented dramatically by one of the most remarkable sources of canyon country history, the Kayenta guest registers, which begin in 1919 and continue to the end of the Wetherill era in the mid-1940s.[23] Although the books contain many entries by guests of presumably humble status, they reveal most significantly the degree to which Kayenta became a refuge for jaded artists and writers during summer flights from the increasing congestion and pressures of urban life. Kayenta never became an artists' colony like Santa Fe during the same period, but as a temporary hideaway from urban ugliness and a retreat where one's creative energies could become recharged and reinspired, it fulfilled the same function.

Artists readily applied their talents to Kayenta scenery and society, often leaving full-page color tributes to their visit. In one amazing sequence of pages in August 1922, for example, Jimmy Swinnerton began with a cartoon of a badger licking an Indian child on the nose, with the caption,

> *That badgers scratch and bite*
> *Is generally supposed.*
> *But this is not one to fight,*
> *He'd rather kiss you on your nose.*

A poem by his wife, Louise Scher, fills out the page. The next page carries a Krazy Kat cartoon by George Herriman. At the top, the mouse, Ignaz, hits Krazy not with the usual brick but with a bucket of paint, while Krazy says, "Et lest I am innitiated among the inna most sicrits of the painted desert, I am now a painted 'ket.'" At the bottom, in one of Herriman's famous surrealistic touches, Krazy and Ignaz observe themselves in the above drama. Krazy says, "The old desert is getting kinda common, Hosteen Nasjit, pipe who's here," while Ignaz responds, "We'll have to give it a new coat of paint, Hosteen Nasja." On the next pages, celebrated western artists W. R. Leigh, Westbrook Robinson, and Maynard Dixon, photographer Dorothea Lange, and Katzenjammer Kids cartoonist P. Dirks created a veritable art gallery, indeed, as Ignaz put it, giving the desert "a new coat of paint."

Poets from the humble to the great flexed their literary muscles on the challenges to their rhyming skill presented by local words:

> *The main road from Bluff to Kayenta,*
> *I don't like and I'll never pretenta,*
> > *But the scenery is grand*
> > *What with rocks, sage, and sand,*
> *And the colors range pink to magenta.*

(Alice Ham Brewer, August 15, 1927)

And,

> *Well I remember and always will*
> *John and Louisa Wetherill.*

(Santa Fe poet Witter Bynner, May 12, 1924)

Not to be left out, writers of prose frequently contributed at least brief comments on the Kayenta environment and accommodations.

Charles Bernheimer signed in on each of his visits, and his literary hero Zane Grey wrote an entire page on September 21, 1929, perhaps his last trip to Kayenta, reminiscing about previous visits and the declining condition of the Indian, which he contrasted with the eternal sameness of the desert.[24] It is an interesting reversal of what he might have observed had he lived to the last decade of the century, with its rising Indian political and economic power in the face of environmental destruction.

During its heyday in the 1920s, Kayenta was big business, with a gross annual income of perhaps $100,000 by the end of the decade. As many as fifty guests surrounded the famous dinner table on summer evenings, enjoying Louisa Wetherill's impromptu dissertations on Navajo culture while Hosteen John smoked his pipe silently by her side. With guest rooms full, tents sheltered some of the overflow, while hardier visitors simply spread their bedrolls outdoors. An immense library of government reports and other scientific literature on the region competed for space on the bookshelves with inscribed first editions of novels left by visiting authors, while Navajo textiles and prehistoric artifacts constituted a museum of local art. Guests were often surprised to find indoor bathroom facilities and also welcomed the shade trees, the expansive lawn, and Louisa's famous flower garden.[25]

The apparent prosperity of Kayenta, though, often masked economic difficulty. Although consistent financial records are not available, a general profile of the operation is possible. Both the Indian trade and the tourist business require the trader to carry a considerable overhead in inventory, pawn, and facilities. Moreover, while the Indian trade provides a relatively consistent income, the tourist business is highly seasonal. Caught between those pincers of consistent expense and inconsistent income, the Wetherill & Colville firm sometimes found itself strapped to meet current obligations. Wealthy clients like Charles Bernheimer and Zane Grey could make a big difference in balancing an annual budget, and Hosteen John courted their business. On the other hand, they could bring disaster if they canceled an expedition after Wetherill & Colville had stretched their credit to procure supplies. This in fact happened in September 1923, when the large Zane Grey–Jesse Lasky party, attempting to film a movie on location on the Kaiparowits Plateau, was turned back by the unseasonably swollen San Juan River. It set

Wetherill & Colville back for the entire season of 1924, forcing Hosteen John to seek an emergency loan of $1,000 from Grey to see him
through the winter. "This is most urgent, a sink or swim proposition,"
his telegram read, "Lasky's failure put us in bad hole."²⁶

Even later in the decade, Wetherill & Colville found themselves
having to seek extensions of credit during the lean days of early
spring. On April 14, 1926, for example, John Wetherill had to ask for
such an extension from the trader Lorenzo Hubbell, Jr., from whom
he had received supplies. "It looks like H___ and it is," he wrote. "I
can't do anything for you now. The prospects are good for the summer. Work here will begin the first of May and continue thro the season. We should be able to clear up things by the first of June. I am
sorry I can't do better." But the following year things were still tight,
and Colville had to write to Hubbell with an unusual proposal that he
send some trade goods and one of his employees from Oraibi to
Kayenta, with Wetherill & Colville's delinquent account to be settled
out of their share of the profits.²⁷

Although the 1930s brought ever increasing scientific parties like
the Rainbow Bridge–Monument Valley Expedition and even movie
crews (though most of those stayed at Goulding's), the decade also
brought the Great Depression. Bernheimer lost most of his money
and made his last major expedition in 1930, whereas Grey's interests
were diverted to his fishing trips. Overgrazing seriously depleted the
Navajo pasturage, bringing the stock-reduction program of the New
Deal and poverty to the Wetherills' Indian customers. By the onset
of World War II, both Wetherills and Clyde Colville were in poor
health, and all three died during the middle years of the decade. Although new owners attempted to keep the business going, even turning the old lodge into a modern motel, Kayenta is no longer the focal
point for tourism that it was during the Roaring Twenties.²⁸

The Wetherills founded other trading posts in the area of this
study besides Oljato and Kayenta. Outside of Kayenta, perhaps the
most important, in terms of longevity and economic vitality, was
Shonto.²⁹ During his explorations of the Tsegi, John Wetherill undoubtedly observed a significant Navajo population on the Shonto
Plateau, and the Shonto Indians certainly traded with him to some
degree at Kayenta after 1910, to which they gained access via the
wagon road through Marsh Pass. In 1915 he and Joe Lee, a grandson
of John D. Lee and an old-timer in the northwestern part of the

reservation, took a wagonload of supplies to Shonto Canyon and set up a temporary tent store in the verdant canyon bottom where a plentiful spring was available. They continued in operation until shortly after World War I, when they sold out to C. D. Richardson.

The Richardsons (C. D. and briefly his nephew Gladwell "Toney" Richardson) built the first permanent buildings—the store, living quarters, and a guest hogan—and developed the spring into a dependable water supply. They sold out to the Babbitts, like themselves a great trading family based in Flagstaff, during the mid-1920s, but the Babbitts made no improvements on the site and sold out in 1930 to Harry Rorick. Rorick brought the trading post pretty much up to its ultimate size and configuration, adding an electrical generator, tourist cabins, shops, and gasoline pumps. Although Rorick had initially intended to develop tourist facilities like those at Kayenta, Shonto under his management remained a conservatively run business, with most of its business in wool and rugs. He made little attempt to tap into new sources of Navajo income, such as the paychecks available from employment on the Santa Fe railroad. Too, the stock-reduction program and general economic retrenchment on the reservation during the 1930s and the war years impeded aggressive development of the trading post. Finally, Rorick was a partial invalid, and after separation from his wife, Elizabeth, was unable to serve his customers personally, so he removed the large counters in the store and placed the goods out where they could serve themselves—the last major alteration in the configuration of the trading post.

In 1945 Rorick sold Shonto to Reuben and Mildred Heflin, Stokes Carson's son-in-law and daughter, who had been running Oljato. The Heflins developed the economic potential of Shonto to its maximum by tightening the traders' ties with the Navajo community through extension of credit, by becoming the claims agent in behalf of the Navajos, and other techniques. It was such aggressive policies that made Shonto a focal point of sharp criticism of trading posts in general during the 1960s and 1970s. The attack began with William Y. Adams's *Shonto: A Study of the Role of the Trader in a Modern Navaho Community*, his Ph.D. dissertation based on several years' employment at Shonto by the Heflins. Adams charged the trading posts with being the "quintessence of paternalism" in retarding Navajo acculturation with the white world. Establishing an ironclad monopoly as the Navajos' contact with the white world was the essential factor in that paternalism, as Adams saw it. The trader did this by discouraging mobility, especially contact with towns like Flagstaff, by credit saturation in which the Navajos' total cash income was committed to the trader by carefully calculated extensions of credit, and even by tampering with the mail to destroy mail-order catalogs and spy upon the amounts of incoming checks.[30] This and similar attacks led to hearings by the Federal Trade Commission in the fall of 1972, which, although they disclosed a good deal of positive functions by the trading posts, recommended considerably greater government regulation.[31]

The other trading posts established in this area by the Wetherills were more modest even than Shonto. Ben Wetherill, who had grown up at trading posts owned by his parents, John and Louisa, spoke Navajo almost as a native language and was fully at home in the canyon country and among its Navajo residents. As a horseman and guide in rough country, he was perhaps the equal of even his father, a reputation well established on expeditions with Herbert E. Gregory and others. After losing an eye, and nearly his life, when he was kicked in the face by a horse as a small boy, Ben became increasingly withdrawn, especially from white society. Eventually his misanthropy would descend into divorce and alcoholism, but during most of his adulthood it manifested itself in a desire to relocate to ever more remote parts of the Navajo country. Clyde Kluckhohn, who would later achieve preeminence as an anthropologist of the Navajos, reflected upon Ben's wanderlust while stopping with him and his wife, Myrle, at Ben's remote Navajo Mountain Trading Post in 1928:

> Only a true son of his father and of the desert would have dreamed of invading this far corner of the Navajo country and establishing a trading post in even more remote isolation. I think the increasing fame of Kayenta, the greater traffic because of Rainbow Bridge and the new oil fields in Monument Valley to the north, had made even Kayenta a bit too crowded for Ben.[32]

Whether Kluckhohn was aware of it, Ben Wetherill had previously run no less than two trading posts at even more remote locations than the one at which Kluckhohn stayed. The first was on Piute Mesa, a short-lived affair of about one year in 1926–27.[33] The Piute Mesa Trading Post consisted of a stone hogan thirty-three feet in diameter and another small hogan nearby in which the traders lived. There were no cash transactions; it was a pure trading post in which Indian livestock, hides, wool, and textiles were traded for white man's trade goods. Water had to be brought to the establishment in drums in a wagon from a spring two miles away, and the trade goods were transported on packhorses. In addition to the remoteness of the location, the venture may have been doomed by a lack of qualified employees, for the two men who assisted Ben had no command of Navajo, and trade fell off sharply when he was absent.

Ben Wetherill's next trading venture was evidently even more brief than the Piute Mesa establishment. There was water at Navajo Mountain, and a site there would be much more accessible than Piute Mesa. At first he built a cabin at War God Spring, a plentiful water source, but too high on the mountain to attract many customers.[34] At last, in 1927, he built a trading post in Cottonwood Canyon, which became the modern Navajo Mountain Trading Post, the primary contact point between whites and Navajos in the Navajo Mountain area. For three months Myrle Wetherill made a home for her husband in a tent while he traded in a nearby stone building, but Ben then built a larger stone residence, which was where Kluckhohn stayed the following year. A notable feature of the residence, to Kluckhohn, was Myrle Wetherill's piano, which Ben had brought the entire distance from Kayenta (a remote enough locale in itself) and placed in an adjoining storeroom for her.[35]

As the Great Depression deepened in 1932, mounting debts, especially to Lorenzo Hubbell, Jr., forced the Wetherills to sell the Navajo Mountain post to Ray and Madelene Dunn. Madelene Dunn, with subsequent husbands Jack Owen and Ralph Cameron, ran the post with only minor interludes under Elvin and Phyllis Kerley and Lloyd Bowles until age forced her to retire in the 1970s.[36]

Like the Wetherills, whom they regarded as implacable rivals and set out to discredit in any way possible, S. I. Richardson, his brothers C.D. and Hubert Richardson and their children were involved in numerous trading ventures on the northern reservation. Most important for the area of this study was Inscription House Trading Post. In 1924 S. I. Richardson built Rainbow Lodge on the southern slope of Navajo Mountain as a base for tourist horseback trips to Rainbow Bridge over the newly developed Bernheimer Trail through Redbud Pass. Tiring of the business after a couple of years, he conceived the idea of building a trading post that would also run tourist excursions into Inscription House, the massive Anasazi ruin in Nitsin Canyon, a tributary of Navajo Canyon. It became, according to his son, writer Gladwell "Toney" Richardson, who worked at the post after 1928, one of the Richardsons' most profitable ventures. "S.I. really needed help when we went there," he recalled,

> three big truckloads of merchandise were required each week to handle his trade. There was no pause between wool-, sheep-, and cattle-buying seasons, due to the different climates in the high and low altitudes from which our customers came. The store became so inadequate we had to close up to stock shelves on rush-day afternoons and, frequently, at night. Our last customer seldom departed before midnight.[37]

Although Toney Richardson was prone to exaggeration, there is no question that Inscription House paid well, both because of its accessibility to the Indians, but also its proximity to the Inscription House ruin (to which S.I. built a spacious trail) and the ruins of the Tsegi as well as Rainbow Bridge. The ultimate physical plant, with store, residence, and ware and guest rooms, was completed in 1929, though electricity was not added until World War II.

In 1954 the old-time trader O. J. "Stokes" Carson purchased Inscription House Trading Post from S. I. Richardson, with the provision that he would maintain a home for him anytime he wished to return.[38] An invalid by this time, Carson had to drop the Richardsons' guide business and concentrate on the Indian trade. Although the market for wool was inconsistent, he traded for it regularly. A major part of his trade, however, was in piñon nuts and saddle blankets. Always a connoisseur of Navajo weaving, Carson recognized that saddle blankets were a neglected economic resource because, although rug collectors were uninterested in them, they sold for low prices and were available in significant quantity. The quality of their weaving was usually not up to that in trade rugs, but their price placed them within reach of less affluent tourists who sought attractive souvenirs of the Navajo country. It brought a new life to Inscription House on a different economic base from that enjoyed by the Richardsons, and Carson and his wife, Jessie, made their home at Inscription House until their deaths in 1974 and 1975.

Goulding's trading post in Monument Valley was even more fa-

mous in some ways than the Wetherill establishment at Kayenta because of the John Ford movies that were filmed there, beginning
with *Stagecoach* in 1939, the movie that made a star of John Wayne.[39]
But Harry Goulding was a sheepman and he and his wife, Leone
(nicknamed Mike), were traders with Monument Valley's Paiutes
and Navajos long before they entered the guide business for tourists
and filmmakers that made them famous.

Harry Goulding first saw Monument Valley from a distance while
trading sheep in the Mormon communities north of the San Juan
River, and a vacation trip there in 1921 convinced him that he
wanted to live there. When he married Leone Knee in 1923, daughter of a Colorado railroad man, he sold her on the idea as well. In
1925 they arrived at the present site of Goulding's trading post in an
old Buick so laden with tents, supplies, and trade goods that it later
reminded Mike Goulding of the Joads' outfit in *The Grapes of
Wrath*. It was to be their home for almost forty years, until age and
health problems forced them to leave.

The first Goulding trading post consisted of three structures: a
brush-roofed shelter similar to a Navajo summer hogan, which
served as an outdoor kitchen in hot weather, and two tents, one for
sleeping and the other for trading. Various people assisted them during the early years, including an old Mexican sheepherder named
Old Jose, an illiterate coyote trapper named Bert Davis, Mike's
brother Maurice Knee, and always, during their entire life at Gouldings, a succession of Navajos who worked for wages. It was a time of
learning: learning the Navajo language, trade practices, how to rotate
their sheep from one water source and range to another, and how to
cope with the capricious and demanding desert climate.

After more than two years in tents, the Gouldings decided to build
a permanent home and store in the shade of the dramatic cliff behind them, where a spring of limited volume was available. Beginning in 1927 with a potato cellar and a small stone cabin, which
served as a temporary home, the Gouldings employed Bert Davis
and a Navajo named Bidaghaa Neez to build the unique (in the
Navajo country) two-story structure eventually memorialized as a set
in the John Ford Westerns: old-fashioned bull pen store and ware-
room on the ground floor, living quarters upstairs. Ford later had the
outside stairway and second-story porch added for one of his movies.

The 1930s was a fateful decade for the Gouldings, as it was for the Indians of Monument Valley and indeed for the nation itself as the Great Depression tightened its grip. On the positive side for the Gouldings were two developments: After a long battle, in 1937 Harry succeeded in getting the state of Utah to sell him the land on which the trading post was located as a school section, thus giving the Gouldings clear title to a small island of private land in the midst of the Navajo Reservation. Also, Harry made his now-famous journey to Hollywood, carrying a packet of photographs of Monument Valley and spurred by the rumor that John Ford was looking for a dramatic location for a new Western movie. His persistence finally earned the rough-hewn sheepman an audience with the famous director, and his salesmanship carried the day. Beginning with *Stagecoach*, Ford made a series of Westerns at Gouldings, including *She Wore a Yellow Ribbon* and *Fort Apache*. At the time, the moviemakers brought much-needed income to the Navajos, who served as crew members and extras. In the long term, Harry's certainty about the dramatic visual appeal of the valley's famous monoliths has been vindicated in a seemingly infinite series of movies and commercial and artistic photographs utilizing them as a backdrop.

Less happily, the Depression precipitated a crisis in the Navajo economy that propelled the tribe into the modern world. John Collier, commissioner of Indian Affairs under the Franklin D. Roosevelt administration, forced the Navajos to reduce the size of their flocks in order to conserve the overgrazed land, and went on to introduce the democratic political system based on representative government in local chapters that continues to the present day. The Collier administration ranks with the Kit Carson campaigns of the 1860s as the two great traumas of Navajo history, and in fact the crisis of the 1930s affected the northern Navajos even more than the earlier one, which they were largely able to flee.

As previously indicated, the Gouldings helped their Navajo neighbors significantly by finding work for them in the movie industry. But the stock-reduction program affected the Gouldings as seriously as it did the Indians, and led to tragedy. Harry kept his own flocks on the reservation as long as possible, but eventually he was forced to move them north of the San Juan River, where they inevitably impinged upon the range of Mormon livestockmen. In an unfortunate mistake (or was it deliberate provocation, as many San Juan County Mormons still believe?), Harry hired an Oklahoma desperado in 1934 named Jimmy (or Clint, as his family and friends called him) Palmer to push his flocks onto the Mormon range. Acting against his orders, so Harry claimed, Palmer drove the Goulding flocks into John's Canyon where he encountered W. A. Oliver and his nephew Norris Shumway with their own sheep. Verbal conflict led to violence, and Palmer murdered both Oliver and Shumway in the most grisly incident in San Juan County history. Palmer's flight eventually led him to Texas, where another crime sent him to a penitentiary there for the rest of his life.[40]

After World War II, the Gouldings increasingly capitalized upon the fame of the Ford Westerns by promoting tourist excursions in the valley. Beginning with two Jeeps that they purchased in 1949, they moved on to a bus, which they drove throughout the valley's most dramatic features. In 1953 they added a row of motel rooms, which replaced the first stone cabins in which the Gouldings themselves had lived.

Always concerned for the welfare of their Navajo customers, neighbors, and friends, the Gouldings saw a need for medical care beyond the simple doctoring most traders tried to offer the Indians. Inspired by the Presbyterian medical mission at Ganado, the Gouldings were able to lure Seventh-Day Adventist medical missionaries to Monument Valley in the 1950s, culminating in the construction of the Monument Valley Hospital in 1961.

Harry's increasing health problems drove the Gouldings from Monument Valley in 1963, after leasing their operation to Knox College in exchange for scholarships for Navajo students. Harry died in 1981 and Mike moved for a time to the Greenhaven community near Page, Arizona. Following the sale of Goulding's to traders Gerald and Roland LaFont of Chinle, Arizona, in the late 1980s, who expanded the motel into a large modern facility and turned the old trading post into a museum, Mike Goulding returned to live in a mobile home provided by the LaFonts. By the time of her death in 1992, it took a long yardstick to measure the changes of the previous seven decades, from the time when traders sold flour, coffee, and sugar out of a tent for Navajo wool, pelts, and rugs, to the modern luxury motel that dwarfs a little building where the old ways are preserved only as museum relics.

NOTES

1. Most of the descriptive data that follows on the traditional trading post is derived from Frank McNitt's classic study, *The Indian Traders* (Norman: University of Oklahoma Press, 1962), 68–80.

2. Clyde Kluckhohn and Dorothea Leighton, *The Navaho* (Cambridge: Harvard University Press, 1946), 131.

3. William Y. Adams, *Shonto: A Study of the Role of the Trader in a Modern Navaho Community*, Smithsonian Institution Bureau of American Ethnology Bulletin 188 (Washington, D.C.: Government Printing Office, 1963), 305–7.

4. McNitt, *The Indian Traders*, Chapter 3 sketches the history of federal regulation of Indian trade and the nature of its primary regulations.

5. Ibid., 98–106.

6. The history of Lee's Ferry after the death of John D. Lee is in W. L. Rusho and C. Gregory Crampton, *Desert River Crossing* (Salt Lake City: Peregrine Smith, 1975).

7. C. Gregory Crampton, *Historical Sites in Glen Canyon: Mouth of Hansen Creek to Mouth of San Juan River*, University of Utah Anthropological Paper No. 61 (Salt Lake City: University of Utah Press, 1962), 8–12. Crampton includes a transcription of a fragmentary diary by Cowles, probably during October 1900, which indicates the difficulty of resupplying the post.

8. P. T. Reilly, interview with Arthur L. Chaffin, December 24, 1966, 3, in the papers of P. T. Reilly, Utah State Historical Society. See also, Crampton, *Historical Sites in Glen Canyon: Mouth of Hansen Creek to Mouth of San Juan River*, 68–71.

9. Reilly interview, 7.

10. Ibid., 7–9.

11. The career of Amasa Barton is discussed by Gary Topping, "Personality and Motivation in Utah Historiography," *Dialogue: A Journal of Mormon Thought* 27 (Spring 1994): 84–88.

12. The 1887 *Report of the Commissioner of Indian Affairs* expressed a suspicion that Barton had been selling guns, and that the heightened potential for violence resulting from that trade was a factor in his death. McNitt, *The Indian Traders*, 51.

13. C. L. Christensen testimony in Colorado River Case, 1929–31, copy at Utah State Historical Society.

14. Doris Valle, *Looking Back Around the Hat* (Mexican Hat, Utah: The Author, 1986), 2, 8–10. Inscriptions on the right bank of the river below Mexican Hat date his arrival, or at least his presence, in 1882.

15. A. C. Ellis, Jr., to E. L. Goodridge, April 25, 1901, in possession of Doris Valle, Mexican Hat, Utah.

16. "Statement of Ben Wetherill—Flagstaff, Arizona, 13 June 1946," in Wetherill Collection at Museum of Northern Arizona, 2–3.

17. See Chapter 2 for Spencer's role in the Paiute conflict. Charles L. Bernheimer, Field Notes, May 29, 1920, copy at Utah State Historical Society. Robert B. Aird, "An Adventure for Adventure's Sake," *Utah Historical Quarterly* 62 (Summer 1994); Valle, *Looking Back Around the Hat*, 16.

18. Bernheimer Field Notes, May 29, 1920.

19. Valle, *Looking Back Around the Hat*, 17–25.

20. The story of the Wetherills' trading career from Ojo Alamo to Kayenta, is told in Frances Gillmor and Louisa Wade Wetherill, *Traders to the Navajos: The Story of the Wetherills of Kayenta* (Boston: Houghton Mifflin, 1934), 45 ff; and Mary Apolline Comfort, *Rainbow to Yesterday: The John and Louisa Wetherill Story* (New York: Vantage Press, 1980), 30 ff.

21. National Register of Historic Places Nomination Form, Utah State Historical Society; Willow Roberts, *Stokes Carson: Twentieth-Century Trading on the Navajo Reservation* (Albuquerque: University of New Mexico Press, 1987), 99–111.

22. Francis Raymond Line, "The Kayenta Mail Run," *Arizona Highways* (January 1991): 29–31.

23. The original books are in possession of Mrs. JohniLou Duncan, a granddaughter of John and Louisa Wetherill. Citations here are from a copy in the author's possession.

24. The text is also given in Comfort, *Rainbow to Yesterday*, 125–26.

25. Ibid., 126–27.

26. John Wetherill to Zane Grey, December 3, 1924 (telegram), in Otis R. "Dock" Marston Papers, the Huntington Library (punctuation added). A note from Grey in the same collection indicates that he made the loan and promised to "try and get Lasky to advance you something."

27. John Wetherill to Lorenzo Hubbell, April 14, 1926; Clyde A. Colville to Lorenzo Hubbell, May 21, 1927, in Lorenzo Hubbell Papers, University of Arizona.

28. Comfort, *Rainbow to Yesterday*, 142–49; Garrick and Roberta Glenn Bailey, *A History of the Navajos: The Reservation Years* (Santa Fe: School of American Research Press, 1986), 184–96; Randall Henderson, "Just Between You and Me," *Desert Magazine* (October 1946): 46–47, mentions immediate post-Wetherill developments at Kayenta.

29. Adams, *Shonto: A Study of the Role of the Trader in a Modern Navaho Community*, 42–53; 156–61; Gladwell Richardson, *Navajo Trader*, 75–82; Roberts, *Stokes Carson*, 116–17; 188–94; Elizabeth Compton Hegemann, *Navaho Trading Days* (Albuquerque: University of New Mexico Press), 265–387.

30. Adams, *Shonto*, 272–96.

31. Roberts, *Stokes Carson*, 165–82.

32. Clyde Kluckhohn, *Beyond the Rainbow* (Boston: The Christopher Publishing House, 1933), 167.

33. Bert Tallsalt, "Ashkii Yazhi: Forgotten Friend of the Navajo," *Navajo-Hopi Observer*, October 19, 1983, says the post was established in 1927, but Ben Wetherill himself said in a "Statement of Ben Wetherill," June 13, 1946, at the Museum of Northern Arizona, "I put in the Teeyahtoh post at Navajo Mountain in the spring of 1927. Before that I had a place across Piute canyon at Piute Mesa for about a year."

34. Tallsalt, "Ashkii Yazhi."

35. Kluckhohn, *Beyond the Rainbow*, 168.

36. Ben Wetherill to Lorenzo Hubbell, Jr., April 10, 1932, in the Lorenzo Hubbell Papers, University of Arizona; Mary Shepardson and Blodwen Hammond, *The Navajo Mountain Community: Social Organization and Kinship Terminology* (Berkeley: University of California Press, 1970), 35–36.

37. Richardson, *Navajo Trader*, 96.

38. Roberts, *Stokes Carson*, 141–49.

39. Samuel Moon, *Tall Sheep: Harry Goulding, Monument Valley Trader* (Norman: University of Oklahoma Press, 1992) supersedes Richard E. Klinck, *Land of Room Enough and Time Enough* (Albuquerque: University of New Mexico Press, 1958) as the standard account of the Gouldings in Monument Valley.

40. Moon, *Tall Sheep*, 85–87. Depositions from Harry Goulding, Palmer's father, H. P. Palmer, and Palmer's girlfriend Lottie Lucile Garrett were collected in anticipation of Palmer's extradition and trial for the Oliver-Shumway murders, and are on

file in the San Juan County archives. Since the extradition and trial never took place, the question of the degree to which Palmer may have been operating under Harry Goulding's orders was never legally determined, and remains a source of bitterness toward the Gouldings among many San Juan County Mormons.

"Beyond the Clay Hills" with Neil Judd

"From ridges that neighbor Kaiparowits Plateau and the Circle Cliffs, far to the west, that siren something which tempts desert pilgrims from their appointed way beckoned me toward the grim silence and the elusiveness of this unknown canyon country."[1] A decade and more after his participation in the discovery of Rainbow Bridge, "that siren something" had lost none of its allure for Neil Merton Judd, and he was making plans for an ambitious expedition that would bring one of its most rugged and elusive regions under the eye of scientific scrutiny. The region was the remote triangle framed by the San Juan and Colorado Rivers and bounded on the east by the Red House Cliffs and the Clay Hills. Forced by extraordinarily bad weather and a missed rendezvous to detour through Grand Gulch, and tugged by nostalgic memories to include Rainbow Bridge on the homeward route, the expedition covered a great deal of additional territory. But the main goal was that elusive natural triangle known at that time only to a very few cattlemen and gold miners. To the scientific world it was a genuine terra incognita. Later recognized by geologist Herbert E. Gregory as a distinct physiographic province and named by him the Red Rock Plateau, in Judd's day it was known to Mormon cattlemen simply as the Lake Country for Hermit Lake, where until 1915 their animals had enjoyed one of the few dependable water sources, or even more vaguely as that mysterious country "beyond the Clay Hills."

Judd had first heard that siren call from the lips of his uncle, Byron Cummings, "the Dean," under whom he was studying classics at the University of Utah in 1907 when Cummings invited him to join his archaeological expedition to White Canyon. It was the great turning point in Judd's life; from that time onward, he dedicated himself with a single-minded intensity to unraveling the prehistoric mysteries of the Southwest. It was a fortuitous moment for a young man of his interests and abilities to be dedicating himself to such a career, for, among all the canyons where our present knowledge of the Anasazis would primarily be derived, only Mesa Verde and Grand Gulch had been scientifically excavated with any degree of thoroughness. Chaco Canyon, Canon de Chelly, and the great ruins of the Tsegi and the Rio Grande were as yet either undiscovered or largely untouched. During his long lifetime (1887–1976), Judd would personally direct the excavations at Betatakin and Pueblo Bonito as well as many lesser sites in Utah, Arizona, New Mexico, and even Central America. In addition, his lengthy affiliations with the National Geographic Society and the Smithsonian Institution enabled him, through both scientific and popular writings and administrative responsibilities, to shape the course of southwestern archaeology in important ways.

Surprisingly, for such a respected and influential scholar, Judd's formal education did not include a Ph.D. He received his B.A. degree from the University of Utah in 1911 and the M.A. from George Washington University in St. Louis in 1913. By the time he began to think of further graduate work, he was employed by the Smithsonian Institution, and the only eastern university offering a program in anthropology that would serve his needs was Harvard. Graduate fellowships and grants were meager in those days, and Judd's personal budget precluded financing a Harvard degree on his own, so he elected to finish his education where he had begun it with Dean Cummings—in the field. It may not have been an ideal choice, but it was not a bad one either, since southwestern archaeology was so much in its infancy in those days that few eastern professors could have taught Judd much more than he learned in the field anyway. And he had the benefit of close personal and professional associations over many years with men like Earl Morris, A. V. Kidder, and A. E. Douglass who, together with Judd, were establishing the basic terms and chronology within which the field would continue to be studied until the present day.[2]

It is perhaps an indication of his exclusive dedication to his work, as well as the social isolation of its setting, that Judd, like his colleague Earl Morris, married late in life. In 1938, only eleven years before his retirement, he married Anne Sarah MacKay. The home they established in Silver Spring, Maryland, was famous both for the azaleas the Judds loved to grow (Judd was official gardener of the

Cosmos Club as well, of which he was a longtime member), and as a hospitable rendezvous point for young anthropologists who found in their host a source of generous professional assistance and stimulating scientific conversation.

One of Judd's most important personal and professional associates, and the one most relevant to the expedition under discussion here, was the legendary John Wetherill, whom he had first gotten to know during his early expeditions with Cummings. Next to the Dean himself, perhaps, Judd seems to have been Wetherill's favorite among the members of the Cummings expeditions. The tone of Wetherill's letters indicate a keen pleasure in the young man's company, and Judd's appreciation of Hosteen John's companionship and backcountry skills was still bright when he penned his reminiscences in 1968:

> I had a deep admiration for John Wetherill. I had known him at Oljeto in 1908 and 1909, when northern Arizona was young and the Navahos were wild. . . . A Quaker by birth and inclination, he could shoe a mule without swearing, and he could lead a pack train where a pack train had never gone before. The Clay Hills country was unmapped and virtually untraveled, but I knew that John Wetherill could take me there if anyone could.[3]

It was a contact between Judd and Louisa Wetherill, rather than John, though, that began the planning for the Clay Hills expedition. Since 1921, Judd had been directing the excavation of Pueblo Bonito. Not content with whatever information on the site he could dig from the ground, he asked Mrs. Wetherill if she would record any Navajo stories she might know regarding Chaco Canyon for possible publication under her name as an appendix to his final report. He was prompted in the request, he says, after reading the first installment of Zane Grey's *The Vanishing American*, which was being serialized in the *Ladies Home Journal*, and "which promises to deal intimately with the Navaho and his tribal life." It is not altogether clear why the Grey story prompted Judd's request. It may be that Judd had little confidence in Grey's ability to fulfill his promise, and knew that he could get more reliable material from Mrs. Wetherill, by then a recognized authority on the Navajo. It is doubtful that Judd knew, or that he could tell from reading no more than the first chapter of the novel, that Grey and Louisa Wetherill had signed a contract to collaborate on a series of Navajo stories, so that she was actually the source for much of the factual basis of the novel.[4] This was the only mention of Grey for the time being, but the man himself, not just one of his stories, would unwittingly play a direct role in Judd's expedition at a later date.

Early in 1923, before he had received a reply from Louisa, Judd wrote to John Wetherill suggesting that they make a trip together, and that if agreeable he could collect the stories from Louisa while in Kayenta preparing for the expedition. He had two areas in mind: the region between the Paria River and the Henry Mountains (basically the Kaiparowits Plateau), and the region "beyond the Clay Hills." In his reply Wetherill ignored the Kaiparowits suggestion, but indicated that he had "been over a great deal of the country" between the San Juan and Colorado Rivers except Moki Canyon, which his brother Clayton said offered considerable archaeological promise. The trips to which he was referring were his own journey to the mouth of Lake Canyon in 1892 with Charles Cary Graham and Charles McLoyd, and Clayton's brief exploration of Moki as a detachment from their brother Richard's 1897 Grand Gulch expedition.[5]

The destination, then, was set. All Judd lacked was an estimate of the expenses so he could submit a formal request for funding to the National Geographic Society. That was forthcoming from Clyde Colville, Wetherill's partner, on March 1. Since Judd's proposed dates included the off-season period of October and November after the work at Pueblo Bonito was finished, and thus after the tourist rush at Kayenta, Colville could reduce the rate on pack animals from $2.00 per head per day to $1.25. Colville recommended fourteen to sixteen animals. John Wetherill's rates were $10 per day plus food, and additional packers could be had for $5 per day.[6]

The size and scope of the expedition as originally proposed by Judd was substantially larger than the project that eventually transpired. The theme of Judd's proposal was that the area to be covered was "almost wholly unknown to men of science," and thus it merited investigation by a team of specialists in several fields. This "blank-spot" aspect, together with its dramatic ruggedness and beauty, rendered it of particular interest to members of the National Geographic Society, and Judd was shrewd enough to refer to the society's publication of Charles L. Bernheimer's article in *National Geographic* the previous year, featuring the Rainbow Bridge area, of which the area north of the river was "practically a continuation."[7]

Although Judd attempted to secure joint funding from the Department of Agriculture, the U.S. Geological Survey, and the Smithsonian Institution, only the Smithsonian proved willing to cooperate in the venture, and even that only for the amount of Judd's salary and that of George B. Martin, his assistant at Pueblo Bonito, and half of their transportation. The eventual amount budgeted by the National Geographic Society was $2,200, which covered a guide and a packer for the forty-day period, a photographer, and the rest of the transportation.[8]

On April 30, 1923, Judd wrote to John Wetherill that the funds for the expedition had been secured, and that he would be prepared to start from Kayenta on October 1. "Unless I become a corpse or a cripple I will be with you," Wetherill replied, "hoping you will be here without fail and promising to keep intruders out." Twice more Judd wrote, advising Wetherill and Colville to expect him and his party sometime between September 20 and 25, the assumption being that a starting date of October 1 was still the plan.[9]

How surprised Judd must have been, then, to receive a letter from Colville on September 5, informing him of a delay:

> In your former letters you spoke as if it would be about the middle of October before you could get out here[.] [O]n this supposition, we have taken on another party which leaves here the 14th of this month and will be out until about the tenth of October and we trust that you can so arrange your plans that this will not delay you.[10]

Judd wrote immediately to express his disappointment and to point out that the intrusion of this other party was causing him a delay of no less than two weeks. Nevertheless, he added, "I believe I know something of this second party and its plans . . . and realizing what the success of its venture means to you, I will endeavor to shape our affairs with good grace." What was the identity of the second party that brought Judd so easily to accept philosophically its intrusion and to wish, on behalf of Wetherill and Colville, for its success? The answer is to be found in the Wetherill trading post guest register where, under the date September 17, 1923, appears the names of the "Zane Grey Party to Nonnezoshe and Wild Horse Mesa."[11]

The Grey party included movie producer Jesse Lasky, who was investigating the possibility of filming Grey's novel *Wild Horse Mesa* on location atop the Kaiparowits Plateau. The trip, incidentally, was a substantial failure. The unseasonal fall precipitation, which was to plague Judd's party later, was the problem. The artist Lillian Wilhelm Smith, who was a member of the party, told the story tersely but poignantly in a note on the back of a painting: "The Muddy San Juan near where we camped Sept. 23 trying to get across to get on Wild Horse Mesa, but no such luck. Flood waters and too little grub made us turn back and to ride back the 100 miles to Kayenta."[12] In spite of Nature's intervention to frustrate the purposes of Grey and Lasky, though, the trip had to have been a rare financial opportunity for Wetherill and Colville, even to the point of leading them to postpone Judd's parsimoniously funded scientific expedition in order to dig into the double treasure chest of Zane Grey and Hollywood. The guides' ethics may have been less than immaculate, but such opportunities presented themselves all too infrequently for a couple of struggling Indian traders to pass them up, as Judd well knew.

Besides, as it worked out, being preempted by the Grey party was not all bad. Judd learned from their experience that it would be futile to try to stick to the original plan of fording the San Juan at Moonlight Creek. Instead, a longer route would be utilized, traveling north from Kayenta through Monument Valley to the swinging bridge that offered precarious passage across the river at the tiny settlement of Goodridge (later known as Mexican Hat). In a final letter to his benefactor, Dr. Coville of the National Geographic Society, Judd reported this change of plans, which required a larger pack string and thus necessitated, if the party were to stay within the allotted budget, shortening the expedition from six weeks to four. A more rapid progress than originally planned would also be required, "with fewer and shorter stops at such ruins as we may find." However, if something of extraordinary merit should be encountered, Judd proposed to linger as long as necessary to do it justice, "and I will meet the difference in cost from my own pocket, pending approval of my report by the Research Committee."[13]

The tone of this last letter before Judd vanished into the unknown hints at frustration in the face of the society's earlier penuriousness in refusing to assume the expense of a biologist and geologist, compounded now by the uncooperative weather, all of which threatened to erode the scientific value of the trip. Presented with a rare opportunity to study a virtually unknown and scientifically promising region, Judd was now being required to cut down both the comprehensiveness and duration of the expedition. It is no wonder that he may have intended to shame the research committee by offering to rescue the research value of the trip by means of funds from his own pocket.

Edwin L. Wisherd, the photographer provided by the society, recorded the departure of the expedition from Kayenta in a memorable photograph that accompanies Judd's *National Geographic* article and which Judd later added to the record of his party in the register book at the Wetherill trading post. In the open area to the east of the trading post, the party's pack animals––all mules––stand, fully loaded and impatient, tossing their heads and pawing the ground. Four of the six members of the party are already mounted, and the expectant tension of the moment is high, as all await Hosteen John's order to move out across Laguna Creek and into Monument Valley.[14]

The romanticism of the moment, though, conceals the shoestring budget and the jury-rigged nature of the outfit. One has to wonder how the contrast between this outfit and Grey's figured in the mind of John Wetherill, and whether he reflected upon the difference in funding between entertainment and science. Neither Martin nor Wisherd—two complete dudes—would be any good with handling the animals, Judd admitted, so both were detailed to carrying and operating the cameras, leaving the mundane duties of camp and trail to Wetherill and his packer, Julian Edmonson. To help reduce the number of animals required, it was planned to pick up additional supplies at Goodridge and at a later rendezvous at Clay Hills Crossing (after the high water would have abated). The Navajo who was to bring the supplies to the rendezvous would continue on with the party and help with the animals. But even that, in this star-crossed expedition, was to fail.

For the first few days everything went well, with the momentary comic relief of the mules' refusal to cross the flimsy suspension bridge with the roaring torrent of the flooding San Juan below. Drawing upon the savvy that made their presence so indispensable, Wetherill and Edmonson scattered some dirt on the floor of the bridge to ease the transition from terra firma, then led Wetherill's horse across first. Thus tricked, the mules followed.

After picking up 150 pounds of oats at Goodridge, the party bade farewell to the last enclave of civilization. Heading northwest past the Goosenecks, they rode up John's Canyon and gained the summit of Cedar Mesa heading for Graham (now Bullet) Canyon which would lead them through Grand Gulch.[15]

In 1923 all of the trails into Grand Gulch were somewhat precarious, and even today Bullet Canyon, which requires negotiating a steep slickrock chute at one point, is best attempted only with animals bred to the canyons. Judd described the trail as "much worn out and steep." Wetherill found a greater adventure awaiting him on the first evening in the canyon, though, when he stood on Judd's shoulders to boost himself into an Anasazi cliff house and found himself looking into the eyes of a rattlesnake.

To the archaeologist, Bullet Canyon—and later Grand Gulch itself—was a mixed experience. Most of the promising ruins had already been excavated, largely by Hosteen John himself on several previous trips. But the canyon still held treasures. Among the ceiling timbers of one kiva, Judd discovered "a thirty-inch war club of mountain mahogany, its handgrip carved and polished through use." And the celebrated Jailhouse ruin in Bullet Canyon impressed Judd greatly with its distinguishing feature, "a window-like opening barred by crossed sticks—a feature unique in my experience. I have never seen anything comparable elsewhere; it resembled a window awaiting six glass panes." Judd's trenchant summary of Grand Gulch's archaeological promise is still true today: "Little if anything written on Grand Gulch; being an important prehistoric center of population it deserves further study even though its best material has gone."[16]

On their way out of Grand Gulch, the party set up camp in a cave near the top of Collins Canyon, which Judd called Adams' cache (for cattleman Franklin Jacob Adams, who purchased the Grand Gulch range in 1918), now known as Collins Cave. It was a comfortable place for a wait of several days while Wetherill and Edmondson rode on to Clay Hills Crossing to meet the Navajo who was to resupply them for their assault on the Red Rock Plateau.[17] Following Wetherill's directions, Judd, Martin, and Wisherd set off on October 17 to explore Grand Gulch below Collins, hoping to reach the natural arch in the lower part of the canyon. Some ten miles downcanyon they turned back without having sighted the arch—a considerable misfortune, for Grand Arch, as it is known today, is only 10.8 miles below

Collins, and Judd would have been highly impressed with the pictographs and other prehistoric remains there. As it was, he was impressed with the immense pictograph panels in that part of the canyon, though he noted that the ruins were fewer and smaller than those in the upper canyon. Also, he noted without elaboration the "deep arroyo which Wetherill says has been cut in the past 30 years [which] has probably destroyed many Basket-maker burials in lower caves."[18] It was the first recorded observation of the ravages of the erosional cycle begun in Grand Gulch by the white men's cattle, a cycle that old-timers like John Wetherill had seen from its inception.

On October 19, Edmondson returned alone to Collins Cave to report that the Navajo had not met them at Clay Hills Crossing, and that Wetherill had crossed the San Juan River on a log the previous evening to bring the supplies from Kayenta himself. With that news, the rest of the party packed up and headed for a rendezvous with Wetherill on the San Juan across from Piute Farms. On the 21st, Wetherill appeared with the supplies and a story worth telling.

After he crossed the river, Wetherill had hiked a dozen miles to an oil rig near Organ Rock, where he borrowed a Model T Ford and drove to Kayenta. There he learned that the Indian had been diverted by a Navajo Squaw Dance and had neglected his responsibility. Wetherill thereupon loaded the oats into Judd's National Geographic Society truck—the only such vehicle available at Kayenta at the time—and returned to the river at Piute Farms. He crossed the oats to the right bank by repeated trips in a folding canvas boat that had seen better days and kept collapsing. He also brought a Navajo named Cauz-zus-see, who knew something of the region beyond the Clay Hills.

For the next couple days, the party followed the old Mormon road through Clay Hills Pass and on to Hermit Lake. Now, roughly forty years after the road had been abandoned, Judd noted that it was "still visible in places, impossible now for wagon to cross."[19] On October 23, fifteen days after leaving Kayenta, Judd caught his first view of the Red Rock Plateau.

Although his fascination with the area is apparent in longer and more detailed diary entries, his overall impression was forbidding: "From west side Clay Hills, country slopes gently to W. as a barren desolate waste. Neither Rio Colorado nor lesser canyons visible." Barren though he found the country to be, Judd nevertheless emphasized its archaeological potential, noting many small ruins along the trail, and one large one, now known as the Fortress, on the rim of the east fork of Lake Canyon.

Now, with Moki Canyon, the main goal of the expedition, within easy reach and the plentiful pasture of Lake Canyon available, Wetherill convinced Judd to leave all but a few animals and supplies there at a base camp and to press on to Moki with a more manageable outfit.[20] It was an inspired decision, for the floor of Moki, drenched by the rains, was a quagmire of quicksand, and Wetherill had his hands full getting even a small party up the treacherous canyon floor. Judd's diary tells the story dramatically:

> First trouble found in crossing steep rock slide near mouth of Moki Canyon—one mule slipped pack and bucked part way down hill with danger of falling into river. Wetherill led off onto quicky sand bar, thence into canyon via stream bed, very narrow in places, lined with over-hanging willows and filled with quicksand. Very dangerous traveling with sand stretching under mules like rubber. Came to falls and built trail around; one mule fell over in climbing steep trail and nearly broke neck. Had to build trail several times where progress blocked.[21]

Once within the canyon, though, Moki proved to be no disappointment. As previously mentioned, Judd knew something of Moki's archaeological promise through Clayton Wetherill's report (the first day in the canyon, the party found an inscription in a cave: "C. Wetherill, 4-4-97"). Even more intriguing to Judd was a specimen of cotton yarn removed from Moki by some anonymous wanderer about 1890. When the yarn had found its way into Judd's hands, he had immediately realized that the canyon offered immense scientific interest, because Moki in his judgment is located too far north to support cotton cultivation, and the presence of such yarn in the canyon indicated the possibility of commerce and perhaps other cultural exchange as well. Although Judd's excavations were too limited to allow him fully to support a theory that Moki and other canyons of the area were a yeasty mixing bowl of cultural contact between the Mesa Verde and Kayenta strains of Anasazi culture—an insight fully realized only during more sustained excavation during the 1950s—his notes do indicate a variety of ceramic types, and contain the observation that "ruins suggest migratory families with short stops only." It is unfortunate, then, given what we know of the later archaeological productivity of Moki, and considering Judd's embryonic insight into Moki's importance as a seedbed of cultural exchange, that his summary of the canyon's archaeological potential is equivocal in its enthusiasm:

> Work in Moki Canyon will prove difficult acc't its accessibility and difficulty of getting in supplies; also, acc't quicksand in canyon. Comparatively little work has been done; much remains for the archaeologist but his rewards would prove far less than those of pothunters in Grand Gulch. Many caves are high and inaccessible without cutting steps.[22]

On one matter, though—the geographical achievement of his exploration of Moki Canyon—Judd was more definite:

> Moki Canyon . . . was represented as about five miles long and enterable, on foot only, in but two places. By boat, it was said, one could reach the slit through which Moki joins the Colorado; eastward, where a huge sand dune folds down over the rim rock, one could slide to the bottom of the gorge.
>
> We made three camps in Moki Canyon, the last fully 18 miles above its mouth and perhaps two-thirds of its total length; we discovered old Indian trails—made, no doubt, by Navajo or Piute hunting parties—and took our mules up both the north and south cliffs.[23]

On October 27 the party climbed up through a dramatic narrow slit in the north wall of Moki, following a faint Indian trail to accomplish the earliest recorded entry of a white man onto Mancos Mesa, "a broad waste of bare sandstone, carved by wind, sand, and the runoff of passing showers. Here and there a tuft of grass or a small bush had found root." Even the mules balked at crossing a region that today, a half-century later, is still one of the most isolated areas in the Southwest, for Judd recorded on the 28th that the "mules hit [*sic*] out during night and Navaho overtook them at fence in branch of upper Lake Canyon, over 20 mi. from present camp." It was enough of an omen that Judd sent the rest of the outfit after them to await the arrival of Wetherill and himself after they had accomplished a little investigation of the mesa. Drawn by the archaeological lure of huge caves near the rim of Knowles Canyon, the intrepid pair continued in a northerly direction. The going was rough, and when they made camp on the night of the 28th, Judd calculated they had traveled fifteen miles to cover a linear distance of about two.

Entering the caves was a perilous undertaking that required crossing steep slickrock stretches at their mouths, with the risk of sliding off into the canyon far below. Following the advice of their Navajo guide, though, Judd and Wetherill found they could negotiate the pitches easily "by running down across the concave sandstone at a speed countering centripetal force—like a bicycle rider on a banked track." Once inside, Judd found the risk repaid in full by an important discovery: a bundle of paired sticks joined by twine to serve as a snare for small animals.[24]

The rest of the journey was conventional in its route and insignificant in its discoveries. After leaving Moki via the immense sand slide at Red Cone Spring (incorrectly labeled Burnt Spring on modern USGS maps), and returning to the rest of the party in Lake Canyon, the explorers followed the old Mormon road to the east as far as Wilson Creek Canyon, then across the San Juan to intersect the old Wetherill trail to Rainbow Bridge. The weather continued to be a problem; quicksand at the river crossing almost cost them a mule, and the insistent rains kept Wisherd's camera out of sight. The good pasturage in Surprise Valley allowed them once again to divide the pack train and take a smaller outfit the rest of the way into the bridge. The weather was so miserable that Judd's second visit to the great span produced in his breast only echoes of the intense emotions he had felt upon first seeing it as a member of the 1909 discovery party, and his descriptions on this trip were mostly reminiscences of that earlier occasion. The return trip did offer some limited exploration of minor ruins in Nasja and Oak Canyons and revisits of Keet Seel and Betatakin in the Tsegi.

Even with the miserable weather experienced on the trail, Judd and the others must have felt fortunate that Nature reserved her full fury until they had reached Kayenta, for they were held there for no less than four days by pounding rain. "Arrived in Gallup at 7 P.M.," Judd's diary concludes on November 16, "with threatening skies daily urging haste and preventing photos."

Judd's final report to the research committee, dated December 13, 1923, focused upon the stated goals of the expedition, "to ascertain whether further, more detailed exploration [in the region] is desirable." He emphasized the delays caused by the weather and the undependable Indian, but also pointed out that any expedition into that rugged and remote country would be in for a rough time because of the scarce water, the difficult terrain, and the necessity of covering large areas for relatively limited scientific returns. "Archaeological investigation awaits the future explorer," he pointed out, though "biological, botanical, and geological research is probably less tempting and less needed because of the relative paucity of material and its probable similarity to that of neighboring regions already studied."[25]

Other than evaluating further research possibilities in the area, Judd seemed to have regarded the geographical knowledge gained to have been the most unqualified success of the trip. "Existing government maps," he observed, "are wholly erroneous and misleading." Local sources of geographical knowledge and even previous explorers were not much more reliable:

> Although Mormon cattle have been ranged for many years over the Clay Hills their owners are only vaguely familiar with the canyons that lead into the Rio Colorado. Early prospectors and, but recently, members of the 1921 federal river survey have penetrated the lower reaches of certain gorges but the entire region, nevertheless, must be regarded as unknown to men of science and still unexplored.[26]

Given this background, the map in Judd's *National Geographic* article, small in scale and lacking in minute detail though it is, fills a large gap in the cartographic history of the San Juan country. Although the maps of the Colorado and San Juan Rivers prepared by the USGS in 1921 were in the main highly accurate, they extended only to the 3,900-foot elevation and thus omitted most of the terrain adjacent to the rivers. That terrain was depicted in Judd's day only by the 1884 USGS maps, which, though of much larger scale than Judd's, were highly inaccurate. Not until Herbert E. Gregory's map accompanying his 1938 USGS Professional Paper on the San Juan country was Judd's map superseded.

Another aspect of that article that no modern student of the San Juan country can fail to appreciate is the liberal collection of Edwin L. Wisherd's photographs that illustrate the nature of the terrain with great effectiveness. Thus, it seems almost unfair of Judd to complain in his report that the expedition's photographic record fails to come up to minimal expectations:

> The recent expedition was not wisely equipped for a satisfactory photographic record and the results, accordingly, are far below expectations. Our apparatus was too cumbersome for speedy manipulation and, what could not be avoided, cloudy skies and drizzly rains frequently interfered. With almost diabolical regularity and throughout the entire expedition rain clouds gathered each time we approached areas offering exceptional photographic opportunity.[27]

One wonders how a better collection of photographs could have been created and selected, for they illustrate important segments of the trail and the archaeological sites studied, the general nature of the terrain, and even include candid views of the pack train. Finally, Wisherd made the first color photograph of Rainbow Bridge, a fact unacknowledged in any of Judd's writings; Judd even failed to mention that Wisherd was using color materials at all. Judd might well have been grateful for Wisherd's presence, too, for his transportation, paid for by the National Geographic Society, enabled Judd to keep a potentially overbudget project well within the allotted funds, and in fact to return a surplus of $83.38.[28]

The Smithsonian Institution and the National Geographic Society must have heard Judd's equivocations more than his enthusiasm, because neither ever sent another expedition "beyond the Clay Hills." Nor did Judd himself ever return, except in his dreams.[29] Hoffman Birney, who knew Judd in later years, told historian Charles Kelly of a meeting with him in 1937 that indicated that the San Juan country still loomed large in his thinking:

> Found time to have lunch with Neil Judd and hear him repeat his plaintive yawp that he'll be able to make just one more trip into the Southwest before he reaches the wheel-chair stage. Like yourself, myself, and other guys that have a faint glimmering of what they're talking about, he considers the archaeology of Utah as barely scratched and hopes to get in to western San Juan County for some real work.[30]

Nor did Judd ever share another trail with John Wetherill, the man who had done so much to introduce him not only to the canyons but to *living* in the canyons as well. And the canyons had, in essential ways, become home for Judd, so that even the hardships had a humor of their own:

> Most trail accidents, if no serious injury is involved, sooner or later disclose humorous possibilities. The personal discomfort of one's saddle companions is always fit subject for jest. And during the rainy season, especially, opportunity knocks frequently. Sodden biscuits are filling, if unpalatable; salted coffee can be drunk. To watch cold, clubby fingers build a fire with soggy wood is indeed amusing. But the very acme of trail humor follows when a tired rider reaches camp at nightfall to discover that his bed tarp has not protected his blankets from a penetrating shower. One can forgive human frailties and omissions, but when the gods take sides the joke is too good to disregard utterly.[31]

The ability to take such misfortunes as they came and to appreciate their humorous possibilities was no doubt one of the things that cemented the bond between the old Indian trader and the young archaeologist. One can almost see the knowing smile cross Hosteen John's face as he read, at the end of Judd's article, that "as a rule, the desert makes brother worshipers of all who venture into its secret places to share its hidden mysteries."[32]

NOTES

1. Neil M. Judd, "Beyond the Clay Hills," *National Geographic* 45 (March 1924): 277.

2. Biographical information on Neil Judd comes from James R. Glenn, "Register to the Papers of Neil Merton Judd," (Washington, D.C.: National Anthropological Archives, 1982); J. O. Brew, "Obituary, Neil Merton Judd, 1887–1976," *American Anthropologist* 80 (June 1978): 352–54; and Waldo R. Wedel, "Obituary, Neil Merton Judd, 1887–1976," *American Antiquity* 43 (July 1978): 399–404.

3. Neil M. Judd, *Men Met Along the Trail: Adventures in Archaeology* (Norman: University of Oklahoma Press, 1968), 95. In a note appended to a letter to Judd from Horace Albright, John Wetherill referred to himself as "your old sidekick." Horace Albright to Neil Judd, July 9, 1932, Utah State Historical Society.

4. Judd to Louisa Wetherill, November 4, 1922, Neil Judd Papers, National Anthropological Archives, Smithsonian Institution. All other Judd papers cited here are

from this collection. The contract between Grey and Louisa Wetherill is in the Otis R. Marston Papers, the Huntington Library.

5. Judd to John Wetherill, January 22, 1923; Wetherill to Judd, January 30, 1923; Judd to Wetherill, February 9, 1923.

6. C. A. Colville to Judd, March 1, 1923.

7. Judd to Frederick V. Coville, March 16, 1923. (The reader will not confuse Coville with John Wetherill's partner at the Kayenta trading post, Clyde *Colville*.) The Bernheimer article Judd cited was "Encircling Navajo Mountain with a Pack-Train," *National Geographic* 43 (February 1923): 197–224. Judd incorrectly cites the March issue. The Bernheimer article had also inspired two college men, Robert B. Aird and John Newell, to see some of the San Juan country earlier in the year. With a horse and burro, they walked from Blanding to the Natural Bridges, down Comb Wash, across the river at Mexican Hat, and through Monument Valley to Oljato. See Robert B. Aird, "An Adventure for Adventure's Sake," ed. Gary Topping, *Utah Historical Quarterly* 62 (Summer 1994): 275–88. 1923 was a busy year in the San Juan country.

8. Judd to Coville, March 28, 1923.

9. Judd to Wetherill, April 30, 1923; Wetherill to Judd, May 9, 1923; Judd to Wetherill, June 6 and August 17, 1923.

10. Colville to Judd, September 5, 1923.

11. Judd to Colville, September 13, 1923; Wetherill Trading Post guest register, September 17, 1923. Copy in possession of author.

12. The painting is in possession of Harvey Leake. On the Grey party, see Ken Wortley, "Zane Grey on the Rainbow Trail," *Westways* (February 1981): 70–73. Wortley and his brother Chester served as packers for the Grey party. He remembers the date of the trip incorrectly as spring instead of September.

13. Judd to Coville, October 4, 1923.

14. Judd, "Beyond the Clay Hills," 276.

15. Judd, *Men Met Along the Trail*, 96. Unless otherwise indicated, the narrative of the expedition that follows is based upon Judd's "Beyond the Clay Hills" and his diary in the National Anthropological Archives.

16. Judd, *Men Met Along the Trail*, 97–98; Judd diary, October 12–15, 1923.

17. Henry R. Lyman, an old-time cowboy in Grand Gulch, photographed the Collins

Cave when it still served as a base camp for the cowboys. See Neal Lambert, "Al Scorup: Cattleman of the Canyons," *Utah Historical Quarterly* 32 (Summer 1964): 307.

18. Judd's article "Beyond the Clay Hills" omits discussion of this exploration of lower Grand Gulch. One therefore has to know his diary to be able to explain Wisherd's photograph on page 290 of the immense pictograph panel some three miles *below* the party's exit point of Collins Canyon. The panel is Site #30 in Kenneth W. Castleton's *Petroglyphs and Pictographs of Utah*, Volume 2 (Salt Lake City: University of Utah Press, 1979), 255.

19. Judd diary, October 22, 1923.

20. Ibid., October 23, 1923. Judd identifies the site as "upper Lake Canyon" where Jacob Adams had a cattle camp. This was probably at the old cabin, now burned, where the modern four-wheel-drive road crosses Lake Canyon.

21. Ibid., October 24, 1923.

22. Ibid., October 25, 1923.

23. Judd, "Beyond the Clay Hills," 291.

24. Judd, *Men Met Along the Trail*, 100; Judd, "Basketmaker Artifacts from Moki Canyon, Utah," *Plateau* 43 (Summer 1970): 16–20.

25. Judd, "Report on the 1923 San Juan Expedition of the National Geographic Society," 3.

26. Ibid.

27. Ibid., 4.

28. Ibid., "Statement of Receipts and Disbursements." Wisherd's color photograph of Rainbow Bridge appeared in "Canyons and Cacti of the American Southwest," *National Geographic* (September 1925): iii. This portfolio also contains color photographs of Monument Valley and other scenes along the trail in 1923.

29. He did return to Rainbow Bridge, however, via houseboat from Wahweap Marina on Lake Powell during the summer of 1966, and wrote an extensive reminiscence of the 1909 discovery expedition, "Return to Rainbow Bridge," *Arizona Highways* 43 (August 1967): 30–39.

30. Birney to Charles Kelly, May 17, 1937. Charles Kelly Papers, Utah State Historical Society.

31. Judd, "Beyond the Clay Hills," 302.

32. Ibid.

Herbert E. Gregory: Humanistic Geologist

Reed W. Farnsworth, a Cedar City, Utah, physician, knew Herbert E. Gregory well during the last dozen years of the great geologist's life. On a pack trip into the Escalante River country of southeastern Utah with Farnsworth and three others in 1944, Gregory revisited the canyon country to which he had devoted a major part of his professional career. Farnsworth was most impressed during that trip, not with Gregory's profound scientific knowledge of the country—though that was also conspicuous—but with his great love for the backcountry he had known so well as a young man. "His eyes sparkled like a child's on Christmas morning," Farnsworth recalled, "as the wind blew his straggly gray locks back from his face. He was seeing visions and dreaming dreams of the happy days he had spent in this area forty years earlier as a field geologist."[1]

The sixty-six professional papers produced during his remarkable career have established beyond question Gregory's reputation as the preeminent field geologist of the Colorado Plateau and one of the finest minds in any discipline ever to encounter that intriguing region. Not all of Gregory's publications by any means concerned the Colorado Plateau; two other absorbing enterprises—the Silliman professorship in geology at Yale University and the directorship of the Bernice P. Bishop Museum in Honolulu—gave his professional career its triangular shape. But it was on the Colorado Plateau that he made his most distinctive and significant scientific contributions. This chapter recounts the story of the blossoming of his great involvement with that region and the development of the formidable analytical prowess that resulted from his surveys during the years 1909–14 of the Navajo country, an area of 25,725 square miles bounded by the Little Colorado, Puerco, and San Juan Rivers and the 108th meridian just east of Farmington, New Mexico. It also discusses his work from 1910 to 1929 in what he calls the "San Juan

Country," the "unknown triangle" of this study plus a substantial part of the region east to the Colorado border, and from 1915 to 1924 in the Kaiparowits region north of Glen Canyon. Those surveys produced several remarkable reports which, almost three-quarters of a century later, have been revised and supplemented but never superseded.[2]

That a geologist who made his primary contribution during the second and third decades of the present century should have been still exploring virgin land seems an audacious idea. It is true, nevertheless, and is a tribute to Gregory's tireless intellectual curiosity as well as to the roughness of the country that had almost completely kept less zealous scientists at bay. "It is unfortunate that [Ferdinand V.] Hayden did not extend his survey westward to the Colorado River," observed C. Gregory Crampton, "as this region—the San Juan Triangle and the Navajo country west of Monument Valley and Marsh Pass—was not covered by any of the three great public surveys [i.e., those of Powell, Wheeler, and Hayden]."[3] One could add as well that a good deal of the country north of Glen Canyon supposedly surveyed by the Great Surveys was done so—if at all—very superficially. Before Gregory's time, for example, the Kaiparowits region was known to science only through two brief visits by members of the Powell survey under Almon Harris Thompson; data reported by the Wheeler survey evidently came at second hand from Thompson's notes and views of the country from remote vantage points.[4]

Gregory's great contribution was to spend roughly twenty years studying those immense neglected regions and reporting on them in intimate detail. Thus it is that Gregory's reports bristle with characterizations of his work as "pioneer undertakings," where "the explorer must rely on his experience and knowledge of topography to find routes and water holes." Fortunately for the automotive tourist, Gregory observed, the scenery available by such a conveyance is "a counterpart of the scenery viewed by the scientific explorer whose routine duties lead him to places difficult of access"—so difficult, in fact, that "saddle horses and pack trains are the only practicable means of transport."[5] Those reports, furthermore, grew from a deeply humanistic perspective and were presented in a warm and felicitous literary style that separated them radically from the naked digests of scientific data that have filled most geological reports in his time and ours.

Although the canyon country, with its striking stream-eroded sedimentary strata, its dramatic downwarps and uplifts, and the occasional igneous punctuation of volcanic dikes and laccoliths, has long been famous as the geologist's laboratory and lecture room, there was little in Herbert Ernest Gregory's background before 1909 that hinted of the contribution he would make there. Born in Middleville, Michigan, in 1869, Gregory seemed destined by his father's ill health and poverty to a life of hard labor supporting his large family. The Gregorys moved to Crete, Nebraska, in 1876 in a futile attempt to find relief for his father's asthma, but when his mother died in 1881, Gregory and the other twelve children had to be abandoned, in their father's destitution, to board with other families. Gregory himself was fortunate in being taken in by a family who loved and accepted him as one of their own, though his youth continued in the typical hard work and drudgery of farm life on the Great Plains.

In school, though, it was a different matter, because Gregory's extraordinary intelligence quickly set him apart from the other students, and he excelled with little effort. His personality developed dramatically during those years as well, as he became the energetic extrovert that brought hundreds of people of all types into his circle of friends. When he became interested in music, he delighted in harnessing his booming baritone voice in the school choir, and it is characteristic of his personality that he abandoned the trumpet for the gigantic tones of the tuba. "I liked to make a big noise," he explained. Chester R. Longwell sketched his personality memorably in a posthumous tribute:

> He was a born extrovert, friendly, talkative, full of good-natured banter. He was vigorous physically, walked with a swinging stride, his keen dark eyes registering everything and everyone around him. Usually he was in company, and his booming voice and infectious laugh drew attention. These qualities remained characteristic of him throughout his entire life. Pictures taken after his eightieth milestone show his face creased with mirth, his eyes keenly alert, his broad mouth twisted in relish as he spoke in the jocular vein.

The academic world opened its arms to him, and he earned no less than three bachelor's degrees (two of them, significantly, in the arts rather than the sciences) before taking the Ph.D. in geology at Yale in 1899. In an instance of academic inbreeding much more common then than now, Gregory taught one year at Yale's Sheffield Scientific School, then was appointed to reorganize the undergraduate program in geology at his alma mater. Yale eventually awarded him the Silliman chair in geology in 1904.[6]

In 1900 Gregory became assistant geologist with the U.S. Geological Survey (USGS) while retaining his position at Yale. The USGS was created in 1879 to supersede in a more centrally directed manner the work of the surveys of Wheeler, King, Hayden, and Powell. It was developed under the guidance of directors such as Clarence King and John Wesley Powell to address a broad variety of scientific problems in the still imperfectly known American West. Many of its best efforts had been on the Colorado Plateau, which Powell himself and other earlier surveys had investigated.[7] By the time Gregory joined the survey, the location and administration of the Colorado Plateau province's meager water resources had emerged, with the passage of the Reclamation Act in 1902, as one of its major challenges.

The water problem was extraordinarily acute in the Navajo country where, since the tribe's return from the Bosque Redondo in 1868, the rapidly expanding population of both people and livestock and the increasing economic dependence of the former upon the latter had placed a severe burden on the region's capricious streams and infrequent springs.[8] To make matters worse, a series of exceptionally dry years between 1897 and 1904 had reduced many of the Southwest Indians to destitution. Gregory's field notes, recorded from interviews with both Indians and whites who had lived through those tragic years, indicate the dimensions of the problem (as well as Gregory's quick appreciation for the humor with which those hardy people viewed their tribulation):

> 1897–1904 Excessively dry years. No grass—no water in springs & streams dry. 1900 Navajo famine year; sheep died, trees— cedar & pinion—died on ridges. No grass anywhere. Crow must carry knapsack. Horses died. Navajos lived on bark & horses.

> Springs at Tuba died down so that crops could not be irrigated. Spring "C" entirely dried out. No water from Moencopi at all.

> In 1902 San Juan entirely dried below Canyon Largo. Few days dry in 1903. Animas dry.[9]

It was not in response to famine, but economic resurgence, though, that Gregory was dispatched to the Navajo country in 1909. The ravages of the Panic of 1893, which destroyed the market for livestock products, had abated by 1900; competition for grazing lands with whites on the margins of the reservation diminished with several expansions of the reservation in the early 1900s; and laws against selling good breeding stock helped the Navajos build their herds and flocks. Although precise statistics are missing, the size of Navajo livestock holdings increased by several times during the first decade of the present century. Obviously, with more land and animals continuous economic progress required development of consistent water supplies.[10]

Gregory's mandate was to locate many, if minor, developable sources of water for livestock. The Navajos, by far the largest of the three tribes—Navajo, Hopi, and Paiute—on the reservation, were primarily herdsmen for whom agriculture played only a supporting economic role. Although the Hopis also raised livestock, they were primarily agriculturalists, but Gregory seemed to share almost the same fatalistic attitude toward their future as they themselves held. Agriculture for the Hopis was always an uncertain enterprise, but over many centuries of practicing it, they had worked out cultivation techniques that in the main worked well enough, and their conservative cultural values probably put them beyond major assistance from the white man, anyway. So discovery and development of sporadic water holes was Gregory's main goal; it was a program directed primarily toward helping the Navajos, and if the Hopis and the Paiutes could profit from it, so much the better.[11]

Gregory's mettle as a man was revealed through the hardships and deprivations that he experienced firsthand in the remote and rugged corners of the reservation where one's survival required coping directly with nature's naked imperatives. Complex topography, intense heat, scarcity of water, or too much of it in the form of flash floods— all these contributed to the difficulties that explorers faced there. It is revealing that the successful forty-year-old Yale professor, who was in great demand in his intellectual environment in the East, was willing to spend a good portion of his summers among the deserted canyons and mesas of the Navajo country.

It was the difficult terrain that fascinated Gregory the most, in particular, the rugged and isolated Navajo Mountain, which he described as

> a symmetrical mound rising 4,000 feet above the flat floor of Rainbow Plateau, an island in the midst of a sea of waterworn and wind-worn brilliantly colored sandstone. . . . Streams in steep-walled canyons reaching up from the Rainbow Plateau are actively eroding the mountain slopes. On the north and northwest sides headward gnawing is particularly vigorous. So deep and so close-spaced are the canyons leading to the Colorado and the San Juan that the interstream ridges stand out like buttresses supporting the mountain from the north. The intricacy and grandeur of the stream-carved sculpture are unexcelled in any other part of the Plateau province.[12]

Gregory's first traverse of that particular part of the reservation was in 1910 in the company of trader John Wetherill. The previous summer Wetherill had told him of the rumored existence of a huge natural bridge north of the mountain, but due to "other obligations," Gregory declined an offer to join what became the discovery expedition of Rainbow Bridge. Although Gregory never recorded disappointment, one might speculate that that lost opportunity helped strengthen his resolve to spend a portion of the following summers there.

Although the view from the summit of Navajo Mountain presents a panorama that is geologically educational, one suspects that it appealed to Gregory for somewhat more subjective reasons. In 1911, limited to the southern part of the reservation because of the resignation of a key assistant, Gregory complained, "Since I can't go to Navajo Mountain I am only working by the day and will be a happy youngster or old man when my days of servitude are done." Plans again failed in 1912, but the following year Gregory was successful in ascending the mountain for the second time. "I'm satisfied that for scenery the Grand Canyon must take second place," he remarked.[13]

Navajo Mountain's harsh environment and isolated setting offered severe challenges to civilized man. It is not unreasonable to postulate that its appeal to Gregory resulted, at least in part, from the opportunity it provided him to test his strength and courage.

His guide, John Wetherill, was not particularly impressed, however, with those traits on their first mutual expedition to the mountain with Gregory's assistants J. C. Pogue and K. C. Heald:

> The Prof [Gregory] & Pogue are no good as help tho at times they think they are helping. Pogue washed the dishes about 2 minutes work & at times they rustle wood & water. . . .

> We left camp & pack horses, to go to the bridge & back. We made it but O. H—, I struck a gate [sic] that I thot would take us there, but Hul [K. C. Heald] was the only one that could keep up the pace over the rough rocks.[14]

As we have seen, Wetherill was already gaining a reputation as the quintessential frontiersman of the northwestern Navajo country. A few years before he had moved his family to Oljato, Utah, a lonely outpost west of Monument Valley where they established trade with the local Navajos and Paiutes. Besides prospectors, his white customers included a few pioneer archaeologists who used the store as a supply point, and Wetherill's knowledge of the country as an aid to locating prehistoric ruins. That particular enterprise was not new to him—he and his brothers had guided visitors to the Mesa Verde cliff dwellings since their discovery in 1888, and their ever-widening interests broadened the scope of their services to cover a large portion of the Four Corners region.

It is little wonder, then, that Wetherill scorned the backcountry ineptitude of newcomers such as Gregory who lacked the advantage of his many years of desert experience. Another factor, though, which may have contributed to his complaints, was that he had just returned from an unplanned trip to Chaco Canyon, New Mexico, where he helped attend to the affairs of his brother, Richard, who had been murdered there shortly before the Gregory expedition was to commence.[15] His mood was undoubtedly still depressed by that ordeal. Despite the initial negative impressions, however, Gregory soon gained the respect of Wetherill and they developed a close friendship that endured the years.

When Gregory began his study of the Navajo country in 1909, he calculated that fully 60 percent of the area had never been described in the scientific literature. The remaining 40 percent, moreover, was known very imperfectly: Only the periphery of the reservation had been studied at all, and even that largely in merely descriptive terms.[16] The area had been mapped, for example, in 1884 by the USGS, but only from a few selected vantage points that failed, in many cases, to disclose accurately the relationships among drainages invisible from those points. Gregory had to conclude that "the 1884 maps are therefore of little practical use."[17]

It was then Gregory's responsibility to penetrate the Navajo heartland, to determine its basic geography, to devise a terminology for the various geographic subregions and geologic formations, and to plot the various structural and physiographic relationships across the reservation and to the better-known geology of adjacent areas. It was a big order, and it was made even more difficult by the immediate pressures of the practical problem of finding and suggesting ways of developing the water resources of the reservation. Although Gregory's water supply paper appeared first in 1916, the 1917 professional paper was its intellectual antecedent, since it sketched the larger geological and geographical context within which the specific problem of the development of water resources could be solved.

The basic document produced by Gregory's surveys was a map, to which the texts of each of his reports could properly be considered simply as commentaries. Each report contains two copies of the map, each with color overlays for specific illustrative purposes. While the map's basic outline includes topographic features like mountains, mesas, and watersheds, and cultural features such as roads, settlements, and state and county lines, Plate I is primarily cultural in emphasis, showing the routes of pre-1909 explorers and the boundaries of Gregory's own twenty-two subprovinces by means of which he conceptualized the basic geography of the Navajo country. Plate II is a geologic map in which the explorers' routes and subprovince boundaries are replaced by another color overlay showing the basic distribution of geologic formations throughout the region. In offering the map, Gregory was conscious of possible defects resulting from the pressures under which it was hastily compiled: "It is too much to hope that the map . . . as presented has a high degree of accuracy, but I believe that it will be found useful by those whose interests call them to this fascinating region." In fact, it served an entire generation well until the development of aerial mapping techniques later in the century, and Gregory's basic conceptualization of Navajo country geography and geology is still the fundamental point of departure for specialized studies.[18]

Gregory sought to devise a comprehensive understanding of the country in terms of both geography and geology. Geographically, he accomplished this by conceptualizing the Navajo country as twenty-two subprovinces definable in terms of some topographic unity—a river, a mountain or mountain range, a valley, a plateau, and so on. That topographic unity, then, would suggest a general approach toward solving that subprovince's economic problems: Obviously the economic problems of the San Juan River valley and those of Navajo Mountain would be considerably different. Most of Gregory's twenty-two subprovinces are still named on maps and used as basic concepts for economic planning.

Likewise, when Gregory began his work, the geological terminology of the Colorado Plateau was so imprecise as to be scientifically almost useless. Earlier geologists like Lester F. Ward and John S. Newberry had lumped together several distinct strata under such generic terms as "variegated shales and marls," and stratigraphic correlation among various geologic regions of the plateau province was almost completely lacking.

Gregory immediately began to impose a terminology for each stratum, which he hoped his published reports would bring into universal usage. Although he revised his own terms as his research and publication progressed, his ultimate nomenclature for the strata of Permian, Triassic, and Jurassic age, which account for most of the Navajo country geology, has indeed been adopted with little refinement by the scientific community.

Gregory was fiercely conservative in developing new nomenclature. In an undated memorandum to the U.S. Board of Geographic Names, he explained that he had derived the names of geographical features and geologic strata on his maps using three primary criteria: long common usage, appearance on previous topographic maps, and, where new names had to be devised, features were named for historic personages "who have taken a leading part in the development of this country and whose names will always be closely associated with its history."[19]

Gregory applied few original names to specific geographical features, but his names for geographical regions and geologic strata were often his own and indicate the degree to which his conceptual-

ization of that country, both at the bird's-eye view and boulder by
boulder down in the canyons, was truly original. Of the seven identifiable geological strata from the Permian to the Jurassic levels, for
example, four were applied by Gregory:

> Moencopi . . . . Lester F. Ward
> DeChelly . . . . Gregory
> Shinarump . . . . John Wesley Powell
> Chinle . . . . Gregory
> Wingate . . . . Clarence E. Dutton
> Todilto . . . . Gregory
> Navajo . . . . Gregory[20]

Gregory's surveys of the Navajo country encompassed much more
than mere geology and geography, because they occurred within a
human dimension and with a human urgency that none of his later
geological projects possessed. In a rare instance of self-revelation,
Gregory began his water supply paper with "A Personal Word," in
which he expressed in embryonic form a primitivistic theory of the
significance of the Navajo way of life and of the nature of the white
man's responsibility to the Navajo:

> To my mind the period of direct contact with nature is the true
> 'heroic age' of human history, an age in which heroic accom-
> plishment and heroic endurance are parts of the daily routine.
> The activities of people on this stage of progress deserve a place
> among the cherished traditions of the human race. I believe
> also that the sanest missionary effort includes an endeavor to as-
> sist the uncivilized man in his adjustment to natural laws. With
> these ideas in mind the opportunity to conduct exploratory
> work in the Navajo country appealed to me with peculiar force.
> . . . To improve the condition of this long-neglected but capable
> race, to render their life more intelligently wholesome by apply-
> ing scientific knowledge, gives pleasure in no degree less than
> that obtained by the study of the interesting geologic problems
> which this country affords.[21]

This, in Arthur O. Lovejoy's terminology, is "hard" cultural primitivism, in which a heroic age when people led simple, virtuous lives,
occurred at an early stage of human evolution, and time since then
has been a story of decline in the basic quality of life.[22] Time has

brought increased knowledge and technology, however, and that is what Gregory proposed to apply to the Navajo economy. Gregory's liberalism, then, had severe limits: Modern science should "assist the uncivilized man in his adjustment to natural laws," but nothing more. This was the extent of what Gregory called his "missionary effort," and the phrase is an implied rebuke to the ethnocentrism of missionaries he no doubt observed.

Although to Gregory the Navajo represented a sort of heroic stage in human evolution, his actual encounters with them during five strenuous field seasons significantly tempered his idealism. In the "Suggestions to Travelers," with which he ends the introduction to his water supply paper, Gregory offers a shrewdly practical appraisal of the Navajo character:

> The Navajo is vigorous, intelligent, and capable of hard work if it is not too continuous. He will render assistance for pay, frequently for friendship, and is loyal and cheerful when fairly treated. He is, however, independent, and will desert with scant ceremony when unjustly treated. He will help himself to interesting trinkets and to food but may be trusted with valuable things and with important missions. He is a past master at driving a bargain. He is an expert horseman but knows little of harness, wagons, and pack outfits. His knowledge of distances and of directions is of such nature as to be of little use to a white man. It is essential to success that the Navajo should understand and approve of you and of your mission, and therefore frankness should characterize all dealings with him.

Of the other tribes inhabiting the Navajo country, Gregory had little to say, except that the Hopi "is indifferent toward you and your mission," and "his chief desire is to be let alone," while "the Piute, in my opinion, is less trustworthy and less skillful than his Navajo and Hopi neighbors."[23]

Following his Navajo country surveys, Gregory turned his attention north of the San Juan to the vast triangle bounded by that river and Glen Canyon, and to the Kaiparowits region north of Glen Canyon. Both areas were almost totally unpopulated except for occasional wandering Indians and stockmen, and a few diehard prospectors along the rivers. Except for the mapping surveys of 1921 along the rivers and a few archaeological expeditions, the areas were almost a scientific blank spot, and Gregory's work represented a great intellectual forward leap.

The Kaiparowits Plateau is one of the most dramatic features in the canyon country. Situated south of the Aquarius Plateau, it separates the Escalante and Paria drainages. Impressive from any vantage point, its most memorable aspect is perhaps its precipitous eastern face known as the Straight Cliffs, some 2,000 feet in height and extending for fifty miles from the town of Escalante to the Colorado River, thus giving rise to its local name, the Fifty Mile Mountain. Its fortresslike appearance from afar is strengthened upon closer inspection, because there are only a very few breaks in its stone walls deep enough to allow passage to its summit.

Although an awareness of the plateau was inescapable from the river, neither of the hurried Powell reconnaissances of 1869 or 1871 had time to study it, nor did the members of the *Canonita* party in 1872. It was the overland arms of the Powell survey in 1872 and 1875 under Almon Harris Thompson that first brought the region under scientific scrutiny. Starting from Kanab to reach the mouth of the Dirty Devil River where the *Canonita* had been cached the previous year, Thompson and his party passed through the gap between the Aquarius and Kaiparowits Plateaus. They initially mistook the Escalante River for the Dirty Devil, as had Jacob Hamblin during his futile attempt to cache supplies for the 1871 Powell river party at the Dirty Devil. Eventually realizing his mistake, Thompson named both the Escalante River, which he erroneously believed to be an original discovery, and the Kaiparowits Plateau, extending the Paiute name for Canaan Peak on its northern end to the entire feature.

Thompson returned in 1875, his last year with the Powell survey, and accomplished the first recorded ascent of the plateau. After exploring along the Fremont River in late July, Thompson and his party crossed the Aquarius Plateau and on August 2 began riding along the Straight Cliffs attempting to reach the southern end of the Kaiparowits. About fifteen miles from the end, they found a break in the cliffs that allowed access to the summit, but only after some arduous trail building. After riding to the end of the plateau, the men returned to its foot via the trail they had constructed.[24]

On his way out, Thompson encountered a group of Mormons from Panguitch who were looking for a place to settle and suggested that they call their settlement Escalante after the river he had

named. Those settlers and their descendants, along with later ar-
rivers, began the first consistent efforts to explore the region, and
Gregory relied heavily upon them for information on the terrain. Although the Escalante settlers farmed, livestock was an important
part of their economy from the beginning, and their quest for grazing
areas led them to explore the nearby plateaus and canyons. Their
early explorations of the Kaiparowits were not promising. Perhaps as
early as 1876 or 1877, Sam and Marion Dorrity tried putting cattle
on the plateau but did not meet with success, perhaps because of the
lack of convenient water sources, and most grazing during those
early years seems to have been done on the Aquarius Plateau and in
the Escalante canyons. By the time Gregory began his surveys in
1915, however, the Kaiparowits was already a well-used sheep
range.[25]

For his venture onto the Kaiparowits in 1915, Gregory relied on
the guide services of the trusted John Wetherill. The party consisted
of Gregory, Wetherill, Ben Wetherill as cook, and John T. Doueghy
as "Jr. Ass't," four saddle horses and four pack mules. The trip was a
reconnaissance of the entire north side of Glen Canyon from Lee's
Ferry to Hite, then across the river to White Canyon and ending in
Monticello. To reach the summit of the Kaiparowits, the party rode
up Last Chance Creek from the Colorado River and searched its upper branches until they found one that allowed access to the summit,
which they rode across to Collett Canyon (also known, confusingly,
as Last Chance Creek at that time) and descended to the Hole-in-
the-Rock road.

Gregory's most extensive exploration of the Kaiparowits occurred
in 1918 on a trip plagued with personnel problems. In Green River,
Gregory engaged Bert Loper as guide and Willard Drake as cook,
rounding out the party with an assistant named Winchell from the
USGS. "Loper," Gregory complained, "is a good worker, faithful, but
slow. [He] is at his best when on foot or in a boat. With horses and
horse trails he is only average."[26] The party was halted in Hall's Creek
as Loper and Drake failed to find a trail across the Waterpocket Fold
to Escalante. Even a local guide, Clarence Brown of Loa, could not
get them across, and Gregory finally decided to use the more familiar
trail through Muley Twist Canyon. Winchell left the party at Escalante. Gregory found guides and oats scarce in late May, because
both were needed for the spring roundup. In time he engaged a man

named Kirchwell to meet them at Fifty Mile Point near the southern end of the plateau in five days to guide them to the summit.

After finding his own way to the summit at Fifty Mile Point and surveying the geology south of the river from that vantage point, Gregory waited three days for Kirchwell, who did not appear, then headed back north toward Collett Canyon. From sheepherders along the way, Gregory "learned that Mr. Kirchwell our 'guide' came down to near 50 mile point could not find us and returned to Escalante. Probably good thing we missed him for a man who does such a fool thing might lead us astray."[27] In the end, the occasional meetings with sheepherders both in the valley and on the Kaiparowits summit proved to be all the guide Gregory needed. Acting upon their advice, he turned up the "Cyote [*sic*] Hole" trail at Panther Seeps, which the sheepman Edward Lay told him was thirty-five miles from Escalante, and gained the summit. Once there, however, he found he was covering much of the terrain he and Wetherill had explored three years previously. And Loper continued to hold things up. Realizing he had left his camera and water bag at Fifty Mile Point, Loper wasted an entire day returning for them, then failed to find the trail down Last Chance Creek by which Gregory and Wetherill had reached the summit on the earlier trip. That part of the trip ended by riding all the way north to Collett Canyon, by which they descended the plateau.

Gregory's last two trips, in 1922 and 1924, were brief. On the 1922 trip, he rode up Rock Creek to the Kaiparowits summit, then all the way across, apparently to Collett Canyon. In 1924 he explored the Paria drainage and attempted to reach the Kaiparowits summit via Wahweap Creek but was dissuaded by his guide, Samuel Johnson of Cannonville. As in 1922, most of his study was devoted to the east and north sides of the plateau.

Gregory began his study of what he called the San Juan country, the triangle between the San Juan and Colorado Rivers, as extensions of his Navajo country surveys and the 1915 survey of the north side of Glen Canyon. The bulk of his investigation occurred, however, during two long field seasons of 1925 and 1927, and were completed during two brief visits in 1928 and 1929.

While Gregory did not enter the Kaiparowits region in 1925, his explorations within the San Juan Triangle were nevertheless a part of his Kaiparowits study as well as a part of his study of the San Juan country. His goal that year, as he put it, was to extend "the survey eastward across Glen Canyon to correlate the geographic and geologic features of the Kaiparowits region with those of southeastern Utah and southwestern Utah."[28] The 1925 expedition began on September 12 in Monticello, where Gregory secured W. H. Christensen and Joseph Adams as guides. The next day they began their trip toward the Bear's Ears and down White Canyon to Fry Canyon, which they followed up to the pass into Red Canyon north of the Tables of the Sun. From Red Canyon they crossed Clay Hills Pass, where they happened to meet John Wetherill, who had been to the mouth of the San Juan River and was evidently returning to Kayenta. They then crossed from Castle Wash to the Lake Canyon drainage, down Johnnie's Hole, and explored lower Castle Wash. On the return trip they explored lower Grand Gulch, evidently entering at Collins Canyon.

In 1927 Gregory engaged two young guides in Blanding, Zeke "Junior" Johnson and Lloyd Young, with four horses and three mules, and set off on May 21 for the farthest reaches of the San Juan country, generally following the old Mormon Hole-in-the-Rock road. Although it was his most productive year in that region, most of Gregory's explorations were accomplished in the face of excruciating pain, evidently from a presumed abdominal rupture sustained when his horse stumbled on the second day of the trip, making walking painful for him. Among the interesting aspects of his field notes are the only scientific description in the literature of Hermit Lake, a description of the annual cycle of cattle herding between western San Juan County and Elk Ridge, and his description of the route from Lake to Moki Canyons and across Mancos Mesa to Trail Cliff. On the latter stretch misfortunes threatened to ruin the trip when Gregory's horse jumped into a pool of water in Cedar Canyon and soaked his camera, and Junior Johnson lost the route to Trail Cliff and the party wound up spending a nearly dry night at the tiny seep called Cedar Spring. On May 28 they camped at the mouth of Red Canyon, "in dirty yard of W. S. Carpenter," who was then living in Bert Loper's cabin and mining a little gold in a gunnysack-lined sluice box. (Carpenter, one of Glen Canyon's famous hermits along with Cass Hite, Bert Loper, and Lon Turner, also fascinated Charles L. Bernheimer who followed essentially the same route on his return trip in 1929.) They followed White Canyon up to the Natural Bridges and the Bear's Ears. At their last camp at the Kigalia Ranger Station on Elk

Ridge, all were eager to head for home the next day: "Both Zeke Johnson Jr and Lloyd Young packers are homesick [or lovesick?—the handwriting is unclear] for Blanding—decide to go." For his part, Gregory's "strained groin seems to be in worse condition than before—Have difficulty in walking & feel pain continuously."[29]

What, then, can be said of Gregory's contributions to our understanding of the canyon country? Scientifically, his reports are gems that gleam among the long drab shelves of rust and tan that contain the USGS Water Supply and Professional Papers. But scientific considerations aside, Gregory was a master of English prose, and his reports are literary gems as well, for in addition to his scientific training, Gregory worked within a strongly humanistic tradition. It is well to remind ourselves at this point that two of his bachelor's degrees were in the arts, and that his reports are filled with cultural and historical facts as well as scientific observations.

For one thing, Gregory's reports are studded throughout with the apt metaphor and the telling phrase that perfectly capture the character of the country and vividly drive home an otherwise prosaic geographical point. To emphasize the ubiquity of Anasazi ruins in some of the canyons, for example, he describes them as being "placed like farm houses along a country highway." To illustrate his point that agriculture on the reservation is severely inhibited by the strong winds that quickly carry topsoil from one locale to another, he employs a telling hyperbole: "It is probable that the reservation could be traversed along a selected route from Carrizo Mountain to Lee's Ferry and from Grand Falls to Bluff without setting foot on soil of local origin."[30]

Gregory was no literary carpetbagger armed with an arsenal of alien terms, and in fact he employed scientific jargon only when it clearly served the interest of scientific precision. He wanted his reports to be as comprehensible as possible both to the scientific community and to the residents of the regions being reported upon. To that end, Gregory often enhanced the literary interest of his reports by including local terminology and folk material in making his points. During sand storms, he tells us,

> the sky is darkened and the swiftly driven sand grains impel man and beast to seek shelter in some friendly arroyo. . . . The

nervous irritation caused by the hot, stifling winds calls to mind the Spanish proverb: "Ask no favor while the solano blows." In the picturesque Navajo mythology the wind People were sent to dry up the earth and "Wind and Night" (sand storm) is the most dreaded expression of these powers for evil.[31]

Another hallmark of Gregory's literary skill was his ability to characterize a large sweep of landscape or indeed an entire province with the appropriate metaphor or the concise, trenchant summary, in a rare blend of science and literature. An excellent example is his description of the four-way drainage system of the Shato (Shonto) Plateau spectacularly visible from the vantage point of Zilnez Mesa. "The Shato Plateau forms the water parting for streams flowing northward into the San Juan, westward into the Colorado, southwestward via Red Lake and the Moencopi into the Little Colorado, and eastward through Tyende and Chinle Creeks into the San Juan. It thus becomes the four-sided roof of the reservation." And his description of the basic topography of the Navajo country immediately puts the reader at home within it:

> Mesa, butte, volcanic neck, canyon, wash, repeated indefinitely, are the elements of the Navajo landscape. Alcoves, recesses, and miniature erosion forms of great variety and rare beauty stand as ornamental carvings on the larger architectural features, and over all is spread an unevenly developed sheet of wind-blown sand.[32]

Nor is the scientific value of Gregory's reports limited to the natural sciences. Gregory never lost sight of the fact that the natural environment is the setting for human activity. In addition to his comments on the culture of the Indians, and his emphasis on the fact that helping them cope with the rigors and capriciousness of their environment was the underlying motive for his water supply paper, Gregory invariably included both historical and contemporary data on white occupation and utilization of the region under investigation. To his historical research in the library, Gregory added interviews with longtime local residents, so that his reports are no less than compendiums of existing knowledge at the time in virtually every field of investigation.[33]

With the staggering expansion of scientific knowledge during the present century, the wide-ranging competence of old-time Colorado Plateau geologists like Gregory, Hugh D. Miser, and Charles B. Hunt is scarcely possible any longer. Nor is their literary elegance any longer a conspicuous feature of scientific monographs. While the extension of knowledge through specialization is to be applauded and encouraged, we cannot permit ourselves to lose the broader human and scientific context Gregory kept constantly before his readers. His reports are a rich blend of science and humanism that grew from a deep love of life and of nature. "The world was his home," Dr. Farnsworth summarized, "and I have never known a person who knew so much about it." [34]

NOTES

1. Reed W. Farnsworth, "Herbert Ernest Gregory: Pioneer Geologist of Southern Utah," *Utah Historical Quarterly* 30 (Winter 1962): 78. The Kanab, Utah, *Kane County Standard*, November 10, 1944, contains an account of that trip, with a list of personnel. Farnsworth's tribute to Gregory unfortunately plagiarizes much of Chester R. Longwell's "Memorial to Herbert Ernest Gregory (1869–1952)," *Geographical Society of America Proceedings*, Annual Report: 1953 (May 1954): 114–23, though his personal recollections of Gregory are valuable.

2. Herbert E. Gregory, *The Navajo Country: A Geographic and Hydrographic Reconnaissance of Parts of Arizona, New Mexico, and Utah*, USGS Water Supply Paper No. 380 (Washington, D.C.: Government Printing Office, 1916); *Geology of the Navajo Country: A Reconnaissance of Parts of Arizona, New Mexico, and Utah*, USGS Professional Paper No. 93 (Washington, D.C.: Government Printing Office, 1917); *The San Juan Country: A Geographic and Geologic Reconnaissance of Southeastern Utah*, USGS Professional Paper No. 188 (Washington, D.C.: Government Printing Office, 1938); and Gregory and Raymond C. Moore, *The Kaiparowits Region: A Geographic and Geologic Reconnaissance of Parts of Utah and Arizona*, USGS Professional Paper No. 164 (Washington, D.C.: Government Printing Office, 1931).

3. C. Gregory Crampton, *Standing Up Country: The Canyon Lands of Utah and Arizona* (New York: Alfred A. Knopf, 1964), 70.

4. Gregory and Moore, *The Kaiparowits Region*, 8–9.

5. Gregory, *The San Juan Country*, 2, 4; Gregory and Moore, *The Kaiparowits Region*, 4–5.

6. Longwell, "Memorial," 115–17.

7. Thomas G. Manning, *Government in Science: The U.S. Geological Survey, 1867–1894* (Lexington: University of Kentucky Press, 1967); A. Hunter Dupree, *Science in the Federal Government* (Cambridge: Harvard University Press, 1957); and John C. and Mary C. Rabbit, "The U.S. Geological Survey: 75 Years of Service to the Nation, 1879–1954," *Science* 119 (May 28, 1954): 741–58.

8. Garrick and Roberta Glenn Bailey, *A History of the Navajos: The Reservation Years* (Santa Fe: School of American Research Press, 1986), 73–104.

9. Herbert E. Gregory Field Notes, Book XI (1914), August 28, 1914. United States Geological Survey Field Records Library, Denver, Colorado. Hereafter cited as "Field Notes."

10. The economic history of the Navajos is obviously much more complex than I have sketched it here. See Bailey and Bailey, *A History of the Navajos*, Chapters 2 and 3. On the economic resurgence of the early twentieth century, see especially pp. 124–39 and the accompanying graphs showing growth in livestock holdings.

11. Gregory, *The Navajo Country*, 76, 103, 113.

12. Gregory, *Geology of the Navajo Country*, 128.

13. Gregory to Edna Hope Gregory, June 21, 1913. Herbert E. Gregory Papers, Museum of Northern Arizona.

14. John Wetherill diary, July 23–24, 1910, Museum of Northern Arizona.

15. Frank McNitt, *Richard Wetherill: Anasazi* (Albuquerque: University of New Mexico Press, 1957), 277–78; Mary Apolline Comfort, *Rainbow To Yesterday: The John and Louisa Wetherill Story* (New York: Vantage Press, 1980), 100.

16. Gregory, *Geology of the Navajo Country*, 9. Among other works, Gregory cites as examples the survey of Amiel Weeks Whipple, the work of J. S. Newberry with the Ives and Macomb surveys, and the surveys of George M. Wheeler and Ferdinand V. Hayden.

17. Gregory, *The San Juan Country*, 5. Gregory was speaking here of the area north of the San Juan River. The maps of the area south of the river were better, but his comment is still applicable.

18. Gregory, *The Navajo Country*, 15.

19. "Memoranda for Board of Geographic Names," undated document in Box 10 of the Herbert E. Gregory Papers, Bernice P. Bishop Museum, Honolulu.

20. Gregory, *Geology of the Navajo Country*, 23–57. Other strata, of course, intervene in this series at various other locations. By the time Gregory's *San Juan Country* appeared in 1938, the Todilto had been renamed the Kayenta. Gregory, *The San Juan Country*, 53.

21. Gregory, *The Navajo Country*, 9.

22. Arthur O. Lovejoy, et al., *A Documentary History of Primitivism and Related Ideas*, Vol. 1: *Primitivism and Related Ideas in Antiquity* (Baltimore: Johns Hopkins University Press, 1935), 7–11. The passage under discussion here also shows Gregory as an evolutionist, a philosophy that anthropologists at the time were beginning to abandon in favor of the cultural relativism of the likes of Franz Boas and Ruth Benedict. On the other hand, Gregory's primitivism put him at odds with older optimistic evolutionists like Lewis Henry Morgan, who considered man's movement from savagery through barbarism to civilization a good thing. Although Gregory refers to the Navajos as existing "on this stage of progress," the context makes it clear that he means by "progress" only cultural change, not improvement. On Boas and cultural relativism, see Abram Kardiner and Edward Preble, *They Studied Man* (New York: World Publishing Co., 1961); Lewis Henry Morgan, *Ancient Society* (Chicago: Charles H. Kerr Co., 1877).

23. Gregory, *The Navajo Country*, 11.

24. Gregory and Moore, *The Kaiparowits Region*, 7–9; Gregory, ed., "Diary of Almon Harris Thompson," *Utah Historical Quarterly* 7 (1939): 123–24.

25. Gregory 1918 Field Notes, Book II, May 29, 1918, reports a conversation with sheepman Edward Lay, who told him he had used the "Coyote Hole" trail to the summit for twenty-five years and before that had used a trail "at 50 miles" near the southern end of the plateau.

26. Ibid., May 18, 1918.

27. Ibid., May 29, 1918.

28. Gregory and Moore, *The Kaiparowits Region*, 2.

29. Gregory, 1927 Field Notes, Book G VIII, May 30, June 1–2.

30. Gregory, *Geology of the Navajo Country*, 28; *The Navajo Country*, 68–69.

31. Gregory, *The Navajo Country*, 67–68.

32. Ibid., 21–22.

33. Gregory's *The San Juan Country* offers perhaps the best example of his broad-ranging research. Both the Introduction and Chapters 1 and 6 are packed with historical data derived both from existing literature and firsthand investigation.

34. Farnsworth, "Herbert Ernest Gregory," 84.

Biology

One of the curious aspects of the history of the San Juan country is the relative lack of interest shown in it by biologists, particularly in view of the extensive attention lavished upon it by geologists and archaeologists. The geology of the region, for example, occupied Herbert E. Gregory over many field seasons, not to mention the more limited investigations of Hugh D. Miser, E. C. LaRue, and others. And although the immense Anasazi remains at Mesa Verde, Chaco Canyon, and Canyon de Chelly attracted much scientific study, archaeological expeditions into the Tsegi, onto the Rainbow and Shonto Plateaus and through Glen Canyon were by no means unusual. But prior to the preinundation surveys of the late 1950s and early 1960s, professional biologists studied the region only briefly and rarely, abandoning the field instead to self-taught amateurs or scientists whose major interests were in some other specialty. The neglect is unfortunate because, as the preinundation surveys of Angus M. Woodbury and his associates demonstrated, the San Juan country offered immense opportunities for studies of a highly diverse ecosystem and its use by and effects upon significant populations of both primitive and civilized man.

Few of the early explorers of the San Juan country included botany or zoology among their interests. Among the Great Surveys, the second Powell expedition included Powell's sister, Ellen Powell Thompson (Mrs. Almon Harris Thompson) as only a quasi-official member of the staff, and she confined her botanical work to the Kanab, Utah, area. Likewise, Townshend Stith Brandegee, with the Hayden survey of 1875, did no investigations west of Recapture Creek.

The first of the San Juan country botanists was Alice Eastwood (1859–1953), whose scientific career did not begin until her thirties, but who became a phenomenal engine of research producing more than 300 scientific publications.[1] Eastwood was born in Toronto and received her elementary education in a convent there, after her mother died and her impoverished father left to seek an income in the American West. She and the other students were expected to live the same life of self-denial as the nuns, and though it was a hard life, it may have been there that Eastwood developed the lack of concern with material comforts and the generosity with her own possessions that characterized her in her maturity. It was certainly at that time that she began her lifelong obsession with botany, acquired from a gardening priest who took her under his wing.

In time, her father became established as a storekeeper in Denver and sent for her and her younger sister. The father's financial status was still shaky enough that Eastwood was barely able to afford to attend East Denver High School, but she persisted and graduated as valedictorian in 1879. Further schooling was out of the question, and she began teaching school herself to keep food on the table. It was the last of her formal education.

Although she taught a bewildering array of subjects and received very little compensation, she was able to save enough and to find time for extensive botanizing in the Colorado mountains, and in time became the leading authority on the state's flora. A high point of her Colorado years was a visit from the English naturalist, Alfred Russel Wallace, co-discoverer with Charles Darwin of the theory of evolution. The two spent three days together botanizing in the Gray's Peak area, to the great delight of the elderly Wallace.

Eastwood and her father eventually scraped together enough money to buy some property in Denver, and it proved to be an extraordinarily good investment, providing her with a modest income that enabled her to quit teaching and devote herself totally to botany. In 1891 she traveled to San Francisco to meet T. S. Brandegee at the California Academy of Sciences, who was highly impressed with her and offered her a position as joint curator of botany and editor of the academy's journal, *Zoe*. Thus began one of the longest professional affiliations in the history of western science, and a career that would produce over 300 professional papers.

Eastwood's research in the San Juan country grew from a botanizing visit to the Wetherills' Alamo Ranch at Mancos, Colorado, in 1889. By this time, the Wetherills were well known for their work at Mesa Verde, and their guest book showed a steadily increasing number of visitors curious about the Cliff Dwellers. Although Eastwood was also interested in the Anasazis, she found the ranch a useful base camp for botanizing expeditions accompanied by Al Wetherill, her favorite among the brothers. The Wetherills were impressed by her energy, her intelligence, and her outdoor living skills.[2]

In addition to local trips in the Mancos area, Al Wetherill accompanied Eastwood, to whom he affectionately referred as the Lady Botanist, or Miss Denver Botanist, on two major botanizing expeditions in Utah. The first took place in the summer of 1892. Botany was only part of Wetherill's reason for the trip; a team of horses the family had bought in Utah had either wandered or been stolen and taken back to Monticello, where they were being held for him. He met Eastwood at the railroad station at Thompson, and they botanized their way south to Monticello, then down Montezuma Creek to the San Juan, and up McElmo Creek and back to Mancos. Although the trip began auspiciously with fine weather, after they left Monticello a fierce thunderstorm moved in. As night approached, Wetherill lowered Eastwood and their supplies into a dry cave in Montezuma Creek while he left to look for a way to get the horses into the canyon. They became separated for the night, but to his evident admiration, "the coyotes and other night-prowling varmints had not frightened her to death (which was far from possible)." And the discomfort did not inhibit her plant collecting, for he noted later that "to judge from the bundles of carefully handled and marked bunches, all with unpronounceable names, the botany business was booming."[3]

In 1895 the pair joined forces again to explore the San Juan River below Recapture Creek and thus to extend Brandegee's botanical reconnaissance during the Hayden survey. Their itinerary took them down McElmo Creek to the San Juan, and down it to John's Canyon (which they called Willow Creek). From Bluff to Comb Wash, they followed the old Hole-in-the-Rock road, then continued along the river to Lime Creek (Epsom Creek, in their terminology) and into the Valley of the Gods, which they called Barton's Range. From there they rode along the foot of Cedar Mesa past the Goosenecks of the San Juan and into John's Canyon. Wetherill could not resist visiting the site of the placer mining operation at the mouth of the canyon, which he and his brothers had worked during the San Juan gold rush, although he had to leave Eastwood and the animals and clamber down the dropoffs by means of ropes.

It was a hard trip on the Lady Botanist because of the rough-riding mule Wetherill had assigned to her. "I was strongly tempted to use the only language mules are supposed to understand," she wrote later, "but 'Confound you' was [*sic*] the strongest swear words I used." Although she complained that her saddle-soreness made it painful during the frequent mounting and dismounting her botanizing required, that her collecting was hampered by the loss of her pick, and that the presence of only one packhorse limited the number of specimens she could collect, it was nevertheless a successful trip. Her final report listed no less than 162 species collected, nineteen of which, she claimed, were previously unknown.[4]

As the first professional botanist to explore the San Juan country of this study, Alice Eastwood's primary importance is naturally in the area of reconnaissance. The 162 species she collected and classified became the basic catalog to which her successors would attempt to add or to modify. But Eastwood was more than just a collector. On her 1892 trip, for example, she observed that some specimens of *Eriogonum inflatum* (desert trumpet, or Indianroot, as Gregory calls it) exhibited more than an inch of swelling at the nodes, while others showed none. The inflated specimens were robust, while the others were "small and weak," and she explained the difference as evidence of the evolutionary process at work:

> The evolutionist would regard the variation as an illustration and living proof of the formation of a new species, and would look upon the plants without inflation as the original from which the inflated forms arose. The inflation is a feature especially beneficial to a desert, slender-stemmed annual and undoubtedly takes the place of the involucral bracts that most Eriogonums possess. It furnished the surface essential to the vital functions of the plant during the ripening of the fruit, since the leaves at the root, by which the plant was enabled to raise its stem and spread out its branches, become dried into dust long before the flowers are gone, and often before they are in bloom. It can easily be seen what an advantage the inflated plants have over the others in the struggle for existence, and they show their superiority in greater size and abundance. They even crowd out other plants and almost usurp the soil.[5]

Also, during visits to Mesa Verde and other Anasazi sites, Eastwood investigated questions of human ecology, both in plant forms used for food, clothing, matting, and house construction, and trade relations suggested by the presence of locally nonexistent items. Nor was Eastwood unaware of geological anomalies that affected vegetal patterns, as when she calls an area along the river above Bluff "a boreal oasis in the midst of a Sonoran desert," perhaps a geological holdover, as Herbert E. Gregory comments, "dating from a time when the climate of the whole San Juan region was colder."[6]

Finally, any account of Eastwood's San Juan research would be incomplete without acknowledging the contribution of Al Wetherill, who, though possessing no formal botanical training, functioned more as a research assistant to Eastwood than as a mere guide and packer. Not only did Wetherill guide her to areas he knew to be rich and various in plant life, but under her tutelage he did some significant collecting on his own. One of Eastwood's scientific papers gives detailed scientific descriptions of several species of plants that Wetherill had sent to her in 1891 and 1894, and Eastwood repaid his help by naming four original plant species after him. "I count my age by friends, not years," Alice Eastwood often said during her later years, "and I am rich in friends." Among the most cherished of those friends was "Mr. Alfred Wetherill, who was my guide, planned the route, managed everything about the camp and horses, helped me greatly in collecting, and, altogether, was as good a friend and as efficient an aid as any botanist could desire."[7]

Zoological investigation got off to a much slower start than botanical. The earliest reports, in fact, on the region's faunal resources were not compiled by professional zoologists, but by the omni-curious geologist Herbert E. Gregory, whose holistic interest not only in the physical structure of the country but also in its ecological features, led him to observe plant and animal life. In his report, *The San Juan Country*, for example, while Gregory could base his account of the region's botany on the reports of Alice Eastwood, there were no such reports on animal life, and he was thus forced to rely upon his own observations, conversations with local residents, and comparisons with published reports on adjacent areas. The result, while sketchy, nevertheless gives the main outlines of the region's zoology, and even goes on to make observations on ecological relationships between man and animals that have considerable significance.[8]

Gregory begins by placing the San Juan fauna in the upper Sonoran, transitional, and Canadian zones as defined for New Mexico by zoologist Vernon Bailey. Then he reports his own observations of animals in several categories: rodents, larger mammals, reptiles, insects, birds, and domestic animals. Some features of his observations are worth calling attention to. In the first place, Gregory had a significant zoological background, as shown especially in his ability to distinguish among several species of mice, which may have eluded a less trained observer. Another is his practice of asking local Indians about faunal changes over the years, which disclosed that large herds of antelope had once lived in the area until the appearance of white hunters, and that buffalo may have been present as well. Changes in domestic animals and conflict between them and native species were also revealed by his observations and conversations with longtime Indian and white residents. He notes the presence of "wild horses and wild long-haired cattle, remnants of the herds brought from New Mexico about 1885," and the near extermination of wolves and cougars by systematic trapping in grazing areas. Finally, Gregory comments on the difficulty of travel in the area because of insects, both the flies encouraged by livestock around residential areas, and mosquitoes that breed in swampy water holes who, "as if resenting the lack of opportunity to live elsewhere, . . . swarm over the pack train and prevent making camp in their vicinity."[9] It is a brief account, but insightful nevertheless, in its focus on the historical changes and human significance of zoological life.

Although archaeology was perhaps its primary emphasis, botany and zoology were also investigated in one of the most remarkable scientific enterprises in the history of the canyon country, the Rainbow Bridge–Monument Valley Expedition (RBMVE). That privately funded field school brought together established scientists and students in several academic disciplines to explore the San Juan country from 1933 to 1938. The project undoubtedly had its ridiculous aspects—its collegiate hijinks emphasized in a Ford Motor Company-sponsored movie, "Rainbow Bridge/Monument Valley—Adventure Bound," led to the characterization of the RBMVE by one Kayenta old-timer as "a bunch of rich college kids looking for a way to spend their summer vacation"—but its scientific contributions were nevertheless impressive. Not only were important additions made to Anasazi anthropology, paleontology, and various areas of biology, but a significant number of young men who later developed distinguished scientific careers of their own received their first field experience with the RBMVE.[10]

The project was one of many creative educational concepts of Ansel Franklin Hall (1894–1962), whom his biographer characterizes as "a rare combination of romantic idealist and practical business man," who as well was "an instinctive teacher" with "a deep feeling for youth as well as for Nature."[11] A native Californian, Hall graduated as a member of the first class in forestry from the University of California, Berkeley in 1917. Following service with the Army Corps of Engineers in France during World War I, Hall entered the National Park Service, where he rose by 1933 to chief of the Field Division. Always a teacher, Hall believed that simply preserving wild areas was not enough, and that the park service ought to develop its educational role through a system of museums and other interpretive programs. Beginning with Yosemite National Park in 1929, Hall created museums and interpretive manuals for use by rangers in several western parks by the beginning of 1930.

The onset of the Great Depression called forth one of Hall's most impressive capacities, his ability to raise funds. Various New Deal programs offered possibilities for continuing his jeopardized educational enterprises, and Hall successfully attracted funds and workers from the Civil Works Administration, the Civilian Conservation Corps, the Works Progress Administration, and others. As a consequence, his park service programs would seem actually to have increased, rather than diminished, during the hard years of the Depression.[12]

Similarly, the Rainbow Bridge–Monument Valley Expedition was conceived not as a relief program in response to the Great Depression, but rather a massive educational and scientific project launched in *spite* of the economic restrictions of that era. By Hall's account, the project began in discussion with John Wetherill during a visit to Kayenta in the fall of 1932. Hall described some of his recent scientific trips in the Sierras and in Central America, collecting geological, paleontological, and biological specimens for the University of California, and Wetherill responded by asking, "Why go to foreign countries? There's plenty of exploring to be done right down in this country; and as for scientific work—well, it's hardly been touched." Irresistibly clinching his argument, Wetherill added that Hall's own boss, Horace Albright, director of the National Park Service, had visited the area the previous summer and expressed an interest in a re-connaissance of scenic and scientific resources that might support creation of a national park in the area. The plan took further shape upon Hall's return to California. In conversation with the director of the California Alumni Association, Hall hit upon the idea of recruiting personnel from among those alumni, and funding the project largely by asking them to volunteer their services. Expenses for each volunteer were estimated at no more than $4.30 per day, including transportation.[13]

As it took shape the program exceeded even Hall's initial expectations. In the first place, personnel far exceeded the ten solicited by the first advertisement in the *California Monthly*, and they included not only scientists in several fields but a large cadre of students with extremely varied levels of education and experience, and not all from within the University of California alumni system. Also, the surprising level of interest exhibited by the respondents suggested to Hall that sources of funding beyond the participants themselves might be available, thus opening up a wider scope of activities and providing financial assistance to potential members from poorer backgrounds. Eventually, during the six years RBMVE put parties into the field, over 250 members participated, with annual personnel lists ranging from approximately thirty to seventy-five. Less well-heeled participants could earn their way as cooks, drivers, or packers.

The canny Hall attracted funding, first, by gaining scientific credibility through appointment of a body of sponsors and advisory staff that included famous scientists like Herbert E. Gregory and anthropologist Alfred L. Kroeber, and public officials like Francis P. Farquhar of the Sierra Club, John Collier of the Bureau of Indian Affairs, and Hall's own boss, Horace M. Albright of the National Park Service. Also, he involved private enterprise by convincing Ford Motor Company that movies and still photographs of a new fleet of Ford cars and trucks negotiating the sand and slickrock of the Southwest would be profitable advertising. A photograph of the vehicles on the 1934 expedition shows no less than eight donated Fords.[14]

The unexpectedly large response to the advertisement for the 1933 expedition allowed Hall to plan ambitiously, in quest of five large objectives: preparation of a base map of the prominent topographic features of the San Juan country to be used to locate sites of scientific interest; an archaeological survey; paleontological exploration; collection of zoological specimens; and a botanical survey. The participants were organized into three teams: the geologists and engineers were to survey sites and prepare a map of the areas adjacent to Monument Valley. The archaeologists were to take a pack train into the area around Navajo Mountain. The biologists could work in conjunction with either team, for they expected to find specimens of interest in either area.

Hall's report on the season's accomplishments was full of high praise. Perhaps the most surprising discovery of the entire six years was made by Navajo packer Max Littlesalt, who found a small fossil dinosaur in the Navajo sandstone of Keet Seel Canyon. Named *Segisaurus halli*, in honor of the Tsegi and Ansel Hall, it is one of the few fossils ever found in that formation. Biologists claimed to have collected over 7,000 insects and potentially to have discovered three new reptiles. On the other hand, the greenness of some of the scientists and the difficulties of the country itself led to some failures. For one thing, members of the geology team came upon Poncho House and claimed it as an original discovery, only to learn later that it had been located by W. H. Jackson of the Hayden survey in 1875 and excavated by S. J. Guernsey in 1923. Also, while the mapmakers succeeded in preparing a small-scale map locating the major landforms of the San Juan country, they abandoned their original goal of a detailed contour map after observing the intricate convolutions of the country as disclosed by their aerial photographs. That goal would have to await the uranium boom of the early 1950s, which prodded the USGS into preparing its 15' and eventually 7½' maps. The aerial photographic survey, in fact, almost had to be abandoned when a hastily contrived airstrip at Mexican Hat proved to be unserviceable, though an almost equally primitive one at Kayenta saved the day.[15]

Although the aerial photographs did not bear fruit in detailed maps, they contributed to the important ecological studies of Angus M. Woodbury of the University of Utah, one of the instructors on the biological team. Although the word *ecology* was first used by the German philosopher and scientist Ernst Haeckel in 1861 to indicate a multidisciplinary understanding of the interrelatedness of various natural phenomena, American scientists had been slow to embrace it, and Woodbury was certainly the first to attempt to integrate southwestern data under its umbrella. During the Glen Canyon survey of the 1950s, Woodbury's conclusions regarding prehistoric human relations with the natural environment would put him at odds with anthropologist Jesse Jennings, but his studies of vegetal distribution based on the RBMVE's aerial photographs were one of the most original products of that project.[16]

In addition to overland expeditions, the RBMVE ran a couple of boat trips down the San Juan River each season. Some, at least, were led by Bayne Beauchamp, whom Hall characterized as "an old-time explorer of the far north who had spent a lot of time on the Yukon and other rivers, mostly in boats that he had himself built." The RB-MVE boats were about a half dozen in number, and were Wilson "Fold Flat" boats in lengths of ten and fifteen feet, constructed of half-inch plywood in such a way as to be collapsible for land transport. The boats, in Hall's estimation, "proved quite seaworthy but were of limited capacity," each only providing room for two occupants.[17] Although Hall's report on the 1933 river expeditions indicated that "further work in these canyons and their tributaries promises to yield important scientific results," it is hard to find reason to regard the river trips as much more than recreational diversions. Perhaps their greatest significance was in providing young Norman Nevills of Mexican Hat, who served as a member of the mapping crew in 1933, with his first interest in running the river.[18]

As Andrew L. Christenson points out, archaeology received the greatest emphasis during all of the RBMVE seasons. Not only were the immense Anasazi ruins in the Tsegi Canyon system the area's most conspicuous and spectacular scientific resources (and thus the most useful in planning appeals for funds), but they were also, through previous scientific exploration, known to be of high potential for adding to scientific knowledge. Accordingly, some of the most celebrated names in southwestern archaeology led the archaeological team: Lyndon Lane Hargrave of the Museum of Northern Arizona was followed by Ben Wetherill, who, although not an academically trained scientist, knew more than most professional archaeologists about the Anasazis; he in turn was followed by E. T. Hall, Jr., Charles Avery Amsden of the Southwest Museum, and finally by Ralph L. Beals of UCLA.

The archaeological accomplishments of the expedition included dendrochronological dating of many Tsegi pueblos, a field in which Hargrave was a leading authority, and collection of ceramic specimens in order to establish a complete cultural sequence for the canyon. Finally, the RBMVE parties were the first to attempt a complete plotting of archaeological sites in the canyon.[19]

Ansel Hall's larger goal of providing data that would justify creation of a national park in the San Juan country failed, as Andrew Christenson observes, perhaps for political, rather than scientific reasons, and Hall himself resigned from the National Park Service in 1937 to assume responsibility for concessions at Mesa Verde National Park. The scientific results of the RBMVE venture were uneven in quality and inconsistently publicized, sometimes only through mimeographed publications of limited distribution. Nevertheless, it provided the first comprehensive, multidisciplinary survey of the scientific resources of the San Juan country, providing a basic repository of data upon which the investigators during the Glen Canyon survey of the 1950s could build. And it provided the first extensive field experience for a whole generation of scientists—Omer C. Stewart, Watson Smith, and George W. Brainerd are a few examples—who would make names for themselves in the Southwest over subsequent decades.[20]

Unimaginative historians of river running have often written of the 1938 Norman D. Nevills expedition from Green River, Utah, to Lake Mead, but mainly as a milestone in the development of commercial river tourism, with barely a nod to the scientific goals that gave birth to the trip and imparted to it its major significance. Elzada U. Clover (1897–1980) was an expert on the vegetation of the lower Rio Grande Valley who had earned her Ph.D. at the University of Michigan and returned as an instructor in the botany department there when she vacationed in southeastern Utah in 1937 and met Norman Nevills at Mexican Hat. While studying the cacti of the region, she became impressed with Nevills's enthusiasm for the river, and the two began seriously discussing the possibility of a botanical expedition through the Grand Canyon, most of which could be reached only by boat. Eventually the trip expanded to include the upper canyons of Labyrinth, Stillwater, Cataract, Narrow, and Glen as well, and they decided to make it the following year.

While Nevills and a USGS employee at Mexican Hat named Laphene (Don) Harris began construction of three special plywood boats for the trip, Clover returned to Michigan to round up some other scientists for the expedition. She settled on two Michigan graduate students, Eugene Atkinson and Lois Jotter, each of whom would pay their own way and help in collecting both zoological and botanical specimens. In addition to Harris, Nevills brought a southern California photographer named Don Gibson. On June 20, 1938, the party pulled away from shore at Green River, Utah.[21]

Nevills was a promotional genius who at this time was attempting to build a reputation as the king of the river runners, a reputation he hoped to turn into a substantial income selling trips to tourists. Although he acquired the reputation, there is no question that his self-created image always exceeded his actual abilities. This "exuberant little windjammer," as P. T. Reilly remembers him, first got beyond himself on the San Juan River in 1936 when he sold a trip from Mexican Hat to Lee's Ferry to former Rainbow Bridge–Monument Valley Expedition member Ernest P. "Husky" Hunt and two friends.[22] They had not been on the river for long, as Reilly puts it, before "the passengers became painfully aware that they had something in common with the guide on which they had not counted—all were seeing the country for the first time."[23] While Nevills was more honest in 1938 in admitting his lack of experience on most of the river they would be traversing, there is no question that he still overestimated his abilities. Consequently, when the party encountered the first big water in Cataract Canyon and became aware of their guide's lack of competence, much of the rest of the trip focused on the simple necessity of getting down the river, and on the interpersonal frictions that developed, to the partial exclusion of scientific matters—an emphasis that subsequent historians have perpetuated.

Nevertheless, the botanists at least (Atkinson seems to have contributed little scientific research) regularly collected specimens through stretches of the river where their mere survival was not a major concern. Clover had brought along a plant press twelve by eighteen inches in size and equipped with blotting paper to dry specimens. She and Jotter collected energetically in Green River and along the placid canyons below, but let up on their efforts during the trials of Cataract Canyon. The sullen Atkinson's hostility to Nevills and other divisive emotions plagued the party through Glen Canyon, and Clover's diary does not indicate a significant amount of collecting there, except in the uppermost miles above Hite, in which she even enlisted Nevills's assistance. "Norm brought in two Sclerocacti last night, also *Opuntia basilaris*," she recorded on July 3. "Lois and I are nearly always up first getting our bed-rolls put away so that we can get breakfast on time and not keep the outfit waiting. Keeps us pretty busy trying to get plants, too. This A.M. I pressed plants. There is quite a growth of *Baccharis* along the river today. It has a funny smell. Plenty of *Ephedra*, too (Brigham Tea)." The next night, July 4, they probably camped near Red Canyon or Ticaboo, for she mentions a talus of red sandstone (mistakenly identifying it as Navajo), and noted "some very large Sclerocacti growing here."[24]

Through the rest of the canyon, the party was more interested in seeking Anasazi sites than in botanizing. Quicksand at the mouth of Moki prevented entry of that canyon, but they did get into Lake Canyon, evidently as far as what was later known as the Wasp House, which Jotter and Atkinson reported as "a well preserved Moki house with polychrome and black on white sherds." The only other mention of cacti in Glen Canyon is Clover's note on the return hike from Rainbow Bridge that there were "numbers of interesting cacti here."[25]

At Lee's Ferry, Harris left the party because of lack of additional vacation time, and Atkinson because of lack of patience with Nevills. With two new boatmen the party continued, and the botanists, perhaps by now accustomed to the hazards of river travel, collected steadily, particularly at Vasey's Paradise, which John Wesley Powell had named in 1869 for a botanist friend.

The scientific results of the expedition were two lengthy collaborative articles by Clover and Jotter.[26] Neither ever returned to the San Juan country, but Clover did some field work in Havasupai Canyon at a later date. Jotter went on to earn her Ph.D., to marry another botanist, and to serve as a member of the botany department of the University of North Carolina.

Nevills's next Grand Canyon expedition, in 1940, also made a significant scientific contribution. The party is best known for the presence of Barry Goldwater, later a longtime senator from Arizona and presidential candidate of 1964, but the scientific work came from another member, Mildred Baker, whom historian David Lavender characterizes as "the secretary of a Buffalo, New York, investment company."[27] She had met the 1938 Nevills expedition at Rainbow Bridge while on a pack trip, and impressed Nevills with her interest in making a river trip with him in 1940. Baker turned out to be an ornithologist of some skill, for she accumulated a list of no less than sixty-two species of birds observed between Green River, Wyoming, and Lake Mead. Her "Annotated Hypothetical Check-list" includes dates and locations of sightings and notes on the frequency of appearance of common species. Several species—the black vulture, the lesser vireo, and the Stephens's Whip-poor-will—are noted as being absent on published Utah checklists.

The first systematic and extensive biological survey of Glen Canyon was the expedition A. W. "Gus" Scott and Robert Robertson of June 20–July 16, 1955 (it will be remembered that the Rainbow Bridge–Monument Valley Expedition worked only on the San Juan and lower Glen, and the biological component of the preinundation survey did not get organized until 1957). With well over three weeks to spend in the canyon by scientists with substantial professional training in both botany and zoology, the Scott-Robertson survey had a much greater opportunity to attain a comprehensive knowledge of Glen Canyon's flora and fauna than any previous expedition.

Both members of the party were Stanford undergraduates who later went on to impressive scientific careers. Gus Scott (1934–), a native Southerner transplanted to Phoenix, had made Glen Canyon trips with YMCA parties in 1953 and 1954, and thus was intimately acquainted with both the canyon and means of safe, comfortable travel in it. Scott was a gregarious and compatible person who made friends easily and eagerly sought out those with experience in areas in which he wished to travel. He was a close friend of Glen Canyon experts Harry Aleson and Dick and Dudy Sprang, who had helped him choose and rig his boat and prepare for a productive trip. In later years his boatman skills and experience increased steadily until he became a well-known figure on all major western rivers, though the Green, Colorado, and San Juan remained his favorites. In later years he received his medical degree at the University of Tennessee Medical School, and practiced beginning in the early 1960s in Richfield, Utah, and later in Prescott, Arizona. Robert Robertson (1934–) was born in England to a stockbroker father who moved to Tahiti, then to the Bahamas about the time Robertson entered Stanford. After the river trip, Robertson went on to earn the Ph.D. in malacology (the study of molluscs) at Stanford. The bulk of his scientific career was spent at the Academy of Natural Sciences in Philadelphia, where he became a renowned authority in his field. This was his only trip through Glen Canyon.

Scott and Robertson were both members of the Stanford class of

1956, and had become roommates there. Their diversity of backgrounds yet common scientific interests made them ideal companions. As a result of conversations at college, the pair decided to spend the summer of 1955 doing biological research in Glen Canyon, then to do the same in the Bahamas in 1956. Both trips turned up impressive results, and in fact the Bahamas expedition produced two new species of molluscs, which were named for their discoverers (*Plagioptycha scotti* and *Microceramus* [*Spiroceramus*] *robertsoni*). The idea of a biological survey of Glen Canyon was not a formal college project, however, though it of course was guided and inspired by coursework both had completed in the natural sciences. Rather, it was simply a way of imparting a theme or a purpose to their river trip beyond that of mere recreation.[28]

The pair used a war surplus ten-man neoprene boat, the *Glen*, which Scott had equipped with a rowing frame patterned after the one invented by the great Glen Canyon riverman Dick Sprang and fashioned under Sprang's tutelage at his Sedona, Arizona, home. This they loaded with supplies for one month, including a backpack outfit to be used during a proposed ascent of Navajo Mountain, a homemade plant press, and a veritable library of biological reference works and notebooks to ensure the accuracy and thorough recording of their discoveries. "Studying botany, ornithology, herpetology, malacology & archeology," they wrote of their purposes in one of the river guest registers. Although the pair worked together on all scientific investigations, it was Scott's primary responsibility to collect zoological specimens, and Robertson's to deal with botany. In addition to a set of 1921 USGS river maps, Scott carried a copy of Harry Aleson's 1950 "Lone Month on the Colorado" journal, one of the most extensive records of geographic, prehistoric, and historic sites in the canyon compiled before the preinundation surveys of the late 1950s and 1960s. With time enough to explore not only the river but many of the side canyons as well, and the knowledge to interpret what they saw, the Scott-Robertson survey was a promising enterprise.[29]

Glen Canyon by 1955 had become a popular place, and in spite of the Sierra Club's characterization of it as "The Place No One Knew," the midsummer Scott-Robertson expedition did not lack for company at virtually any point on the river. "*Smallest* (!) expedition down the river this year," they recorded under their names in the guest register at Music Temple, as Boy Scouts, commercial and private parties, and motorboat tourists from Lee's Ferry all turned up at various times. But the Scott-Robertson party brought something new—science. On June 22, as they hiked up Warmspring Creek, a side canyon at Mile 136.7, right bank, the echoes of the steep canyon walls encouraged them to shout such scientific terms as "prezygapophysis and other words which have probably never echoed from these walls."

Proceeding on their leisurely way down the canyon, the pair collected and identified numerous specimens, both plants and animals, and explored the lower parts of both Forgotten Canyon (which had probably not been revisited since its discovery by Canyon Surveys in 1952) and Smith Fork. On June 25 they made an original geographical discovery. Like Forgotten Canyon at Mile 132.1, the USGS mapmakers of 1921 had failed to explore and to indicate on their maps another left bank canyon at Mile 130.2. This canyon Scott and Robertson proposed to explore.

Thick brush at the mouth had no doubt helped keep other explorers out, as had a large beaver pond about one-third mile up the canyon. "Human footprints to pool, not past," Scott noted. But others had been beyond in the distant past, for a set of Moki steps on the left bank led to a ledge above, "very steep and dangerous," which the explorers did not climb. For the first couple of miles additional beaver sign was common. At about three miles, a waterfall appeared, which they bypassed via a talus slope that led to the plateau above, then returned to camp at the mouth. It was the first recorded exploration of the canyon. They named it Beaver Canyon for the prolific beaver activity in its lower reaches. Canyon historian Otis R. "Dock" Marston, contributing to the confusing multiplicity of Glen Canyon place names, later recommended naming it Crystal Springs Canyon to avoid what he thought was potential confusion with Cha (Beaver, in the Navajo language) Canyon north of Navajo Mountain on the San Juan. Marston's name stuck.

By the time the party reached Ann's Canyon, they had explored Hall's Crossing, Lake Canyon, and other sites, and were ready for a layover day. While Robertson brought his notes up to date and reported having collected thirty-four plants to that point, Scott read through some of their library and recovered from indigestion. Farther down, at the Rincon, science encountered materialism as they talked to a couple of uranium prospectors in a helicopter who reported to them that the area was already claimed by previous uranium men. And between Bown's Canyon and the Escalante, Robertson brought the Caribbean to Glen Canyon by singing a calypso as they drifted along while Scott recorded the words in his journal.

In camp at the Escalante, and then again at Rainbow Bridge, Scott copied names recorded in guest registers, as he had previously copied historic inscriptions at various sites. His journal thus preserves historic records as well as scientific data lost by the canyon's inundation.

"Been up 13 side canyons," they recorded when they reached Music Temple, but the greatest adventure of the trip awaited them at the mouth of Forbidding Canyon, as they set out to climb Navajo Mountain, a feat rarely if ever accomplished from the river. On July 6 they arose early and loaded their backpack for an anticipated five-day hike. To save weight, one carried the pack while the other carried two rolled-up blankets. The plan was to reach the summit via upper Bridge or Oak Canyons, descend to the San Juan via Nasja or Oak Canyons, build a raft and float back down to their camp at Forbidding.

After a couple of cold nights that forced them to supplement the meager warmth of the blankets by building campfires, they reached the summit, but as they were low on water and the descent on the north side of the mountain promised to be difficult, they elected instead to head down the south side to Rainbow Lodge and to return via Cliff Canyon and the Bernheimer Trail through Redbud Pass. It was a fortunate decision, because in spite of finding a small spring on the way down, they were very dry and tired when they reached the old lodge site, and were happy to find some uranium prospectors there who offered them cold water and three pounds of peaches, as well as feeding them breakfast in the morning.

"Great to be back on river again, almost like being home," Scott wrote after their return to camp and setting off down the river. The rest of the trip was a relatively uneventful continuation of their past activities, with the exception of some improvised trigonometric calculation of the height of the canyon walls in Labyrinth Canyon (Mile 35.45), which they had been told were 1,500 feet high. By roughly measuring angles with a compass and pencil, Scott calculated the wall to be only about 464 feet. On July 16 they came into sight of Lee's Ferry and the trip was done.

Although Robertson never returned to the river, the trip made an indelible impression upon him. On the way back to Phoenix, they stopped at the Grand Canyon, where they attended a lecture on geology and a naturalist's workshop and visited the library maintained by the park service. "Went to look at the canyon," he recorded; "Impressive, but not as good as Navajo Mtn!"

The Scott-Robertson expedition was possibly the best documented river trip ever made anywhere, and compares favorably with almost any other scientific survey. Both members kept elaborate diaries with lists of equipment and provisions and even a daily menu for all three meals. Most impressive, though, was their final report on their scientific work. It begins with Robertson's introduction to Glen Canyon botany, which discusses each division, class, subclass, and family in the Linnaean classification system in which specimens were collected, with collection numbers from their subsequent catalog. This is followed by a mile-by-mile dated list of the sixty-five specimens collected. The zoological section is organized by amphibians (five species of frogs and toads), reptiles (twelve species of lizards and snakes), birds in Glen Canyon (eighteen species) and on Navajo Mountain (nine species). Finally, W. B. McDougall of the Northern Arizona Society of Science and Arts provided a list of the Linnaean Latin names for each of the botanical specimens and verified Robertson's initial classifications.

Given the scientific rigor of the Scott-Robertson expedition, it is unfortunate that both of its members were deeply engaged in graduate studies in other fields when the preinundation surveys were at work, because their findings might have saved the later scientists at least some of their work. Like the geographic work of Canyon Surveys, the Aleson-Sprang-Thomas group of the early 1950s, the Scott-Robertson work was never published, and some great science never went beyond personal enrichment on a great river trip.

Over the next few years, the preinundation surveys under the Glen Canyon Salvage Project would bring to some degree of completion a good deal of prior work in three primary disciplines: geology, archaeology, and biology. Of those fields, the preinundation surveys had the least to do in geology because of the systematic studies of Herbert E. Gregory. Knowledge in the other two fields, however, was sketchy because of the uncoordinated manner in which it had been accumulated and the meager amount that had been published.

NOTES

1. Carol Green Wilson, *Alice Eastwood's Wonderland* (San Francisco: California Academy of Sciences, 1955); Marcia Bonta, "Alice Eastwood," *American Horticulturalist* (October 1983): 10–15. For material on Alice Eastwood, the author gratefully acknowledges the research assistance of Nancy Warner in the archives of the California Academy of Sciences.

2. Eastwood's expeditions with the Wetherills is recorded by Al Wetherill in his autobiography, *The Wetherills of the Mesa Verde*, ed. Maurine S. Fletcher (Rutherford, N. J.: Fairleigh Dickinson University Press, 1977), Chapter 11.

3. Ibid., 199–202; Alice Eastwood reminiscences, California Academy of Sciences archives; Eastwood, "General Notes of a Trip Through Southeastern Utah," *Zoe* 3 (January 1893): 354–61.

4. Alice Eastwood reminiscences, California Academy of Sciences Archives; Eastwood, "Report on a Collection of Plants from San Juan County, Southeastern Utah," *California Academy of Sciences Proceedings* [2nd Series] 6 (August 1896): 271–329.

5. Eastwood, "General Notes of a Trip Through Southeastern Utah," 356.

6. Eastwood, "Notes on the Cliff Dwellers," *Zoe* 3 (January 1893): 375–76; "Report on a Collection of Plants from San Juan County, Southeastern Utah," 274; Herbert E. Gregory, *The San Juan Country*, USGS Professional Paper No. 188 (Washington, D.C.: Government Printing Office, 1938), 23.

7. Eastwood, "Two Species of Aquilegia from the Upper Sonoran Zone of Colorado and Utah," *California Academy of Sciences Proceedings* [2nd Series] 4 (March 1895): 559–61; Ella Danes Cantelow and Herbert Clair Cantelow, "Biographical Notes on Persons in Whose Honor Alice Eastwood Named Native Plants," *Leaflets of Western Botany* 8 (January 1957): 83–101; Eastwood, "General Notes of a Trip Through Southeastern Utah," 355.

8. Gregory, *The San Juan Country*, 26–27.

9. Ibid., 27.

10. The original records and specimens of the RBMVE deposited at the Museum of Northern Arizona were significantly augmented during the 1980s by anthropologist Andrew L. Christenson, who collected various diaries and memoirs of surviving members of the project and compiled annual personnel lists. Records cited here,

unless otherwise attributed, are from that collection. Christenson summarized his research in "The Last of the Great Expeditions," *Plateau* 58 (1987). "Rainbow Bridge/Monument Valley—Adventure Bound," produced originally as an advertising film by Ford Motor Company, is commercially available in videotape form from Interpark, of Cortez, Colorado. The "rich college kids" reminiscence comes from Mrs. JohniLou Duncan of Prescott, Arizona, a granddaughter of John and Louisa Wetherill.

11. Watson Smith, "Ansel Franklin Hall, 1894–1962," *American Antiquity* 29 (October 1963): 228–29.

12. Ansel Franklin Hall, "A Brief Outline of my Work for the National Park Service," details this phase of his career.

13. Ansel Franklin Hall, "Wanted: 10 Explorers," *California Monthly* 30 (May 1933): 49–50; and "In Navajo Land," *California Monthly* 31 (September 1933): 17–18 ff.

14. Christenson, "The Last of the Great Expeditions," 4–7, 21; and "The Rainbow Bridge–Monument Valley Expedition, 1933–1938: A Listing of Sponsors, Staff, Crew Members, and Other Personnel."

15. Christenson, "The Last of the Great Expeditions," 26–27; Hall, "In Navajo Land," 123–24; Thorn L. Mayes to Thorn Mayes, Jr., December 3, 1973, copy in possession of the author.

16. Christenson, "The Last of the Great Expeditions," 27; Jesse D. Jennings, *Glen Canyon: A Summary*, University of Utah Anthropological Paper No. 81 (Salt Lake City: University of Utah Press, 1966), 11–30.

17. Bayne Beauchamp to Ansel Hall, July 8, 1935; Ansel Hall to Otis R. Marston, July 13, 1950; September 29, 1952, and November 28, 1952, in Marston Papers, the Huntington Library; Arthur W. Nelson Diary, 1936, 30–58.

18. Hall, *General Report Rainbow Bridge–Monument Valley Expedition of 1933* (Berkeley: University of California Press, 1934), 11; Arthur W. Nelson, Jr., Diary, 1936, 30-58; Christenson, "The Rainbow Bridge–Monument Valley Expedition, 1933–1938."

19. Christenson, "The Last of the Great Expeditions," 28–30.

20. Smith, "Ansel Franklin Hall, 1894–1962," 229; Christenson, "The Last of the Great Expeditions," 30–31.

21. In addition to Clover's diary, a copy of which is in the Nevills Collection, Marriott

Library, University of Utah, this account is based on William Cook, *The WEN, the BOTANY, and the MEXICAN HAT* (Orangevale, Calif.: Callisto Books, 1987); and P. T. Reilly, "Norman Nevills: Whitewater Man of the West," *Utah Historical Quarterly* 55 (Spring 1987): 181–200; and Reilly, "Norman Nevills as I Knew Him," manuscript at Utah State Historical Society. Less valuable is Nancy Nelson, *Any Time, Any Place, Any River: The Nevills of Mexican Hat* (Flagstaff, Ariz.: Red Lake Books, 1991).

22. Reilly, "Norman Nevills as I Knew Him," 1.

23. Reilly, "Norman Nevills as I Knew Him," 1; "Norman Nevills: Whitewater Man of the West," 186.

24. Clover diary, July 3, 1938.

25. Ibid., July 6, 1938.

26. E. U. Clover and Lois Jotter, "Floristic Studies in the Canyon of the Colorado and Tributaries," *American Midland Naturalist* 32 (1944): 591–642; and "Cacti of the Colorado River and Tributaries," *Bulletin of the Torrey Botany Club* 68 (1941): 409–19.

27. David Lavender, *River Runners of the Grand Canyon* (Tucson: University of Arizona Press, 1985), 98. Nelson, *Any Time, Any Place, Any River*, 22, calls her "a middle-aged schoolteacher." A copy of Baker's checklist of birds is in possession of the author.

28. Personal information of Scott and Robertson and the background of their trip comes from an interview by the author with Gus Scott, June 30, 1994.

29. This account of the Scott-Robertson expedition is based on Scott's diary and other records of the expedition at the Utah State Historical Society, Robertson's diary in possession of the author, and conversations with Gus Scott.

The Cliff Dweller from Manhattan

The Rainbow Plateau region south of Glen Canyon was one of the last areas in the lower forty-eight states to be systematically explored. Extremely rugged and isolated, it was neglected by the great federal surveys of the late nineteenth century, which brought most of the Colorado Plateau into public knowledge. Geologist Herbert E. Gregory, who named the Rainbow Plateau and conducted several expeditions into the area, called it

> the most inaccessible, least known, and roughest portion of the Navajo Reservation. . . . The deep canyon trenches are practically impassable and the buttresses flanking the cathedral spires are so narrow, smooth, and rounded that passage from one to another and access to the capping mesas have so far not been attained. Whether the ancient cliff dwellers made use of these mesa tops is yet undetermined. . . . The experience of my party indicates that exploration in this canyoned land may be accompanied by hardships.[1]

The deep and circuitous Forbidding Canyon nearly bisects the Rainbow Plateau. Its sculptor, Aztec Creek, flows northerly to the Colorado River, dividing the Navajo Mountain country to the east from Cummings Mesa to the west. Abrupt sandstone walls dominate the scenery along the length of the canyon, making it nearly inaccessible. Drop-offs and quicksand in the creek bed further discourage human intrusion.

The most famous of Forbidding Canyon's tributaries is Rainbow Bridge Canyon. Hidden from public knowledge until 1909, Rainbow Bridge was soon publicized by enthusiastic visitors such as Zane Grey and Theodore Roosevelt. Their popular accounts accentuated the mystique of the uncivilized Navajo Mountain region and extolled its scenic potential. There were few, however, who could afford the substantial effort, time, and money required to make the long trip to Rainbow Bridge, despite the availability of commercial pack trips. In the decade following its discovery, fewer than 200 visitors had signed the register at the arch.

A few of those who did make the trip included in their itinerary the narrow five-mile defile between the arch and the Colorado River, but there is no record that any of the early tourists explored Forbidding Canyon above its junction with Rainbow Bridge Canyon. That venture was the goal of the 1921 and 1922 expeditions of Charles L. Bernheimer, a goal that proved so elusive in its achievement that members of the 1922 party elected to change the very name of the canyon, originally known blandly as West Canyon, to the more descriptive Forbidding Canyon.[2] The success of those expeditions lured Bernheimer back to the same area in 1924 and to other parts of the canyon country in 1923, 1926, 1927, 1929, and 1930. Of those other trips, only those of 1927 and 1929 are relevant to the area of this study.

Of all those who ventured forth into the canyon country by pack train, surely none was as improbable as Charles Leopold Bernheimer (1864–1944). Utterly unqualified by heritage, training, or physique for geographical and archaeological investigations in the harsh climate and terrain of the desert Southwest, Bernheimer nevertheless made fifteen such expeditions from 1915 to 1936. The wild horses of Bernheimer's imagination fed upon the novels of Zane Grey and drew him again and again to the slickrock country where the eastern urbanite, who was at home in congressional hearing rooms and the drawing rooms of New York's most wealthy and powerful classes, became equally at home beside a lonely desert campfire. Several of the Bernheimer expeditions reported previously undiscovered geographical features and collected important archaeological artifacts under the auspices of the American Museum of Natural History and other institutions of which he was an important benefactor.

Bernheimer, a German Jew, was born at Ulm-on-Danube, Württemberg, and educated in Geneva. He came to the United States in 1881 to work in New York City as an office boy in the cotton cloth wholesaling business of his uncle Adolph. Through the years, Bernheimer rose steadily in the organization, serving as its president during 1907–28 and thereafter as chairman of the board of directors.

The civic-minded Bernheimer was an active Republican and achieved an international reputation as a leader in commercial arbitration. Though he scorned a newspaper article that referred to him as a multimillionaire, he nevertheless became a very wealthy man, only to lose most of it during the Great Depression of the 1930s.[3]

Bernheimer's marriage in 1893 to Clara Silbermann, daughter of Jacob Silbermann, a New York silk manufacturer, was an event of the highest significance in his life, for she was his true supporter and the marriage was a love match of the deepest order. Though she was unable to brave the rigors of desert life and join her husband on his southwestern expeditions, she understood the pull the desert had on him and encouraged him to follow his desires. "Charlie, go and see the Rainbow Bridge as soon as possible," she admonished him; "you won't rest until you have done it." Though he was away from her side and out of communication for periods of a month or more during the summers he spent in the Southwest, she was his constant partner. He telegraphed and wrote to her whenever the rare opportunity presented itself, and wrote his field notes in the form of a letter to her. "Dearest Clarchen," the early field notes begin, and other pet names are interspersed throughout. The ultimate tributes to her were the naming of mesas discovered by him in 1921 for her and their two daughters, Helen and Alice, of Clara S. Bernheimer Natural Bridge, discovered in 1927, and the dedication of his book to her. She died in 1932.[4]

Bernheimer was more than just a wealthy businessman; he was a man of considerable culture as well. His literary skill is amply demonstrated in his book, his articles, and his field notes, where he shows a fine ear for the nuances of the language in his depiction of the rigors of the trail and the beauties of the desert vistas, as well as for the intricacies of the personalities of his colleagues. He was an artist of considerable skill. He mentions carrying a sketchbook in which he frequently made pencil drawings of striking geographic features, and his field notes, particularly those of 1929, contain numerous sketches illustrating and supplementing his verbal narrative. Finally, he was a pianist of at least modest skill, who, at the request of a missionary, accompanied the singing at a religious service in Kayenta in 1921. "To my sorrow," he reported, "years of neglect had made my playing rusty, but I agreed to do my best for him." In retrospect, Bernheimer recalled poignantly the religious feeling of the occasion to which his music contributed: "There were gathered Jew and Gentile, Mormon, Quaker, and Polytheist, but all were enraptured by a single thought, each was speaking to his Creator in his own way. On that evening I believe I was lifted more nearly heavenward than ever before."[5]

On his southwestern expeditions Bernheimer was the quintessential tourist whose pocket camera recorded everything from the sublime Rainbow Bridge down to the most mundane details of camp life. Like most tourists he spent nearly as much time in front of the camera as behind it, and the dozens of snapshots in which he appears reveal a skinny, sunken-chested little man whose physique contrasts dramatically with the robust cowboys and packers who accompanied him. "If one met him about 1910, and saw his frail body," his colleague Julius Henry Cohen recalled, "one might have said that a man with such physical handicaps should, with good fortune, live to be sixty, but not much beyond that. To live to eighty, was a sheer triumph of spirit over body." Bernheimer exacerbated the handicap of his frail physique with what, to the detached observer, was a nearly hilarious hypochondria. Both his book, *Rainbow Bridge: Circling Navajo Mountain and Explorations in the "Bad Lands" of Southern Utah and Northern Arizona*, and his voluminous field notes record in detail his alcohol rubs, his potions, poultices, and balms through which his obsessive concern for his health manifested itself. His medicine satchel, the contents of which he inventories in an appendix to the book, included such concoctions as Argyrol ("solution for eyes"), Aristol, Ichthyol Salve, and Fraser's Bismuth Sub. No. 2 ("for Dysentery")—surely the most elaborate apothecary ever seen in that country.[6]

Bernheimer dressed like a westerner, though his clothes always seemed too big for his bony frame. He wore the same heavy leather boots and high leggings that his guides did, but his English riding breeches added a sartorial touch they lacked. With a loose wool shirt and well-worn campaign hat, his appearance was not radically different from his colleagues. Eastern ways died hard, though, and his book contains a description of the process by which he experimented with different types of high Victorian collars that would enable him to wear a necktie comfortably in the desert heat, only to yield in the end to the popular loose bandanna. In his field notes for his 1919 expedition, a brief pack trip with Zeke Johnson into the Natural

Bridges in southern Utah, he mentions that one of the packhorses carried his "dress suit case."[7] The image of Bernheimer dressing for dinner in the wilds of White Canyon lingers in the mind.

Thus the easterner offered much to the ridicule of famously irreverent westerners. Florence and Robert Lister, biographers of Earl Halstead Morris, the archaeologist who accompanied Bernheimer on some of his most important expeditions, report that Bernheimer often regaled his companions around the campfire by reciting page after page of the hyperromantic prose of Zane Grey, whose novels had played a major role in luring him to the canyon country. His red wool skating cap, which he wore to bed on chilly nights, was a source of snickering amusement to the rough-hewn cowboys. And the nauseating aroma of his cheap Between the Acts cigars, which he kept properly moistened in a humidor packed with wet sheets of newspaper, fumigated every trail and campsite. "He smoked the worst kind of five cent cigar you ever heard of," Cohen recalled:

> He nearly killed me in Washington, D.C. during the winter of 1943 and the spring of 1944, staying up until the early hours of the morning while Paul Fitzpatrick (the night owl) and I worked over drafts and memoranda for Senate committee members.... Through it all, Bernheimer smoked these "stinkadoras," as I called them. For Christmas I sent him a box of good cigars and suggested that he might smoke them, at least when he was with me in our dissipations. But, these he gave away to friends.[8]

It is noteworthy, then, that Bernheimer actually attracted little or no behind-the-back ridicule on his expeditions; in fact, he was both respected and loved by his associates. Clarence Rogers, who served as a packer on the 1930 expedition to the Lukachukais, recalled with pleasure Bernheimer's genteel manners and the old man's sincere gratitude when Rogers helped him onto his horse: "Thank you, sir, thank you." When guide Dudy Thomas arrived in Kayenta after one of Bernheimer's visits in the 1930s, John Wetherill greeted her by saying, "You just missed old Bernheimer. He's a strange old duck . . . But I like him."[9]

The remarkable consistency in the personnel of the Bernheimer expeditions, especially the constant presence of the two guides, John Wetherill and Zeke Johnson, could be explained in economic terms: Bernheimer had plenty of money and spent it lavishly on his trips, and Wetherill and Johnson made major parts of their livelihood guiding such people. But there is every reason to believe that they continued to accept his bookings because they enjoyed his company, finding him an easy and appreciative companion in the rough country he loved as intimately and felt as much at home in as they did. And Bernheimer did literally feel at home in the desert: "We camp on the precise spot we did last year," he wrote to his wife in 1921. "My bed will be on the same precise spot. Does it surprise you then that it feels like a home—indeed like home? I am writing these notes sitting under the same pinion tree under which I wrote you last year."[10]

Part of their liking for Bernheimer resulted from their realization that he understood and admired their hard-won skills in negotiating the rugged country. He missed no opportunity, both in his published and unpublished writings, to pay due tribute to the skill of his guides. Upon arriving at Rainbow Bridge on July 5, 1922, after arduously blasting and hacking a trail around Navajo Mountain to the south and west, a feat that Bernheimer regarded as one of the great achievements of his career, he awarded the glory not to himself, as leader of the party, but to John Wetherill:

> By our reaching the Rainbow Arch at 10 A.M. to-day we have succeeded to circumnavigate Navaho Mountain with 26 heads of stock. My chief thought at this time is that posterity may recognize and appreciate the ability of John Wetherill at finding and constructing the trail through Red Bud Pass [*sic*] which after 4 full days of labor yielded to his genius.[11]

Bernheimer's humility and self-deprecating sense of humor was no doubt another endearing quality. In the "Dramatis Personae" that introduced the characters at the beginning of his book, he described each in admiring terms. John Wetherill: "Discoverer of Rainbow Natural Bridge, guide, student, geologist, and expert on matters relating to the American Indian"; Louisa Wetherill: "A woman of extraordinary ability in handling Indians"; Zeke Johnson: "Man of great experience as guide, possessing extraordinary knowledge of the country and Indians of Arizona and Utah"; and on down the list. He listed himself last, as "Charles L. Bernheimer, Tenderfoot and cliff dweller from Manhattan." When devising the text for the plaque that, at Wetherill's suggestion, the old guide installed for him in 1937 at Clara S. Bernheimer Natural Bridge in Monument Valley, Bernheimer apologized for listing Wetherill and Johnson as guides and himself as leader: "I did not like to use the 'leader' next to my name, but I could not find any other in its stead. I assure you it was not done out of conceit, but for the purpose of indicating that I am the husband of Clara Bernheimer, without saying so."[12]

It was deeds, not mere words, that earned the respect of both Wetherill and Johnson, respect they did not hand out lightly. Each, in his own way, tested him—tests Bernheimer welcomed—and gave him high marks for passing. He ran the Wetherill gauntlet in 1921 when he made the dangerous climb into Keet Seel, refused to dismount at steep places until the others did, and kept in the saddle for three hours after Wetherill had suggested that "Mr. B." might like to stop for the night. Bernheimer had met Johnson's challenge in 1919 when he booked the guide for the Natural Bridges trip. The Mormon co-op at Blanding, Johnson's source for provisions, had run low on supplies, and Johnson was hesitant to take the frail New Yorker into the backcountry with only such spartan fare as he himself might subsist upon. "Of course if you are afraid to start with such supplies as are available, we shall have to wait," Bernheimer taunted. "Not I," was Johnson's response. "Nor I," said Bernheimer quickly.[13]

The scientific successes of the Bernheimer expeditions were a result of the fortunate combination of his money and innocent enthusiasm for the remote canyon country, the archaeological sophistication of Earl Morris on the five trips of which he was a member, and the profound knowledge and backcountry skills of the two guides, John Wetherill and Zeke Johnson. The process through which Bernheimer met Wetherill and Johnson is unclear in each case, though it was inevitable, given his interest in the country, that he should have done so, for they were the two most famous and knowledgeable guides in the area. Though the two were peers in skill, knowledge, and experience, they were polar opposites in style and personality: the one a silent, stoical Quaker, the other a gregarious, voluble Mormon.

Why two guides? The answer is not entirely clear. Bernheimer quoted a ploy of Sir Walter Raleigh to the effect that it was a division of expertise. As Queen Mary was the best dancer in Scotland and Queen Elizabeth the best dancer in England, he said, so Wetherill was the best guide south of the San Juan River and Johnson the best on its north. It is, however, an inadequate answer. There is a certain symbolism lending support to Bernheimer's claim in that Wetherill was located in Kayenta and was official custodian of Rainbow Bridge and Navajo National Monuments, while Johnson, who lived in Blanding, was custodian of Natural Bridges National Monument; but in fact the knowledge of the two men overlapped greatly. Johnson had herded cattle, hauled freight, and prospected south of the river for many years, while Wetherill had an impressive record of archaeological investigation with his brothers in Grand Gulch and other canyons north of the river, as well as guiding scientists like Herbert E. Gregory and Neil M. Judd through the area. Bernheimer's background in diplomacy seems to hold a more satisfying answer: Though the two guides were friends and held high respect for each other, there was more than a little rivalry between them, and Bernheimer may have seen that his best interest lay in exploiting their friendly competition.[14]

John Wetherill (1866–1944) has already been introduced as a partner of his brothers in their archaeological and geographical discoveries, and as leader of the Rainbow Bridge discovery party. Ezekiel Johnson (1869–1957), who was fifty years old when he met Bernheimer in 1919, had lived a rough and diverse life.[15] He was the twenty-fourth child of Mormon polygamist and Kane County pioneer Joel H. Johnson, a cold and tyrannical father. The rigors of life on the southern Utah frontier meant a harsh existence in which a child was expected to grow up fast and assume a productive role in the family economy. As a very young child, Zeke began helping the men in the fields, and at the age of fourteen he worked for his older brother Nephi riding the mail route from Kanab to St. George. In 1886 he took up the life of a cowpuncher on the Arizona Strip, and two years later entered into an unhappy marriage with the first of five wives, most of whom he outlived.

Although Johnson abandoned the life of a cowboy briefly during the 1890s to join the gold diggers of the San Juan Canyon, he spent most of that decade hunting wild cattle for the Bluff co-op, an experience that enhanced his formidable and intimate knowledge of the San Juan country. "See all those trees down there?" he asked a tourist party on Elk Ridge once. "Sure thick. And I've had a wild cow tied to every one of 'em." Catching wild cattle in brush country, as the writings of J. Frank Dobie and Ben K. Green attest, is a rough business, requiring not only special horses and horsemanship, but a high degree of plain toughness as well. Zeke Johnson was one of the toughest. Even in rough canyons where, one student of the wild cattle business on the San Juan says, "a horseman here might well be frustrated when trying to ride through this snaggled labyrinth at a jog trot," Johnson "rode at full speed, flinging himself violently from side to side of his horse's withers or ducking clear down below his saddle horn to avoid being swept off by low limbs as his eager cow pony strained to catch a fleeing critter."[16]

In 1898, presumably on one of his cattle-hunting expeditions, he saw the Natural Bridges for the first time. "I was just thrilled," he recalled, "and resolved that I would be their protector," a wish that came to pass when he was appointed the first custodian of the Natural Bridges National Monument, at a salary of one dollar per month with the guide and horse rental concessions.[17]

It is one of the miracles of the human spirit that one such as Zeke Johnson could emerge from a life of hardship and sorrow with such a famously buoyant personality, for he became known in the canyon country as an unparalleled wit and raconteur. His stories, jokes, and songs were in ubiquitous evidence on the trails and in the campsites of the Bernheimer expeditions, to the latter's great delight. "Johnson is an incorrigible optimist," Bernheimer wrote. "If at a difficult place the mules kick and bite each other and slip their loads, he sings either some fancy song someone else composed or a dockerel [*sic*] of his own. He laughs and jokes and is perpetual sunshine."[18] Bernheimer even interrupted his narrative of the day's events in his field notes to record Johnson's songs:

> *Put on airs—put on airs,*
>   *Tis so everywheres;*
> *If you do as folks and fashions do;*
>   *You got to put on airs.*[19]

Although Earl Halstead Morris (1889–1956) participated in only five of the Bernheimer expeditions (1921, 1922, 1923, 1929, and 1930), his importance transcends mere time spent on the trail, for it was through Morris that most of the important archaeological contributions of the Bernheimer expeditions were made. The influence was mutual, too, for Bernheimer's money made it possible for Morris to spend extensive time in locales he would never have been able to visit on his own. Perhaps most important, it was through Bernheimer's guide, John Wetherill, that Morris became acquainted with Canyon del Muerto where he made his first extensive study of the Basketmakers.

When Morris met Bernheimer in 1921, he was already well on his way to becoming one of the greatest of southwestern archaeologists.[20] He had begun his career at about the earliest possible age, uncovering his first Anasazi artifacts at the age of three while digging in some ruins in the Farmington, New Mexico, area with his father, Scott N. Morris, an ambitious young Pennsylvanian who had migrated to New Mexico to seek his fortune in the freighting business. The murder of Scott Morris in 1904 by a business associate was a profoundly important tragedy for the son. His mother became a recluse for the rest of her life (although Bernheimer found her to be charming, bright, and well educated) and dependent upon her son. Morris himself became bitter; his shyness and introspective nature intensified, and for the rest of his life he knew few pleasures besides those he could dig from the earth. Archaeology became his hobby, his profession, and his life. His skill with the shovel, the whisk broom, the camel's-hair brush, and the other tools of the trade became legendary, as did his seemingly preternatural instinct for knowing where to dig. Time and again he made amazing discoveries at sites previously thought to have been exhausted.

Morris entered the University of Colorado in 1908, an institution to which he remained deeply loyal throughout his life, even though he spent most of his career in the employ of more handsomely endowed eastern institutions. By the time he terminated his formal education with the M.A. degree in 1915, he had made the profound transition from pothunter to scientist and had come under the lasting influence of such then-prominent men as Edgar L. Hewitt, Jesse W. Fewkes, and Byron Cummings. Although the younger generation of which Morris was a part considered the work of men like Hewitt and Fewkes, who operated under a heavy romantic bias, to be shallow and misleading, he did learn from them professional field techniques that later served him well.

Morris was a part of virtually every important development in the infancy and early maturity of southwestern archaeology. Beginning in the summer of 1915 he worked with Nels C. Nelson of the American Museum of Natural History on a dig on the upper Rio Grande, where Nelson was devising ways to apply the principle of stratigraphy, previously developed on the ruins of the ancient Mediterranean, to south-western sites. In 1919 Morris became converted to the dendro-chronology dating project of Professor A. E. Douglass, an astronomer at the University of Arizona. Over the years Morris contributed innumerable tree specimens to Douglass from ruins in which he was working and helped in a major way to establish the basis for dating southwestern sites. It was, he asserted late in life, to his estimation his most important contribution to the field. Morris's role in the Pecos conference in August 1927, which established the basic terminology and chronology for the Basketmaker-Pueblo culture was of central importance. Finally, his work on the Basketmakers of Grand Gulch, Falls Creek, the Animas Valley, and Canyon del Muerto was of vital importance in establishing both the chronology and diagnostic features distinguishing the various stages of development and the fact that they represented an unbroken cultural continuity.

At the time he met Bernheimer, Morris's fame as an archaeologist rested upon his excavation and restoration of the ruins at Aztec, New Mexico, an ambitious and precedent-setting, though controversial, project. Morris gave his life to Aztec as to no other site. By an arrangement with the American Museum of Natural History in 1919, he actually built a home at the ruin and enjoyed, as the Listers point out, a situation previously known only by Richard Wetherill at Pueblo Bonito, of an archaeologist living in the midst of his work. He lived at Aztec until 1955 when he retired and moved to Boulder, Colorado. Morris's restoration of the Great Kiva at Aztec, though criticized by purist colleagues as artificial and speculative, became a model for similar projects and was clearly one of the crowning achievements of his career.

Although Morris wrote a number of articles on southwestern pre-history and an important monograph on Anasazi basketry, his perfectionism prevented him from producing the quantity of publications that his career would have supported. Nevertheless, when he died in 1956 he was recognized as one of the truly seminal figures in the field, a reputation that has remained unchallenged.

Morris's relations with Bernheimer were respectful and cordial, though perhaps more formal than the relationships Bernheimer enjoyed with the other long-standing members of his expeditions, Wetherill and Johnson. Wealthy patrons were obviously crucial to the success of southwestern archaeology, a fact that Morris vividly realized, and he was careful to cultivate Bernheimer and to keep his interests in the country alive and directed toward the most scientifically promising areas and projects. He first met Bernheimer through Clark Wissler of the American Museum of Natural History. Morris was the only employee of the museum located within the area of Bernheimer's interest, and Wissler referred to him Bernheimer's request for a trained professional who could explain the archaeological meaning of ruins such as Betatakin, Keet Seel, and Inscription House. In spite of his archaeological interests, Bernheimer at the time was captivated by the scenic attractions of Rainbow Bridge and the idea of making another trail to it south and west of Navajo Mountain. Morris's mission, from the perspective of the American Museum of Natural History, was to get Bernheimer interested in science and to encourage him to finance expeditions into regions with more archaeological promise than the Navajo Mountain area.

The first significant Bernheimer expeditions were those of 1921 and 1922 on the Rainbow Plateau. Bernheimer's first visit to the area was a 1920 trip to Rainbow Bridge under the guidance of Wetherill and Johnson. Except for an excursion to the top of Navajo Mountain, it comprised little more than Wetherill's standard tourist itinerary. However, it aroused Bernheimer's interest in the region and set the stage for a number of subsequent expeditions that were far more significant. His summary of the accomplishments of the more daring 1921 trip is also valid for his later explorations: "Much new territory never visited by white men was traversed. Many erroneous reports can now be controverted. A large number of unnamed places, canyons and mesas, received appropriate names which we hope may become permanent."[21]

The dual objectives of the 1921 expedition were to explore the western half of the Rainbow Plateau and to blaze a new trail to Rainbow Bridge around the west side of Navajo Mountain. It is not clear who suggested this particular itinerary, but Bernheimer was obviously enthusiastic about it—especially about the challenge of locating a "northwest passage" to the arch. As a consequence, the 1921 Bernheimer expedition became the first to explore Forbidding Canyon systematically and to document many of its geographical features. The published accounts of the trip revealed to the nation that the West had not yet been completely explored.

The personnel of the expedition included Bernheimer, Wetherill,

Johnson, and two wranglers supplied by Wetherill: Al Smith, who had been on the 1920 expedition, and Shadani, a Navajo from Nakai Canyon.

After traversing the now familiar Tsegi Canyon, a visit to Inscription House ruin introduced Bernheimer to the Navajo Canyon drainage which forms the southern boundary of the Rainbow Plateau. A local mustached Navajo named Not-si-san (Navajo Mountain) was hired to lead the entourage to the Colorado River in an attempt to find the Crossing of the Fathers. Although they missed the actual location of the ford by about five miles, the reconnaissance of the country west of Cummings Mesa was of value in providing the explorers with a better perception of the geography of a section of the country that had been inadequately mapped and that had never been described in print before.

For some inexplicable reason, Bernheimer found Navajo Canyon depressing. A campsite on Jay-i Creek, a northern tributary that joins Navajo Creek near its midpoint, he ungratefully named Do-ya-shon-da, which is Navajo for "No Good." Camp No Good eventually proved to be more useful than first thought, serving as headquarters for the 1924 expedition to Cummings Mesa and the mouth of Navajo Canyon, but Bernheimer's feeling toward the area persisted. "I always dreaded Navajo Canyon, which may account for my being attracted to it as a fly is to the fire," he later admitted.[22]

Before leaving Navajo Canyon for the uninhabited country to the north, the guides determined that additional feed was needed for the livestock. Shadani was sent on an excursion to procure grain from the local Navajos but returned with the discouraging news that he was able to obtain only one bag of corn. This caused Bernheimer even more anxiety. "Now I understand, as never before, what it means to get out into wild, unknown regions, to depend on what one can carry along and what one can wrench from Mother Earth in her sternest mood," he wrote.[23] Despite the risk, which perhaps was not as great as he imagined, the party proceeded northerly up Jay-i Creek toward Forbidding Canyon, following a primitive trail Wetherill had traversed approximately ten years earlier.

Beyond the divide of the two canyon systems they encountered a vast depression named the Kettle. Morris described it as "a maze of tortuous canons winding in and out among dumpling-like knobs of rock, too hopelessly rough to be crossed by a pack train."[24] To Bernheimer, "it had the characteristics of a crater but might have been a blowout of natural gas, an indication of the presence of oil."[25] It is actually the broad, deep head of the eastern branch of Forbidding Canyon. The outlet, a narrow slit, is barely detectable from the rim and gives the impression that the sides form a continuous bowl.

The party skirted the obstacle because, as Bernheimer explained, "no one could climb down a kettle's side." Access to the drainage was possible via the western branch, which they called Ferguson Canyon in honor of an earlier explorer who had left a record of his visit. "With the exception of Wetherill, Morris, myself, and a man by the name of Ferguson who had carved his name on a rock, I believe no white men have been in this vicinity," said Bernheimer.[26]

Bernheimer, whose previous trips had been over established trails, was continually impressed by Wetherill's ability to find ways through rough country, although he did not view the skill as romantically as he had the year before. At that time he had written, "Mr. Wetherill is of course a genius and has a sixth sense which one riding behind him feels guides and directs him."[27] In 1921 he observed that Wetherill's "memory of the faint and intermittent Indian trails is most remarkable. We strayed but rarely. He is beyond all doubt the typical pathfinder or pathmaker."[28] Bernheimer's fear of becoming lost was perhaps diminished by the realization that the passable routes had already been discovered by the Indians and that it was not clairvoyance that was required of a guide by rather the ability to detect the sometimes subtle signs of earlier usage.

His confidence, however, was soon dashed:

> At six o'clock that evening we found we had lost our way. This was due to the fact that there were no trails hereabouts to be depended on. Such as there were proved misleading. They were merely old tracks made by sheep and goats that come into this region to graze when there is extreme drought elsewhere; and at best goat trails are notoriously undependable and far from serviceable for a packtrain.[29]

And the next morning an event occurred that left Bernheimer even more bewildered:

> Wetherill this morning on foot went off early scouting for trails down West Canyon. . . . He, being a perfect type of the individ-

ualist, did not say why he went afoot, when he would be back, whether he would travel on the slick rocks to the right or left of the canyon, whether he was looking for a way out of it.[30]

Shortly after lunch, Wetherill returned with the

disheartening news that the lower canyon was impassable except on foot and that he had not been able to find an alternate route to the canyon rim. Morris best described the cause of the predicament: An adequate conception of the ruggedness of this particular region cannot be conveyed in words. . . . In looking from the foot of Cummings Mesa toward Navajo Mountain, the foreground might be likened to a sea driven in the teeth of a hurricane, the waves of which at their height had been transfixed to salmon-colored stone.[31]

It was across that sea that they needed to pass, and it was Johnson who finally found a route that he described as "not so bad." Bernheimer quipped, "If Johnson's 'not so bad' signified anything at all, I should say his 'bad' must be impossible." [32]

The party covered only a few miles that day, but at the end of their trail they found a delightful glen in a side canyon. "Here was Goldenrod Canon, a natural garden," Morris noted, "and just across that ridge, Navajo Canon, desolation incarnate."[33] But Morris had further reason for enthusiasm, for he observed prehistoric remains in several caves as they ascended the base of Navajo Mountain. Although the ruins were all small, they offered much more scientific promise than the sites in Forbidding Canyon. At the time, Morris suspected that Wetherill had bypassed larger ruins in the interest of later study by his more established clients such as Byron Cummings, but he subsequently realized that there simply are no large ruins in the canyon.

To the north the men observed a saddle between Navajo Mountain and "the nameless mesa to the west of it," but Wetherill advised against attempting to reach Rainbow Bridge by that route because of the uncertainty of success and the limited provisions on hand. "Altogether it is difficult to describe the obstacles that must be overcome on a 'first journey' by which I mean a journey never before tried by white man under white man's conditions," Bernheimer said with disappointment.[34] If the arch was to be reached that year, it would have to be over the trail around the north side of the mountain. Although

Bernheimer had already been over that route, they decided to proceed anyway.

"The bridge is not more than six or eight miles in an air line from Clematis and Goldenrod camps [in Forbidding Canyon], but to get there we had ridden fully fifty miles, and in so doing had made almost the complete circuit of Navajo Mountain," Morris wrote.[35] "Almost" was not enough to satisfy Bernheimer.

The following summer, 1922, he returned and his dream finally became reality with the aid of determination, planning, and a mule load of "dynamite, TNT, and black powder." This accomplishment was a source of great pride for the now-seasoned explorer, and his popular accounts of the feat in a book and a *National Geographic* article were destined to create a generation of canyon country enthusiasts, many of whom eventually made the trip to the arch over the new Bernheimer Trail. Incidental to that achievement, and of greater scientific significance, was the Bernheimer party's exploration of Cliff Canyon, lower Forbidding Canyon, and No Name Mesa.

As Bernheimer's field notes reveal, the logistics of the undertaking were difficult enough to dissuade all but the most resolute:

> Our cavalcade is very large this year. There is Wetherill, Johnson, Morris, Al and Jess Smith, . . . Sagi-nini-jazi, and myself. We have twenty seven animals . . . [and] tools, all very heavy, which we carry in order to work our way through. Three sledge hammers, three shovels and spades, two picks, drills, and other heavy iron tools . . . and . . . of course, feed.[36]

Although Morris participated in the 1922 expedition, he was not particularly happy to be spending another season on the Rainbow Plateau. He had proposed a trip into the unexplored and archaeologically promising Lukachukai and Carrizo Mountains on the border of Arizona and New Mexico. Bernheimer's mind was made up, though, and Morris yielded to his wishes in hope of convincing his benefactor of the value of a future expedition devoted primarily to archaeology. Perhaps in an attempt to make the best of a less than ideal situation, Morris set off by himself into the upper tributaries of Forbidding Canyon while the rest of the group looked for a route to Rainbow Bridge. The most imposing ruin he visited had already been excavated by Cummings, but he found several smaller sites.

Meanwhile, the others scouted on foot to determine whether the pass they had seen the year before between Navajo Mountain and the mesa to the west of it could be negotiated by pack animals. The mesa, which stretches from high on the mountain to the sheer walls of Forbidding Canyon, was one of the major obstacles that had thwarted the 1921 plans. Bernheimer now referred to it as Nameless Mesa, and later in the trip as No Name Mesa. Given his penchant for naming geographical features, it is a mystery why he did not choose a less enigmatic title for such an imposing landmark.

Wetherill climbed to the saddle and reported that although the route appeared to be traversable, it would require descent into a deep canyon north of No Name Mesa, which they called Cliff Canyon. A few cairns along the thousand-foot ascent marked an ancient trail. "It was not," Bernheimer commented, "the kind of trail we associate at home with woodcraft."[37]

The descent into Cliff Canyon was treacherous. The 2,000-foot drop is still impressive and difficult, though eased somewhat in later years by a well-used trail. And many modern-day hikers have been tempted to echo Bernheimer's melodramatic exclamation upon discovering the dry creek bed at the bottom: "To turn back was impossible[;] confronting us was the unknown!"[38] Fortunately a perennial water source exists a few miles downstream.

The next day the group found a better campsite about a mile farther west near a Basketmaker site Morris had identified. They split up from there in an attempt to find a route into Rainbow Bridge Canyon, a tributary of which they correctly supposed to be the next canyon to the north. Bernheimer and Johnson followed Cliff Canyon to its junction with Forbidding Canyon and proceeded down the latter a few miles until halted by a deep pool and steep walls. Before turning back they observed

> an immense cave shelf at least three hundred feet long and one hundred and fifty feet deep, a perfect concave dome. Its floor space fully half an acre was strewn everywhere with charcoal. Dozens of ancient fire places large and small, some shrine-like, covered the floor.[39]

The two men scratched their names into the sandstone at the back of the cave.

In the meantime, Wetherill explored the area north of camp and Morris climbed to a high vantage point. In the afternoon the party reassembled, all with discouraging reports. Wetherill declared that the obstacles in Forbidding Canyon would have to be overcome, but after Johnson and Bernheimer reiterated the difficulties, he decided to look at the side canyon north of camp once more.

That route, which was to become known as Redbud Pass, was already familiar to Wetherill, but he evidently hesitated to recommend it because of the difficulties it presented in making it passable for the animals. Wetherill's initials are inscribed in the cliff near the northern terminus of the pass along with the date "3-14-1911," and a note added to a 1911 entry in the Rainbow Bridge register explains that he had "walked over mountain while hunting trail around to north and west of mountain. Found place where trail was afterward built by Bernheimer in 1922."[40] Although he had previously visited the area, he reserved the credit for the opening of the pass for Bernheimer. Wetherill sometimes used such a means of honoring his clients for the accomplishments of expeditions they financed and downplayed the significance of his own contributions. "The Indians found it long before the white men came," he said of Rainbow Bridge.[41]

Four days of backbreaking work were required to clear the way for the animals and their packs. At one place the walls were only two feet apart and had to be chipped away. As Morris described it,

> The major obstacle was fissure between great vertical slabs of stone, perhaps 3 ft. wide at the bottom and thirty feet deep. We rolled loose blocks of stone down into it from the cliffs on the W. side, then shot down and sledged to pieces the two vertical leaves of stone at the W. side of the fissure, until the slit was filled and widened enough for the animals to climb down it.[42]

Johnson was unable to help for the first couple of days because of a leg injury, though he proved to be "a recalcitrant patient" under the ministrations of Wetherill and Bernheimer. Bernheimer himself suffered—somewhat less, one suspects—from a back problem and mosquito bites, but his efforts to embrace western ways helped him look at such hardships philosophically.[43] Actually, Bernheimer had it easy compared to the men who were doing the work: while they spent long days wielding picks and sledgehammers in the hot sun he was resting in the shade, writing voluminous notes, and taking baths in a pool in Cliff Canyon.

On July 5 the pack train negotiated Redbud Pass and proceeded downcanyon to Rainbow Bridge. Bernheimer was almost ecstatic but credited the success to Wetherill's ingenuity. Wetherill, Morris, and packer Jess Smith continued on foot to the mouth of Rainbow Bridge Canyon and then up Forbidding Canyon. The rest of the men took the stock back through Redbud Pass and met the hikers at Charcoal Cave in Forbidding Canyon. Wetherill pointed out his initials on the slope above the creek bed opposite the cave, which marked the southern limit of an earlier excursion up the canyon.

Morris described the major barrier there as "the largest pool in the entire country aside from the Colo. River." Although he was not unfamiliar with the occasional severity of desert weather, he recorded that conditions at the time were really extraordinary:

> The heat this day was the worst I have ever experienced. The wind blowing over the hot rocks actually burned one's eye balls and made one gasp for breath. The night was also hot. One could not lay naked because of the mosquitos, and beneath even a canvas perspiration ran in streams. Water in the pails was above body temperature on the morning of the 6th.[44]

Despite the heat, Wetherill set out in an attempt to ascend Forbidding Canyon to the point where he was stymied the year before. He found that it was too hopelessly rough to be developed as an alternate route. In the meantime, Morris dug through the debris in Charcoal Cave and found a skeleton that he declared to be that of a Basketmaker. He considered it significant that evidence of this early culture was found so far west. The men also found some sandals at a site above the mouth of Cliff Canyon and named the place Sandal Cave.

The ascent of No Name Mesa was the objective of the next two days. It was not evident that there was a way to breach its sheer sides, but Johnson found a cleft across from the mouth of Redbud Pass, which, with great difficulty, he used to reach the first bench above the canyon floor. Morris, Wetherill, and Jess Smith succeeded in reaching the mesa top the second day via "Johnson's Hole" but found it to be "the most trying mountaineering experience that they ever had." They saw no sign of prior human intrusion except for what appeared to be a cairn.[45]

The Bernheimer party used Redbud Pass again on the return trip to Kayenta, this time to gain access to the original Rainbow Bridge trail. Thus, in Bernheimer's words, "The rugged forbidding giant rock, Navajo Mountain, the War Gods' Dwelling Place was circumnavigated."[46]

The only significant portion of Forbidding Canyon not explored by the 1921 and 1922 expeditions was the mysterious Kettle. The 1924 Bernheimer expedition discovered an incredibly rough trail to its bottom, and it, too, succumbed to Bernheimer's passion to go where white men had apparently never been. "We followed Forbidding Canyon in its course to its beginning," he wrote in his journal. "Its whole life history is like its birth place. Rough threatening life and limb. Comparatively narrow though the Kettle is, it was difficult to pick a way which did not necessitate retracing."[47] The 1924 expedition also accomplished the second recorded ascent of Cummings Mesa and extensive exploration of Navajo Canyon and its tributaries.[48]

Now submerged in its lower reaches by the Lake Powell reservoir, Forbidding Canyon is the most-visited of all the reservoir's tributaries, as tourist boaters by the thousands motor up as far as Rainbow Bridge Canyon and turn in to dock almost beneath the great arch. Many, too, proceed on up Forbidding for some miles to enjoy the dramatic scenery. Beyond the head of the estuary, though, the canyon still presents to hikers the obstacles that earned its name; one may still view the drop-offs and pools that brought the 1921 Bernheimer expedition to a halt and rendered necessary the creation of Redbud Pass as an alternative overland route to Rainbow Bridge. In those upper reaches the canyon and its tributaries are today almost as little known as they were in Bernheimer's day, and without Bernheimer's field notes and publications they still would be largely a geographical mystery.

Rainbow Bridge was the original and the greatest attraction to the canyon country for Bernheimer. Lured to it by Zane Grey's novel *The Rainbow Trail*, Bernheimer found that it fully justified Grey's lurid prose. By the time he had visited the famous arch several times and had supervised the building of the new trail to it through Redbud Pass, Bernheimer began to look about for new projects.

The later trips were grandiose in scale. The 1927 expedition to the Tsegi, Navajo Canyon, and Monument Valley, for example, used forty-two animals, and the 1929 trip north of the San Juan River and beyond the Clay Hills had no less than forty-six. Bernheimer could scarcely fail to notice the increased size of the pack trains. "The men seem to increase their packtrain from year to year," he noted in 1927, but tried to put a favorable face on it by speculating that "It is probably because we have no certainty as to our requirements." Later, he admitted the truth:

> It seems to me we are doing more camp loafing than ever, but that is probably because I am not pressed for doing things as formerly, because I want to save myself a bit. I am a year older than in 1926. Then, too, when riding I am urging for a slower pace, so that my horse and mule need not be urged to keep up, which is a tiring process. In other words, I am a dude-explorer, and must refer once more to the foolishness of having 42 animals with all the care they need.[49]

Another reason for the ever larger packtrains, seemingly not suspected by Bernheimer, was that the guides, John Wetherill and Zeke Johnson, provided the animals and were paid a daily rate for each. More animals meant more money.

The camp loafing of which Bernheimer complains is a considerable benefit to the historian, for Bernheimer used much of the idle time to write his field notes, which occasionally reveal much about the man and his relationship to the country. The 1927 trip, for example, began with an automobile drive from Flagstaff to Kayenta, during which Bernheimer complained of being exposed to the bad cold that his driver, Earl Sisk, had. He refused to drink from their water container, which he suspected Sisk of contaminating, and hung his head out the window every time the unfortunate man sneezed or coughed. After ten days on the trail, though, Bernheimer's habitual hypochondria had so far vanished that he could say of the imperfectly washed eating utensils:

> Everything is antiseptic. Even the fact that there was one spoon and one cup for each (aluminum, and how well cleaned one does not examine), that no one thinks of washing before the meal, that a pocket knife is used instead of a can opener, does not change the deliciousness of the perfect repast.[50]

The 1927 expedition had two goals, one paleontological and the other geographical. In the first place, Bernheimer wished to relocate dinosaur tracks fossilized in tributaries of the Tsegi and Navajo

Canyons observed on previous expeditions. Then he wished to locate a reported natural arch in Monument Valley that Old Mike, who knew where it was, claimed was "bigger and finer than Rainbow [Bridge]."⁵¹

Both sets of tracks were located with little difficulty, but problems began when Bernheimer decided they should somehow be removed and taken to the American Museum of Natural History. Having no adequate rock-cutting tools, the men decided to ruin one of their axes chopping a set of tracks out of the rock. Bernheimer supplemented these fossils with measurements of the length of stride and other data, and with photographs laboriously made by sweeping out the tracks, then marking them with charcoal or chalk or filling them with water to obtain the desired contrast. Some were recorded by means of casts molded with an improvised mixture of mud and flour pressed into tracks greased with lard. Eventually one of the men was sent back to Kayenta for better tools and materials, and though he was unable, in that isolated community, to locate rock-cutting implements, he did bring a supply of cement, which made better molds than the mud-flour mixture.

The expedition's greatest triumph, the discovery of the arch, ironically came close to being abandoned because of Bernheimer's disgust with the Paiute guide, Old Mike. "And then we have the Ute," he complained on May 25, "useless and ignorant hereabouts. We believe he has no special knowledge of the Natural Bridge being bigger and finer than Rainbow, as he bragged. He just prevaricated. We shall probably send him home in a day or so."

Fortunately that intention was abandoned, for Old Mike did know of a large arch in Monument Valley previously unseen by whites. Although it is far smaller than Rainbow Bridge and less esthetically pleasing (largely because it is situated lengthwise at the head of a tight box canyon, rather than across a large canyon as Rainbow Bridge, and thus does not permit a long, dramatic view beneath its chord), Bernheimer was highly pleased with the discovery, and expressed his pleasure by naming it after his wife, Clara Silbermann Bernheimer. "Thus Clara, the veiled lady, had her veil lifted today to humanity, white and Indians," Bernheimer exulted.⁵² An inscription was left on one of the arch abutments recording the name given the arch and the discovery date. In 1936 Bernheimer shipped a twelve-by-eighteen-inch bronze plaque to Wetherill and asked him to install it on the arch near the inscription. The plaque records the name and discovery date, with the names of Bernheimer, Wetherill, and Johnson. "I know it will be troublesome for you to get to the bridge," Bernheimer wrote Wetherill, "but I am asking you to do this not because you suggested it, but because it is a matter of sentiment with me to have my poor little wife's name perpetuated."[53]

In 1929 Bernheimer made his only trip north of the San Juan River. After a paleontological prelude in which Bernheimer, with Barnum Brown from the American Museum of Natural History, and Earl Morris explored various fossil sites in New Mexico and Montezuma Creek, Utah, the huge Bernheimer pack train of forty-six animals and nine men left Blanding on May 25. Morris was a member of the party, the main goal of which was to reach the confluence of the San Juan and Colorado Rivers, investigating archeological sites along the way in Grand Gulch, Lake, Moki, and Slickrock Canyons.

The last two canyons mentioned provided the only significant scientific results, but the scenery all along the route impressed Bernheimer mightily. "Ten miles of Grand Gulch is no ten cent movie," the old man exulted, "it is grand opera." Immediately upon entering the Kane Canyon access to Grand Gulch, Bernheimer was delighted by the views. "A more thrilling, concentrated bit of travel in exquisite, weird scenery I have not come across," he exclaimed.

Previous scientists and pothunters had so depleted the Anasazi sites in Grand Gulch that Morris found little to investigate, though he did find a promising beam from which he took a tree ring sample. (It was while Morris was in Grand Gulch that A. E. Douglass's tree ring chronology of southwestern prehistory was completed by discovery of the sample at Showlow, Arizona, that filled the last gap.) A misunderstanding between Wetherill and Johnson led to establishment of their camp fifteen miles farther down the canyon than they had planned, leading to much backtracking and wasted time.

The scenery, however, remained spectacular. Leaving Grand Gulch via Collins Canyon on June 1, the party crossed Grand Flat and ascended Clay Hills Pass, whose Chinle colors drew some of Bernheimer's most breathless prose:

> As we approached the Clay Hills, if romantically inclined, we could have gone into ecstasy. The "painted desert" in all its glory grew more brilliant as we advanced. . . . Color photography

would have been welcome. We were helpless and descriptive
words are futile. . . . It was like dwelling in a rainbow. All its colors and hundreds of demi-tone shadings gambolled around us. I
shall never forget Clay Hills Pass.

After camps at Irish Green and Bed Rock Springs in Castle Wash,
the party crossed the divide between the San Juan and Colorado
River drainages and camped in the east fork of Lake Canyon. Although the vestiges of the Hole-in-the-Rock road could have guided
them to Cottonwood Canyon near the confluence, Johnson and
Wetherill struck out into country unfamiliar to both, in an attempt to
find some unexcavated sites in Glen Canyon's left bank tributaries.
After some scouting, Johnson located a route that probably brought
them to the river at the Gretchen Bar, from which they continued
downstream to Slickrock Canyon. There Morris excavated several
caves, finding a Basketmaker mummy and other artifacts, including
what appeared to be the shell of a drum.

June 7 was the most difficult day yet, as the party sought a route to
Gray Mesa. Wisely, most of the men and animals were sent back to
Lake Canyon, while Johnson, Wetherill, Morris, and Bernheimer,
with eight animals, went ahead to the confluence of the rivers. The
bank of the Colorado was choked with "almost impenetrable vegetation necessitating the play of the axe, and many an innocent tree and
bush had to make room for the march of civilization." The mouth of
Wilson Canyon was so brushy it took two hours to cross it, and the
axe-wielding men, in their frustration, gave it an impromptu name,
which Bernheimer delicately rendered in Latin as *Filius canis.*

Bernheimer's field notes at this point contain uncharacteristic errors and omissions probably ascribable to after-the-fact composition
and confusing geography. The guides were aware of a cowboys' trail
at or near the Rincon, but were unable to find it, and instead improvised an ascent up the small box canyon just east of the Rincon where
Aleson Arch (formerly Flying Eagle Arch) is situated. Bernheimer
inexplicably failed to mention the arch, and instead, even more mysteriously, reported seeing *two* natural arches a mile east of the center
of the Rincon. The only plausible explanation seems to be that he
confused this stretch of the trail with the two natural arches farther
along, near the confluence of the two rivers, the only place in that region where such a phenomenon exists.

After reaching the confluence, the party returned along the old Mormon road to Lake Canyon, where the rest of the group awaited them. The goal now was Moki Canyon, whose untapped archaeological potential was well known to both Wetherill and Johnson. It was an easy ride across the plateau of the Lost Cowboy country to reach the Moki rim, but a different matter to gain access to the canyon floor. After a lengthy search, Johnson located the immense sand slide at Red Cone Spring, and the party proceeded downcanyon to a campsite at a plentiful spring about one-quarter mile below what has come to be known as Bernheimer Alcove.

Morris's excavations at Bernheimer Alcove and another cave upcanyon from it were highly productive, including no less than seven Basketmaker mummies and a fending stick (which Bernheimer characterized as a boomerang). They proved to be the best archaeological finds of the expedition.

Instead of retracing their steps through Clay Hills Pass, the guides proceeded to Mancos Mesa via what is today known as Harrison Canyon, a dramatic cleft in the right bank of Moki Canyon about four miles upcanyon from the Red Cone sand slide. Their next camp was at Jane's Tank, a cave and plentiful water source in Cedar Canyon. The route from there to Trail Cliff at the Little Rincon whereby access to the Colorado River is possible down a precipitous cowboy trail was largely unfamiliar to the guides, and Johnson's attempt to cheer the party up by calling it a "promenade" drew Bernheimer's sarcasm. Only after lengthy scouting and Bernheimer's suffering from the heat and bugs, did Johnson finally locate the trail. The last leg of the journey proceeded up the riverbank to White Canyon and the Natural Bridges, where an automobile awaited Bernheimer.

The cliff dweller from Manhattan made one more pack trip in to the canyon country, an archaeological expedition into the Lukchukai Mountains in 1930. But age was catching up with him, and the long days in the saddle and other grueling conditions of backcountry travel possible to him in the springtime of his life were denied him in its autumn. And his fortune, out of which the lengthy and expensive western trips had been funded, withered in the Great Depression. Bernheimer made occasional trips to Kayenta during the last decade of his life, keeping in touch with the old guides who had brought such pleasure and significance to him in country of which few other New Yorkers were aware. Although the geographical and archaeological results of the Bernheimer expeditions were not insignificant, their greatest value is undoubtedly in the elaborate field notes and photographs that document one of the most improbable, and yet the happiest, encounters between Man and Nature in the history of the canyon country.

NOTES

1. Herbert E. Gregory, *The Navajo Country: A Geographic and Hydrographic Reconnaissance of Parts of Arizona, New Mexico, and Utah*, USGS Water Supply Paper No. 380 (Washington, D.C.: Government Printing Office, 1916), 44–45.

2. Charles L. Bernheimer, *Rainbow Bridge: Circling Navajo Mountain and Explorations in the "Bad Lands" of Southern Utah and Northern Arizona* (Garden City, N. Y.: Doubleday, Page & Co., 1924), 96.

3. Julius Henry Cohen, *They Builded Better Than They Knew* (New York: J. Messner, 1946), 149-61; *The National Cyclopedia of American Biography* (New York: James T. White & Co., 1938), vol. E, 1937–38, 196–97; *New York Times*, July 2, 1944; Bernheimer, *Rainbow Bridge*, 28–29. In addition to his book, Bernheimer's major published writings are "Encircling Navajo Mountain with a Pack-Train," *National Geographic* 43 (February 1923): 197–224, and "Cave Treasures of the Lukaichukais," *Touring Topics* 23 (September 1931), unpaginated photographic supplement.

4. *The National Cyclopedia*, 196–97; *New York Times*, October 13, 1932; Charles L. Bernheimer Field Notes (hereafter referred to as CLB Field Notes), May 19, 1920; July 4, 1921, originals in American Museum of Natural History, New York City, copies at Utah State Historical Society.

5. Bernheimer, *Rainbow Bridge*, 14, 30–32.

6. Bernheimer's negatives and albums of photographic prints are in the American Museum of Natural History, New York City; duplicate albums are at the Utah State Historical Society; Cohen, *They Builded Better*, 150; Bernheimer, *Rainbow Bridge*, 180–82.

7. Bernheimer, *Rainbow Bridge*, 101; see the photograph opposite p. 52, which shows Bernheimer in a necktie at Inscription House; CLB Field Notes, June 28, 1919.

8. Florence C. and Robert H. Lister, *Earl Morris & Southwestern Archaeology* (Al-

buquerque: University of New Mexico Press, 1968), 106–9; Bernheimer, *Rainbow Bridge*, 36, 112; Cohen, *They Builded Better*, 150.

9. Clarence Rogers Oral History interview, January 8, 1974, Utah State Historical Society, 17; oral communications with Richard W. Sprang, Dudy Thomas's husband.

10. CLB Field Notes, July 9, 1921.

11. Rainbow Bridge Register, copy in Otis R. "Dock" Marston Papers, the Huntington Library.

12. Bernheimer, *Rainbow Bridge*, xi; there are similar references in the CLB Field Notes, e.g., July 1, 1921; Bernheimer to John Wetherill, September 10, 1936, copy in Marston Papers, the Huntington Library.

13. Bernheimer, *Rainbow Bridge*, 17–18.

14. Ibid., 13.

15. Unless otherwise attributed, the Johnson biographical material given here comes from "Zeke: A Story of Mountain and Desert," anonymous MS in Special Collections, Marriott Library, University of Utah.

16. Karl Young, "Wild Cows of the San Juan," *Utah Historical Quarterly* 32 (Summer 1964): 252, 254, 262–63.

17. Utah Writers Project, *Utah: A Guide to the State* (New York: Hastings House, 1941), 501–7; Charles Kelly and Charlotte Martin, "Zeke Johnson's Natural Bridges," *Desert Magazine* (November 1947): 12–15.

18. CLB Field Notes, May 22, 1920.

19. Ibid., June 1, 1929.

20. Unless otherwise cited, the following material on Morris is based on Lister and Lister, *Earl Morris and Southwestern Archaeology*.

21. CLB Field Notes, July 15, 1921.

22. Ibid., June 19, 1924.

23. Bernheimer, *Rainbow Bridge*, 63.

24. Earl H. Morris, "An Unexplored Area of the Southwest," *Natural History* 22 (November-December 1922): 508.

25. Bernheimer, *Rainbow Bridge*, 65.

26. Ibid., 66. Bernheimer failed to notice the names of G. Emerson, J. P. Miller, and M. S. Foote inscribed in the cliff. It is likely that these men had come into the canyon from Navajo Mountain in the early 1800s in search of the rumored Mitchell-Merrick silver mine.

27. CLB Field Notes, May 22, 1920.

28. Bernheimer, *Rainbow Bridge*, 65–66.

29. Ibid., 66.

30. CLB Field Notes, July 8, 1921.

31. Morris, "An Unexplored Area," 508–9.

32. Bernheimer, *Rainbow Bridge*, 70.

33. Morris, "An Unexplored Area," 509–10.

34. CLB Field Notes, July 9, 1921.

35. Morris, "An Unexplored Area," 512.

36. CLB Field Notes, July 1, 1922.

37. Ibid., June 29, 1922. The somewhat inaccurate 1892 Geological Survey "Marsh Pass" topographical map shows a trail in the general vicinity, but the field records of the surveyors, Arthur P. Davis and H. M. Wilson, apparently have been lost or destroyed. It is possible that they, or members of their crews, utilized the trail during their 1883–84 field work.

38. Bernheimer, "Encircling Navajo Mountain with a Pack Train," 213.

39. CLB Field Notes, June 30, 1922.

40. Rainbow Bridge Register, copy in Marston Papers, the Huntington Library. The possibility of pre-1909 sightings of Rainbow Bridge is one of the most vexed questions of Utah historiography, and the present essay can only note that some of the supposed early visitors claim to have reached the arch by means of what later became known as the Bernheimer Trail through Redbud Pass. James W. Black, for example, recorded a notarized statement on September 27, 1930, that in January 1892 he was prospecting in the Navajo Mountain area and "crossed over the mountain into a large canyon now known as Cliff Canyon, and through a pass now called Red Bud Pass [*sic*]." An Indian trader, William Franklyn Williams, made the improbable claim that he and two others "had no trouble taking their horses through what is now known as Redbud Pass" to a sighting of Rainbow Bridge in 1884. Weldon F. Heald,

"Who Discovered Rainbow Bridge?" *Sierra Club Bulletin* 40 (October 1955): 24–28.

41. John Stewart MacClary, "Trail-Blazer to Rainbow Bridge," *Desert Magazine* (June, 1938): 34.

42. Earl H. Morris Field Notes, July 2, 1922, University of Colorado.

43. CLB Field Notes, July 4, 1922.

44. Earl H. Morris Field Notes, July 5, 1922.

45. CLB Field Notes, July 8, 1922.

46. Ibid., July 14, 1922.

47. Ibid., June 17, 1924.

48. The first recorded ascent of Cummings Mesa was made by Byron Cummings and John Wetherill in 1919. Lyndon Lane Hargrave, *Report on Archaeological Reconnaissance in the Rainbow Plateau Area of Northern Arizona and Southern Utah* (Berkeley: University of California Press, 1935), 14; Bernheimer, *Rainbow Bridge*, 178.

49. CLB Field Notes, May 21–22, 27, 1927.

50. Ibid., May 21 and 31, 1927.

51. Ibid., May 25, 1927.

52. Ibid., June 8, 1927.

53. Bernheimer to Wetherill, September 10, 1936, Otis Marston Papers, the Huntington Library.

Charles Kelly's Glen Canyon

Ventures and Adventures

He was born with a chip on his shoulder. Quick to take offense, slow to forgive, arrogant, self-righteous, Charles Kelly (1889–1971) was a walking argument, a fight waiting for a place to happen. His photographs reveal a man small in stature but compensatingly pugnacious, often with a week's growth of beard and a defiant cigar jutting from his mouth. Savagely antireligious, he lived squarely in the midst of Mormon country and dared the Mormons to do something about it. As one of the founding fathers of the Utah Ku Klux Klan in the 1920s, Kelly hated even when there was nothing to hate and confided to his diary that he hoped it would be good for business.[1]

And yet there was good in the man, too. He made friends as fiercely as he made enemies, and though he lost some of them through real or imagined affronts, he remained loyal to most. As a historian, he was a bloodhound on a trail, and if he occasionally followed a false scent, he more often treed his prey. And he followed his quarry into some of the most remote country Utah had to offer: He took the first automobile across the Salt Lake Desert on the Donner trail, and floated Glen Canyon several times in the years when it was known only to a few gold miners, explorers, and Indian traders. If he later applauded the flooding of Glen Canyon and rushed into print with the suggestion that the reservoir be named Lake Escalante, he was a formidable defender and student of the backcountry. As the first custodian of Capitol Reef National Monument, he compiled an immense body of interpretive information that fifty years later still serves rangers and visitors alike, and resigned bitterly in the face of excessive park service bureaucratization.

The first great hate of Kelly's life was his father, a preacher in the mode of Elmer Gantry. Although Kelly danced on his father's grave, he ought to have recalled that he learned two valuable skills during his forced service to his father's profession: music and printing. Always employable through one or the other, Kelly was never without a job, even in the worst of the Great Depression. Following service in World War I, Kelly settled in Utah with his bride, Harriette Greener. The marriage and the place of residence lasted the rest of his life. His interest in history came later, as a result of an idle curiosity about the Donner emigrants, but it stuck just as deeply, and resulted in a torrent of books and articles, both scholarly and popular, on a variety of subjects including trails, mountain men, Mormons, outlaws, and the deserts and canyons of the Colorado Plateau, all characterized by exhaustive library research, as well as interviews and field investigations.[2]

It is not clear just how and when Kelly became interested in Glen Canyon, but it matters little, since Kelly's omnivorous curiosity led him everywhere, and Glen Canyon, one of the earth's most endlessly enchanting places, worked its irresistible spell upon many. It is certain that the people with whom he would share his first river trip in 1932 came into his circle of friends through publication of his *Salt Desert Trails* (1929). The first of those was Hoffman Birney, a prolific writer on western themes then living in Tucson and working on an article about the Mormons. One of his latest books was *Roads to Roam*, an entertaining account of an automotive odyssey through seven western states during the summer of 1928. Birney shared Kelly's love of the backcountry and its history, his lack of religion and general irreverence for cultural sacred cows, and his racism. The two took to each other naturally, and began a collaboration on a book about the Mormon avenger Porter Rockwell, which appeared in 1934 under the title *Holy Murder*. The Kelly-Birney friendship cooled after Birney stole an idea Kelly suggested for a book about the Donners and published it on his own. But in 1932, their friendship was at high tide. "My acquaintance with Birney last summer, which continues by correspondence," Kelly wrote, "was one of the highlights of the year. He is a real guy." He further noted that they were talking about a trip on the Green River, though Kelly also wanted to run the Dirty Devil.[3]

That their plans shifted to Glen Canyon was a result of Kelly's meeting with Dr. Julian H. Steward, then professor of anthropology at the University of Utah. Steward (1902–1972) was one of Utah's first professionally trained anthropologists and a creator of the department at the university. Trained during the 1920s at the University of California at Berkeley under Alfred L. Kroeber, Robert H. Lowie, and the eccentric Jaime d'Angulo, Steward developed "a broad orientation to the holistic aspects of anthropology, a concern for seeing mankind from the biological, cultural, historical, and linguistic viewpoints," and became, during his later career at Columbia and the University of Illinois, one of the important theorists in the profession. During his brief tenure at the University of Utah (1930–1933), he accomplished some important studies in the Great Basin area, through which he met Kelly, and made two expeditions into southern Utah, one into the Paria and Johnson Canyons, and the other through Glen Canyon with Kelly and Birney. In fact, the archaeological promise of Glen Canyon and Steward's offer of university funding for the trip led Kelly and Birney to change their river trip plans.[4]

The party as finally constituted included, in addition to those three, Byron O. "Barney" Hughes, whom Kelly identifies as "some kind of assistant flunkey" whom Steward had taken under his wing during a previous teaching job at the University of Michigan, and John "Jack" Shoemaker, a son of Birney's Philadelphia publisher. Personal conflicts developed almost immediately. "When final arrangements were being made for the trip Steward acted so flighty that Birney took a great dislike to him," Kelly noted. That dislike was hardly mitigated when, at Torrey, Steward claimed that there had been a misunderstanding and that he expected everyone to pay their own expenses. Birney lost his temper and expressed the intention of leaving the party, but later decided thirty dollars was a cheap enough fee for three weeks in Glen Canyon even if he had to pay it himself, and stayed. The damage was done, though, because, according to Kelly, the incident "caused a breach in the expedition, Birney taking every opportunity to rub it into Steward for the rest of the trip."[5] As things worked out, he would have plenty of opportunities.

Getting from Hanksville to Hite in 1932 was inevitably an adventure. The Kelly party built roads and pushed the two cars and boat trailer over rough places until they reached the Wolgamott ranch, where they hired a wagon and some horses for the worst stretch of the journey, the roadless route down the floor of North Wash to the river. Another adventure awaited them at the mouth of North Wash, where an old prospector, John Young, had somehow heard of their impending arrival, and awaited their assistance in ferrying a stranded partner, Harry Correll, from the other bank of the river. Correll and another friend, Sam Gates, had wrecked a raft trying to cross the river. Gates had fallen into the water and drowned, and Correll had been marooned on the other side for nine days without food. Steward and Hughes ferried the dazed and starving man back to the right bank, fed him, and witnessed a recovery so remarkable that the following day he was ready to take up mining again.[6]

After spending a day in camp to get the boats ready and to hike up to the mouth of the Dirty Devil River, the party embarked on July 6. None were experienced boatmen. Their two boats, the *Dirty Devil* and the *Bright Angel*, were folding canvas craft borrowed from David Dexter Rust, an old riverman and guide from whom they also received their only information on what awaited them, beyond a set of 1921 USGS river maps Birney had gotten from their author, Col. Clarence H. Birdseye, in Washington, D.C. At least they looked the part, as they banned razors by mutual agreement, and all soon took on the scruffy appearance characteristic of Kelly's style in the outdoors. Birney, appraising the party's appearance on July 7, observed that "Kelly, Steward, and I, being darker, are the most savage looking, with little to choose between us. Steward, cavorting naked on a sandbar, looks like *Homo neanderthalis*."[7]

The neophyte rivermen ran their first rapids, a little riffle at the mouth of North Wash, with no trouble: "The 'rapid' didn't even joggle the boat," Birney reported. If that experience fed their confidence, Trachyte Rapid, a half mile below their camp at White Canyon, destroyed it the following evening as they unaccountably attempted to run it in the dark. Few experienced boatmen would have regarded Trachyte as a significant obstacle, but it nearly upset both of their boats in a comic display of miscommunication, misunderstanding of the river channel, and poor vision in the darkness. Unaware that Birney was at the oars of the other boat, Steward and Hughes had managed to land above the rapid. They ran it in the dark, hoping to rescue swimmers after what they presumed would be a capsize. All wound up safe, though separated, and the mutual accusations made tempers rise. "Steward and Barney swear the waves were six feet high," Birney jibed. "They were probably all of twenty inches." Kelly wrote, "Everybody was mad, Birney pulled out his bottle of Rainbow Bridge wine, and we killed it." (This was a bottle purchased to celebrate their arrival at the famous arch. Half of it already had been consumed after the rough day building road south of Hanksville.)[8]

And so they continued down the river. "To those who have passed through the perils of Cataract Canon and the real rapids there, the tiny riffles of Glen Canon would be a joke," Birney thought. "To us— utterly inexperienced watermen—the rapids of Glen Canon seem quite serious. We stop and study them all." Unfortunately, their study seems to have produced little understanding, for they still ran everything the wrong way. At their first camp below Hall's Crossing, they got separated when they disagreed upon a landing site and spent the night apart. Much more serious, though, was a near disaster at the mouth of the Escalante River, which, swollen by sudden rain storms, was creating tricky waves and a large eddy below its mouth. Hughes broke an oar, but Shoemaker plied a paddle and got the first boat across. Birney had a rougher time, getting caught in the eddy, shipping buckets of water, and in spite of portaging what seemed to be the worst of the rapids, found he was still in jeopardy of a series of sandwaves.[9]

The combination of hazards proved to be too much for poor Steward, who simply lost his nerve. Birney and Kelly preyed upon his weakness, as reported in Birney's diary:

> Steward, incidentally, has gone yellow. The river has his goat. The high water at the Escalante, plus the little experience with the sandwaves, seems to have him buffaloed. He was awake until after three last night, pacing up and down the beach, planting sticks at the water's edge so he could gauge the rise or fall of the Colorado, and otherwise indulging in a lot of useless worry. I entertain him with tales of San Juan floods, their suddenness and terrific violence, which Kelly seconds most admirably.

Later, he says that he and Kelly rocked the boat in rapids to try to scare Steward, whom he describes as being "like a hen on a hot griddle." In fact, according to Kelly, personal relations within the group had almost completely deteriorated by that time:

> Birney was aggravating and unnecessarily bossy, making trouble over trivial incidents. Steward and Hughes were flighty, kept to

themselves, and acted like two old maid morphadites. In place of intelligent conversations around camp in the evenings, all but Shoemaker and myself spent the time singing and composing filthy limericks. . . . The scenery was marvelous and the whole journey intensely interesting to me, but would much rather have made it in different company.

To Birney the whole thing remained a big joke even years later. During a 1937 visit to Washington, D.C., Birney learned that Steward was in the same city and tried to contact him, evidently with the main purpose of teasing the unfortunate man even more about the river trip. "We called him twice," Birney reported to Kelly, "but he wasn't in his office and they didn't know where he was hiding — so that's that. I'd have liked to shouted 'Horsecock' or 'Sandwaves, Barney' in his ear."[10]

Granted, then, that the trip in human terms was a miserable failure, was it of any scientific value? Birney and Kelly, predictably, gave Steward low marks as an archaeologist. Kelly, whose archaeological acumen was limited to pothunting, thought Steward lazy for the deliberate pace at which he worked. Be that as it may, Steward's published report gives detailed data on twenty-eight sites that he excavated in an attempt "to discover the place and manner in which those culture elements which had been chronologically differentiated in the San Juan area had become blended into a single culture and spread northward into the Northern Periphery [of the Anasazi area]." His conclusion was that Glen Canyon was not that place; rather it was "a kind of no-man's land which had been very slightly settled by outposts from both Mesa Verde and Kayenta and which had come into contact with the Northern Periphery but had not strongly influenced it."[11] This, one would submit, was a considerable accomplishment for a scant twenty-three days in the canyon, many of which were archaeologically barren.

While Kelly and Birney were also interested in archaeology (though without any serious knowledge of the field), their main stated purpose in making the trip was to investigate sites of historical interest. They found many: inscriptions, cabins, trails, and mining remains. Of greatest interest to them, however, was the point at which it was then supposed that the Franciscan Fathers Dominguez and Escalante had crossed the river on November 7, 1776, on their return to Santa Fe after exploring much of Colorado and Utah. Kelly was aware also of the Mormon pioneer Jacob Hamblin's crossings at Kane Creek, and noted that it was understood that the two crossings were one and the same, a realization reached at about the same time by Dr. Russell G. Frazier, a Bingham Canyon physician who became a well-known river runner and Antarctic explorer.

After study of Escalante's diary, Kelly became convinced that the Crossing of the Fathers could not have been at Kane Creek, though he found nowhere else on the 1932 trip that met the description. Frazier visited the locale in 1933 and agreed with Kelly. There the matter stood for four years, until Frazier met a young prospector named Byron Davies, who reported having seen another set of steps cut into the rock about a mile below the previously known crossing. Frazier suspected that the steps were those cut by Escalante. Accompanied by Davies and Kelly, Frazier took a motorboat up from Lee's Ferry in August 1937 and determined that Davies's steps were very old but that they also did not exactly meet the padre's description. He returned in October with a pack train from Cannonville and succeeded in getting the animals all the way to the river via Davies's steps. On that occasion he found yet others that Davies had not previously noted. It was this last set of steps, at what he named Padre Creek, that best matched Escalante's diary. In a *Desert Magazine* article written by Kelly but appearing under Frazier's name, Frazier speculated that the first set of steps discovered by Davies were also Spanish in origin, but later, perhaps around 1800.[12]

Kelly was on the river again in 1938, this time as part of an expedition led and financed by Julius F. Stone (1885–1947). It was not the first money Stone had sunk in Glen Canyon. He had been a leading financier of the ill-fated Hoskaninni Mining Company promoted by engineer Robert Brewster Stanton during the years 1897–1902. Stanton had located contiguous mining claims throughout the whole of Glen Canyon, gambling a great deal of his investors' money that he could extract the powdery gold from the river sands. He proved to be unable to deliver on his promise, and his immense wrecked dredge remained visible in the river just above Bullfrog Creek until the flooding of the canyon, a silent reminder of the elusiveness of Glen Canyon wealth.[13]

Stone lost a lot of money on the venture, but the river was in his blood. In 1909 he led and financed a trip down the entire river, guided by the celebrated riverman Nathaniel Galloway, and devoted to photographic documentation of the geological theories of Clarence Edward Dutton. Now, late in life, Stone was interested in placing plaques at Separation Rapid in the lower Grand Canyon where the two Howland brothers and William Dunn had left the 1869 John Wesley Powell party, and at Frazier's Padre Creek crossing in Glen Canyon. On the latter trip, Stone also wished to investigate the 1642 and 1837 inscriptions near Lake Canyon.[14]

The Glen Canyon trip took place during late September and early October 1938. In addition to Stone, Kelly, and Frazier, the personnel included Stone's son George, their Ohio friend William Chryst, boatman Frank Swain (a river partner of Frazier's), and Dr. A. L. Inglesby, a dentist-turned-rockhound who had become a considerable expert on the backcountry of southern Utah. Stone was eighty-three years old at the time, and Inglesby insisted upon making him comfortable by installing an easy chair in his boat. The party carried the flag of the Explorers Club, of which both Stone and Frazier were members. Two of the three tin boats were named *Amos* and *Buzz* after Amos Burg and Haldane "Buzz" Holmstrom, who were at that very time making their historic voyage down the river (Burg was using the first inflatable boat on the Colorado, and Holmstrom would become the first man to run every rapid on a single trip). As Holmstrom's financial backer on the 1938 trip, Stone had a special interest in its success, and Holmstrom had acknowledged that assistance by naming his boat, in return, the *Julius F.*[15]

In order to give him, as Stone titled an article about the trip, "Another Fling at Colorado River Rapids," Swain first turned the boats upstream from North Wash on September 24, motoring up through Narrow Canyon, then the lower reaches of Cataract Canyon in an attempt to top the mighty Dark Canyon Rapid, which the 1909 party had elected not to run. Even with only Stone in the bow and Swain in the stern, the underpowered craft was unable to prevail against the current. With the throttle wide open, the boat remained motionless in the river, spray breaking over the happy old man for a few minutes until Swain recognized the futility of the venture and turned downstream. The party spent the night below the rapids, and one may well imagine that the sound of booming water in his ears all night brought Stone dreams of remembered rides through rapids in years gone by.[16]

The drama done, oar power became the order of the day as the boats drifted back down the river and entered Glen Canyon. Memories rushed in anew as the boats passed Ticaboo, where Stone had met Cass Hite in 1896 and again in 1909, and Stone related the story of how the old miner had given him his only thermometer to replace Stone's broken one and to enable him to continue recording temperatures during the rest of the trip. On September 28 they drifted past Camp Stone, Stanton's headquarters during the mining venture and, in a now famous episode, they stopped at the wreck of the old dredge and built a fire from some of its boards to make coffee. Stone quipped that he calculated that pot of coffee cost him $5,000.[17]

Frazier and Kelly stopped at Lake Canyon to look for a reported 1534 inscription, but found instead the 1642 date, which Stone surmised "may and probably does have some historical significance if it can be identified and properly interpreted." Less mysterious were the inscriptions of the 1871 Powell expedition in Music Temple, which the Stone party then varnished over to protect them from further deterioration. Finally they arrived at their major goal, Padre Creek, where Frazier had identified the Escalante steps, and Swain, working from a precarious footing on his boat, drilled the holes and affixed Stone's plaque at the mouth of the canyon.[18]

They arrived at Lee's Ferry two days before their transportation to Salt Lake City was due. To their surprise and delight, they discovered that their history-laden trip offered yet another experience when they learned that the remains of Powell's boat, the *Nellie Powell*, was rotting in the earth at Leo Weaver's ranch, where they were camped. What they found was a few charred fragments left from a brushfire, but they were still identifiable from the stout construction and blue paint as Powell's boat. "This midnight discovery of an old boat used by the first men ever to pass down the great river seemed a fitting climax to our journey," Kelly wrote.[19]

Successful as the 1938 trip was, Kelly and Frazier were unsatisfied that they had located all the Spanish inscriptions in Glen Canyon. In fact, they had virtually no evidence of any such inscriptions at all, for a supposed Escalante inscription near Padre Creek had turned out to be meaningless erosional markings, and the reported 1534 inscription at Lake Canyon was nonexistent. All they had for their searches was the 1642 inscription, which they were unable to corroborate as genuine nor to connect with any known person. Both men seem to have fallen under the romantic thrall of the area's popular legends of lost Spanish mines and trails, legends that have run far in advance of the meager solid evidence.

At any rate, they set out again in the spring of 1942 on what was to be the last river trip for both men, in search of Spanish inscriptions. Their partner on this trip was Willis D. Johnson, whose first river experience had come in 1938, when he had been selected from several applicants at Green River, Utah, to complete the voyage with Burg and Holmstrom as a general camp roustabout. Since that time, he had made other trips separately with both Burg and Holmstrom, and had gathered considerable river knowledge, both through his own experience and from watching his partners, two of the most skilled boatmen of their day. Little of that skill, unfortunately, was in evidence on the 1942 trip, which turned out to be a genuine adventure.

Actually, skill was hardly a factor at all, since any skill the three may have possessed was negated by the unsuitability of their boats. Perhaps Kelly and Johnson had been seduced during previous trips into thinking that Glen Canyon's mild rapids offered no serious challenge, and that any type of boat could make the journey. Kelly, of course, should have known better from his 1932 experience, but Johnson and Frazier had only been through the canyon with skilled boatmen and superb equipment, and probably underrated the hazards. Their boats, at any rate, were ludicrously inadequate. Frazier's sixteen-foot rubber kayak was the only one that stood much of a chance of making the trip, and in fact he was the only one who escaped serious trouble. The others were far too small: Kelly had a six-foot inflatable boat, and Johnson an eight-foot one. Frazier and Johnson propelled their boats with paddles, but Johnson switched to oars almost immediately when he careened out of control in Trachyte Rapid. Even at that, the oars he and Kelly used were so short they offered little leverage, and were attached to the boats only by means of hard rubber oarlocks, glued to the tubes and inadequate to sustain hard rowing. To complete the problem, the boats were too small to carry all the gear and supplies they needed for the trip; they had to abandon some of their outfit at Hite and even then loaded the boats far too high for stability. They were floating accidents, and the old riverman Arthur Chaffin, examining their outfits at Hite, told them he thought they were crazy.[20]

The first few days, however, were uneventful. Ticaboo Rapid was "all covered and smooth" in the high water, and Kelly estimated that they were being pulled along at about eight miles per hour—fast current on any river. They noted a great deal of mining activity, and stopped at Smith Fork where Johnson showed them the big petroglyph panel. It was one of the most impressive panels in the whole canyon country, well known on the river, and one wonders that they had not found it before. On their second day out (April 12), they landed at Moki Canyon, their first major stop, where they intended to explore a supposedly untouched ruin that Johnson had noticed in 1938. The climb to the ruin presented a real challenge. It was, by Kelly's estimate, nearly 500 feet above the canyon floor and required use of a series of "Moki steps"—footholds chiseled into the rock by the ancients and now eroded dangerously. Kelly and Johnson were admitted amateurs at rock climbing, and Frazier was probably not much better, though he had done some in the Antarctic. Equipped with only rubber-soled shoes (one of Frazier's soles came off during the climb), "a length of cotton sash cord" (probably not of a large enough diameter to permit an adequate handgrip), and a prospector's pick, they set off. Though the climb presented some tense moments, they negotiated it with no accidents—only to find a mysterious inscription, "W. W. Jones, 1922," on the cave wall beside the ruin. They had risked life and limb to no purpose.[21]

Drifting on down to Lake Canyon, they revisited the 1642 inscription and came to the decision that it was a hoax perpetrated by one C. Burt, whose name was just beneath the date and of the same apparent age and style. So vanished their last illusion of Spanish romance. Other stops produced more solid historic interest, as they took advantage of the rapid progress made possible by the fast water to stop more often than on previous trips and to explore more extensively. They explored some ruins, visited Dr. W. H. Schock's mining cabin, and climbed to the top of Hole-in-the-Rock, where they found some artifacts associated with the 1879–80 Mormon emigrant party and noted the new automobile road that had been built in 1941.[22]

The trouble began just below the mouth of the San Juan River, as the additional silt began to produce sandwaves. Johnson missed the first series, but Frazier and Kelly got into the midst of them, and Kelly shipped water in waves that, as he said, seemed to be ten feet high. More sandwaves and minor rapids gave them trouble; Kelly had difficulty landing at Aztec (Forbidding) Creek for the hike to

Rainbow Bridge and shipped water again. The big trouble was yet to come, though, and the terse prose of Kelly's diary tells the story well:

> Two miles above Wild Horse Bar ran into combination of rapid and sand waves. Tried to pull to left bank, but got sucked in. Doc was ahead, got into worst of it, but was able to pull through. Willis followed, was turned over by a big sand wave. Went under, but hung on to the boat. I tried to pull down to him, but no chance. Then I got dumped out, but boat stayed right side up. Crawled back in and tried to ride the waves, but got sucked into whirlpool on right bank. Went back upstream with the back eddy and tried to pull into rapid again, but was thrown out at same place. Fought it for half an hour, bouncing like a cork, but couldn't get anywhere. Finally grabbed a rock and landed, then had hell of a time to pull boat along shore. Pulled it down to big flat rock and over into quiet water below. Couldn't see anything of Doc or Johnson. They couldn't get back to me. Willis swam ashore with boat, badly winded. Doc picked up two cans of food and landed, waited for me. When I got out we landed on bar below and built a fire to dry out. Had lunch. My pack partly wet. Bedding dry. Willis' stuff all wet. Both of us were pooped.[23]

It was, fortunately, the last major trouble, though they put in another wet day and had to row for their lives in another set of sandwaves. The gusto of rapids-running, if Kelly had ever felt it, was now gone: "Came on down," he noted, "taking all the inside curves" (thus avoiding the main current, which follows the outside of river bends, and also bypassing the sandwaves that would develop there). With this heightened caution, the trio made it the rest of the way to Lee's Ferry, but it is difficult to quarrel with Kelly's own assessment of the cause of their trouble: "Our little rubber rafts were much too small for the kind of water we found on this voyage."[24]

Kelly's last involvement with Glen Canyon occurred after the "discovery" of Gregory Natural Bridge in a tributary of the Escalante River by the Norman Nevills expedition of 1940. Although previously known to Garfield County cattlemen and visited by W. R. Chenoweth of the 1921 USGS mapping party, the arch remained largely unknown to the general public until Nevills's enthusiastic publicizing of it.[25] Nevills hoped his sensational descriptions of the arch would help revive what was by then becoming the moribund proposal of Harold Ickes's expansionist Interior Department in the late 1930s to create an immense Escalante National Monument. The monument would embrace the entire Green-Colorado River system from Green River and Moab, Utah, to the Arizona border, including the San Juan River below Bluff and much of the rivers' backcountry environs.[26]

Kelly, a much more skilled writer and publicist than Nevills, added his pen to the crusade. In a February 1941 *Desert Magazine* article, Kelly offered his judgment that "this section contains more natural attractions than any other equal area in the West," and assured potential visitors that the two arduous "trails" to the Hite area—one down North Wash and the other down White Canyon— would soon be improved and joined by a ferry. The article went on to list and describe the area's more memorable attractions, mostly emphasizing those in Glen Canyon. "Even after roads have been built into this magnificent section, it will be generations before its hidden recesses have been fully explored," he concluded, "—and therein lies its fascination."[27]

This published effusion, however, masked a considerable personal distaste for further exploration of those "hidden recesses," at least by boat. Dick Sprang knew Kelly well in later years after Kelly had become superintendent of Capitol Reef National Monument (a much more modest reservation adjoining the proposed Escalante Monument) and both were living in Wayne County, Utah. Sprang tried on more than one occasion to draw Kelly into a comparative discussion of their Glen Canyon river trips, but Kelly declined. He was through with the river, and did not remember his experience on it fondly. Thus it is not surprising that Randall Henderson reported in *Desert Magazine*, on the eve of construction of the Glen Canyon dam, that Kelly was one of the project's enthusiastic supporters: "Kelly is looking ahead to the day when a great new reservoir will be formed behind the proposed Glen Canyon dam in the Colorado River. He would name it Lake Escalante. . . ."[28]

The Kelly river trips, then, like most human endeavors, were a mixed success. Kelly's own personality was such that it took a particular type of companion to get along with him. Dr. Frazier was that type—"He is a good guy, and has helped me much," Kelly wrote, "besides being damn good company on desert trips"—as Steward and Birney, who were immensely capable people in their own ways, were not.[29] Group compatibility, though, seems to have been related to the scientific results of his trips only in a negative ratio, for the conflict-ridden 1932 trip was also the one that produced the most and best findings. Kelly's personality, too, prevented him in some way from achieving compatibility with the river itself, from feeling its rhythms and meeting its imperatives, as all great boatmen, indeed outdoorsmen, come to understand their environment. Nevertheless, something kept drawing him back to the river, and the body of archaeological and historical knowledge he helped to build are an impressive monument to a man who left so little else.

NOTES

1. Kelly's diary and autobiography are in the papers of Charles Kelly at the University of Utah. See also Randall Henderson, "Kelly of Capitol Reef," *Desert Magazine* (November 1955): 4–6, Randall Henderson, "Just Between You and Me," *Desert Magazine* (August 1956): 42, and A. Russell Mortensen, "In Memoriam," *Utah Historical Quarterly* 39 (Spring 1971): 199–200. Kelly's Klan involvement is recounted in Larry R. Gerlach, *Blazing Crosses in Zion: The Ku Klux Klan in Utah* (Logan: Utah State University Press, 1982), 28–31.

2. Mortensen, "In Memoriam"; Kelly diary, August 20, 1936. A full bibliography of Kelly's publications by Howard Foulger is in the papers of Charles Kelly at the Utah State Historical Society.

3. Kelly, *Salt Desert Trails* (Salt Lake City: Western Printing Co., 1929); Birney, *Roads to Roam* (Philadelphia: Penn Publishing Co., 1930); Kelly and Birney, *Holy Murder* (New York: G. P. Putnam's Sons, 1934); Kelly diary, February 3, 1931, January 4, 1932. On Birney's career, see *New York Times*, June 4, 1958, and *Who Was Who in America*.

4. Robert F. Murphy, "Introduction: The Anthropological Theories of Julian H. Steward," in Jane C. Steward and Robert F. Murphy, eds., *Evolution and Ecology: Essays on Social Transformation by Julian H. Steward* (Urbana: University of Illinois Press, 1977), 1–16; Steward, *Archaeological Reconnaissance of Southern Utah* (Washington, D.C.: Government Printing Office, 1941).

5. In addition to Kelly's main diary entry of July 31, 1932, which summarizes the river trip, he kept a separate diary during the trip, and it is also in the Kelly Papers at the University of Utah. A copy of Birney's 1932 river diary is also in the Kelly collection at the University of Utah. All passages quoted here are from those three diaries.

6. Both Kelly and Birney record the rescue of Correll in their diaries, and Kelly wrote an article about it, "Gold Hunters Are Like That!," *Desert Magazine* (July 1942): 13–15.

7. Birney diary, July 7, 1932.

8. Ibid., July 6 and 8, 1932; Kelly river diary, July 7, 1932.

9. Birney diary, July 8 and 13, 1932; Kelly river diary, July 13, 1932. Experiences like these belie Kelly's claim in his article about the trip, "Down the Colorado," *Utah Motorist* (August 1932): 5–8, that "The entire trip was made without accident of any kind."

10. Birney diary, July 15, 1932; main Kelly diary, July 13, 1932. Birney to Kelly, May 17, 1937, Kelly Papers, Utah State Historical Society.

11. Main Kelly diary, July 31, 1932; Steward, *Archaeological Reconnaissance*, 281–82; 329; 354–56.

12. The Frazier Papers are at the Utah State Historical Society. Dr. Russell G. Frazier, "El Vado de los Padres," *Desert Magazine* (July 1940): 3–5. Kelly's authorship of the article is claimed in his diary, December 11, 1939. Although the Frazier party correctly identified the Escalante steps, it was not an original discovery. Otis Marston, "River Runners: Fast Water Navigation," *Utah Historical Quarterly* 28 (July 1960): 307, proves that David Dexter Rust knew where and what they were at least as early as 1926.

13. The story of the Hoskaninni Mining Company is told by Stanton himself in *The Hoskaninni Papers: Mining in Glen Canyon, 1897–1902*, University of Utah Anthropological Paper No. 54, C. Gregory Crampton and Dwight L. Smith, eds. (Salt Lake City: University of Utah Press, 1961).

14. A full account of Stone's 1909 trip is in his book, *Canyon Country: The Romance of a Drop of Water and a Grain of Sand* (New York: G. P. Putnam's Sons, 1932). Much of the story of the Separation Rapid plaque installation is told in correspondence in the Frazier Papers, and of its later removal to higher ground above the advancing waters of Lake Mead, in the Harry L. Aleson Papers at the Utah State Historical Society. Stone's account of his 1938 Glen Canyon trip is "Another Fling at Colorado River Rapids," *Ohio State University Monthly* 30 (November 1938): 17–18. Stone not only paid for the entire trip, but he even refused a check from Kelly for a share in the payment for the latter's *Saturday Evening Post* article about it. See Stone to Frazier, January 7, 1938, and January 27, 1939, Frazier Papers; and Kelly diary, February 2, 1939.

15. Haldane "Buzz" Holmstrom Papers, Utah State Historical Society and the Burg and Holmstrom diaries at the Oregon Historical Society document the relationship with Julius Stone. The easy chair used on that trip by Stone is now at the Utah State Historical Society.

16. Stone, "Another Fling"; Charles Kelly, "At Eighty-three He is an Explorer," *Saturday Evening Post* (May 6, 1939): 20–21. Kelly also kept a laconic diary of the trip, which is in the Kelly Papers at the University of Utah.

17. Ibid.

18. Stone, "Another Fling," 18.

19. Kelly, "At Eighty-three He is an Explorer," 77.

20. Kelly river diary, April 10–11, 1942. Photographs of the equipment are in the Utah State Historical Society's general photograph collection and in two Kelly articles: "River Gold," *Desert Magazine* (October 1942): 15–17; and "Sand Waves," *Arizona Highways* (April 1944): 36–39.

21. Kelly, "We Climbed to the Moki Ruin," *Desert Magazine* (January 1943): 5–8.

22. Kelly river diary, April 14, 1942.

23. Ibid., April 17, 1942.

24. Ibid., April 18–19, 1942; Kelly, "Sand Waves," 39.

25. Jared Farmer, "Undiscovered to Undiscoverable: Gregory Natural Bridge," *Utah Historical Quarterly* 63 (Spring 1995): 107–9.

26. Norton Allen's map accompanying Kelly's "Proposed Escalante National Monument," *Desert Magazine* (February 1941): 20, shows the geographic extent of the monument. See also Elmo Richardson, "Federal Park Policy in Utah: The Escalante National Monument Controversy of 1935–40," *Utah Historical Quarterly* 33 (Spring 1965): 109–33.

27. Ibid., 22.

28. Randall Henderson, "Just Between You and Me," *Desert Magazine* (August 1957): 42. Dick Sprang conversations with Gary Topping.

29. Main Kelly diary, February 2, 1939.

The Lure of the Desert

Much of the final chapter of the history of the San Juan country was written by a different breed of explorer. This new explorer may not have possessed an interest in scientific aspects of the region, but if he did, it was an avocational interest. That it was avocational does not necessarily mean his science was sloppy or superficial; it merely means that it was adjunct to his main interest, which was recreation. And many of these new explorers had no scientific interest whatever. Possessed of leisure time and money to spend enjoying it, they responded enthusiastically to photographic essays on the canyon country in popular magazines and hired professional guides to show the country to them. Most of those recreationists are known to history only laconically, by their names recorded in visitors' registers at places like Rainbow Bridge or Kayenta, sometimes with brief enthusiastic comments. Others were highly articulate, describing their experiences on the trail and their reactions to the beauties and hardships of the region in articles and books that afford an intimate view of their motives and of the effects of the country upon them.

The literate recreationist began to appear in the San Juan country prior to World War I. Tourism in the West, including the canyon country, during those early years was largely for the wealthy who could afford the high railroad fares, and for the hardy who were willing to endure long hours in the saddle and to camp under very primitive conditions, because tourist accommodations were largely nonexistent.[1] The development of inexpensive and reliable automobiles after the war, and the Good Roads Movement during the 1920s, which promoted development of paved surfaces on which to drive them, democratized tourism. From that time until the terminal date of this study (and beyond!), western tourism grew immensely in popularity, with only temporary setbacks during the Great Depression and World War II.[2]

It was Rainbow Bridge that lured most of the early tourists to the San Juan country well into the 1930s, before the movie industry revealed the dramatic beauty of Monument Valley and Norman Nevills popularized river running. The first photographs of the bridge were made on the very day of discovery, August 14, 1909, and those and other images of the bridge lost no time in reaching the public through magazine articles. Soon tourists began making the arduous desert ride (and later the almost equally arduous automobile trip) to Kayenta, where they could engage the guide services of the bridge's discoverer himself, John Wetherill, who was perhaps the only white man able to find his way over the tortuous route to the bridge. The trip, which ordinarily lasted a little over a week, required significant horsemanship and the willingness to undertake the risk of accident or inclement weather, but the rewards were contact with the colorful Navajo and Paiute Indians, views of some of the world's most spectacular scenery including Rainbow Bridge, and a feeling of accomplishment at having negotiated one of the roughest trails in the West.

One of the earliest of the literate tourists to make the journey was Zane Grey, who engaged Hosteen John to take him there in April 1913. Grey at the time was only on the threshold of the literary fame that would make him a household word synonymous with western fiction and one of the wealthiest American writers.[3] Trained as a dentist at the University of Pennsylvania, Grey had abandoned his practice in New York City to devote himself to writing. His early efforts, a trilogy of historical novels based on his ancestors' experiences on the Ohio River frontier, were both literarily and financially unsuccessful. In 1907 he spent part of the summer in Arizona with C. J. "Buffalo" Jones, photographing Jones's adventures roping mountain lions on the Kaibab Plateau and gaining his first experiences with cowboys, Mormons, and the plateaus and canyons of the Southwest, which would furnish him with his most important literary material. In 1910 his first successful novel, *The Heritage of the Desert*, was published by Harper & Brothers. In 1912, after a fierce struggle between Grey and his publisher over the apparently anti-Mormon content of his next manuscript, Harper & Brothers finally agreed to publish *Riders of the Purple Sage*, which became the best-known and best-selling Western of all time.

Grey's meeting with John Wetherill at Kayenta in April 1913 began a complicated relationship that lasted until Grey's last visit in

1929. On the one hand, Grey was starstruck by the great frontiers-man, whom he saw as an embodiment of the virtues of hardy western living, and used him as a character in some of his novels like *The Rainbow Trail* and *Lost Pueblo*. On the other hand, although most of Grey's fame and wealth lay in the future, his arrogance was already beginning to emerge, and for all his admiration of John Wetherill, he treated him as a servant, addressing him as "Wetherill" and ordering him about.[4] For his part, Hosteen John ordinarily abided Grey's im-periousness silently, both because of his Quaker peaceableness and because his fledgling guide business needed the income. Neverthe-less, it is easy to read a considerable reluctance in Grey's statement that "after three trips to Marsh Pass and Kayenta with my old guide, Al Doyle of Flagstaff, I finally succeeded in getting Wetherill to take me to Nonnezoshe [Rainbow Bridge]."[5] And in private, Hosteen John was known to vent his frustration in a humorous parody of Grey, with huge six-guns and batwing chaps slapping about his thighs, that he acted out around the campfire for the amusement of other clients.[6]

The 1913 Grey party included Nasja Begay ("Nas Ta Bega" in Grey's writings) and Joe Lee, both of whom delighted Grey, the for-mer because of Grey's romanticized ideas of the American Indian and because of Nasja's membership in the original bridge discovery party, and the latter because he was a real-life Mormon, whom Grey also romanticized because of the Mormons' exotic social practices and skill in coping with the harsh desert. After giving Grey a tour of Monument Valley, Hosteen John turned up the Tsegi on what was becoming his standard tourist itinerary to Rainbow Bridge. The Tsegi afforded an opportunity to show his clients the immense cliff dwellings, a good campsite at Bubbling Spring, and easy access to the summit of Piute Mesa.

Grey was highly impressed by the vista from Piute Mesa (although he mistook Glen Canyon for the Grand Canyon, an error he re-peated in his novel about the area, *The Rainbow Trail*) and gloried in the precipitous descent into Piute Canyon. While crossing the slick Navajo sandstone domes between Cha and Bald Rock Canyons, which he would later dub "the glass mountains," one of the horses slipped and escaped destruction, according to Grey's account, only by Lee's great strength at the end of a lasso and Grey's assistance in boosting the horse to safety. It was, indeed, the stuff of romance.

The greatest romance, though, awaited him at the great bridge itself. As they camped beneath it that night, the moonlit span and the presence of the exotic Nasja Begay who seemed as primeval as the stone formation itself, moved Grey to some of his purplest prose:

> Dark, silent, statuesque, with inscrutable face uplifted, with all that was spiritual of the Indian suggested by a somber and tranquil knowledge of his place there, [Nasja Begay] represented to me that which a solitary figure of human life represents in a great painting. Nonnezoshe needed life, wild life, life of its millions of years—and here stood the dark and silent Indian.[7]

Extravagant as it seems to the jaded modern reader, it was prose such as that, some of which Grey used verbatim in his 1915 novel *The Rainbow Trail*, that lured innumerable other tourists to the bridge. Grey never lived to see the irony in the fact that his own descriptions of the Rainbow Bridge country would defeat his prophecy that the bridge

> was not for many eyes to see. The tourist, the leisurely traveler, the comfort-loving motorist would never behold it. Only by toil, sweat, endurance and pain could any man ever look at Nonnezoshe. It seemed well to realize that the great things of life had to be earned.[8]

Although Rainbow Bridge lured many famous visitors, certainly the most illustrious was Theodore Roosevelt, who went there in August 1913, the same year as Grey's visit. Roosevelt's postpresidential years were filled with frustration as he helplessly watched his hand-picked successor, William Howard Taft, betray the Progressive movement by an apparent shift toward conservatism. Roosevelt returned to politics in 1912, only to find himself denied the Republican presidential nomination, and when he formed his own party and ran anyway, he found that he only divided the Republican vote and ensured the election of the detested Democrat, Woodrow Wilson. Wilson's pacifist policies at the outbreak of World War I enraged the bellicose Roosevelt, and once the United States did enter the war, the hero of San Juan Hill was denied an army commission.

Always a man of action, Roosevelt alleviated some of his frustrations by extensive travel, to Africa, to the American Southwest, and to South America. A trip to the Kaibab Plateau, Rainbow Bridge, and the Hopi Mesas in 1913 formed the subject matter for three chapters in one of his last books, *A Book-Lover's Holidays in the Open* (1916). Accompanied by his sons Archie and Quentin and their cousin Nicholas, Roosevelt hunted mountain lions with "Uncle" Jim Owens, engaged John Wetherill to take them to Rainbow Bridge, then witnessed the celebrated Snake Dance of the Hopis.

Like Zane Grey before him, Roosevelt found that the larger-than-life canyon country inspired him to some larger-than-life prose, and the foreword to *A Book-Lover's Holidays* contains some ebullient passages that might even have made Grey blush. Always an advocate of what he called "the strenuous life," Roosevelt had spent most of his own years attempting to overcome his boyhood asthma, his frail physique, and his nearsightedness.[9] In the foreword, he paid extravagant tribute to those hardy outdoorsmen whose daily lives are filled with the risks, hardships, and adventures that sedentary urbanites like himself can only experience through books or on brief vacations such as the ones he was about to narrate. Roosevelt painted a lurid picture of the perils inherent in their lives:

> Wearing toil and hardship shall be his; thirst and famine he shall face, and burning fever. Death shall come to greet him with poison-fang or poison-arrow, in shape of charging beast or of scaly things that lurk in lake and river; it shall lie in wait for him among untrodden forests, in the swirl of wild waters, and in the blast of snow blizzard or thunder-shattered hurricane.[10]

The Roosevelt party, guided by John Wetherill and Nasja Begay, left Kayenta for Rainbow Bridge on August 10. The route followed was identical to that taken by the Grey party the previous spring, and Roosevelt's reactions to the various scenic views and perils along the trail were not dissimilar to those of Grey: "On we went, under the pitiless sun, through a contorted wilderness of scalped peaks and ranges, barren passes, and twisted valleys of sun-baked clay."[11] Rainbow Bridge itself Roosevelt found to be "surely one of the wonders of the world. It is a triumphal arch rather than a bridge, and spans the torrent bed in a majesty never shared by any arch ever reared by the mightiest conquerors among the nations of mankind."[12] Later, the portly Roosevelt floated on his back in a pool of water under the bridge and sat up late that night in firelit conversation (no word of approval was recorded for the action of his hated successor, William

Howard Taft, in creating Rainbow Bridge National Monument in 1910).

Upon returning to Kayenta, Roosevelt was apparently as impressed by Louisa Wetherill's knowledge of and work with the Navajos as he had been with the natural phenomenon of Rainbow Bridge. To his delight she transcribed and translated three Navajo prayers for him, and he offered an enthusiastic endorsement of her efforts in helping the Indians learn to function in white civilization and her intentions to establish a "half-way house" toward that end. Like the anthropologist Lewis H. Morgan, with whose *Ancient Society* Roosevelt was probably familiar, Roosevelt held an evolutionary view of the American Indian, who had passed from savagery to barbarism, but was still inferior to civilization as represented by the white man.[13] Roosevelt applauded the efforts of "traders of the right type" such as the Wetherills, who "have rendered genuine, and ill-appreciated, service" in assisting the Indian in his upward evolution, and whose "stores and houses are centres of civilizing influence."[14] He warned, however, that such evolution must proceed slowly and be guided by the kind of wisdom and knowledge exhibited by Louisa Wetherill.

During the 1920s the packtrain Grey and Roosevelt used gave way to the automobile, at least as a means of transportation to the remote trading posts where the more primitive conveyance could be arranged. Though often equipped with large balloon tires to negotiate the sandy wagon tracks, many early automobiles became mired as they attempted to reach Wetherill's or Goulding's. Nevertheless, the automobile tourists persevered, and by the end of the decade even drove to Navajo Mountain.

Among those early automobile tourists were two adventurous young Bostonians, Winifred Hawkridge Dixon and Katherine Thaxter ("Toby"), who in 1919 drove an eight-cylinder Cadillac touring car on an amazing cross-country odyssey that included Kayenta and a pack trip to Rainbow Bridge.[15] Published in 1924, Dixon's *Westward Hoboes: Ups and Downs of Frontier Motoring* is narrated in the hipsterish Jazz Age vernacular of the decade, and includes an account of one member of her party—the Golfer—who took a golf club and some balls to Rainbow Bridge and became the first to drive a golf ball over the famous structure. Beneath the stylish irreverence, though, one can find a sincere appreciation for the country and an attempt to experience it on its own terms. Dixon greatly admired the Wetherills of Kayenta and the civilized amenities of their remote home. "At the Wetherell's [*sic*]," she wrote, "we found homeliness, a bountiful table, and marvel of marvels, the bath-tub furthest from an express office in the States." By contrast, she continued, "a few miles further north, all traces of civilization drop out of sight, and you are living the Day after Creation."[16]

Camped at Betatakin, Dixon found herself, as it were, living in a real-life Western movie: "Sleep that night was more romantically staged than under ordinary circumstances. The cold, glacial tang of high altitude nipped us pleasantly. The cliffs shut us in, not forbiddingly but protectingly." Even more significantly, she discovered she was "finding herself," just as characters in Western movies are supposed to do. "We had a sense of courage toward life new to us all. The mere fact of our remoteness helped us shake off layers of other people's personality, which we had falsely regarded as our own and showed us new selves undreamed of." At Rainbow Bridge, even the irreverence of the golf episode could not erode the enchantment of the place as the moon crept high in the night sky over the bridge. "It was not surprising that the Navajos held this spot in superstitious reverence, as the haunt of gods," she mused. "We were all, I think, in a state of suspended attention, waiting for something to happen which never did happen." The moon rose, and "when I waked Toby to watch it, we lay there, almost holding our breath, until the shadow had made its arc down the side of the cliff and disappeared."[17]

Back at Kayenta, after baths, a luxurious meal with linen tablecloth and napkins, and shopping in the store, the guests were treated to a serenade by a group of young Navajos. Sitting on wool sacks, the wide-eyed New Englanders witnessed by lantern light a primordial ritual they never forgot. "They started with a mild song of hunting or love, but soon they were singing war songs. Our blood stirred to an echo of something we knew many lives ago. The lantern light made a wilder, wider arc; the shouts became more fierce; the group swayed faster and swung into a wide ellipse. . . . The blackness, the orange hills, the swinging light, the shouts, the listening stillness of the desert,—that will always be Kayenta for me."[18]

Another example of the literate tourist who made the transition from pack train to automobile during the 1920s was Clyde Kluckhohn, who later became the great anthropologist of the Navajos. In two little-known but memorable books, *To the Foot of the Rainbow*

(1927) and *Beyond the Rainbow* (1933), Kluckhohn's warm prose and self-deprecating humor told the story of several footloose college summers during which he wandered about the Navajo country, eventually reaching the Grand Canyon, Rainbow Bridge, and even once crossing the formidable San Juan and Colorado Rivers to reach the Kaiparowits Plateau.[19]

Kluckhohn's adventures began in the summer of 1923 when, on vacation as a Princeton undergraduate, he made a remarkable horseback journey from Ramah, New Mexico, through the New Mexico pueblos and north to Mesa Verde, then west to Kayenta, Rainbow Bridge, and all the way to the Grand Canyon before turning back to Ramah. Although he began alone, he soon joined forces with a jaded New Yorker named Roy "Andy" Anderson, who was also on a lone horseback trip fleeing for a time the pressures of eastern big-city life. As the pair limped on their low-budget way across the desert, trading one exhausted horse at a time for other mounts usually little better, they slowly found themselves acquiring valuable desert skills in packing and handling half-wild animals and building their Navajo vocabulary.

Arriving at Kayenta, they sought to engage John Wetherill to take them to Rainbow Bridge, but learned that he was already on the trail with the ill-fated Zane Grey–Jesse Lasky expedition that was turned back by the swollen San Juan River. As it turned out, Hosteen John's absence mattered little, because they were unable to afford the $10 per day guide fees quoted to them by Clyde Colville. Undaunted, and armed with a crude hand-drawn map, they set out alone. Somewhere between the Tsegi and Piute Canyon they met the returning Lasky party in two groups a day apart. Camping one night with Lasky, they found him to be "a delightful man, quiet, unassuming, and a ready worker." The next day they met Grey and Hosteen John coming up the perilous ascent from Piute Canyon. "The narrow trail did not permit of many niceties, but we had a chance to look at Z. G. and to shake Mr. Wetherill by the hand," Kluckhohn reported.[20]

As they approached the bridge, Kluckhohn feared it would be no match in reality for Grey's purple prose descriptions, but his fears proved to be unfounded. "This sight," Kluckhohn exulted, "was more than recompense for the hardships and dangers of the trail. It awed and thrilled us as a wonderful symphony or a painting from the brush of a great master. And more—for was this not the eternal handiwork of the Great Master?"[21]

Kluckhohn returned briefly in 1926 with two student comrades from the University of Wisconsin, to which he had transferred from Princeton. Inspired by Neil Judd's "Beyond the Clay Hills" article in *National Geographic*, the trio hoped to reach Rainbow Bridge, then cross the San Juan to see the country Judd described. But it was not to be: A bucking horse threw one of the members of the party, breaking his leg, and there was, as one of his chapter titles announces, "no rainbow this summer."[22]

Kluckhohn brought four more Wisconsin friends back to the canyon country in 1927. Their goal was the mysterious Kaiparowits Plateau, the Wild Horse Mesa of Zane Grey that had intrigued Kluckhohn from a distance on previous trips, and which he supposed no white man had ever visited. The group drove from Kluckhohn's Iowa home to Tonalea, where the trader, Skeet Stiles, convinced them to rent horses from a Navajo rather than buying them. All but Kluckhohn were complete dudes, two of the men having been on horses only once before, and as they prepared their outfit, they presented a strange spectacle:

> Nel [Hagan] and Bill [Gernon] looked professional with their sombreros aslant and their six-shooters strapped to their sides. Lauri [Sharp] wore an immense ten-gallon cowboy hat which made him look like a moving picture director. Jim [Hanks] and I hadn't been able to find hats big enough for our heads, and so we tied bandanas about them in Navajo fashion.[23]

It turned out to be Kluckhohn, though, the experienced desert rat, who almost sabotaged the expedition by poor arithmetic in negotiating the animal rental. Their first night out from Tonalea, the shrewd Navajo, who knew all along that he had been shortchanged, caught up with them and demanded the balance of the agreed-upon price, thinking they would not yield to the inconvenience of abandoning the trip at that late moment. He had not reckoned with the depths of student poverty, however, and the college men elected instead to re-outfit with lesser, though cheaper animals.

It was a fatal choice, for three of the four horses died from exhaustion before they party reached Rainbow Bridge, and a fourth was abandoned, also presumably to die. While recuperating in Surprise Valley, the men captured two horses belonging to Paiute Indians. Although their stolen horses got them the rest of the way to the bridge, they nearly cost them personal injury when the Indians caught up with them and angrily recovered the animals.

The trip did have its positive aspects, though it failed in its objective. The group located a nice spring in Forbidding Canyon where they splashed around for several days, and they succeeded in climbing Navajo Mountain via the headwaters of Nasja Creek. But they failed to descend Nasja Canyon to its mouth to resolve the question of its drainage into the San Juan or the Colorado (their maps disagreed on the point). And they failed to cross the swollen Colorado River. Jim Hanks, although a strong swimmer, was unable to reach an island with 1,200 feet of rope that would help them ferry themselves and their animals across, and they turned back.

Success at last was theirs in 1928. The 1927 party reconvened as the Filthy Five, now a bunch of seasoned desert rats. Outfitting at Tonalea again, they added a Navajo guide named Dogi at Ben Wetherill's Navajo Mountain Trading Post and proceeded to their old camp in Forbidding Canyon, where they enjoyed several days of relaxation. They were probably the most literary group ever to visit the place: Kluckhohn and Sharp were studying Homer in the original Greek; Hanks had Pepys's diary, and Gernon had a one-volume Shakespeare from which they read a play each evening, each of the men reading an act and improvising comical additions.

Although they succeeded this time in clambering down the precipitous Nasja Canyon and verifying its drainage into the San Juan, they found fording the river impossible at that point. More disappointment awaited them upon their return to Ben Wetherill's establishment where, while they were resupplying for another assault on the Kaiparowits, they learned that Ben and his father had taken Herbert E. Gregory there in 1915, that Mormon cattlemen regularly grazed their stock there, and that a Navajo then at the trading post had hunted deer there the previous winter. It was hardly an unexplored area.

The Kaiparowits nevertheless proved to be worth the effort to get there. After fording the San Juan at Trail Canyon and crossing over to the Hole-in-the-Rock road, they rowed across the Colorado in a leaky homemade boat left there by trappers Howd Teeples and Billy Hay the previous spring.[24] Once on the plateau, Kluckhohn found, instead of the desert he had expected, an Edenic scene:

> Our first glimpse of this fair valley as we climbed over the Mesa
> rim was a moment of ecstasy, one of those fleeting instants, trea-

sured forever in memory, when the soul's longing is completely satisfied and the spirit soars, when all the dark corners of one's mind and all the unhappy tangents of thought are for a time blotted out and washed into oblivion, when there is a place only for rapture. We had expected Inferno, but we found Paradise.[25]

Not surprisingly for a group who had attained such a long-sought and rewarding goal, they stayed as long as their food held out, exploring the immense mesa individually and in groups, enjoying the scenery and the many Anasazi ruins. Returning to civilization seemed to them like leaving paradise for purgatory.

Kluckhohn's last pack trip, in 1929, was anticlimactic. None of the Filthy Five could join another assault upon the Kaiparowits, so Kluckhohn enlisted three visiting Oxford students. Driving to Navajo Mountain in Kluckhohn's Buick with guide Grant Hamblin, the men engaged a Navajo packer and set out. When Hamblin turned back with appendicitis, another Navajo was hired. But it was all futile, for once again the flood-swollen San Juan proved an impassable barrier. "Despite our disappointment," Kluckhohn confided, "I am a little glad that our last effort was repulsed, that Wild Horse Mesa proved itself still a stronghold not lightly to be taken."[26]

While Kluckhohn and his partners were on the Kaiparowits in 1928, the writer Hoffman Birney was in the midst of a lengthy automobile journey through the West. His purpose, at least in part, was to demonstrate the degree to which the auto could serve as practical transportation in the hitherto undeveloped West. *Roads to Roam* (1930) was his narrative of the 7,250 miles he put on his Chrysler roadster, "Betsy," through seven western states during that summer.[27] In a foreword, Birney's editor was at some pains to explain that the narrative was informally composed to accompany several hundred photographs the author made during the trip. To the modern reader, however, the photographs appear quite undistinguished in comparison with the text, which, though written in the breezy slang of the Jazz Age, is nevertheless an engaging tale of early western automobile travel.

A major purpose of the book, as mentioned, was to advertise the practicality of the automobile and to encourage western tourism. "I made no more preparation for the trip," Birney says, "than I would to drive down town, and had no mechanical trouble whatever beyond a broken spring"; and "The only moral that adorns this tale, is that such expeditions are exceedingly simple and can be duplicated by anyone." Birney acknowledged his role as tourist promoter explicitly: the West "is a land you must see and know if you would understand it. But if these scribblings of mine succeed in making you want to see it and to follow the dim trails and seek the foot of the Rainbow with me, I am content and repaid."[28]

Birney's trip to "the foot of the Rainbow," however, was by automobile only as far as Navajo Mountain, where he and four others outfitted a pack train. His companions were young Sid Stallings, a University of Arizona student and member, like Birney, of the Phi Delta Theta fraternity there; a mutual friend named Ed Adams; and Ventress Wade, their guide, who was a nephew of Louisa Wetherill and also a Phi Delta Theta member. A Paiute named Dick (also referred to as Hotshot) was engaged as a wrangler, but Wade and Birney did the packing.

The itinerary was the then-standard Wetherill route, which Wade had been over repeatedly, and was unusual only in a chance meeting in Surprise Valley of a party outfitted by the Richardsons at Rainbow Lodge and including a Quaker couple from Philadelphia named Burnham, who turned out to be related to some friends of Birney, who had grown up in that city. But visiting the great bridge itself was an overwhelming experience for Birney and his companions. They celebrated their arrival with a strange banquet of corned beef hash ("don't laugh, that's noble chow if it's cooked right," Birney warned) spiced up with green peppers and pimiento and accompanied by "fried potatoes, lima beans, asparagus salad, biscuits, jam, and sliced peaches." Perhaps their weariness or their feeling of triumph over daunting obstacles increased their appetites, because Birney said, "We stuffed, sighed, and returned to stuff some more."[29]

At the time Birney was in the midst of a religious crisis that eventually led him from the residual Protestantism of his youth into what he termed "non-militant atheism."[30] The sight of Rainbow Bridge in the moonlight inspired him to some purple prose ("the curving crest of the arch was touched by the light, splashed suddenly with silver paint, dripping from the moon"). But also to an outburst of religious emotion: "Nothing could be more marvelous, nothing more beautiful; nor could anything more perfectly attest the definite existence of a Supreme Being, a mighty Architect of the universe, and the wonders of which He is capable."[31]

Demonstrations by Birney and others of the automobile's practicality during the 1920s went a long way toward democratizing tourism. Unfortunately, their demonstrations occurred on the eve of the Great Depression, which put recreational funds for most Americans into short supply, and the Second World War, which curtailed travel through rationing of such commodities as gasoline and rubber. Nevertheless, interest in the new democratic automobile tourism continued to surge. Popular western magazines, both inside and outside the Four Corners states, encouraged the new tourism through informative and attractively illustrated articles on the canyon country. In Utah, *The Utah Magazine* and *The Utah Motorist* were good examples, as were *Progressive Arizona* and, of course, *Arizona Highways* in Arizona, and *Touring Topics* in California. But the most consistent and effective advocate of canyon country tourism was *Desert Magazine*, which began publication in November 1937 in El Centro, California. After two years the magazine moved to its permanent home in Palm Desert, where it continued until the early 1970s. Particularly under its founder, Randall Henderson (1880–1970), who served as editor until 1958, *Desert* taught frustrated urban dwellers what the open country of the Southwest offered, and how they could live there in comfort, either temporarily or permanently.

Henderson was an Iowan who hopped a freight train to California in 1907 after finishing high school. He tried San Francisco, but soon moved to Los Angeles, where he put himself through the University of Southern California with a journalism major. After a brief apprenticeship at the *Los Angeles Times*, Henderson moved east to work on the Parker *Post*, then he and a partner started the Blythe *Herald* and later bought the Calexico *Chronicle*. A desert editor had been born.[32]

Desert Magazine was a precarious proposition in the beginning. While Henderson recruited writers (but wrote most of the copy himself at first), his partner, J. Wilson McKenney, hit the road, soliciting advertising and selling copies of the magazine. Although the idea was a bit ahead of its time, history shortly caught up with it. President Roosevelt's Small Tract Act of 1938 opened up the public domain to small homestead sites of five acres, bringing a wave of what were called "jackrabbit homesteaders" to the desert country. And the entry into the civilian market after World War II of the popular four-wheel-drive Jeeps, the transportation heroes of the war, opened up much of the backcountry previously accessible only on foot or horseback. *Desert Magazine* began to develop a public.

During its maturity in the 1940s and 1950s, *Desert Magazine* assembled a stable of desert writers, many of whom had not published before but who blossomed under Henderson's editorial tutelage. Charles Kelly, Nell Murbarger, Richard Van Valkenburg, and not least, Henderson himself, were writers who could express themselves authoritatively and yet colorfully on subjects of interest to aficionados of the arid lands. If the magazine exhibited such idiosyncrasies as the articles of Marshall South, a back-to-nature type who adopted an Indian-like existence with his family in the southern California desert, its more solid contributors lured many new converts to the joys and variety of life in the desert, and taught them to travel and live there with understanding and comfort.

The credo of this new class of desert dwellers and writers was an editorial by Henderson that appeared in the first issue of the magazine. It is a stirring piece of expository prose that was frequently quoted, cited, reprinted, and reread by his writers and readers alike. The main body of the essay is a panoramic history of man's encounter with the American desert, from the Spanish explorers and the mountain men, through the Mormons and miners, and right up the jackrabbit homesteaders and sun seekers of his own day. Such modern developments as a thriving economy, a good highway system, and inexpensive desert land tempted increasing numbers of urban dwellers to visit and even consider taking up residence in the arid regions. Henderson pointed out, though, that not all those who visited the desert were happy with the experience. The desert must be taken on its own terms, he warned, to appreciate it fully. Americans typically had not been willing to do this, preferring instead to attempt to exploit it in the interest of preconceived desires and goals: imperial aggrandizement, mineral wealth, religious freedom, or perpetual leisure. The real riches of the desert, he continued, disclosed themselves only to those who bring open-minded curiosity, tolerance, and a willingness to forgo immediate comforts in the interest of a greater ultimate understanding and enjoyment. Henderson concluded in a remarkable peroration from which he took the title of the editorial, "there are two deserts":

> One is a grim, desolate wasteland. It is the home of venomous reptiles and stinging insects, of vicious thorn-covered plants and trees and unbearable heat. This is the desert seen by the

stranger speeding along the highway, impatient to be out of the "damnable country." It is the desert visualized by those children of luxury to whom any environment is intolerable which does not provide all the comforts and luxuries of a pampering civilization. It is the concept fostered by fiction writers who dramatize the tragedies of the desert because there is a market for such manuscripts.

But the stranger and the uninitiated see only the mask. The other desert—the real desert—is not for the eyes of the superficial observer or the fearful soul of a cynic. It is a land which reveals its true character only to those who come with courage, tolerance and understanding. . . .

To those who come to the desert with tolerance it gives friendliness; to those who come with courage it gives new strength of character. Those seeking relaxation find in its far horizons and secluded canyons release from the world of man-made tensions. For those seeking beauty the desert offers nature's rarest artistry. This is the desert that has a deep and lasting fascination for men and women with a bit of poetry in their souls.

This is the desert I have undertaken to reveal in the pages which follow—the desert which lies beyond the golf courses, the cocktail bars and the heated swimming pools—beyond the forbidding mask of aridity.[33]

As noted above, the first recreationists in the San Juan country long antedated Randall Henderson and *Desert Magazine*. After the heyday of the gentlemen explorers like T. Mitchell Prudden around the turn of the century, democratized tourism began to emerge. Riverman David Dexter Rust began guiding fold-boat trips through Glen Canyon well before World War I. Rust led the parties himself, but the members were expected to paddle their own boats in a participatory approach that has lately become popular once again on commercial river trips.[34]

After the war, though, tourism in the San Juan country really began to boom. Indian traders like the Gouldings and the Wetherills were the first to feel its effect, as they found their guest rooms drawing more business than their trading posts. Harry and "Mike" Goulding came to Monument Valley in 1924 to raise sheep and trade with the San Juan Paiutes and Navajos. Homesteading a school section on the edge of the Tse-begay, the famous rock formations that have appeared in innumerable pictorial features, advertisements, and movies, the Gouldings found the scenery that had attracted them to the location to be as appealing to travelers and vacationers. They began guiding visitors to some of the most photogenic viewpoints and were so encouraged by the response that Harry, in a celebrated daring venture, journeyed to Hollywood to show Monument Valley photographs to movie director John Ford, who was reported to be looking for a set for a film called *Stagecoach*. Goulding's persistence paid off, and Monument Valley eventually became as much of an American icon as the lanky young star of the movie, John Wayne.[35]

John and Louisa Wetherill had been in the San Juan country much longer, but by moving from out-of-the-way Oljato to Kayenta in 1910, they had placed themselves in the midst of a natural transportation route through the Indian country, and during the 1920s they began to cash in on the tourist business much as the Gouldings were doing. Hosteen John's fame as discoverer of Rainbow Bridge and guide to Zane Grey and Theodore Roosevelt placed him in great demand as guide for pack trips, and Louisa's renown as an expert on Navajo culture appealed to tourists desiring more than a superficial encounter with the region and its people. The cool, comfortable accommodations in the large stone guest quarters lured visitors in increasing numbers over the long, sandy roads and through the steep defile of Marsh Pass to Kayenta. During what the Wetherills' biographer has called "the Roaring Twenties at Kayenta," the large guest registers filled to bursting with names of visitors both common and famous. Poets like Witter Bynner signed in verse, while artists like Jimmy Swinnerton and George Herriman filled entire pages with colorful and humorous depictions of the canyon country and its denizens. Many are the reminiscences of dinners at Kayenta made memorable by Louisa's sophisticated discourses on the Navajos, surrounded by the Wetherills' magnificent library of the science, history, and literature of the San Juan country, while Hosteen John ate silently by her side.[36]

A similar boom in river tourism began during the late 1930s in response to the efforts of one of the West's great tourism promoters, Norman D. Nevills of Mexican Hat, Utah.[37] Although Nevills's egotism outran his river skills, he both shaped and embodied the persona of the salty, devil-may-care river guide that fulfilled people's expectations during his own day and has continued in hundreds of dude-herders since then. Nevills began as a local boatman and camp wrangler employed by the Rainbow Bridge–Monument Valley Expedition in the 1930s, and branched out from there to begin taking guests at his parents' Mexican Hat Lodge on short river runs in crude homemade boats.

As discussed in Chapter 11, his national reputation got a big boost from a highly publicized 1938 scientific expedition led by him and University of Michigan botanist Elzada Clover from Green River, Utah, to Lake Mead in three wide-beamed plywood skiffs of his own design and construction. From then until his death in an airplane crash in 1949, Nevills was the king of the commercial river runners, whose seven Grand Canyon expeditions and many San Juan runs established a style that has long outlived him. To the great delight of his guests, Nevills lectured (often inaccurately) on river history and natural history, guided short hikes to interesting side canyon attractions, and indulged in various personal antics on the river and around the campfire. Several rivermen who later achieved fame in their own right as explorers or proprietors of commercial river-running companies gained some of their initial experience as Nevills's boatmen: Otis R. "Dock" Marston, P. T. Reilly, Harry Aleson, J. Frank Wright, and others.

Nevills's fame largely precluded competition during his lifetime, though he made a number of enemies who would have liked to drive him out of business. Although his equipment and the name Mexican Hat Expeditions were taken over after Nevills' death by J. Frank Wright and Jim Rigg, they could not sustain the near monopoly he had enjoyed over commercial river running, and others began to enter the field. Among the significant newcomers were Harry Aleson and his backer, Charles W. Larrabee, who had each fallen out with Nevills during the 1940s. Aleson made at least two important innovations: He procured a fleet of war surplus neoprene landing craft that were much more spacious and comfortable than the Nevills boats, and he began promoting trips in Glen Canyon and on the San Juan that emphasized not just whitewater adventure (though Aleson also did that), but rather luxurious accommodations and leisurely side trips led by a guide who really knew the country and its literature.[38]

Other guides, whether they followed the Nevills or the Aleson pattern, began to proliferate. In addition to the Wright-Rigg and Larrabee-Aleson firms, river runners like Bus Hatch and his family, "Moki Mac" (Malcolm Ellingson), Ken Sleight, Georgie White, and many others were on the river well before construction of the Glen Canyon Dam. But not all the activity on the river was commercial. YMCA trips, for example, gave later river explorers like Dr. A. W. "Gus" Scott his start, and Boy Scout trips guided by Bert Loper, John Cross, and others were common. The scientific interest of Glen Canyon and the San Juan, with the region's unparalleled beauty, spacious campsites, and relatively easy whitewater, led some people to scorn the expense, the regimentation, and the silly Hollywood hijinks of commercial river trips in favor of going it on their own. With an inexpensive neoprene boat, a little outdoor savoir faire, some background reading in scientific and historical literature, one could make his own trips. Alone, or accompanied by a few compatible friends, one could proceed at his own pace, making his own discoveries—and inevitably his own mistakes—and engaging the country in whatever way and at whatever level he wished.[39]

One of the primary areas for tourism first promoted by river runners was the Escalante River. Although the river itself is a very minor flow, and is in fact navigable only for brief periods during spring floods, its canyon is one of the scenic gems of the Glen Canyon region. Paralleling the east side of the Kaiparowits Plateau, its as-the-crow-flies length of roughly fifty miles is multiplied many times on the convoluted canyon floor before reaching the Colorado River. Several lengthy side canyons of its own drain both sides of the river and contain much spectacular scenery, including no less than nine natural rock arches. First publicized as a tourist destination during the 1940s, it has since become a backpackers' Shangri-la for its ease of access, the dramatic scenery of its colorful sheer walls, and its friendly campsites.

Before that time, it was known only to a few cattlemen. The mouth of the river was first discovered by the second Powell expedition of 1871–72, simultaneous with the exploration of Potato Valley by Mormon pioneers, which led to their creation of the town of Escalante in 1875. That agricultural community had become prosperous enough by the end of the decade to have played an instrumental role in supplying the desperate Hole-in-the-Rock party (at allegedly exorbitant prices). Although cattle accompanied the earliest settlers, the business was not substantial enough to have merited listing in the census until 1890. By the turn of the century, however, Garfield County had eclipsed even mighty San Juan County in number of cattle, and it is presumably around that time that cattlemen began their acquaintance with the Escalante River canyons.[40]

The most famous recreational visitor to the Escalante region was a starry-eyed young poet and artist from southern California named Everett Ruess. So much paper and ink have been expended on Ruess, especially on speculations regarding his mysterious disappearance from an Escalante side canyon in 1934, that it almost seems an environmental crime to add to the expenditure, but a summary account of his life, at least, is necessary.[41]

Ruess was the younger of two sons of Christopher and Stella Ruess, a couple of free-thinking Unitarians from Los Angeles. Stella Ruess was herself an artist and poet of some note, and Everett, who was born in 1914, received every encouragement toward the life of an esthete, which he adopted. The talented but undisciplined youth passed in and out of various California schools, but frequently succumbed to a wanderlust that led him to prolonged encounters with nature on the beaches and in the mountains of his native state. By 1931 he had discovered the canyon country of the Four Corners region and over the next three years undertook several lone journeys there with a dog and pack burros.

In the history of the Southwest Ruess has become the most prominent symbol of the sensitive soul communing deeply with Nature and interpreting its essence in art, poetry, and poetic mystical letters to his parents and brother. His early demise, which incidentally enhanced his mythic, symbolic status as the "sensitive soul," nevertheless came almost certainly from his recklessness and incompetence in coping with the imperatives of life in the desert. That incompetence came into focus in his testy relationships with Indian traders and guides John Wetherill and Harry Goulding, who criticized his headstrong disregard of their advice and his mistreatment of his animals. For his part, Ruess depended upon the traders for supplies and geographical information, but held them in contempt as greedy exploiters of the noble Indians.

Ruess's naiveté apparently caught up with him in 1934. After a brief sojourn in Escalante, Utah, he set off into the canyons of the Escalante toward an undisclosed destination after warning his family that he would not be able to communicate for several weeks. He was last seen in Davis Gulch, where his burros were discovered by searchers after he failed to reappear within his projected schedule.

What happened to Everett Ruess? An intensive search failed to provide a definite answer, and even though several canyon experts like Harry Aleson and Ken Sleight made their quest for information about his ultimate fate a lifetime preoccupation, the mystery is as baffling today as it was in 1934. Was he mistaken for a law enforcement officer by cattle rustlers and murdered? Did he underestimate the dangers of crossing the Colorado River—or perhaps the San Juan if he succeeded in crossing the Colorado and reached the latter river via Grand Gulch? Or did he deliberately vanish, perhaps to Mexico, where he assumed a new identity? "When I go, I leave no trace," he wrote to a friend in June 1934.[42] It must be his epitaph, for the mystery of his demise or whereabouts remains unresolved.

Ruess's disappearance notwithstanding, it was Gregory Natural Bridge in Soda Gulch, one of the Escalante's lower tributaries, that first sparked tourist interest in the Escalante. Well known by Indians and cattlemen who often camped beneath it, the bridge first came to scientific notice during Herbert E. Gregory's studies of the Kaiparowits region and was visited by William R. Chenoweth during his 1921 mapping survey of Glen Canyon. But it was Norman Nevills's 1940 river trip duplicating the first Powell expedition from Green River, Wyoming, to Lake Mead that made the official "discovery" of the span. Nevills had saved this event as one of the highlights for his passengers, because he already knew the general location of the arch, and exaggerated its dimensions as he was wont to exaggerate his other achievements in the interest of publicity.[43]

Harry Aleson also accomplished several important early explorations of the Escalante River in his own idiosyncratic way—by boat. The 1940 Nevills expedition brought together two men who would become Nevills's enemies and rivals during the latter part of the decade. Charles Larabee, a wealthy California businessman, was a Nevills passenger who became disgusted with what he saw as the leader's incompetence and arrogance. As the party neared the end of their voyage in the Grand Canyon, they met Aleson and a friend, Louis West, who had motored up from Lake Mead to meet them and volunteer to tow the rowboats across the lake. Aleson sought to share some of Nevills's glory (Grand Canyon river trips were big news events at the time) and to offer Nevills a partnership in which Aleson would help secure customers and tow the expeditions across the lake at the end of the trip. The partnership became a reality but did not endure, and when Aleson broke with Nevills, Larabee found a chance to vent his anger at Nevills by backing Aleson as his competitor.[44] Aleson eventually became a celebrated guide, particularly in Glen Canyon, but in the late 1940s he struggled to attract customers and hoped to do it by accomplishing feats that would attract the press coverage that had generated Nevills's fame.

Running the Escalante River seemed to Aleson to offer his best chance at that publicity. It was, in the first place, a difficult run because of the limited stream flow. Although Aleson used the smallest boats he owned, navy surplus seven-man neoprenes, they still required a fair amount of water and were difficult to pull or portage through the shallow stretches. Nevertheless, the canyon offered such spectacular scenery that its tourist potential was obvious. Finally, Aleson hoped to lure *Desert* publisher Randall Henderson on one of his trips because *Desert* offered the best advertising outlet, and Henderson had resisted accepting Aleson's advertisements because of doubts about his competence. Henderson, though, was passionately interested in the Everett Ruess disappearance, and Aleson hoped to play that card to persuade Henderson to join one of his trips so he could demonstrate his competence as a guide.

Like many of Aleson's schemes, this was a crazy one, born in the mind of a man seeking a shortcut to glory. In all, Aleson ran the Escalante three times in 1948 and 1949, the last time with Randall Henderson and his wife, an experience summarized in the title of Henderson's *Desert* article, "When the Boats Wouldn't Float—We Pulled 'Em."[45] Surprisingly, Aleson's strange strategy seemed to have its desired effect upon Henderson, who evidently overlooked the travel hardships in his delight at the Ruess sites visited, and a warm friendship between him and Aleson resulted.

Aleson's greatest contribution to recreational enjoyment of Glen Canyon, however, probably did not come from his guided trips. It came through his own leisurely off-season explorations of the place as part of a team that came to call itself Canyon Surveys.

"Let's go live in Glen Canyon."

Those words inaugurated eight of the most scientifically and recreationally significant trips ever made through the 162.5 miles of Glen

Canyon. They were the words of Dick Sprang, ghost artist during the 1950s of Batman comic books, to his wife, Dudy Thomas Sprang (and after her death in 1957, to a later wife, Elizabeth Lewis Sprang, who enjoyed two Glen Canyon trips with him), and Harry Aleson, during his off-season explorations of the river and its associated backcountry.[46]

Sprang's proposal contained the essence of the *Desert Magazine* approach to the canyon country. Note, in the first place, that he proposed that they *live* in the canyon; he did not suggest that they merely run the river. The river, to be sure, was a major focal point of their trips; as Sprang later expressed it, the river is the *theme* of that country, "a country *shaped* by the river." But the river was presently important to them mainly as a vehicle of transportation; it was the ancient products of river erosion—the immense sandy beaches that provided luxurious campsites, the cliff faces that offered scenic delights, and the side canyons that contained Anasazi dwellings and other exploratory possibilities—that ultimately attracted them back to the canyon again and again.

What did Sprang mean by *living* in the canyon? None of their trips lasted less than a month, and several extended to six weeks, in a canyon that commercial parties commonly traversed in *one* week. Illustration: Both Sprang and Aleson were obsessed by a boyish love of flying. On each of their trips, they scheduled at least one check-up flight and airdrop of a few luxury items (bourbon, beer, steaks, ice cream—or Cracker Jacks, a favorite snack of Dudy Thomas) by their friend Joe Moser, of Sedona, Arizona. On one trip of a planned six-weeks' duration, Moser set out up the canyon at Lee's Ferry, looking for the group, after they had been on the river for a month. He expected to find them in the lower canyon, almost ready to end the trip. But after futilely checking such likely locations as Navajo Canyon, Forbidding Canyon, Hidden Passage, and the mouth of the San Juan, he began to worry. He flew on up: Hole-in-the-Rock, the mouth of the Escalante, the Rincon. Nothing. He opened the throttle. Lake Canyon, Hall's Crossing, Bullfrog Creek, Moki Canyon. Where did he find them? Serenely camped at the mouth of Hansen Creek at Mile 129.5 — only thirty-three miles from Hite, Utah, their embarkation point. They had averaged only one mile per day over the first month of the trip.

Who were these people? Richard W. Sprang was a phenomenally talented young commercial artist in the 1940s who was cutting a big swath in the New York City artistic scene when he realized the big city was not for him. He discovered the canyon country of the Southwest during lunchtime visits to bookstores where he purchased, literally for pennies, volumes from Frederick S. Dellenbaugh's personal library, and other primary sources on the canyon country, like Herbert E. Gregory's indispensable USGS Professional and Water Supply Papers. The turning point in his life came when he received a contract as a primary illustrator of comic books featuring Bob Kane's character, Batman. "You can live anywhere there's a mailbox," he was told, and he appeared shortly in Sedona, Arizona, in the heart of the country whose literature he had been collecting.

There he met Dudy Thomas, ex-wife of a well-known tourist guide, and longtime and well-known resident of the canyon country, a close friend of John and Louisa Wetherill and many other Indian traders and canyon characters. If Dudy introduced Dick to the canyons, he deepened her appreciation of them, with his intuitive artist's understanding of maps and topography and his scientist's soul, which guided him through mastery of a vast literature and shrewd analysis of primary sources that were both fugitive and contradictory.

Their first Glen Canyon trip, in the fall of 1950, included their Sedona friend Elmer Purtymun, a salty, grizzled, egotistical character born for and aspiring to, but inexperienced in, the tourist business. Their transportation was Sprang's WW II surplus ten-man neoprene assault boat, purchased for $45 and rigged with an impressive rowing frame of varnished 2 x 6's and steel strapping, created out of Sprang's Teutonic engineering orientation that would build a mousetrap to last for a millennium. Sprang was acquiring his river knowledge the hard way—on the river—for his oars were too short and his boat handling technique embryonic.

Late in the afternoon of October 10, one of the fateful encounters in Glen Canyon history occurred. During the long run from the Rincon to the Escalante, the Sprang party discovered that the sheer cliffs provided impressive echoes. As Purtymun (no doubt it was he) reveled in his repeating shouts, he was mystified by some echoes returning at irregular intervals. He stood up in the boat to investigate the phenomenon, and the echo said, "Sit down, you're rocking the boat"! Everyone laughed. It was Harry Aleson, camped for several days at the mouth of the Escalante and just completing an expedition he later termed his Lone Month on the Colorado.

A veteran of World War I, Aleson suffered from chronic gastrointestinal problems that eventually claimed his life in 1972. His first marriage had ended in 1939, and he did not remarry until 1962. Years of living alone had bred a mysterious sense of humor and an unpredictable personality that made him a genuine canyon country character.

As they camped together that night, new friends became old friends. Through drawings in the sand in the erratic light of the campfire, Aleson explained old rivermen's techniques for making graceful landings in the full current along a sheer wall, or below an eddy, how to align a boat at a very acute angle when entering rapids to avoid shipping water, and why one camps most safely on the beach *above* the outwash of a side canyon, to avoid being wiped out by a surprise flash flood.

Subsequent trips in 1951 honed Sprang's quick grasp of navigational techniques and exponentially advanced his knowledge and love of Glen Canyon. By 1952 his canyoneering skills equaled or exceeded those of most Glen Canyon old-timers, and he was ready to make Aleson an offer.

"Herewith a brainstorm," he wrote Aleson on March 17. "See sample sheet enclosed." It was a system for "the orderly and permanent filing of notes re: our explorations of Glen Canyon." Here is the system:

> Each mile of the river would be given a full sheet in a loose-leaf notebook containing 162 sheets. . . . Each sheet would be divided into 10 sections representing tenths of a mile, and in each section all notes applying would be entered. The heading of each sheet provides space for the noting of photo references and map references applying to that sheet's area. . . .

> At proper intervals throughout the book would be inserted sheets that bear a pasted on section cut from the river survey sheets [the USGS river maps of 1921] . . . the sectional maps would be further sectioned in sequence and each section mounted and inserted just before the group of mile note sheets that cover area represented on map section.

> I can see the book or books even containing stereo pairs [of aerial photographs] inserted into envelopes which are ring-bound into book at proper points.

"Ambitious?" he concluded. "God! Never in our lives could we fill all those blank spaces. But the system would perhaps provide to those who follow us an orderly and complete record of OUR findings, and graphically show them by means of the unfilled sections the areas left untouched for THEIR explorations." In their final version, the forms exhibited those "unfilled sections" even more conspicuously than the original proposal, for they wisely covered only one-half mile per sheet, making 324 sheets in the set rather than 162, thus allowing more room in the blanks left for recording data.

By the time the trio shoved off from Hite in the fall, equipped with a sheaf of blank forms and a fierce love of the canyon, they had decided to call themselves Canyon Surveys, and to indicate their presence at important junctures in the canyon by means of a symbol: an upright arrowhead scratched in the rock, surrounding the letters CS.

Their gear that year was typical of all their later trips. "We *lived* in the place," Sprang wrote many years later,

> luxuriated in the most comfortable camps I've ever known, camps made possible by the marvelous wooded bars; we brought pounds of reading matter with us, and our 10-man assault boats, built for the invasion of Japan, seemed capable of hauling tons of food of infinite variety.

Photographs of their boats under way look, as their friend Gus Scott observed, like a floating garage sale. "This may be the shortest river trip on record," Sprang warned his wife once while trying to load their groaning boat at Hite. "As soon as the boat was loaded, it sank!"

Anyone who saw them on the river (and few ever did, because they always made their trips in October or November, well after commercial trips and other visitors had ceased) would have remarked at the presence of Pard, Dick's dog, and Micky, Dudy's leonine black-and-white alley cat, who ran every river and hiked every canyon with them. One would have to go back to Rags and Cataract, the Airedale dog and the bear cub Clyde Eddy took through the canyons in 1927, to find more exotic river companions than Pard and Micky. Yet they fit in perfectly, submerging their natural suspicions of each other, and apparently enjoying the canyons as much as their human partners.

Another typical aspect of their approach to the canyons was their congenital hatred of national parks and other government-regulated areas that tended to diminish one's direct encounter with nature, an encounter that called forth the best in people and equipment, but made possible the greatest rewards of outdoor living. None of this trio ever bought a government permit. Operating in a country, as P. T. Reilly characterizes it, where God lost His boots, they were willing to assume the risks and enjoy the rewards. "What does Zion National Park have that this place doesn't?" Sprang asked Aleson in upper Moki Canyon, one of the most spectacular places on the whole Colorado Plateau. Aleson's reply was instantaneous: "Park rangers."

The 1952 trip had a special goal. The USGS river maps of 1921 showed, at Mile 132 LB across from Smith Fork Canyon, a truncated canyon pinched off at the 3,900-foot elevation about one-half mile from the river. In 1951 Sprang purchased a complete set of U.S. Soil Conservation Service aerial photographs in stereographic pairs, and he immediately reported to Aleson that they proved to be *"very interesting!"* Viewed in stereo, low-level aerial photographs, with their exaggerated relief and pinpoint detail, are visually stunning—they can make one give up television—and as a navigational device in rough country are far superior to maps in almost every way. For that reason, and also because good 15' USGS maps of southeastern Utah were only then beginning to be issued in response to the uranium boom, Canyon Surveys used aerial photographs almost exclusively in their explorations away from the river.

But what Sprang undoubtedly had in mind in this case was the fact that the photographs showed not just a tiny half-mile gorge at Mile 132 LB, but a mighty canyon approximately nine miles long that debouched on the Colorado River at that point. (It is perhaps worth noting here that a similar LB side canyon only a mile farther down the river, across from Hansen Creek, was similarly ignored on the maps. Known today as Crystal Springs Canyon, it was explored in 1955 by the Scott-Robertson expedition.) When Sprang observed that although the 1921 maps ignored the canyon, it had almost certainly been known to early miners and trappers, Dudy responded, "Correct. Let's say the canyon has been forgotten, and for our purposes call it that." It appears today on maps as Forgotten Canyon.

Gaining access to the canyon was an intimidating prospect. Aleson's maps show that he had previously explored a little side canyon of Forgotten that enters near its mouth, but the main canyon itself confronted the visitor with a narrow slot filled with deep ice water and bordered by sheer cliffs. On earlier trips, Canyon Surveys had noted heavily eroded Anasazi steps, however, ascending to a plateau just downstream from the mouth of the canyon. By using rock-facing tools and rigging a safety line, the trio enlarged the steps and by-passed the slot just as their Anasazi predecessors had done. On October 23, 1952, they entered the main canyon, the first human beings to do so, so far as evidence existed, since the Anasazis had left.

In the absence of cattle, the canyon floor was brushy, and hiking was difficult. The party made slow progress. They stopped for lunch, then continued upcanyon. Shortly after 3:00 P.M., Sprang suddenly stopped. "Look at that," he said.

In an alcove high above them on the right bank canyon wall was a large Anasazi ruin. To the right of the ruin were three menacing white pictographs, leaping figures brandishing weapons and shields. Aleson named it the Three Warriors Ruin. They memorialized the discovery by placing in the ground a group of rocks in the shape of a "D." It represented, according to Aleson, "Dick, Dudy, and the Dumb Norwegian." It might also have stood for Defiance House, which is the name currently applied to it by the park service. It is the largest ruin and the most popular Anasazi site on the current Lake Powell reservoir.

Stabilization of the ruin with concrete has recently been made necessary by mobs of motorboating vandals. Even the University of Utah Press has vandalized the pictograph panel: A prudishly emasculated version of one of the figures serves as their logo. It was different on October 23, 1952. Then, as Sprang reminisced,

> The silence was tangible, a permeation uninterrupted through the centuries. To me, the stillness possessed the hush of reverence. . . . We were aware that we were keeping our voices low. We smiled at that. When Harry called his description to Dudy on the canyon floor and broke the spell, we smiled at that, too. Noisy mankind had returned.

No other discoveries could top that one, but the 1952 trip was equally important for the immense amount of data on inscriptions, prehistoric sites, and geography recorded on the Canyon Surveys forms and in Aleson's ninety-eight page journal, which ranks in accuracy and thoroughness with the other great classic journals of western exploration, and is one of the most valuable documents in existence describing Glen Canyon.

In 1953 the trio turned their attention to the San Juan River and to overland exploration of the vast poorly known area between the San Juan and Colorado Rivers, which geologist Herbert E. Gregory called the Red Rock Plateau. The spring river trip, from Mexican Hat to Lee's Ferry, was extraordinarily taxing because of the low water (1,500 cfs) which was frequently insufficient to float their boats, and a fiercely persistent upriver wind. The highlight of the trip was a three-day hike up Grand Gulch almost to Collins Canyon. Aleson kept no record of that trip, but Sprang's diary and the sites he recorded on tissue overlays of his aerial photographs constitute the only systematic survey of historic and prehistoric sites ever undertaken in that lower part of the canyon.

They returned to Grand Gulch in the fall in Aleson's 1946 Dodge Power Wagon to complete their survey from Collins to Polly's Island and downcanyon to their spring turnback point. Later, they drove through Clay Hills Pass and out to the Hermit Lake area on the Hole-in-the-Rock road.

Canyon Surveys' last Glen Canyon trip was a six-week stay in 1955, but the trip was scientifically much less important than the previous ones. By that time, the trio had found the rigors of scientific discipline to be less alluring than the relaxed living in their scenic and luxurious camps. In 1957 Dudy Thomas Sprang died during an operation to remove a brain tumor.

Aleson and Sprang both continued their involvement with Glen Canyon, though separately. Sprang married Elizabeth Lewis, an artist and canyon aficionado, but a contrary personality to Aleson's. "I'll marry you," she told Sprang, "but you'll have to be the one to handle Harry Aleson." The couple made two Glen Canyon trips in the late 1950s under the shadow of the new Glen Canyon Dam. Elizabeth collected rubbings of much of the prehistoric rock art that would be inundated, as well as sketching scenic views. Perhaps prodded by Elizabeth's sketching, Sprang did some drawing as well, satirizing their trip in several hilarious cartoons.

Today, in an age when people line up to buy tickets to run rivers, the Canyon Surveys trips offer a dramatic contrast. They remind us that those who wish to engage the canyon country at a serious level can do so on their own, with immense enjoyment and intellectual significance. Their trips went far toward redefining both science and recreation, and especially in the marriage of the two.

The group's greatest shortcoming was that they published virtually nothing. Some few scientists like Gene Foster, Angus Woodbury, and Dean Brimhall were aware of their accomplishments and took advantage of them in published reports. But when the Glen Canyon survey of the 1950s studied the entire canyon to record the historic and prehistoric sites that would be destroyed by the dam, they virtually had to begin from scratch. Plans for augmentation of Canyon Surveys' findings by others were never in fact much more than a vague hope, for the forms have remained in Dick Sprang's possession instead of being called to the attention of the scientists who conducted the Glen Canyon survey. Bitterness over the impending dam, Dudy Sprang's untimely death, and the trio's fierce distaste for publicity all must have influenced their unspoken decision to shelve their scientific investigations. It was an unfortunate and unforeseen end to one of Glen Canyon's most promising projects.

NOTES

1. Earl Pomeroy, *In Search of the Golden West: The Tourist in Western America* (New York: Alfred A. Knopf, 1957), Chapter 1, "Palace Cars and Pleasure Domes," sketches the upper-class nineteenth-century tourist.

2. Ibid., 127–31; in spite of its social and economic significance for the region, the Good Roads Movement and automotive tourism in the Colorado Plateau states have largely escaped the attention of historians. Three master's theses, however, bear upon the subjects: Jay Melvin Haymond, "A Survey of the History of the Road Construction Industry in Utah," (M.A. thesis, Brigham Young University, 1967); Lewis Wetzler, "Arizona Highways," (M.A. thesis, University of Arizona, 1937); and Gary Topping, "A History of *Arizona Highways* Magazine," (M.A. thesis, Northern Arizona University, 1970).

3. Frank Gruber, *Zane Grey: A Biography* (New York: World Publishing Co., 1970).

4. Most of the extant Grey-Wetherill correspondence in the Otis Marston Papers at the Huntington Library and in the possession of Harvey Leake, of Phoenix, Arizona, illustrates Grey's imperiousness.

5. Grey, "Nonnezoshe," in *Tales of Lonely Trails* (New York: Harper & Brothers, 1922), 3.

6. Frank McNitt, *The Indian Traders* (Norman: University of Oklahoma Press, 1962), 272.

7. Grey, "Nonnezoshe," 16.

8. Ibid., 17.

9. Edmund Morris, *The Rise of Theodore Roosevelt* (New York: Coward, McCann & Geoghegan, 1979) recounts Roosevelt's prepresidential years. Pending completion of Morris's biography, Henry F. Pringle's *Theodore Roosevelt* (New York: Harcourt, Brace & Co., 1956) is the standard account of the later years, though Roosevelt's postpresidential period has never been adequately studied.

10. Theodore Roosevelt, *A Book-Lover's Holidays in the Open* (New York: Charles Scribner's Sons, 1916), vii–viii.

11. Ibid., 48.

12. Ibid., 49.

13. Lewis H. Morgan, *Ancient Society* (Chicago: Charles H. Kerr & Co., 1877).

14. Roosevelt, *A Book-Lover's Holidays*, 53.

15. Dixon's book does not give the year of the journey, but she signed the Wetherill guest register on May 17, 1919, under her maiden name, Hawkridge. Copy in possession of the author.

16. Winifred Hawkridge Dixon, *Westward Hoboes: Ups and Downs of Frontier Motoring* (New York: Charles Scribner's Sons, 1924), 263.

17. Ibid., 274, 290.

18. Ibid., 295.

19. Clyde Kluckhohn, *To the Foot of the Rainbow* (New York: The Century Co., 1927); *Beyond the Rainbow* (Boston: The Christopher Publishing House, 1933).

20. Kluckhohn, *To the Foot of the Rainbow*, 220, 222.

21. Ibid., 235.

22. Kluckhohn, *Beyond the Rainbow*, 194.

23. Ibid., 71.

24. Kluckhohn had no idea who had built or abandoned the boat, but Teeples later identified it to Dick Sprang by means of Kluckhohn's photograph in *Beyond the Rainbow*, opposite p. 184. Dick Sprang statement on Hite, Utah, Utah State Historical Society, 38–45.

25. Kluckhohn, *Beyond the Rainbow*, 194.

26. Ibid., 271.

27. Hoffman Birney, *Roads to Roam* (Philadelphia: The Penn Publishing Co., 1930).

28. Ibid., 17, 18, 305.

29. Ibid., 289.

30. Birney recounts his religious development in *"Non Credo*: The Evolution of a Non-militant Atheist," a manuscript in the Charles Kelly Papers, Utah State Historical Society.

31. Birney, *Roads to Roam*, 290–91

32. [Randall Henderson,] *"Desert's* First 11 Years," *Desert Magazine* (November 1948): 17–20; Randall Henderson, "Fifty Years a Desert Reporter," *Desert Magazine* (December 1961): 13–15; Jack Pepper, "Randall Henderson, Man of the Desert," *Desert Magazine* (March 1964): 23–24; Jack Pepper, "In Memory of 'Mr. Desert,'" *Desert Magazine* (September 1970): 7; and J. Wilson McKenney, *Desert Editor: The Story of Randall Henderson and Palm Desert* (Georgetown, Calif.: Wilmac Press, 1972).

33. McKenney, *Desert Editor*, 186–87 quotes the last three stirring paragraphs of the essay; Randall Henderson, *On Desert Trails, Today and Yesterday* (Los Angeles: Westernlore Press, 1961), 19–35 gives the entire text.

34. David Dexter Rust, testimony in Colorado River Case, Utah State Historical Society, and "Boating on the Colorado," *Improvement Era* 4 (May 1901): 507–12.

35. Richard Klinck, *Room Enough and Time Enough* (Albuquerque: University of New Mexico Press, 1953); Samuel Moon, *Tall Sheep* (Norman: University of Oklahoma Press, 1992).

36. Mary Apolline Comfort, *Rainbow to Yesterday: The John and Louisa Wetherill Story* (New York: Vantage Press, 1980); the Kayenta guest registers are in possession of Mrs. JohniLou Duncan, Prescott, Arizona. One of the most memorable descriptions of the Wetherills' facilities at Kayenta is Elizabeth Compton Hegemann, *Navaho Trading Days* (Albuquerque: University of New Mexico Press, 1963), 224–39, with its accompanying photographs of both interior and exterior.

37. By far the best analysis of Nevills's career and contribution to river travel is P. T. Reilly, "Norman Nevills: Whitewater Man of the West," *Utah Historical Quarterly* 55 (Spring 1987): 181–200; but other works include Nancy Nelson, *Any Time, Any Place, Any River: The Nevills of Mexican Hat* (Flagstaff, Ariz.: Red Lake Books, 1991); and William Cook, *The WEN, the BOTANY, and the MEXICAN HAT: The*

Adventures of the First Women Through Grand Canyon, on the Nevills Expedition (Orangevale, Calif.: Callisto Books, 1987). Contemporary accounts of Nevills's trips include Ernie Pyle, *Home Country, 1939* (New York: William Sloan Associates, 1947), 397–401; Wallace Stegner, *The Sound of Mountain Water* (Garden City, N. Y.: Doubleday, 1969), 102–20; and Alfred M. Bailey, "Desert River Through Navajo Land," *National Geographic* (August 1947): 149–72.

38. Gary Topping, "Harry Aleson and the Place No One Knew," *Utah Historical Quarterly* 52 (Spring 1984): 165–78.

39. An excellent example of such a trip, made in 1946 in two foldboats, is George O. Bauwens, "Down the Colorado: A Fold Boat Trip Through Glen Canyon," *The Utah Motorist* (October 1946): 30–31 ff.

40. Garfield County Daughters of Utah Pioneers, *Golden Nuggets of Pioneer Days: A History of Garfield County* (Panguitch, Utah: Garfield County News, 1949), 92, 98; Don D. Walker, "The Cattle Industry of Utah: A Historical Profile, 1850–1900," *Utah Historical Quarterly* 32 (Summer 1964): 191.

41. Randall Henderson, publisher of *Desert Magazine*, took a particular interest in Ruess and his disappearance, and edited a compilation of his poems, art, and letters, with photographs of Ruess that had appeared in the magazine: *On Desert Trails with Everett Ruess* (Palm Desert, Calif.: Desert Magazine Press, 1940). It is now superseded by W. L. Rusho, *Everett Ruess: A Vagabond for Beauty* (Salt Lake City: Peregrine Smith Books, 1983). Wallace Stegner, "Artist in Residence," in *Mormon Country* (New York: Duell, Sloan & Pearce, 1942), 319–30 is a concise summary and interpretation of Ruess's life.

42. Ruess to Bill Jacobs, June 19, 1934, in Henderson, ed., *On Desert Trails With Everett Ruess*, 52.

43. Jared Farmer, "Undiscovered to Undiscoverable: Gregory Natural Bridge," *Utah Historical Quarterly* 63 (Spring 1995): 100–21.

44. Gary Topping, "Harry Aleson and the Place No One Knew," 165–78.

45. *Desert Magazine* (September 1950): 5–13.

46. Ibid. The rest of this chapter is based on Aleson's 1950 and 1952 diaries, correspondence, and motion pictures at the Utah State Historical Society, interviews with Dick Sprang, and Elizabeth Sprang's *Good-bye River* (Reseda, Calif.: Mojave Books, 1979). See also Barry Scholl, "Double Identity: The Two Lives of Dick Sprang," *Salt Lake City* (May-June 1996): 42–45 ff.

The End of Glen Canyon

Although Arthur L. Chaffin (1885–1979) was the last of the Glen Canyon gold miners, to call him only that would be to sell him short. In spite of the fact that he brought two successive wives to the canyon and was thus no hermit, he shared fully with his friends Cass Hite, Bert Loper, and Lon Turner the rigors and joys of life in the canyon. Although there were rumors that an unsolved murder in the Hite area had been committed by Chaffin, no evidence or charges were ever brought, and his appearance certainly suggested no violent propensities. With his balding head, steel-rimmed glasses, round belly, benevolent smile, and soft voice, Arthur Chaffin was the type of person one would want to represent Santa Claus.[1]

Chaffin's older brothers, Louis and George, were among the first miners attracted to Glen Canyon by Cass Hite, and young Arth (it was never "Art") joined them at Moki Bar as a freighter and miner in the late 1890s.[2] During his long life on the river, which ended only with the filling of the Lake Powell reservoir in the early 1960s, Chaffin did virtually everything that could be done on the river. At various times he was a miner, freighter, boatman, watchman at the Stanton dredge, Indian trader, ferry builder and operator, and tourist promoter. He was, as his old friend Dick Sprang remembers, a master "riverbank engineer," whose expertise at improvising and handling tools and riggings to move and operate heavy equipment by himself was without parallel. During various periods when Sprang actually lived at Hite while completing work on the season's last Batman comic book drawings that would finance his extended vacations in the canyon, he had ample opportunity to study Chaffin's extraordinary creativity in improvising solutions to difficult engineering problems far from machine shops and heavy equipment. "I was fairly good with my hands," Sprang recalled,

and up at his tool shed at the ranch and down at the shop at the
ferry house, Arth showed and described many splendid hard-
used tools of a far older time that were ideally suited to riverbank engineering, very cleverly adapted or actually created to
handle special problems with the moving and maintaining of
heavy mining machinery, and all manner of other kinds of machinery including his remarkable ferryboat.

It was on another occasion, however, and in a location far from the
river that Sprang developed his ultimate appreciation for that great
wizard of the river:

> Once years later I watched Chaffin splice a heavy steel cable up
> at Jackson's sawmill in Teasdale. I had learned to splice manila
> hausers and lines as a boy on Lake Erie, but when I saw his
> gnarled old fingers weave the stiff strands of steel cable, I knew
> I was watching a master.[3]

As a miner, Chaffin worked first with his brothers, then with Cass
Hite, with Frank Bennett in the Henry Mountains, and at Camp
Stone, where he was employed as caretaker of the Stanton dredge after the Hoskaninni Mining Company went out of business. Eventually he made his home at Hite, from which he ranged down the river,
working various mining operations either alone or accompanied by
his wife. In the early years they used a small boat for those trips, but
in one of the quirks of human nature that keeps history interesting,
they always slept on old iron bedsteads Chaffin had hauled down to
favorite campsites. Later, he borrowed some ten-man neoprene
boats from Harry Aleson and lashed them together into a giant raft
with some fifty-gallon drums, which he then floored over and
equipped with a regular bed inside a wall tent, a full-size cookstove,
and a large outboard motor.[4]

The Chaffin ranch at Hite became legendary as a canyon garden
spot, with its prolific fruits and melons and scenic environs. And it
became a tourist attraction as well after 1946, when Chaffin built the
first ferry, eventually motorized, for transporting automotive traffic
across the river, linking Wayne, Garfield, and San Juan Counties for
the first time by an effective and scenic transportation route.[5] It was
Arthur Chaffin who wrote a large part of the last chapter of Glen
Canyon history, and it is one of history's ironies that he, the original

Glen Canyon tourism promoter, wrote it as an opponent of the Glen Canyon Dam, which created the canyon country's ultimate tourist attraction, Lake Powell.

The Glen Canyon Dam's origins arose from the curiously inconsistent mixture of reason and unreason that seems to motivate much of what we Americans do.[6] On the one hand, the economic needs of an expanding western population suggested a network of dams that would provide impoundments for irrigating the otherwise almost useless arid western lands, flood control, and hydroelectric power both for western homesteads and industry. The first two of those needs, at least, had been foreseen in the creation of the Newlands Reclamation Act of 1902, which provided for construction of dams funded by proceeds from western land sales and irrigation water. On the other hand, Americans had long been gripped by a love for the grandiose, particularly the technologically grandiose, beginning at least as early as construction of the transcontinental railroads and the immense factory system of the Gilded Age, the Panama Canal, and the war machines of our two great industrialized world wars. Somewhere along the way a sense of practicality, of esthetics, and of environmental consequences became lost in a headlong compulsion to build ever bigger things and therein somehow vindicate America's essential soundness and strength. Some kind of control of the Colorado River's devastating floods and harnessing its hydroelectric potential in the interest of agricultural and industrial development in southern California surely made sense. But in retrospect, at least, the idea of flooding the historically and scenically unparalleled Glen Canyon, even though the dam does produce 1,300 megawatts of relatively cheap and clean power, has been hotly debated, particularly as it brings no benefits whatever in flood control or irrigation.

The idea of damming the Colorado River had its inception in a succession of floods that devastated agriculture around Yuma, Arizona, and in California's Imperial Valley during the early part of this century. The rapid population growth in southern California after World War I brought into focus the importance of that agriculture as well as the increasing need for water and electrical power for that region. California, however, was unable to act unilaterally to utilize the river, for the river drained no less than seven western states, each of which had to be guaranteed its share of the water as well. Before an apportionment could be made, the engineers and politicians involved had to gather scientific data on this least known of all major American rivers to ascertain how much water was available, and also where suitable dam sites might be located. Pointing up the urgency of the matter, the United States Geological Survey was joined in this fact-gathering venture by Southern California Edison, a power company that stood to make a good deal of money from hydroelectric development. In 1921 the two organizations prepared a series of topographic maps of the Colorado River from its confluence with the Green to Lee's Ferry and the San Juan River below Chinle Creek (the survey was extended through the Grand Canyon by 1923). The maps, which extended from the river bed to the 3,900-foot elevation, were obviously prepared with the plotting of dam sites in mind (the maximum pool level for Lake Powell was established at 3,700 feet). Although the maps had their inaccuracies, they were the first river maps created by modern instrument survey techniques. And they served a generation of scientists, miners, and river runners well until preparation by the USGS of complete 15' topographic maps of the region based on aerial photography in response to the uranium boom of the early 1950s (ultimately these were replaced during the 1980s by even more detailed and accurate 7½' maps).

Of the two mapping projects, Glen Canyon and the San Juan, the latter is much better documented.[7] Beginning at Sand Island several miles west of Bluff on July 18, 1921, the party reached the mouth of the river on October 3. The USGS was represented by topographic engineer Kelly W. Trimble, leader of the expedition, and Hugh D. Miser, a portly geologist from Arkansas. Robert N. Allen, a civil engineer with a B.S. from California Technological Institute in Pasadena, left a young wife in Los Angeles to represent Southern California Edison in the party as recorder. The other party members were locals: The legendary miner and boatman Bert Loper was head boatman. Heber Christensen did double duty as cook and boatman before his lack of skills at the oars led to his replacement in that capacity early in the trip by rodman Henry Elwyn Blake. Another rodman, Hugh Hyde of Bluff, rounded out the crew.[8]

The boats immediately proved inadequate to the task. Made by a firm called Fellows in San Pedro, California, and furnished by Southern California Edison, they were shipped by train to Green River, Utah, then trucked to Bluff. Their length was adequate—sixteen feet—and they were flat-bottomed for maneuverability. But they were constructed of fragile redwood, the only virtue of which is its lightness, and they were entirely open with no watertight compartments. At least one more boat should have been added to the fleet, for Blake recalled that over the stretches of river in which all seven men, their instruments and supplies had to be loaded simultaneously into the boats, their sixteen-inch sides had only four inches of freeboard left, an unsafe margin in rough water. In addition, one of the boats simply broke apart after striking a rock in the rapids now known as False John's Canyon Rapid, an accident the boatmen ascribed to faulty doweling in construction.[9]

Although the San Juan Canyon is very narrow and steep in places, in other areas it broadens out greatly, and one of the great values of the San Juan mapping expedition is that carrying their line to the 3,900-foot elevation sometimes meant surveying a great deal of the surrounding country as well as just the river. In addition, Miser's curiosity led him even farther afield on some occasions than the 3,900-foot contour required. Once, for example, he ventured into Monument Valley via Organ Rock as far as Train Rock. On the other side of the river, he and Loper hiked approximately twenty-five miles from Clay Hills Crossing to the Red House at the mouth of Red Canyon, then to the summit of Clay Hills Pass, a grueling ordeal in the August heat that made them grateful even for the tadpole-infested water in the reservoirs at Red House.[10]

Arriving at the mouth of the San Juan a few days early for their intended rendezvous with the Colorado River mapping party, the Trimble party decided to hike and row upstream a few miles to Hole-in-the-Rock, then drifted back to the confluence. On October 5 the two parties made their rendezvous, and Miser proceeded to Lee's Ferry with the Colorado River team with a brief detour to Rainbow Bridge, while the Trimble team continued the river survey to Lee's Ferry.[11]

The Colorado River survey began at Green River, Utah, on September 10, 1921, in four boats, one of which was the historic *Edith*, taken through the canyons in 1911–12 by the Kolb brothers, Ellsworth and Emery, who were boatmen on this trip. Of the other three boats (provided by Southern California Edison), the *Edison*, the *L.A.*, and the *Static*, one was equipped with a motor that though balky helped them make better time through the placid stretches of Labyrinth and Stillwater Canyons than would have been possible while rowing. The motor yielded to oars while running rapids. Personnel of the party included the USGS topographical engineer William R. Chenoweth, geologist Sidney Paige, and hydraulic engineer Eugene Clyde LaRue as the scientific staff, with five others in addition to the Kolb brothers. After five days the party reached the confluence of the Green and Colorado where their mapping began.[12]

Chenoweth had previously surveyed Glen Canyon overland from Hansen Creek to the mouth of the Dirty Devil, so the Cataract Canyon survey ended on October 2 when, in Ellsworth Kolb's words, "Mr. C, completed his line to the Freemont [*sic*] and tied into his old line." At Hansen Creek the party divided, with the chef, recorder, and two rodmen remaining with Chenoweth to continue the overland survey along the right bank to a point opposite the mouth of the San Juan, and the others continuing to rendezvous with the San Juan party. The Chenoweth party retained the *L.A.* and was supplied by caches left by the rest of the party at Hall's Creek and earlier caches left by Chenoweth.[13]

Few of those, no doubt, who lived on or utilized the river after the turn of the century realized the degree of the threat the dam proposals represented to their way of life. The mapmakers and engineers who traveled down the river in the early 1920s were few in number, studious and silent by nature, and soon gone, leaving the old ways of life apparently untouched. Armed with the data provided by the mapmakers, though, the politicians continued on a course that would eventually doom Glen Canyon.

Eugene Clyde LaRue had been advocating a Glen Canyon dam since 1916 as a flood control and water storage facility that would aid all seven affected states.[14] When a conference was announced for Santa Fe in the fall of 1922 to work out an apportionment of the water, LaRue persuaded a party of engineers from the USGS, the Bureau of Reclamation, Southern California Edison, and several representatives of Utah state government and the Mormon Church to make their way to the conference via Capitol Reef to the mouth of Hall's Creek. There they would be met by a group of boats and journey through Glen Canyon to Lee's Ferry, then overland to catch the Santa Fe train at Flagstaff. His idea was to waylay the delegates and to convince them of the advantages of a Glen Canyon dam.

The river trip was memorable for having been recorded in detail by two members of the party, Mormon apostle and irrigation expert

John A. Widtsoe, who was representing the state of Utah at the Santa Fe conference, and Lewis Ransome Freeman, a budding writer seeking adventure on the river, who signed on as one of the boatmen.[15] For Widtsoe, the ten-day trip was an excursion through a wonderland:

> Sleeping on the sweet sand was full of romance. Darkness closed in with multiplied whisperings of silence. Shadows climbed up the vertical side of the narrow canyon in huge and awesome forms. Then with the first light of morning, the canyon rioted with changing color. As the sun rose, though the canyon remained in the shadows until the sun was high, a glorious moving, colorful, ever-changing panorama played on the canyon walls. We watched it in breathless wonder.

Perhaps it was those beauties that impressed Widtsoe more than LaRue's pleas for the dam, for he concluded his reminiscence of the trip with the hope that in time a good road down Hall's Creek and another good one to Lee's Ferry would encourage other tourists to enjoy a similar river trip.[16]

Freeman's narrative is much less poetic, emphasizing instead, through self-deprecating humor, the earthy and watery realities of piloting Southern California Edison's boats left over from the previous summer's mapping parties, all now equipped with motors, over 119 miles upstream in Glen Canyon from Lee's Ferry to Hall's Crossing. The crew was under the supervision of Tom Wimmer, an old Green River boatman of many years, and most recently boatman for the U.S. Coast and Geodetic Survey of Glen Canyon, which took place simultaneously with the mapping survey. Although Freeman, a foppish Stanford graduate, made the mistake of showing up in LaRue's office for his interview with Wimmer clad in crisp white flannels and sporting a walking stick, he impressed his future boss enough to get the job. "I struck him," Freeman reported, "as being too fat, both above and below the ears, and . . . he kind of distrusted on general principles dudes that wore ice-cream pants and silk socks and carried a cane." But Wimmer had faith that Freeman had more grit than he exhibited. To Freeman's immense surprise, the other boatman were just as effete in background as he—all college men and mostly scions of wealthy families.[17] In the end, the river called forth the best in each of them as they attempted to keep the battered and leaky boats afloat and to keep the motors running as the sandy water ground through seals and bearings.

The result of the Santa Fe conference was the Colorado River Compact of 1922, ratified by six of the seven states (Arizona did not join until 1944). The compact divided the river drainage into two basins with the dividing line at Lee's Ferry. The Lower Basin states, Arizona, Nevada, and primarily California, were guaranteed at least 7.5 million acre-feet of water annually, and they almost immediately began a succession of dams on the lower river beginning with Boulder (later Hoover) Dam near Las Vegas in order to meet the increasingly urgent power, water, and flood control needs of southern California.

The Upper Basin states, still sparsely populated, undertook no immediate water storage projects, content merely with the assurance that the compact had guaranteed their share of the water whenever the need for it would develop. That need eventually materialized during the Great Depression and World War II, when water for agricultural expansion became desirable, and electrical power became necessary for the region's large military installations and defense-related industries. In response to this need, the Bureau of Reclamation began planning the Colorado River Storage Project, which historian Mark W. T. Harvey characterizes as "a giant package of reclamation projects, storage dams, and power facilities that promised to transform this part of the American West, much as TVA had done for an important region of the South."[18]

Exactly what that package would consist of took shape only after an immense debate during the late 1940s and early 1950s among various engineers and scientists, political constituencies, and conservation organizations. The Bureau of Reclamation's chosen site for the primary storage facility was Echo Park, near the confluence of the Yampa and Green Rivers. But conservationists, in a dramatic come-from-behind victory against the Bureau and its powerful Upper Basin political constituency, capitalized on the fact that the dam would impinge upon Dinosaur National Monument, a component of the National Park System, and mustered a polyglot constituency that defeated the idea of a dam at that point. Where, then, could such a dam exist? As an alternative, the Bureau turned then to Eugene Clyde LaRue's by then almost ancient idea of a Glen Canyon dam. While few conservationists were happy about flooding Glen Canyon, they had just won a major battle against a powerful government agency and its constituency and did not think they could win another such battle this soon without incurring the onus of willful obstructionism against western economic development, a very popular movement during those immediate postwar years. In addition, Glen Canyon was unprotected public domain, without the toehold of national park designation the conservationists had gripped so tenaciously in defeating the Echo Park project. Although the Sierra Club's David Brower mounted a last-ditch but impotent gesture to save Glen Canyon, it was insufficient. The Sierra Club admitted the ignorance underlying its decision not to fight for Glen Canyon as it had for Echo Park in publishing a book of Glen Canyon photographs by Eliot Porter called *The Place No One Knew* in 1963, the year the gates were closed on the Glen Canyon Dam. The title was an absurd revelation of Sierra Club solipsism; C. Gregory Crampton, who had written no less than six books on Glen Canyon by 1963 and was one of those who knew the canyon well, has quipped that it should have been called "The Place the Sierra Club Didn't Know."[19] Nevertheless, there was a tragic kernel of truth in the title, for those politically astute environmentalists who could have saved the canyon clearly did not know the place, and became aware of it only after it was lost.[20] Those who did know the canyon were a motley group of river runners, tourists and other recreationists, cowboys, miners, and scientists who individually were politically inarticulate and possessed no political identity as a group.[21]

Ironically the canyon did become known, as it were, on its deathbed. The National Park Service, which would administer the new Glen Canyon National Recreation Area, was obligated under the Historic Sites Act of 1935 to collect as much data as possible on the cultural resources—that is, historic and prehistoric activities—in the area to be flooded. Closely following on the passage of the Colorado River Storage Project Act of 1956, the park service awarded contracts to two public agencies to collect such data. The University of Utah Department of Anthropology, under the direction of Jesse D. Jennings, had by far the largest role—to survey and excavate sites in Glen Canyon above the mouth of the San Juan, and on the right bank of Glen Canyon from the mouth of the San Juan to the dam site. The Museum of Northern Arizona, under the direction of Alexander J. Lindsay, Jr., was given the responsibility of studying the area to be inundated on the San Juan River and Glen Canyon's left bank from the mouth of the San Juan to the dam site. Historical sites within the entire area were to be studied by C. Gregory Crampton of the Department of History at the University of Utah as part of the contract awarded to the Department of Anthropology.[22]

All three of the surveys, prehistoric and historic, experienced methodological and financial problems and had to develop original ways of defining and accomplishing their goals within those strictures. Although the University of Utah had the largest budget, it also had the largest area to survey, and Jennings found himself forced to develop private funding sources and to rely upon volunteer labor in some instances to supplement the inadequate public money. The Museum of Northern Arizona's appropriation fell far short of supporting exhaustive excavations, and the institution deemed it wise to restrict its work to problem-oriented explorations of a relatively few sites, and to extending, with limited support, the survey begun by Miss Gene Foster as a volunteer some years before. Crampton's historical survey received only $25,000, a pittance to support six summers in the field plus the preliminary documentary and oral history work. Although he was fortunate in being able to use University of Utah vehicles for land transportation, and in having editorial and publication costs absorbed by the Department of Anthropology, most of his budget went for a boat and supplies, and both he and his graduate student assistants worked for no wages.[23]

For the director of the salvage project, Jesse D. Jennings (1909–), the Glen Canyon Dam came along at a vital juncture in his career. Born in Oklahoma and educated at a small Baptist college and the University of Chicago, his position at the University of Utah, which he had begun in 1948 after several years as a National Park Service archaeologist, had just about exhausted its professional challenges and opportunities for him. Stymied in his desire to create a natural history museum at the university, but almost finished with the formal report on his excavations at Danger Cave near Wendover, Utah, which would bring him prizes and international renown, Jennings was wondering if the time was right to move to a more prestigious position with better opportunities elsewhere. Directing the Glen Canyon project "promised to be a tremendous research and student training opportunity that would come only once in a lifetime," and he felt compelled to accept, "with no hesitation, but many misgivings."[24]

It was a fateful decision that kept him in Utah for the rest of his career, and it brought him even greater fame than Danger Cave had done, because the Glen Canyon project became a methodological model for salvage archaeology.

Although the park service asked Jennings to undertake the project in 1956, a contract was not negotiated until June 1957, which gave him about one year to investigate the site and devise a plan. Careful planning was essential, because his misgivings resulted from the intimidating vastness of the area and its remoteness from supply bases, the unavailability of experienced Anasazi archaeologists, and the large amount of money that must be administered efficiently to accomplish a great deal of work in a short time. During that year Jennings read all the historical and descriptive literature available on the area, accomplished both an aerial and land reconnaissance, and encouraged the Anasazi archaeologist Robert H. Lister to take the 1957 academic year off from the University of Colorado to conduct a pilot project that would establish the logistics and methods to be followed by Jennings's crews. By the beginning of the 1958 season, Jennings was ready to begin work in earnest.

The necessity of simultaneously training, feeding, equipping, and guarding the physical well-being of a group of student archaeologists with, in most cases, no experience in a remote desert setting like Glen Canyon required establishing a rigid set of rules and procedures and sticking to them. In spite of his own lack of experience in the canyon country, Jennings was well equipped, both in his intelligence, his willingness to seek expert advice, and not least his imperious manner, to create and enforce the necessary discipline. Jennings's manner in the field, which he himself characterized as "abrupt and direct," became famous. Known by intimidated employees as Yahweh or the Dark Lord, for his "looming presence" on a site, Jennings would often greet a new crew chief with the words, "So, _____, you're making the mistakes on this site." "When someone did question a decision or a set of instructions," Jennings recalled,

> I merely said, "That is not a debatable subject." In field schools, when the group was in camp and I was responsible for not only the field research but also crew health, safety, cleanliness, and camp comfort, I was even more curt. When any student resisted the routine or any rules or decisions, I made a quick offer: "Ei-

ther shut up and do it, or pack your gear so I can get you to the
bus station and ship you back to Salt Lake City." In all the years,
only one person chose the bus.[25]

One can assume that the remoteness of Glen Canyon from any bus
stations imparted even greater weight to Jennings's authority.

Jennings's system for Glen Canyon consisted of small, largely au-
tonomous excavation projects of six to eight crew members under
the supervision of a chief. Two to four of these parties would take the
field each summer. Jennings himself directly supervised no crew, but
visited each of the sites several times each season to ensure that
things were going well. The crews worked ten days, then had four
days off. No alcohol was permitted in camp, no work or sightseeing
was permitted alone, and each crew member was equipped with a
first-aid kit containing a snakebite kit and various salt tablets, aspirin,
laxatives, and diarrhea remedies. Because construction of the dam
was already well under way, it was imperative to begin at the lower
end of the canyon that would be flooded first and work upstream, fo-
cusing initially on the main canyon, then branching off into the main
tributaries.[26]

The equipment provided the parties was simple. Jennings had
special ten-by-twelve-foot tents with four-foot walls made, and provided two tents for each party: one for cooking and the other for personal gear, supplies, and office. A Dutch oven or two was provided,
and Jennings recruited a cook from among each party's members,
training him and providing him with a few simple recipes. Jeeps and
boats were employed for transportation to and among the excavation
sites. River travel was a particular problem for Jennings, who was
mortally afraid of water, but he forced himself to learn to handle a
boat under J. Frank Wright's tutelage, and became competent
enough to instruct his crews in basic techniques. The boats were two
flat-bottomed aluminum craft called Arkansas Travelers, powered by
two outboard motors, and if ugly, they were nevertheless serviceable
in transporting gear and people. Supply bases were set up in Escalante, Kanab, or Blanding.

The results of the Glen Canyon project were highly satisfying to
Jennings. In addition to the biological and historical reports, a total
of about thirty anthropological papers were published, many of
which led to graduate degrees or employment for crew members,

who published the papers under their own names, not Jennings's. Besides planning and supervising the entire project, Jennings confined his involvement only to writing the final summary report. For himself Jennings reminisced that

> learning the Glen and working in and near it for six or seven summers was a rich, emotionally charged period of my life. The vastness, the isolation, the stillness, the overwhelming beauty of the land, even (especially) the heat, the still starlit nights, the blue and brassy midday sky, all combined to make me constantly aware of my good fortune. . . . In retrospect, . . . I fear I loved every minute of it.[27]

According to William Y. Adams, whose history of archaeology in Glen Canyon provided a starting point, the archaeologists were hampered in their work by several factors. One was a lack of a cumulative body of knowledge handed down by previous investigators. Before the Glen Canyon survey, archaeologists had devoted their attention simply to random artifact removal—pothunting—or systematic excavation of a relatively few easily accessible sites, most of which had previously been worked. The result was that only a tiny number of sites had been investigated in a series of unrelated excavations that had given no basis for large generalizations about prehistoric life in the canyon. Nor had sites difficult of access or located in unscenic locales been studied. Finally, archaeological survey techniques had to be invented virtually from scratch, for most prior archaeology in Glen Canyon and elsewhere had been directed to investigation of specific problems in a few specific sites. As noted, the Museum of Northern Arizona was unable, both from expertise developed in previous projects and from limited funding, to depart from a problem-oriented approach to a limited number of sites. However, the University of Utah was able to field a larger number of investigators at any given time, and accomplished both a comprehensive survey of a large number of sites and thorough excavation of a limited number of sites of extraordinary potential interest. Methodological experimentation by the University of Utah teams extended as far as the very implements used in digging, according to Jennings. Instead of spending "10,000 cramped hours . . . in alternate checkerboarded 5 foot squares slowly wearing away sterile fill with whisk brooms" according to traditional excavational procedures, Jennings admonished his crews to "use the coarsest tool which will do the work—i.e., re-cover the data." According to that approach, "a shovel can be as use-ful as a trowel, a road patrol or scraper as useful as a shovel, or a dragline as useful as a pick, in the hands of an excavator who is free of ritual compulsiveness."[28]

Crampton, too, found himself forced to improvise as the conven-tional methods of the historian proved inadequate. While a doctoral student at Berkeley under Herbert Eugene Bolton, Crampton had learned the importance of field work in any aspect of history that has a geographical component. Thus he was intellectually resilient enough to work out solutions to the "problems [that] confront the historian when he leaves the library and the archives and goes into the field to study environmental and material remains," matters "about which handbooks on historical method say little." Crampton found that he could learn a great deal from archaeological methods, which employed an initial reconnaissance, than a more detailed site survey. Crampton's reconnaissance of Glen Canyon began in 1949 when, at the end of his fourth year as a history professor at the Uni-versity of Utah, a Realtor friend, O. Coleman Dunn, invited him along on a Glen Canyon river trip. It was a great turning point in his life, not only because of the relaxed and scenic life on the river but also because of the obvious physical remains of historical activity no-ticeable at various points. When he began the historical survey in earnest in 1957, he built upon what he knew from general western history—the Dominguez-Escalante and Powell expeditions, for ex-ample—and from dramatic remains of historical activity he had seen in the canyon—the Stanton dredge and the Hole-in-the-Rock cross-ing. To that history, during seven field seasons, 1957–63, he added a catalog of sites discovered while hiking along riverbanks and up side canyons from his little seven-man navy surplus neoprene boat. The resulting reports were thus based upon a creative blend of documen-tary and oral sources long used by historians, and the shoe-leather techniques of the archaeologist. "Indeed," Crampton noted, "the final reports are so unlike historical treatises that it is not altogether inappropriate that they will be part of the *Anthropological Papers* published by the University of Utah Press. Historical archaeology, as its name implies, represents the bridging of historical and archaeo-logical techniques."[29]

A final component to the preinundation survey was the biological research supervised by Angus Munn Woodbury (1886–1964). A son of Mormon pioneers in St. George, Utah, Woodbury received his education at Brigham Young University, the University of Utah, and the University of California, Berkeley, which granted him his Ph.D. in zoology in 1931. Although trained as a herpetologist, Woodbury's interest early in his professional career shifted to ecology, the study of the interrelatedness of biological organisms with each other and with their inanimate environment. From 1957 until the death of him and his wife in an automobile accident in 1964, Woodbury planned and directed the biological studies in Glen Canyon.[30]

Woodbury's research design was ambitious. After a preliminary trip that would identify several typical ecological sample areas, a five-year study of those plots would produce a vegetation map, a study of the relation of zoological organisms including even parasites to that vegetation, a study of the effects of the natural setting of Glen Canyon on prehistoric human inhabitants, and finally a study of the effects of the reservoir on Glen Canyon's natural setting over a period after the completion of inundation. Although some of Woodbury's work was published posthumously, only the long-term study of the effects of the reservoir was not completed, and even it was taken up at a later date by the Lake Powell Research Project, funded by the National Science Foundation and other sources.[31] Like the anthropological and historical surveys, it was the first time a concerted effort, supported by at least reasonably adequate funding, had been applied to the study of Glen Canyon natural history, and it is not surprising that the results went far beyond the casual botanizing of an Alice Eastwood or an Elzada Clover.[32]

Woodbury's conclusions regarding prehistoric human interaction with the environment were sharply contested, however, by Jesse Jennings. While acknowledging that some of Woodbury's work had to be published posthumously in incomplete form and with only tentative conclusions, Jennings pointed out nevertheless that the biologist, "knowledgeable as he was, cherished about the American Indian some highly subjective and stereotyped views not consonant with views held by anthropologists." Primary among those questionable views was the conception of "the Indian as a wretched, improvident creature engaged in a losing battle with a hostile world against which his technology was inadequate," and reacting against that world in a wholly passive way.[33] In contrast, Jennings admired the Anasazis of

Glen Canyon as tenacious and resourceful hunters and farmers who adapted creatively to a parsimonious environment that they occupied more or less consistently for a thousand years. Furthermore, in Jennings's view, the Glen Canyon Anasazis offer scientists a better appreciation of that Puebloan resourcefulness than do the relatively fertile environments that sustained the great cities of the Tsegi, Mesa Verde, and Chaco Canyon.[34]

The Glen Canyon Salvage Project was an obituary written while the patient was on his deathbed. As Glen Canyon died, there was a transitional generation bridging the gap between the old rivermen like Arthur Chaffin and Dick Sprang and the multitude of modern recreationists who know Glen Canyon only from the deck of a rental houseboat after its metamorphosis into Lake Powell.[35] Among those was Woody Edgell, who ran the Hite ferry briefly after the departure of Arth Chaffin and while the lake was rising. The loquacious Edgell, who cleaned up the junkyard Hite had become after the departure of the Chaffins, was full of futile optimism that his ferry would link Highway 95 across Lake Powell, ignoring the state's plans for a complete realignment of the highway and construction of the three bridges, over the Dirty Devil, Narrow, and White Canyons, by which motorists now gain access to San Juan County.[36] J. Frank Wright, a Nevills boatman and inheritor of the Nevills business with his partner, Jim Rigg, opened a small marina at Hall's Crossing as the lake was rising.[37] The riverman who made the best transition to the lake, however, was the legendary Art Greene, a salty character and fine businessman who made a comfortable living as a tourist promoter on both river and lake.[38]

Greene's background as a cowboy remained apparent in his clothing and his speech, but it was as a trader and tourist promoter that he made his reputation. And he was a family man, who involved his wife, their two daughters and sons-in-law, and even their grandchildren in various aspects of the business. Stan Jones, his friend of later years, remembered people saying of him that "Art has been out here and accomplished so much in so few years without doing a lick of work . . . because he had the *family* doing all the work."[39] From 1945 to 1950 the Greenes ran Ramon Hubbell's trading post at Marble Canyon at the west end of Navajo Bridge where the road to Lee's Ferry intersects with Highway 89. When that contract expired, they moved a few miles up along the Vermilion Cliffs toward Kanab and went into competition with Hubbell, building a similar establishment called Cliff Dwellers Lodge.

The gregarious Greene was a famous raconteur, whose cowboy clothing and toothless grin endeared him to tourists as a real western "character," yet veteran river people respected his wisdom and knowledge of the country. "The river is dropping so fast the catfish are wearing straw hats," he told one party of dudes. "I ain't afraid of the river," he told Dick Sprang, "and I hope you ain't, but man, I respect it! You gotta respect it or the goddam son of a bitch will GET YA!"[40]

Greene's most famous venture during river days was his airboat excursions from Lee's Ferry to Rainbow Bridge. The boat, christened the *Tseh Na-ni-ah-go Atin* ("the trail to the rock that goes over," in Navajo) was powered by an airplane engine and propeller near the stern. One imagines Greene's customers were relieved to find that Rainbow Bridge is one of the most spectacular scenic sites in the world, for a lesser destination would not have justified the ear-splitting transportation. In time, Greene replaced the airboat with a more conventional inboard craft that made conversations possible between guide and passengers in voice rather than sign language and removed the necessity for issuing ear plugs to those boarding the boat.

When the Glen Canyon Dam was finished, Greene had already recognized the business potential of the lake, and he opened the first marina in the vicinity of the dam. It was the most advantageous location on the lake, not only because the lake itself would first develop there (in fact years before it eventually reached Hite at the upper end), but also because of the proximity of the community of Page, Arizona, where additional food, lodging, and other support services for his guests were available. Greene's first marina was in Padre Bay where the lake initially developed, but access to it required negotiating a rough road to a fairly remote site. Consequently, as the lake continued to rise, he moved to Wahweap Bay, where he put in a little dock and continued his Rainbow Bridge excursions in addition to other modest services. Greene's pioneering efforts at Wahweap led eventually to creation of by far the largest and most profitable of concessions on the lake.

The transitional generation is also well represented by Stan Jones, a writer and photographer who arrived in Page, Arizona, at about the time the reservoir was beginning to fill and became the observer of the last days of the canyon as he became the promoter of the new Lake Powell.[41]

Born in 1918, Jones grew up in a middle-class family in Winnetka, Illinois, a suburb of Chicago. The scarcities of the Great Depression instilled in him a deep work ethic, which has sustained a largely self-employed writing career. An early athletic talent that led to high school diving championships and a swimming instructorship in the navy during World War II prepared him for the rigors of canyon country exploration. A successful career in newspaper writing and editing led to employment as a publicist with Walt Disney, where he promoted the budding career of Fess Parker in the mid-1950s. As he and his wife, Alice, noted the deteriorating health of their young son as a result of the Los Angeles air pollution, they found it necessary to leave Disney and relocate to Tucson, Arizona. There he found work as a publicist for the University of Arizona and on his own produced his first book, *Arizona's Future*, for the Arizona Republican Party, which the party used in 1964 to help secure the presidential nomination of Barry Goldwater. It was a time of gestation for his career as promoter of Lake Powell; he spent days in the university library studying the history and natural features of his adopted state—knowledge he would put to powerful use in his later writings.

When Lake Powell began to form, Jones moved his family to the tiny community of Page, which at that time was still mostly a construction camp for the dam workers, but was making its transition to the tourist support center it has since become. The lake at that time consisted only of a few shallowly inundated areas right around the dam, and Jones found his creativity taxed to produce photographs illustrating recreational opportunities that would soon exist but that had not yet really developed. Accordingly, he staged a photograph, for example, of some friends lounging on lawn chairs under beach umbrellas on a tiny expanse of sand that would soon be several hundred feet under water. Wishing to illustrate the dramatic waterfalls that occasionally develop in the canyon country, he photographed a tiny trickle of water over a cliff near Page, only to learn later that it was overflow from a leaky lawn sprinkler system at a park ranger's home.

In his zeal to acquire firsthand knowledge of the canyons that the lake would soon make available to tourists, Jones acquired a small, narrow boat that he nicknamed the Cigar, powered by a small outboard motor and ideally suited for exploration of narrow canyon slots. On the boat he carried an aluminum ladder, which enabled him to reach ledges above the lake level that contained Anasazi remains or scenic vantage points. Thus he became the original explorer of many parts of the canyon inaccessible since the disappearance of the Anasazis, if even then. The enterprise was not without its dangers. One was the necessity of safely anchoring the ladder, which he accomplished by grinding automobile engine valves to a sharp point and driving them into the sandstone as pitons to which he could lash the ladder. Another peril was the immense flocks of birds whose previously inaccessible rookeries he was able to invade from the rising water. At times he found himself being dive-bombed and forced into retreat by protective nesters. But he persisted, and became perhaps the first person to have explored every one of Glen Canyon's tributaries thoroughly, a possibility opened by motorized transportation.

Exploring Glen Canyon's scenic areas fell far short of exhausting Jones's interest. He had a lifelong love of history and knew from his studies in the University of Arizona library that the history of northern Arizona and southern Utah was long and rich. In later years he laughed at his naiveté as a researcher in those days, which failed to lead him to Crampton's studies of the canyon until he had duplicated much of their research himself. But whether by the easy way or the hard way, Jones has become one of the most respected experts on Glen Canyon history, and one of the appealing features of his best-selling maps of the lake, "Stan Jones' Lake Powell Country," is their historical data, which deepens the visitors' experience far beyond the scenery. Even beyond other visitors, Jones was captivated by the awe-inspiring beauty of Rainbow Bridge, which he has photographed memorably on hundreds of occasions. That interest led him to plan a book on the vexed history of its discovery, and while the book is still uncompleted at this writing, Jones has become the acknowledged expert on the subject, as the immense files in his office demonstrate.

Thus the history of the canyon has passed from the records of the original explorers and inhabitants through a transitional generation to later visitors and scholars across a wide spectrum of interests. If few of those who know that history prefer the lake to the canyon, the lake is nevertheless the reality with which we must deal, and Glen Canyon has been one of America's success stories in effective preservation of historical knowledge of an area destroyed in the name of modern progress.

Arthur Chaffin's Glen Canyon mining career, along with his other enterprises, ended in acrimonious litigation during the mid-1960s as he sought compensation for his mining and tourism interests as they were destroyed by Lake Powell. In spite of employing river historian Otis R. "Dock" Marston as a witness, and expert photographer and riverman Dick Sprang to photograph the scenic resources of the Hite area, the Chaffin trial ended on January 7, 1966, with an award of only $8,000, "not enough to pay the expense & worry of fighting them," Chaffin wrote to Sprang. "We did learn that the B.L.M. & [Bureau of] Reclamation are so 'rotten' that no citizen should be proud of them."[42]

The following Christmas, in the North Hollywood home of historian P. T. Reilly, Chaffin reminisced about the old days in Glen Canyon: his days as a trader at Camp Stone, placer mining, and his old friend Cass Hite. He could not have foreseen, of course, the major social problems Lake Powell would bring, the ultimate, one hopes, being a 1992 story in the *Salt Lake Tribune* titled, "Drinkers, Fighters, Fornicators," in which police were reported as having witnessed "a woman openly engaged in a sex act involving a funnel, a rubber hose and beer."[43] His most poignant observations instead related to the effects of the then-rising Lake Powell on the natural features of the old canyon, particularly the beaver. Beavers have existed in plentiful enough numbers to have provided an income for trappers perhaps as far back as the shadowy mountain man Denis Julien in the 1830s, and certainly including Nathaniel Galloway around the turn of the century and even Chaffin himself. The same lake that was buoying Stan Jones into his exploration of Glen Canyon's hidden marvels was driving beavers onto ever higher ground in the tributary canyons in quest of survival. "Poor things," Chaffin lamented, "they're having a tough time of it." At the mouth of Smith Fork, for example, he had observed beavers living under some fallen rock ledges near the famous petroglyph panel—by then also flooded—that had been an imperative stop for river parties.

> When I was down doing that backhoe work and we was over there, I seen where they'd been, and different places along the side of the river where there wasn't no dirt to dig . . . their holes,

why they just got in under the rocks. They'd get up in the top of the trees and cut the trees off to get something to eat.

Then, after a reflective silence, Chaffin added quietly, in the saddest voice ever heard, "Yes, it's a different story down there [now]."[44]

NOTES

1. Several people have suspicions of Chaffin's involvement in at least one murder and, less seriously, he was known for taking advantage of associates or customers in business dealings. See, for example, Harry Aleson's confidential note to Otis Marston, November 22, 1966, and his reminder to Chaffin of some of their business dealings, Aleson to Chaffin, February 1, 1967, both letters in the Harry Aleson Papers, Utah State Historical Society.

2. Arthur L. Chaffin testimony, Colorado River Case, 1929, Utah State Historical Society.

3. Dick Sprang, recorded reminiscences of Hite, Utah, Utah State Historical Society. Other Chaffin material here comes from Chaffin's testimony in the Colorado River Case, Utah State Historical Society; interviews with P. T. Reilly, Reilly Papers, Utah State Historical Society; Charles Kelly, "New Road into the Utah Wilderness," *Desert Magazine* (February 1947): 10–14; and Joyce Rockwood Muench, "They Run the Ferry at Hite," *Desert Magazine* (February 1952): 22–26.

4. Ibid., 13–14; Kelly, "New Road Into the Utah Wilderness," 10–14; Muench, "They Run the Ferry at Hite," 22–26.

5. The story of the building and dedication of the Hite ferry is told in a pamphlet, [Wm. E. Rice,] "Hite, September 17, 1946," available at the Utah State Historical Society and other repositories. The Hite ferry built by Chaffin was the first only in the sense that it was the first designed for general traffic. A copper miner, Benjamin Harshberger, had maintained a large cable-anchored ferry for a brief period in 1907 or 1908 to transport his ore from the Fry Canyon area to Green River. It was located at Mile 165.8, about 3.3 miles above the Chaffin ferry. C. Gregory Crampton, *Historical Sites in Cataract and Narrow Canyons, and in Glen Canyon to California Bar*, University of Utah Anthropological Paper No. 72 (Salt Lake City: University of Utah Press, 1964), 36.

6. The background of the Glen Canyon Dam has been told in various places: Russell Martin, *A Story That Stands Like a Dam: Glen Canyon and the Struggle for the Soul of the West* (New York: Henry Holt, 1989); Loren D. Potter and Charles L. Drake,

Lake Powell: Virgin Flow to Dynamo (Albuquerque: University of New Mexico Press, 1989); Philip L. Fradkin, *A River No More: The Colorado River and the West* (New York: Alfred A. Knopf, 1981). Its relationship to the Echo Park dam proposal is a major focus of Mark W. T. Harvey's *A Symbol of Wilderness: Echo Park and the American Conservation Movement* (Albuquerque: University of New Mexico Press, 1994).

7. Miser's Field Notes are in the USGS Field Records Library, Denver, Colorado; his report is *The San Juan Canyon, Southeastern Utah: A Geographic and Hydrographic Reconnaissance*, USGS Water Supply Paper No. 538 (Washington, D.C.: Government Printing Office, 1924); see also Pearl Baker, "Man Against the River: 7,000 Miles of Rapids with Bert Loper," *Utah Humanities Review* 1 (April 1947): 113–21; and *Trail on the Water* (Boulder, Colo.: Pruett Press, 1969); Richard Westwood, *Rough-Water Man: Elwyn Blake's Colorado River Expeditions* (Reno: University of Nevada Press, 1992). W. L. Rusho, ed., "River Running 1921: The Diary of E. L. Kolb," *Utah Historical Quarterly* 37 (Spring 1969): 269–83, mainly covers the Cataract Canyon survey and devotes only a week to Glen Canyon, which, as Rusho points out (n. 11), was mainly surveyed by land parties operating out of Lee's Ferry; E[ugene] C[lyde] LaRue, *Water Power and Flood Control of the Colorado River Below Green River, Utah*, USGS Water Supply Paper No. 556 (Washington, D.C.: Government Printing Office, 1925).

8. Miser, *San Juan Canyon*, 2; Henry Elwyn Blake to Otis Marston, November 11, 1947, Marston Papers, the Huntington Library; Robert N. Allen testimony in Colorado River Case, Utah State Historical Society.

9. Henry Elwyn Blake to Otis Marston, December 1, 1947, Marston Papers; Robert Allen testimony in the Colorado River Case; Henry Elwyn Blake testimony in Colorado River Case.

10. Miser Field Notes, August 11–12, 23, 1921.

11. Miser, *San Juan Canyon*, 2; Miser Field Notes, October 5–8, 1921. Blake reported a dispute between Allen and Trimble precipitated by LaRue's disputation of Trimble's instrument readings at the mouth of the San Juan, which led to Allen and Christensen leaving the party on October 14. Blake to Marston, December 1, 1947; Allen testimony in Colorado River Case; Westwood, *Rough-Water Man*, 61–63.

12. Rusho, ed., "River Running 1921," 269–74.

13. Ibid., 279–80.

14. Eugene Clyde LaRue, *Colorado River and Its Utilization*, USGS Water Supply Paper No. 395 (Washington, D.C.: Government Printing Office, 1916).

15. A. R. Mortensen, ed., "A Journal of John A. Widtsoe," *Utah Historical Quarterly* 53 (1955): 195–230; John A. Widtsoe, *In a Sunlit Land* (Salt Lake City: Deseret News Press, 1952), 178–85; Lewis R. Freeman, *Down the Grand Canyon* (New York: Dodd, Mead and Co., 1924), 71–215.

16. Widtsoe, *In a Sunlit Land*, 180.

17. Freeman, *Down the Grand Canyon*, 73–75; 79–83.

18. Harvey, *A Symbol of Wilderness*, 43.

19. C. Gregory Crampton interview with Jay M. Haymond, November 15–17, 1994, 58, Utah State Historical Society.

20. Eliot Porter, *The Place No One Knew* (San Francisco: Sierra Club Books, 1963); C. Gregory Crampton interview with Jay Haymond, November 17, 1994, Utah State Historical Society; Martin, *A Story That Stands Like a Dam*, Chapters 1–4.

21. See, for example, Gary Topping, "Harry Aleson and the Place No One Knew," *Utah Historical Quarterly* 52 (Spring 1984): 165–78. Aleson had concocted a harebrained scheme in which he would fight the dam by arranging to be called as an expert witness, presumably to defend the project, then reverse himself and deliver a ringing denunciation—surely not an effective kind of political action.

22. In addition to the massive reports published by both institutions, there are several summary accounts of the Glen Canyon Salvage Project: Martin, *A Story That Stands Like a Dam*, Chapter 5; Jesse D. Jennings, *Glen Canyon: A Summary*, University of Utah Anthropological Paper No. 81 (Salt Lake City: University of Utah Press, 1966); Jennings and Floyd W. Sharrock, "The Glen Canyon: A Multi-discipline Project," *Utah Historical Quarterly* 33 (Winter 1965): 34–50; William Y. Adams, *Ninety Years of Glen Canyon Archaeology, 1869–1959* (Flagstaff: Northern Arizona Society of Science and Art, Inc., 1960), 9-29; Crampton interview with Jay Haymond, November 15–17, 1994, *Outline History of the Glen Canyon Region, 1776–1922*, University of Utah Anthropological Paper No. 42 (Salt Lake City: University of Utah Press, 1959), and *Ghosts of Glen Canyon: History Beneath Lake Powell* (St. George, Utah: Publishers Place, 1986), 15–16; Charles S. Peterson, "In Memoriam: C. Gregory Crampton, 1911–1995, *Utah Historical Quarterly* 63 (Fall 1995): 370–73.

23. Jennings, *Glen Canyon: A Summary*, 4–5; Adams, *Ninety Years of Glen Canyon Archaeology*, 9–11; Crampton interview with Jay Haymond.

24. Jesse D. Jennings, *Accidental Archaeologist: Memoirs of Jesse D. Jennings* (Salt Lake City: University of Utah Press, 1994), 205.

25. Ibid., 195–96, xiii–xiv.

26. Ibid., 210–11, gives a season-by-season summary of the area studied; p. 206 explains the geographical responsibilities assumed by the two institutions involved, the Museum of Northern Arizona and the University of Utah.

27. Ibid., 216–17.

28. Adams, *Ninety Years of Glen Canyon Archaeology*, 19; Jennings, *Glen Canyon: A Summary*, 6–7.

29. C. Gregory Crampton, "Historical Archaeology on the Colorado River." In Robert G. Ferris, ed., *The American West: An Appraisal* (Santa Fe: Museum of New Mexico Press, 1963), 216–17; Crampton interview with Jay Hammond; Martin, *A Story That Stands Like a Dam*, 103–7.

30. Vasco M. Tanner, "Angus Munn Woodbury, 1886–1964," *Great Basin Naturalist* 25 (December 31, 1965): 81–88; Stan Rasmussen, "Adventure in the Glen Canyon of the Colorado," *Reclamation Era* (May 1958): 41–45; Olive W. Burt, "He Brands Snakes," *Desert Magazine* (October 1950): 9–12.

31. Angus M. Woodbury, *Ecological Studies of Flora and Fauna in Glen Canyon*, University of Utah Anthropological Paper No. 40 (Salt Lake City: University of Utah Press, 1959); Potter and Drake, *Lake Powell: Virgin Flow to Dynamo*.

32. A complete list of publications of the Glen Canyon Survey, including the ecological studies of Woodbury and his associates, is given in Jesse D. Jennings, *Glen Canyon: A Summary*, 70–84.

33. Jennings, *Glen Canyon: A Summary*, 39.

34. Ibid., 30; Jennings, *Accidental Archaeologist*, 216.

35. On the transformation of Glen Canyon from river to reservoir, see Jared Farmer, "Field Notes: Glen Canyon and the Persistence of Wilderness," *Western Historical Quarterly* 27 (Summer 1996): 211–22.

36. Dick Sprang statement on Hite, 51–54.

37. Choral Pepper, "Caves, Canyons, and Caches," *Desert Magazine* (September 1964): 16–19 ff.

38. Joyce Rockwood Muench, "Art Greene: A Friend by the Side of the Road," *Arizona Highways* 40 (January 1964): 44–47; Randall Henderson, "When the Boats Wouldn't Float—We Pulled 'Em," *Desert Magazine* (September 1950): 5–6; Ralph Gray, "Three Roads to Rainbow," *National Geographic* 111 (April 1957): 547–61;

Frank Jensen, "Riverman," *Desert Magazine* (July 1962): 26–27; Al Hall and Hubert Lowman, "We Saw a Rockfall in Glen Canyon," *Desert Magazine* (January 1957): 9–10; Stan Jones interview with Gary Topping, March 24–25, 1995, Utah State Historical Society.

39. Jones interview with Gary Topping, 28.

40. Gray, "Three Roads to Rainbow," 550; Elizabeth Sprang, *Good-bye River* (Reseda, Calif.: Mojave Books, 1979), 1.

41. Jones is a prolific author of newspaper columns and magazine articles, best known for his ubiquitous "Stan Jones' Lake Powell Country," a large color map of the lake packed with illustrations and historical and geographic data that has been sold by the thousands at various tourist outlets in the area for almost thirty years in annually revised and improved editions. Other major publications include *Spectacular Lake Powell Country* (1978); *Fishin' Lake Powell* [with Bob Hirsch] (1983); and *Glen Canyon Dam and Steel-Arch Bridge Souvenir Guide Book* (1984), all published by his own Sun Country Publications in Page, Arizona. Biographical data based on Stan Jones interview with Gary Topping, March 24–25, 1995, Utah State Historical Society.

42. Chaffin to Sprang, January 16, 1966, in records of *Chaffin vs. United States*, papers of Milton R. Oman, Utah State Historical Society.

43. *Salt Lake Tribune*, June 5, 1992, A1–A2.

44. Chaffin, interview with P. T. Reilly, December 24, 1966, 59–61. Reilly Papers, Utah State Historical Society.

Epilog

Beginning at least as early as Eliot Porter's *The Place No One Knew* (1963), denouncing the "loss" of Glen Canyon has become a favorite pastime, not only among river runners, environmentalists, and wild-eyed Earth First! activists, but also by almost anyone who knows or at least has heard anything about the subject. Glen Canyon has become a symbol in the American mind for the triumph of American materialism and greed over esthetics and science. Of course this is not a baseless rage—Glen Canyon was a place of unparalleled beauty and interest, though the uninformed nature of much of that rage merits a heavy discount. Although some few visitors like Charles Kelly applauded the flooding of the canyon, most who knew the area even casually were appalled. But the lovers of the canyon lost, because of their fragmentation, political ineptitude, and abandonment by such organized political acumen and weight as the Sierra Club could have provided. The post–World War II ethos of development, progress, technical mastery, and triumph over Nature was a juggernaut that might have annihilated even a vigorous resistance.

There are, of course, some compelling points to be adduced in defense of Lake Powell. The Glen Canyon Dam, for one thing, produces an immense amount of inexpensive electrical power (something one supposes southern California Sierra Clubbers have not been willing to deny themselves in protest over the dam) with low staff and maintenance costs. And, once one reconciles oneself to the *fait accompli* of the environmental effects of the submersion of Glen Canyon, it is totally "clean" power, with none of the hazards of nuclear reactors nor the smoke-spewing pollution of such coal-powered plants as the Navajo Generating Station, ironically located within view of the Glen Canyon dam. And, partially compensating for the submersion of the vast majority of Glen Canyon's archaeological sites and many of its scenic attractions, the lake has made possible access to treasures like Rainbow Bridge to anyone with the price of a tour boat ticket.

Still, it is hard to dispute Wallace Stegner's judgment that Lake Powell was a questionable compromise: "In gaining the lovely and the usable, we have given up the incomparable."[1] And P. T. Reilly's warning against replicating such projects in the future surely merits serious reflection: "Even nuclear power does not remove the need to build dams because they also provide for crop irrigation. A major question now before us is whether we can afford to build dams purely for power generation."[2]

Both sides in the controversy are welcome to anything they think they can mine from the foregoing pages in support of their positions, for I do not intend to provide either a promotional tract or a jeremiad—both redundant and futile enterprises. Rather, my is purpose to promote Glen Canyon as a subject inherently worthy of historical examination, as a theater in which the great drama of Man in Nature has been played out to an intricately detailed script.

It was a unique play, in which the stage settings severely limited and shaped the scope and course of human activity. It may well be, as John Wetherill said, that the desert will take care of you, but as Hosteen John well knew, the desert has to be taken on its own terms. Robert Brewster Stanton, author of the two most ambitious attempts in Glen Canyon history to bend Nature to human designs—the riverbank railway and the gold dredge—learned most bitterly of Nature's recalcitrance. The most successful of Nature's exploiters, by contrast, may have been the modest agricultural enterprises of the Anasazis, the meager flocks of the Navajos, the easy placer mines of Cass Hite and Arthur Chaffin, and the river tours of Norman Nevills and Harry Aleson. "Let's go live in Glen Canyon," Dick Sprang used to say. Genuine living was possible there, and many accepted the invitation.

Far from merely a stern barrier to human intrusion and exploitation, Nature in fact exerted an active influence on those who entered the San Juan country. It was Zane Grey—himself the most arrogant of dudes—who created the literary paradigm for the experience of countless refugees from urban, industrial American culture who "found" themselves through contact with the primeval realities of the canyon country. The archetypal Grey hero or heroine in his books about southern Utah and northern Arizona—*The Heritage of the Desert, Riders of the Purple Sage, The Rainbow Trail, The Man of the Forest*, and *The Call of the Canyon* are all good examples—is a physically weak and morally confused easterner who comes west and enters an environment where, one might say, the chips are always down in a life-and-death struggle against clearly evil villains and the unforgiving imperatives of desert living. The easterner responds positively to those challenges, finding clear purpose in life, physical strength, and—inevitably—love.

In some cases, like that of Charles L. Bernheimer, who was intimately familiar with Grey's writings, it may have been life imitating art, but we have seen numerous instances of the profound emotional effects on visitors to the canyon country, even upon such presumably hardened scientists as Neil M. Judd and Herbert E. Gregory. Turning even a few pages in the Kayenta guest registers must impress one with the essential validity of the Grey paradigm.

Of course it was not that those "hardened" scientists simply capitulated to their emotional reactions; Glen Canyon and the San Juan country remained a great—though unsystematically exploited—scientific laboratory from the initial pothunting forays of Graham and Mcloyd in the 1890s to the hurried investigations of the Glen Canyon Salvage Project of the late 1950s and early 1960s. It is surely a great misfortune that a systematic scientific survey like those of Powell, Wheeler, or Hayden was not dispatched to the San Juan country in time to go about its work at an appropriate pace and level of sophistication. Instead, scientific work in all fields, while not insignificant, was generally sporadic, amateur, and unpublished before the improvised salvage project undertaken beneath the lengthening shadow of the dam. The tragic consequence was that the scientific potential of the region was largely squandered.

So what was Glen Canyon, then, in its permanent significance? A Brigadoon, as Dick Sprang calls it, a vanished utopia that will never reappear except in our dreams? A symbol of American exploitative excess, an inspiration for riverbank rhetoric and cocktail party hand wringing? A "muddy ditch," as one Lake Powell marina employee put it, a useless wasteland that was finally tamed by technological triumph?

It was all of those things and none of those things. The best answer I can offer is simply given in the previous chapters, which explain the place the best I can. Glen Canyon is still there, its lowest elevations, to be sure, submerged. But to the explorer skilled with boat and boot, with compass and map, with four-wheel-drive and Dutch oven, with book and manuscript, and driven by a love for Nature's secret places, Glen Canyon has lost only some of its allure, and even in its diminished scale remains the most enchanting place on earth.

NOTES

1. Wallace Stegner, "Glen Canyon Submersus." In *The Sound of Mountain Water* (Garden City, N. Y.: Doubleday & Company, 1969), 128.

2. P. T. Reilly, "The Lost World of Glen Canyon," *Utah Historical Quarterly* 63 (Spring 1995): 134.

Illustrations

The purpose of the following photographs is to illustrate some of the historical persons and places discussed in the text. Purely scenic photographs have been omitted. Glen Canyon was, however, a famously scenic place, and fortunately there are several published collections of photographs to which the reader interested in the beauty of Glen Canyon may turn. The best is Eleanor Inskip's *The Colorado River Through Glen Canyon Before Lake Powell: Historic Photo Journal 1872 to 1964*, a beautifully produced series of mostly color photographs illustrating important historic and scenic sites in geographic sequence from Hite to Lee's Ferry. P. T. Reilly's "The Lost World of Glen Canyon," reveals the canyon in black and white, both from the air and the water, including unique views of erosion caused by Lake Powell's advancing waters in 1968. The pioneering work of C. Gregory Crampton in *Standing Up Country: The Canyonlands of Utah and Arizona* offers an illustrated history of a larger region that includes Glen Canyon and the San Juan River, with both historic and scenic views in color and black and white. Many of his photographs are reproduced in his *Ghosts of Glen Canyon: History Beneath Lake Powell*, which, like Inskip's book, is arranged in geographical sections. E. Tad Nichols, "Glen Canyon As It Was: A Photographic Record," is a collection of black and white photographs by an explorer of the 1930s. Readers interested in artistic photography should not deny themselves the pleasure of Eliot Porter's famous *The Place No One Knew: Glen Canyon on the Colorado*. Unfortunately, Porter's closeup lens revealed little of Glen Canyon's uniqueness in the sweep of its scenic vistas. Most of his photographs could have been taken almost anywhere in the canyon country, and in fact a few of them are not Glen Canyon scenes at all.

All photographs in this section are from the Utah State Historical Society unless otherwise credited.

Cass Hite, Hosteen Pish-la-kai ("Mister Silver") to his Navajo friends, at about the time he became Glen Canyon's first permanent white resident in 1883. Although he lured many other miners to unprofitable digs in the 1890s, he himself earned a comfortable income from the placers in the "Bank of Ticaboo."

Platte DeAlton Lyman, de facto leader of the Mormon San Juan mission, the Hole-in-the-Rock expedition. Banished from the leadership hierarchy at Bluff, he became the first cattleman in the Lake Country.

John Albert Scorup, the first great cattleman of the canyons, who defeated the Texans and the Bluff Pool to create a cattle empire that included most of San Juan County, Utah.

Byron Cummings, "the Dean," as his students affectionately called him. Professor at the Universities of Utah and Arizona, Cummings's archaeological methods were primitive, but he accomplished the first investigations of many prehistoric sites and participated in the discovery of Rainbow Bridge.

Herbert Ernest Gregory, the great geologist of the canyon country and Navajo land. Gregory's reports for the U.S. Geological Survey brought the first comprehensive scientific understanding of the structure of much of the Colorado Plateau by embracing anthropology, biology, history, and folklore as well as geology.

Charles L. Bernheimer, the Cliff Dweller from Manhattan, as he modestly called himself. Lured by the writings of Herbert E. Gregory and Zane Grey, Bernheimer returned again and again during the 1920s to explore the canyons. His field notes and other writings are an invaluable record of an eastern dude's encounter with the desert backcountry.

Members of the Nevills party prepare for their 1938 expedition at Mexican Hat, Utah. The party included the two botanists Lois Jotter (L) and Elzada Clover (R). The women are flanked by Eugene Atkinson on the left and Norman Nevills on the right.

The Wetherill establishment under construction in Kayenta. During the years after 1910 this compound, which included home, trading post, tourist resort, and the most remote post office in the United States, became a celebrated outpost for exploration and recreation in the canyon country. *Photo courtesy of Harvey Leake.*

The combative Charles Kelly strikes a pose in Glen Canyon, 1932. Kelly was a competent historian and a fine writer, but not much of a river runner. His Glen Canyon trips were marked by dissension, inadequate equipment, and poor boatmanship.

Ezekiel Johnson, cowboy, miner, guide, and raconteur whose exploits are featured prominently in the writings of his most famous client, Charles L. Bernheimer.

Arthur L. Chaffin spent nearly a lifetime in Glen Canyon as a miner, trader, and
ferryman. His friends included Cass Hite, Hoskinnini, and virtually everyone who
had anything to do with the river from the 1890s to the creation of the Glen
Canyon Dam. His life on the river ended bitterly in the 1960s with a lawsuit over
eminent domain as Lake Powell flooded his property.

"Hosteen John" Wetherill, explorer, archaeologist, and trader who made
some of the most remarkable discoveries in the history of the Southwest. After
accomplishing the first excavations at Mesa Verde with his brothers, he explored
Grand Gulch and discovered Betatakin, Inscription House, and Rainbow Bridge.
"The desert will take care of you," he said, and no one was more at home there
than Hosteen John.

John Wetherill at the Goodridge (Mexican Hat) swinging bridge. Built toward the end of the nineteenth century by prospector Emery Langdon Goodridge, the bridge was destroyed more than once by the treacherous San Juan River, but it remained a much more dependable crossing than the sporadic ferries and fords it replaced. On the back of this photo, Hosteen John poked fun at the remoteness and barrenness of the place: "Kayenta—45 (?) mi.; Bluff—27 mi.; Hell—1 mi." *Photo courtesy of Harvey Leake.*

Robert Brewster Stanton, the engineer who mounted the two most ambitious attempts at economic exploitation of Glen Canyon: the water-level railroad from Colorado to California, and the Hoskaninni gold dredge. The railroad was never built and the dredge failed to turn a profit, but Stanton never lost interest in the country and became the first historian of the Colorado River.

Earl H. Morris, the archaeologist who accompanied several of the Bernheimer expeditions. Morris was a prominent contributor to development of Anasazi chronology and tree-ring dating. He excavated the ruins at Aztec, New Mexico, and restored the great kiva.

Robert Robertson (L) and Gus Scott at Lee's Ferry, July 16, 1955. During a month in Glen Canyon, the two Stanford undergraduates explored Forgotten Canyon, discovered and explored Beaver (now Crystal Springs) Canyon, climbed Navajo Mountain, and accomplished an impressive botanical and zoological survey of the canyon. *Photo courtesy of Gus Scott.*

Theodore Roosevelt (R) and two of his family companions at Kayenta, 1913. T. R. experienced some of what he called "the strenuous life" on the trail to Rainbow Bridge. *Photo courtesy of Harvey Leake.*

The writer Hoffman Birney in Glen Canyon, 1932. Birney's dislike for the anthropologist Julian Steward ruined the 1932 expedition, but his *Roads to Roam* was an engaging invitation to Southwestern tourism.

Zane Grey and his horse, White Stockings, negotiating a rough spot on the Rainbow Trail in 1913. Grey's melodramatic novels of southern Utah and northern Arizona made him a wealthy man and established a romantic vision of that country for generations of tourists. *Photo courtesy of Harvey Leake.*

Bibliography

ARCHIVES AND MANUSCRIPT COLLECTIONS

Although every repository consulted during the research for this book is listed below, only major collections in those repositories are given. The provenance of individual manuscripts or records is given at the point of first citation of those items in the footnotes.

American Museum of Natural History, New York City
    Charles L. Bernheimer Papers
    Richard Wetherill Papers

Arizona Historical Society, Tucson
    Byron Cummings Papers

Arizona State Museum, Tucson
    Byron Cummings Papers
    John and Louisa Wetherill Papers

Bernice Bishop Museum, Honolulu
    Herbert E. Gregory Papers

California Academy of Sciences, San Francisco
    Alice Eastwood Papers

Henry E. Huntington Library, San Marino, California
    Otis R. Marston Papers

Museum of Northern Arizona, Flagstaff
    John and Louisa Wetherill Papers
    Rainbow Bridge–Monument Valley Expedition Papers

National Anthropological Archives, Smithsonian Institution, Washington, D.C.
    Neil Merton Judd Papers

United States Geological Survey Field Records Library, Denver, Colorado
    Herbert E. Gregory Field Notes

Northern Arizona University, Flagstaff
    Gladwell Richardson Papers

University of Arizona Special Collections, Tucson
    Lorenzo Hubbell Papers

University of Utah Special Collections, Salt Lake City
    Dean Brimhall Papers
    Charles Kelly Papers
    Norman Nevills Papers

Utah State Historical Society, Salt Lake City
    Harry Aleson Papers
    Colorado River Case Archives
    Charles Kelly Papers
    Russell G. Frazier Papers
    Milton R. Oman Papers
    P. T. Reilly Papers

SELECTED BIBLIOGRAPHY

This is a severely restrictive listing of only the most important books and articles utilized in or closely related to this study. Additional newspaper articles, oral history interviews, and ephemera are cited in the footnotes to individual chapters. A much more extensive bibliography, nearly exhaustive for works published through about 1985 and covering a somewhat larger geographic area, is on deposit at the Utah State Historical Society.

Articles

Adams, Eleanor B. "Fray Francisco Atanasio Dominguez and Fray Silvestre Vélez De Escalante," *Utah Historical Quarterly* 44 (1976): 40–58.

Aird, Robert B. "An Adventure for Adventure's Sake," ed. Gary Topping. *Utah Historical Quarterly* 62 (Summer 1994): 275–88.

Alter, J. Cecil. "Father Escalante's Map," *Utah Historical Quarterly* 9 (1941): 64–72.

Auerbach, Herbert S. "Father Escalante's Route," *Utah Historical Quarterly* 9 (1941): 73–80.

———. "Father Escalante's Itinerary," *Utah Historical Quarterly* 9 (1941): 109–28.

————. *Father Escalante's Journal, 1776–77*. Salt Lake City: Utah State Historical Society, 1943.

Austin, Thomas E. and Robert S. McPherson. "Murder, Mayhem, and Mormons: The Evolvement of Law Enforcement on the San Juan Frontier, 1880–1900," *Utah Historical Quarterly* 55 (Winter 1987): 36–49.

Babington, S. H. "On the Painted Desert and the Black Mesa of Arizona: 1936 Rainbow Bridge Expedition," *Pacific Magazine* 4 (Spring 1937).

Bailey, Alfred M. and Fred G. Brandenburg. "Desert River Through Navajo Land," *National Geographic* 92 (August 1947): 149–72.

Baker, Pearl. "Man Against the River: 7,000 Miles of Rapids with Bert Loper," *Utah Humanities Review* 1 (April 1947): 113–21.

Barber, Edwin A. "The Ancient Pueblos, or the Ruins of the Valley of the Rio San Juan," *American Naturalist* 12 (September 1878): 606–14.

Beals, Ralph L., George W. Brainerd, and Watson Smith. "Archaeological Studies in Northeast Arizona: A Report on the Archaeological Work of the Rainbow Bridge–Monument Valley Expedition," *University of California Publications in American Archaeology and Ethnology* 44 (1945).

Benson, Seth B. "A Biological Reconnaissance of Navajo Mountain, Utah," *University of California Publications in Zoology* 40 (1935).

Bernheimer, Charles L. "From Kayenta to Rainbow Bridge," *Natural History* 20 (November-December 1920): 553–59.

————. "Encircling Navajo Mountain with a Pack Train," *National Geographic* 43 (February 1923): 197–224.

————. "Discovering a New Trail to the Rainbow Bridge," *Progressive Arizona* 3 (December 1926): 18–19 f.

————. "The Fifth Bernheimer Expedition to the Southwest," *Natural History* 27 (May-June 1927): 248–56.

————. "Cave Treasures of the Lukaichukais," unpaginated, *Touring Topics* 23 (September 1931).

Bigham, Barbara. "Grand Old Man of the Colorado," *American West* 13 (March-April 1976): 26 f.

Bolton, Herbert E. "Spanish Exploration in the Southwest, 1542–1706." In *Original Narratives of Early American History*, Vol. 2. New York: Scribners, 1916.

————, ed. "Pageant in the Wilderness: The Story of the Escalante Expedition to the Interior Basin, 1776, including the Diary and Itinerary of Father Escalante Translated and Annotated," *Utah Historical Quarterly* 18 (1950): 1–250.

Boyers, L. Morgan. "List of Birds Collected by the 1933 Rainbow Bridge–Monument Valley Expedition and Deposited with the University of California Museum of Vertebrate Zoology," *Rainbow Bridge–Monument Valley Expedition Bulletin* 4.

————. "Check List of Mammals Collected by the Rainbow Bridge–Monument Valley Expedition, Field Season of 1933," *Rainbow Bridge–Monument Valley Expedition Bulletin* 5.

Bradley, George Y. "George Y. Bradley's Journal, May 24–August 30, 1869," William Culp Darrah, ed. *Utah Historical Quarterly* 15 (1947): 31–72.

Brew, John Otis. "Neil Merton Judd, 1887–1976," *American Anthropologist* 80 (June 1978): 352–54.

Brugge, David M. "Vizcarra's Navajo Campaign of 1823," *Arizona and the West* 6 (1964): 223–44.

Burt, Olive W. "He Brands Snakes," *Desert Magazine* (October 1950): 9–12.

Burton, Robert E. "Preliminary Report on the Flora of Water Lily Canyon, with a Check List of Plants Collected During 1934," *Rainbow Bridge–Monument Valley Expedition Bulletin* 9.

————. "Report on Grasses Collected in the Rainbow Plateau Area During 1934," *Rainbow Bridge–Monument Valley Expedition Bulletin* 7.

Camp, Charles L. "A New Type of Small Bipedal Dinosaur from the Navajo Sandstone of Arizona," *University of California Bulletin of the Department of Geological Sciences* 24 (November 30, 1936): 39–56.

Cantelow, Ella Dales and Herbert Clair Cantelow. "Biographical Notes on Persons in Whose Honor Alice Eastwood Named Native Plants," *Leaflets of Western Botany* 8 (January 16, 1957).

Clark, C. C. "Zoology of Navajo Mountain," *Rainbow Bridge–Monument Valley Expedition Preliminary Bulletin, Biological Series* 4 (1935).

————. "Mammals of the Tsegi Drainage Area," *Rainbow Bridge–Monument Valley Expedition Preliminary Bulletin, Biological Series* 4 (1935).

Clover, E. U. and Lois Jotter. "Cacti of the Colorado River and Tributaries," *Bulletin of the Torrey Botany Club* 68 (1941): 409–19.

————. "Floristic Studies in the Canyon of the Colorado and Tributaries," *American Midland Naturalist* 32 (1944): 591–642.

Colton, Harold S. "A Brief Survey of the Early Expeditions into Northern Arizona," *Museum Notes* 2 (March 1, 1930): 1–4.

————. "Steamboating in Glen Canyon of the Colorado River," *Plateau* 35 (Fall 1962): 57–59.

Conrotto, Eugene L. "America's Last Indian War," *Desert Magazine* (March 1961): 32–34.

Correll, J. Lee. "Navajo Frontiers in Utah and Troublous Times in Monument Valley," *Utah Historical Quarterly* 39 (Spring 1971): 145–61.

Crampton, C. Gregory. "Historic Glen Canyon," *Utah Historical Quarterly* 28 (July 1960): 274–89.

————. "Historical Archaeology on the Colorado River." In Robert G. Ferris, ed., *The American West*, (Santa Fe: Museum of New Mexico Press, 1963): 213–18.

Crotty, Helen K. "Honoring the Dead: Anasazi Ceramics From the Rainbow Bridge–Monument Valley Expedition," *UCLA Museum of Cultural History Monograph Series* 22 (1983).

Culmer, Harry L. A. "Personal Diary of H. L. A. Culmer," *Southwest Monuments Special Report* 18 (June 1937).

————. "The Natural Bridges of White Canyon: A Diary of H. L. A. Culmer, 1905," Charlie R. Steen, ed. *Utah Historical Quarterly* 40 (Winter 1972): 55–111.

Cummings, Byron. "The Great Natural Bridges of Utah," *National Geographic* 21 (1910): 157–66.

————. "The Kivas of the San Juan Drainage," *American Anthropologist* 17 (1915): 272–82.

————. "Arizona Navajo National Monument," *Art and Archaeology* 10 (July-August 1920): 27–36.

————. "White Man's Discovery of the Natural Bridge," *Progressive Arizona* 3 (July 1926): 22–24.

————. "Prehistoric Pottery of the Southwest," *Kiva* 1 (1935): 1–8.

————. "Navajo Sand Paintings," *Kiva* 1 (March 1936): 1–2.

————. "Early Days in Utah." In *So Live the Works of Men: Seventieth Anniversary Volume Honoring Edgar Lee Hewett*. Albuquerque: University of New Mexico Press, 1939.

Cummings, Malcolm B. "I Finished Last in the Race to Rainbow Bridge," *Desert Magazine* (May 1940): 22–25.

————. "Recollections of Discovery of Rainbow Bridge," *Cummings Publication Council Bulletin* 1 (1959): 15–16.

Danson, Edward B. "The Glen Canyon Project," *Plateau* 30 (1958): 75–78.

Darrah, William Culp. "Powell of the Colorado," *Utah Historical Quarterly* 28 (1960): 223–31.

————. "John Welsey Powell and an Understanding of the West," *Utah Historical Quarterly* 37 (Spring 1969): 146–51.

Dellenbaugh, Frederick Samuel. "F. S. Dellenbaugh of the Colorado: Some Letters Pertaining to the Powell Voyages and the History of the Colorado River," C. Gregory Crampton, ed. *Utah Historical Quarterly* 37 (Spring 1969): 214–43.

Douglass, Andrew Ellicott. "The Secret of the Southwest Solved by Talkative Tree Rings," *National Geographic* 56 (December 1929): 737–70.

Douglass, William B. "The Discovery of Rainbow Natural Bridge," *Our Public Lands* 5 (1955): 8–9 f.

Dyar, W. W. "The Colossal Bridges of Utah, a Recent Discovery of Natural Wonders," *National Geographic* 15 (September 1904): 367–68.

Eastwood, Alice. "General Notes of a Trip Through Southeastern Utah," *Zoe* 3 (January 1893).

———. "Lists of Plants Collected in Southeastern Utah," *Zoe* 4 (July 1893).

———. "Two New Species of Aquilegia from the Upper Sonoran Zone of Colorado and Utah," *California Academy of Sciences Proceedings* (2) 4 (March 1895).

———. "Report on a Collection of Plants from San Juan County, Southeastern Utah," *California Academy of Sciences Proceedings* (2) 6 (August 1896): 271–329.

Eaton, Theodore H., Jr. "Report on Amphibians and Reptiles of the Navajo Country Based upon Field Work with the Rainbow Bridge–Monument Valley Expedition During 1933," *Rainbow Bridge–Monument Valley Expedition Bulletin* 3 (June 1935).

———. "Amphibians and Reptiles of the Navaho Country," *Copeia* 3 (October 15, 1935).

Farmer, Jared. "Field Notes: Glen Canyon and the Persistence of Wilderness," *Western Historical Quarterly* 27 (Summer 1996): 211–22.

———. "Undiscovered to Undiscoverable: Gregory Natural Bridge," *Utah Historical Quarterly* 63 (Spring 1995): 100–21.

Farnsworth, Reed W. "Herbert Ernest Gregory: Pioneer Geologist of Southern Utah," *Utah Historical Quarterly* 30 (Winter 1962): 76–84.

Foster, Gene. "A Brief Archaeological Survey of Glen Canyon," *Plateau* 25 (1952): 21–26.

———. "Petrographic Art in Glen Canyon," *Plateau* 27 (1954): 6–18.

Fowler, Don D. and Catherine S. Fowler. "John Wesley Powell, Anthropologist," *Utah Historical Quarterly* 37 (Spring 1969): 152–72.

———, eds. *Anthropology of the Numa: John Wesley Powell's Manuscripts on the Numic Peoples of Western North America, 1868–1880.* Smithsonian Contributions to Anthropology 14 (ca. 1972).

Frazier, Russell G. "El Vado de Los Padres [The Crossing of the Fathers]." *Desert Magazine* (July 1940): 3–5.

Gaines, Xerpha M. "Plants in Glen Canyon," *Plateau* 30 (1957): 31–34.

Gillmor, Frances. "The Wetherills of Kayenta," *Kiva* 11 (November 1945): 9–11.

Goetzmann, William H. "The Wheeler Surveys and the Decline of Army Exploration in the West." In Ferris, Robert G., ed., *The American West: An Appraisal*, Santa Fe: Museum of New Mexico Press, 1963, 37–47.

Gray, Ralph. "Three Roads to Rainbow," *National Geographic* 111 (April 1957): 546–61.

Gregory, Herbert E. "Scientific Explorations in Southern Utah," *American Journal of Science* 243 (October 1945): 527–49.

Grey, Zane. "Down into the Desert," *Ladies Home Journal* (January 1924).

———. "Trails Over the Glass Mountains," *Outdoor America* (January 1924). Reprinted in: Zane Grey, *The Undiscovered Zane Grey Fishing Stories*, 1983, 145–59.

———. "Breaking Through: The Story of My Life," *American Magazine* (July 1926): 11–13.

Hafen, Leroy R. "Armijo's Journal," *Huntington Library Quarterly* 11 (1947): 87–101; also published as "Armijo's Journal of 1829–30; the Beginning of Trade Between New Mexico and California," *Colorado Magazine* 27 (April 1950): 120–31.

Hall, Al and Hubert Lowman. "We Saw a Rockfall in Glen Canyon," *Desert Magazine* (January 1957): 9–10.

Hall, Ansel Franklin. "Wanted: 10 Explorers," *California Monthly* 30 (May 1933): 49–50.

———. "In Navajo Land," *California Monthly* 31 (September 1933): 17–18 f.

———. "General Report, Rainbow Bridge–Monument Valley Expedition Field Season of 1934," *Rainbow Bridge–Monument Valley Expedition Bulletin* 6.

———. "Exploring the Navajo Country," *American Forests* 42 (1936): 382.

———. "The Field Program of the Rainbow Bridge–Monument Valley Expedition," *Rainbow Bridge–Monument Valley Expedition Bulletin* 8.

———. "General Information for Members of the Rainbow Bridge–Monument Valley Expedition," *Rainbow Bridge–Monument Valley Expedition Bulletin* 10.

———. "The Northern Navajo Country: Annotated Reading List," *Rainbow Bridge–Monument Valley Expedition Bulletin*.

Hall, E. T., Jr., "Report on Archeological Survey of Main Tsegi," *Rainbow Bridge–Monument Valley Expedition Preliminary Bulletin*, Archeological Series no. 3.

Heald, Weldon F. "Who Discovered Rainbow Bridge?" *Sierra Club Bulletin* 40 (October 1955): 24–28.

Henderson, Randall. "When the Boats Wouldn't Float—We Pulled 'Em," *Desert Magazine* (September 1950): 5–11.

Hill, Joseph John. "Spanish and Mexican Exploration and Trade Northwest from New Mexico into the Great Basin, 1765–1853," *Utah Historical Quarterly* 3 (January 1930): 3–23.

Hite, Cass. "Colorado River Gold," *Utah Historical Quarterly* 7 (1939): 139–40.

Holmes, E. F. "The Great Natural Bridges of Utah," *National Geographic* 18 (1907): 199–204.

Hunt, Charles B. "Around the Henry Mountains with Charlie Hanks," *Utah Geology* 4 (Fall 1977): 95–104.

Ives, Ronald L. "Bert Loper—The Last Chapter," *Journal of Arizona History* 17 (Spring 1976): 49–54.

Jackson, William Henry. "A Notice of the Ancient Ruins in Arizona and Utah Lying About the Rio San Juan," *Bulletin of the Geological and Geographical Survey of the Territories* 2 (1876).

———. "Report on the Ancient Ruins Examined in 1875 and 1877." In Hayden, F. V., *Tenth Annual Report* (1878), 409–50.

Jacobs, G. Clell. "The Phantom Pathfinder: Juan Maria Antonio de Rivera and His Expedition," *Utah Historical Quarterly* 60 (Summer 1992): 200–23.

Jennings, Jesse D. "The Aboriginal Peoples," *Utah Historical Quarterly* 28 (July 1960): 211–22.

———, and Floyd W. Sharrock. "The Glen Canyon: A Multi-discipline Project," *Utah Historical Quarterly* 33 (Winter 1965): 34–50.

Jensen, Frank. "Riverman," *Desert Magazine* (July 1962): 26–27.

Jones, Kumen. "First Settlement of San Juan County, Utah," *Utah Historical Quarterly* 2 (1928): 8–11.

Judd, Neil M. "Basketmaker Artifacts from Moki Canyon, Utah," *Plateau* 43 (Summer 1970): 16–20.

———. "Beyond the Clay Hills," *National Geographic* 45 (March 1924): 275–302.

———. "Byron Cummings, Archeologist and Explorer," *Science* 120 (1954).

———. "Byron Cummings, 1860–1954," *American Anthropologist* 56, Pt. 1 (1954): 870–72.

———. "Byron Cummings, 1860–1954," *American Antiquity* 20 (1954): 154–57.

———. "The Discovery of Rainbow Bridge," *Cummings Publication Council Bulletin* 1 (1959): 8–13.

———. "The Discovery of Rainbow Bridge," *National Parks Bulletin* 54 (November 1927): 6–16.

———. "Explorations in San Juan County, Utah." In *Explorations and Field-Work of the Smithsonian Institution in 1923. Smithsonian Miscellaneous Collections* 76 (1924): 77–82.

———. "On Some Names in Natural Bridges National Monument," *National Parks Magazine* (October 1967): 16–19.

———. "Pioneering in Southwestern Archeology." In Erik K. Reed and Dale S. King, eds. *For the Dean*, 1950, 11–27.

———. "Rainbow Trail to Nonnezoshe," *National Parks and Conservation Magazine* 47 (November 1973): 4–8.

———. "Reminiscences in Southwestern Archeology," *Kiva* 26 (1960): 1–6.

———. "Return to Rainbow Bridge," *Arizona Highways* 43 (August 1967): 30–39.

Kelly, Charles. "Down the Colorado," *Utah Motorist* (August 1932): 5–8.

———. "At Eighty-three He is an Explorer," *Saturday Evening Post*, May 6, 1939.

———. "Lost Silver of Pish-la-ki [*sic*]," *Desert Magazine* (December 1940): 5–8.

———. "Hoskaninni [*sic*]," *Desert Magazine* (July 1941): 6–9.

———. "Proposed Escalante National Monument," *Desert Magazine* (February 1941): 21–22.

———. "Gold Hunters Are Like That!" *Desert Magazine* (July 1942): 13–15.

———. "River Gold," *Desert Magazine* (October 1942): 15–17.

———. "We Climbed to the Moki Ruin," *Desert Magazine* (January 1943): 5–8.

———. "Autographs in Stone," *Desert Magazine* 6 (June 1943): 9–12.

———. "The Three Who Lost," *Desert Magazine* (April 1945): 4–6.

———. "Mormon Crossing at Hole-in-the-Rock," *Desert Magazine* (May 1947): 10–14.

———. "New Road into the Utah Wilderness," *Desert Magazine* (February 1947): 10–14.

———. "Sand Waves," *Arizona Highways* (April 1949): 36–39.

———. "Chief Hoskaninni," *Utah Historical Quarterly* 21 (July 1953): 219–26.

———. "The Poke and Posey Wars," *Desert Magazine* (May 1965): 18–19.

———, and Charlotte Martin. "Zeke Johnson's Natural Bridges," *Desert Magazine* (November 1947): 12–15.

Kerr, Walter A. "Byron Cummings, Classic Scholar and Father of University Athletics," *Utah Historical Quarterly* 23 (1955): 145–50.

Kidder, Alfred Vincent. "Earl Halstead Morris—1889–1956," *American Antiquity* (April 1957).

———. "Reminiscences in Southwest Archaeology, I," *Kiva* 25 (1959): 1–32.

Krutch, Joseph Wood. "Lightning Water." In Alan Ternes, ed., *Ants, Indians, and Little Dinosaurs*, New York: Charles Scribner's Sons, 1975, 288–91.

Lambert, Neal. "Al Scorup: Cattleman of the Canyons," *Utah Historical Quarterly* 32 (Summer 1964): 301–20.

Lavender, David. "Mormon Cowboy," *Desert Magazine* (October 1940): 4–8.

Leake, Harvey and Gary Topping. "The Bernheimer Explorations in Forbidding Canyon," *Utah Historical Quarterly* 55 (Spring 1987): 137–66.

Lee, Joe. "My Wonderful Country," *Frontier Times* (February-March, 1974): 6-15 ff.

Lee, Katie. "Glen Canyon Diary, 1956," *Journal of Arizona History* 17 (Spring 1976): 54–56.

Lindsay, Alexander J., Jr., "Saving Prehistoric Sites in the Southwest," *Archaeology* 14 (1961): 245–49.

Lister, Robert H. "Salvage Archaeology Today and the Glen Canyon Project." In Ferris, Robert G., ed., *The American West: An Appraisal*, Santa Fe: Museum of New Mexico Press, 1963, 219–25.

————, and Florence C. Lister. "The Wetherills: Vandals, Pothunters, or Archaeologists," *Prehistory and History in the Southwest. Archaeological Society of New Mexico Papers* 11 (1985): 147–53.

Longwell, Chester R. "Memorial to Herbert Ernest Gregory (1869–1952)," *Geological Society of America Proceedings*, Annual Report: 1953 (May 1954): 114–23.

Lyman, Albert R. "The Land of Pagahrit," *Improvement Era* 12 (October 1909): 934–38.

————. "A Relic of Gadionton: Old Posey as I Knew Him," *Improvement Era* (July 1923): 791–801.

————. "First White Men in San Juan County, Utah," *Utah Historical Quarterly* 2 (January 1929): 11–13.

————. "Pahute Biscuits," *Utah Historical Quarterly* 3 (1930): 118–20.

————. "Memories of the Pagahrit," *Desert Magazine* (April 1963): 24–25.

MacClary, John Stewart. "Trail-Blazer to Rainbow Bridge," *Desert Magazine* 1 (June 1938): 4–5 f.

————. "Shortcut to Rainbow Bridge," *Desert Magazine* (May 1939): 3–6.

McKean, Frank. "They Really Dig It at Glen Canyon," *Utah Alumnus* (October 1959): 16.

McPherson, Robert S. "Paiute Posey and the Last White Uprising," *Utah Historical Quarterly* 53 (Summer 1985): 248–67.

————. "Navajos, Mormons, and Henry L. Mitchell: Cauldron of Conflict on the San Juan," *Utah Historical Quarterly* 55 (Winter 1987): 50–65.

————."Canyons, Cows, and Conflict: A Native American History of Montezuma Canyon, 1874–1933," *Utah Historical Quarterly* 60 (Summer 1992): 238–58.

Marston, Otis R. "River Runners: Fast Water Navigation," *Utah Historical Quarterly* 28 (July 1960): 291–308.

————. "Early Travel on the Green and Colorado Rivers," *Smoke Signal* (Fall 1965): 231–36.

————. "The Lost Journal of John Colton Sumner," *Utah Historical Quarterly* 37 (Spring 1969): 173–89.

————. "With Powell on the Colorado." In *Brand Book 2 of the San Diego Corral of the Westerners*, 1971: 64–76.

Miller, David E. "The San Juan Mission Call," *Utah Historical Quarterly* 26 (1958): 161–68.

————. "Discovery of Glen Canyon, 1776," *Utah Historical Quarterly* 26 (1958): 221–35.

————. "Murder at Rincon," *Salt Lake Tribune*, March 23, 1958.

————. "Hole-in-the-Rock," *Desert Magazine* (September 1959): 19–21.

Miller, G. B. "Mexican Hat," *Desert Magazine* (January 1941): 18.

Miller, William C. and David A. Breternitz. "1957 Navajo Canyon Survey: Preliminary Report," *Plateau* 30 (January 1958): 72–74.

————. "1958 Navajo Canyon Survey: Preliminary Report," *Plateau* 31 (July 1958): 3–7.

Morgan, Dale L., ed. "The Exploration of the Colorado River in 1869," *Utah Historical Quarterly* 15 (1947).

————, ed. "The Exploration of the Colorado River and the High Plateaus of Utah in 1871–72," *Utah Historical Quarterly* 16–17 (1948–49).

Moseley, M. Edward. "The Discovery and Definition of Basketmaker," *Masterkey* 40 (October-December 1966).

Mott, Dorothy Challis. "'Natani Yazi': Little Captain," *Arizona Highways* 15 (October 1939): 4–5 f.

Muench, Joyce Rockwood. "They Run the Ferry at Hite," *Desert Magazine* (February 1952): 22–26.

————. "Art Greene: A Friend by the Side of the Road," *Arizona Highways* 40 (January 1964): 44–47.

Nichols, E. Tad. "Glen Canyon as It Was: A Photographic Record," *Journal of Arizona History* 17 (Spring 1976): 57–68.

Pattison, N. B. and L. D. Potter. "Prehistoric and Historic Steps and Trails of Glen Canyon-Lake Powell," *Lake Powell Research Project Bulletin* 45 (May 1977): 1–84.

Pepper, Choral. "Caves, Canyons, and Caches," *Desert Magazine* (September 1964): 16–19 f.

Peterson, Charles S. "In Memoriam: C. Gregory Crampton, 1911–95," *Utah Historical Quarterly* 63 (Fall 1995): 370–73.

Pogue, Joseph E. "Nonnezoshe—The Great Natural Bridge of Southern Utah," *Science* 33 (March 3, 1911): 355.

————. "The Great Rainbow Natural Bridge of Southern Utah," *National Geographic* 22 (November 1911): 1048–56.

————. "Great Rainbow Natural Bridge," *Grand Valley Times*, April 12, 1912.

Powell, John Wesley. "Major J. W. Powell's Report on His Explorations of the Rio Colorado in 1869." *Utah Historical Quarterly* 15 (1947): 21–27.

————. "Major Powell's Journal, July 2–August 28, 1869," William Culp Darrah, ed. *Utah Historical Quarterly* 15 (1947): 125–31.

————. "Journal of W. C. Powell, April 21, 1871 to December 7, 1872," Charles Kelly, ed. *Utah Historical Quarterly* 16-17 (1948–49): 257–478.

Prudden, T. Mitchell. "A Summer Among the Cliff Dwellers," *Harper's Magazine* 94 (September 1896).

———. "An Elder Brother to the Cliff-Dwellers," *Harper's Magazine* 95 (June 1897): 56–62.

———. "The Prehistoric Ruins of the San Juan Watershed," *American Anthropologist* 5 (April-June 1903): 224–28.

———. "The Circular Kivas of Small Ruins in the San Juan Watershed," *American Anthropologist* 16 (January-March 1914): 33–58.

———. "A Further Study of Prehistoric Small House Ruins in the San Juan Watershed," *American Anthropological Association Memoirs* 5 (1918): 3 f.

———. "Prehistoric Small House Ruins," *El Palacio* 5 (1918).

Rabbitt, John C. and Mary C. "The U.S. Geological Survey: 75 Years of Service to the Nation, 1879–1954," *Science* 119 (May 28, 1954): 741–58.

Rasmussen, Stan. "Adventure in the Glen Canyon of the Colorado," *Reclamation Era* (May 1958): 41–45.

Redd, Charles E. "Short Cut to the San Juan." In *1949 Brand Book*. Denver: Denver Posse of the Westerners, 1950.

Reebel, Mollie B. "Navajo Mountain: A Community and Health Experiment in the Wilderness," *National Association of Indian Affairs Bulletin* 24 (1935).

Reed, Erik K. "The Distinctive Features and Distribution of the San Juan Anasazi Culture," *Southwestern Journal of Anthropology* 2 (1946).

Reilly, P. T. "How Deadly Is Big Red?" *Utah Historical Quarterly* 37 (Spring 1969): 244–60.

———. "Norman Nevills: Whitewater Man of the West," *Utah Historical Quarterly* 55 (Spring 1987): 181–200.

———. "The Lost World of Glen Canyon," *Utah Historical Quarterly* 63 (Spring 1995): 122–34.

Richardson, Elmo R. "Federal Park Policy in Utah: The Escalante National Monument Controversy of 1935–1940," *Utah Historical Quarterly* 33 (Spring 1965): 109–33.

Richardson, Gladwell [Maurice Kildare]. "Murder at Rincon," *Frontier Times* (May, 1971): 26–28 f.

Richardson, Gladwell [Toney]. "Traders at Tonalea," *Desert Magazine* (January 1948): 17–20.

Richardson, Sullivan C. "Hole-in-the-Rock," *Improvement Era* 43 (January 1940): 18–21 f.

Rinaldo, John B. "An Archaeological Reconnaissance of the San Juan and Colorado Rivers," *Rainbow Bridge–Monument Valley Expedition Preliminary Bulletin*, Archaeological Series no. 5.

————. "Review of Survey and Excavations in Lower Glen Canyon, 1952–1958," *American Antiquity* 28 (1962): 111–12.

Roberts, Frank H. Jr. "A Survey of Southwestern Archaeology," *American Anthropologist* 37 (1935): 1–35.

Roosevelt, Theodore. "Across the Navajo Desert," *Outlook* 105 (October 11, 1913): 308–17.

Rusho, W. L. "Charlie Spencer and His Wonderful Steamboat," *Arizona Highways* 38 (August 1962): 34–39.

————, ed. "River Running 1921: The Diary of E. L. Kolb," *Utah Historical Quarterly* 37 (Spring 1969): 269–83.

Rust, David D. "Boating on the Colorado," *Improvement Era* 4 (May 1901): 507–12.

Scholl, Barry. "Double Identity: The Two Lives of Dick Sprang," *Salt Lake City* (May-June 1996): 42–45 ff.

Scott, Kenneth W. "The Heritage of the Desert: Zane Grey Discovers the West," *Markham Review* 2 (February 1970): 10–14.

Smith, Dwight L. "The Engineer and the Canyon," *Utah Historical Quarterly* 28 (1960): 263–73.

————. "A Survey of the History of Exploration of the Colorado River." In *Denver Westerners Brand Book*, 1962.

————. "Hoskaninni: A Gold Mining Venture in Glen Canyon." In K. Ross Toole, ed., *Probing the American West: Papers from the Santa Fe Conference*. Santa Fe: Museum of New Mexico Press, 1962.

Smith, Watson. "Ansel Franklin Hall, 1894–1962," *American Antiquity* 29 (October 1963): 228–29.

————. "Who Didn't Discover the Bernheimer Bridge?" *Kiva* 43 (1977): 83–87.

Stearns, Frederic A. "Rainbow Bridge Exploration Trip via the Colorado River," *Pacific Mutual News* (October 1931): 378–83.

Steward, John F. "Journal of John F. Steward, May 22–November 3, 1871," William Culp Darrah, ed. *Utah Historical Quarterly* 16-17 (1948–49): 181–251.

Stone, Julius F. "Another Fling at Colorado River Rapids," *Ohio State University Monthly* 30 (November 1938): 17–18, 36.

Sumner, John C. "J. C. Sumner's Journal, July 6 to August 31, 1869," William Culp Darrah, ed. *Utah Historical Quarterly* 15 (1947): 113–24.

Tallsalt, Bert. "Ashkii Yazhi: Forgotten Friend of the Navajo," *Navajo-Hopi Observer*, (October 19, 1983), 6.

Tanner, Clara Lee. "Byron Cummings: 1860–1954," *Kiva* 20 (October 1954): 1–20.

Tanner, Vasco M. "Angus Munn Woodbury, 1886–1964," *Great Basin Naturalist* 25 (December 31, 1965): 81–88.

Thompson, Almon Harris. "Diary of Almon Harris Thompson," J. Cecil Alter and

Herbert E. Gregory, eds. *Utah Historical Quarterly* 7 (1939): 3–140.

Topping, Gary. "Charles Kelly's Glen Canyon Ventures and Adventures," *Utah Historical Quarterly* 55 (Spring 1987): 120–36.

———. "Harry Aleson and the Place No One Knew," *Utah Historical Quarterly* 52 (Spring 1984): 165–78.

———. "Herbert E. Gregory's Navajo Country Surveys," *Canyon Legacy* 24 (Summer 1995): 9–15.

———. "Personality and Motivation in Utah Historiography," *Dialogue: A Journal of Mormon Thought* 27 (Spring 1994): 73–90.

Turner, Christy G. II. "Mystery Canyon Survey: San Juan County, Utah, 1959," *Plateau* 32 (April 1960): 74–80.

———. "Further Baldrock Crescent Explorations: San Juan County, Utah, 1960," *Plateau* 34 (April 1962): 101–12.

———, and William C. Miller. "1960 Northeast Navajo Mountain Survey," *Plateau* 33 (January 1961): 57–68.

Utley, Robert M. "Reservation Trader in Navaho History," *El Palacio* 68 (Spring 1961).

Visher, S. S. "Herbert Ernest Gregory, 1869–1952," *Association of American Geographers Annals* 42 (December 1952): 322–23.

Walker, Don D. "The Carlisles: Cattle Barons of the Upper Basin," *Utah Historical Quarterly* 32 (Summer 1964): 268–84.

Warner, Ted J. "The Significance of the Dominguez–Vélez de Escalante Expedition." In *Charles Redd Monographs in Western History: Essays on the American West, 1973–1974* 5 (Provo, Utah: Brigham Young University Press: 1975): 63–80.

Wedel, Waldo R. "Neil Merton Judd, 1887–1976," *American Antiquity* 43 (July 1978): 399–404.

Wetherill, Ben W. "General Report of the Archaeological Work," *Rainbow Bridge–Monument Valley Expedition Preliminary Bulletin*, Archaeological Series no. 1.

Wetherill, Fanny. "The Navaho People," *Masterkey* 11 (January 1937): 16–17.

Wetherill, John. "Navajo National Monument," *Southwestern Monuments Monthly Report* (March 1934): 2–6.

———. "Navaho Indian History and CWA Work," *Southwestern Monuments Monthly Report Supplement* (April 1934): A–D.

———. "Notes on the Discovery of Betatakin," *Plateau* 27 (April 1955): 23–24.

———. "Notes on the Discovery of Kiet Siel," *Plateau* 27 (January 1955): 18–20.

———, Pat M. Flattum, and Frederic A. Stearns. "Early Trip up the Colorado from Lee's Ferry to Rainbow Bridge, January 1931," *Plateau* 34 (October 1961): 33–49.

Wetherill, Louisa Wade [Lulu] and Byron Cummings. "A Navaho Folk Tale of Pueblo Bonito," *Art and Archaeology* 14 (1922): 132–36.

Wetherill, Marietta. "Prisoners of the Paiutes," *Desert Magazine* 15 (April 1952): 17–20.

Wetherill, Milton A. "Betatakin Ruins," *Kerley News*, July 6, 1936, 17.

———. "Conversation with: Milton Wetherill," *Western Gateways* 7 (Summer 1967): 43–45 f.

Wheat, Carl I. "The 1954 Navajo Canyon Expedition," *Explorers Journal* 45 (December 1967): 249–62.

Widtsoe, John A. "A Journal of John A. Widtsoe," A. R. Mortensen, ed. *Utah Historical Quarterly* 23 (July 1955): 195–231.

Wilson, Carol Green. "The Eastwood Era at the California Academy of Sciences," *Leaflets of Western Botany* (1953): 58–64.

Woodbury, Angus M. "The Colorado River—The Physical and Biological Setting," *Utah Historical Quarterly* 28 (1960): 199–208.

Woolley, Edwin G. "Journal of Two Campaigns by the Utah Territorial Militia Against the Navajo Indians, 1869," C. Gregory Crampton and David E. Miller, eds. *Utah Historical Quarterly* 29 (1961): 148–76.

Woolley, Franklin B. "Military Reconnaissance in Southern Utah, 1866," C. Gregory Crampton, ed. *Utah Historical Quarterly* 32 (1964): 145–61.

Wortley, Kenneth. "Zane Grey on the Rainbow Trail," *Westways* 73 (February 1981): 70–73.

Young, Karl. "Wild Cows of the San Juan," *Utah Historical Quarterly* 32 (Summer 1964): 252–67.

Young, Stuart M. "In the Canyons of the Cliff-Dwellers," *Western Monthly* 12 (January-February 1911): 11 f.

———. "Statement of Stuart M. Young Concerning the Discovery of Rainbow Bridge," *Cummings Publication Council Bulletin* 1 (1959): 14.

Books and Government Reports

Adams, William Y. *Ninety Years of Glen Canyon Archaeology, 1869–1959*, Museum of Northern Arizona Bulletin 33, Glen Canyon Series no. 2. Flagstaff: Northern Arizona Society of Science and Art, Inc., 1960.

———. *Shonto: A Study of the Role of the Trader in a Modern Navaho Community*, Smithsonian Institution Bureau of American Ethnology Bulletin 188. Washington, D.C.: Government Printing Office, 1963.

———, Alexander J. Lindsay Jr., and Christy G. Turner II. *Survey and Excavation in Lower Glen Canyon, 1952–1958*. Flagstaff: Northern Arizona Society of Science and Art, 1961.

————, and Nettie K. Adams. *An Inventory of Prehistoric Sites on the Lower San Juan River, Utah*. Flagstaff: Northern Arizona Society of Science and Art, 1959.

Ambler, J. Richard, Alexander J. Lindsay, Jr., and Mary Anne Stein. *Survey and Excavations on Cummings Mesa, Arizona and Utah, 1960–1961*. Flagstaff: Northern Arizona Society of Science and Art, 1964.

Amsden, Charles Avery. *Prehistoric Southwesterners from Basketmaker to Pueblo*. Los Angeles: Southwest Museum, 1949.

Anderson, Keith M. *Archaeology on the Shonto Plateau*. Globe, Ariz.: Southwest Parks and Monuments Association, 1969.

Atkins, Victoria M., ed. *Anasazi Basketmaker: Papers from the 1990 Wetherill-Grand Gulch Symposium*. Salt Lake City: Bureau of Land Management, 1993.

Bailey, Garrick and Roberta Glenn. *A History of the Navajos: The Reservation Years*. Santa Fe: School of American Research Press, 1986.

Baker, Arthur A. *Geology of the Monument Valley-Navajo Mountain Region: San Juan County, Utah*, USGS Bulletin 865. Washington, D.C.: Government Printing Office, 1936.

Baker, Pearl. *Trail on the Water*. Boulder, Colo.: Pruett Press, 1969.

Baldwin, Gordon C. *The Ancient Ones: Basketmakers and Cliff Dwellers of the Southwest*. New York: W. W. Norton & Co., 1963.

Bartlett, Richard A. *Great Surveys of the American West*. Norman: University of Oklahoma Press, 1962.

Benally, Clyde. *Dineji Nakee Naahane: A Utah Navajo History*. Monticello, Utah: San Juan School District; Salt Lake City: University of Utah Printing Service, 1982.

Bernheimer, Charles L. *Rainbow Bridge: Circling Navajo Mountain and Explorations in the "Bad Lands" of Southern Utah and Northern Arizona*. Garden City, N. Y.: Doubleday, Page & Co., 1924.

Birney, Hoffman. *Roads to Roam*. Philadelphia: Penn Publishing Co., 1930.

Bolton, Herbert E. *Pageant in the Wilderness: The Story of the Escalante Expedition to the Interior Basin*. Salt Lake City: Utah State Historical Society, 1950.

Briggs, Walter. *Without Noise of Arms: The 1776 Dominguez-Escalante Search for a Route from Santa Fe to Monterey*. Flagstaff, Ariz.: Northland Press, 1976.

Castleton, Kenneth B. *Petroglyphs and Pictographs of Utah*, Vols. 1–2. Salt Lake City: University of Utah Press, 1979.

Chamberlin, Ralph Vary. *The University of Utah: A History of Its First Hundred Years, 1850 to 1950*. Salt Lake City: University of Utah Press, 1960.

Chapin, Frederick H. *The Land of the Cliff-Dwellers*. Boston: W. B. Clark, 1892.

Chavez, Angelico, tr. Ted J. Warner, ed. *The Dominguez-Escalante Journal: Their*

Expedition Through Colorado, Utah, Arizona, and New Mexico, in 1776. Provo, Utah: Brigham Young University Press, 1976.

Clark, Georgie White and Duane Newcomb. *Thirty Years of River Running.* San Francisco: Chronicle Books, 1977.

Cohen, Julius Henry. *They Builded Better Than They Knew.* New York: J. Messner, 1946.

Cole, LaMont C. *Report on the Herpetology of the Navajo Country.* Berkeley: Rainbow Bridge–Monument Valley Expedition, 1935.

Colton, Harold S. *Black Sand: Prehistory in Northern Arizona.* Albuquerque: University of New Mexico Press, 1960.

Comfort, Mary. *Rainbow to Yesterday: The John and Louisa Wetherill Story.* New York: Vantage Press, 1980.

Cook, William. *The WEN, the BOTANY, and the MEXICAN HAT: The Adventures of the First Women Through Grand Canyon, on the Nevills Expeditions.* Orangevale, Calif.: Callisto Books, 1987.

Crampton, C. Gregory. *Ghosts of Glen Canyon: History Beneath Lake Powell.* St. George, Utah: Publishers Place, 1986.

——. *Historical Sites in Cataract and Narrow Canyons, and in Glen Canyon to California Bar*, University of Utah Anthropological Paper No. 72. Salt Lake City: University of Utah Press, 1964.

——. *Historical Sites in Glen Canyon, Mouth of Hansen Creek to Mouth of San Juan River*, University of Utah Anthropological Paper No. 61. Salt Lake City: University of Utah Press, 1962.

——. *Historical Sites in Glen Canyon, Mouth of San Juan River to Lee's Ferry*, University of Utah Anthropological Paper No. 46. Salt Lake City: University of Utah Press, 1960.

——. *Outline History of the Glen Canyon Region 1776–1922*, University of Utah Anthropological Paper No. 42. Salt Lake City: University of Utah Press, 1959.

——. *The San Juan Canyon Historical Sites*, University of Utah Anthropological Paper No. 70. Salt Lake City: University of Utah Press, 1964.

——. *Standing Up Country: The Canyon Lands of Utah and Arizona.* New York: Alfred A. Knopf, 1964.

——, and Steven K. Madsen. *In Search of the Spanish Trail, Santa Fe to Los Angeles, 1829–1848.* Salt Lake City: Gibbs Smith, 1994.

Cummings, Byron. *The Great Natural Bridges of Utah*, University of Utah Bulletin 3, Part 1. Salt Lake City: University of Utah Press, Nov. 1910.

——. *The Ancient Inhabitants of the San Juan Valley*, University of Utah Bulletin 3. Salt Lake City: University of Utah Press, Nov. 1910.

———. *Indians I Have Known*. Tucson: Arizona Silhouettes, 1952.

———. *First Inhabitants of Arizona and the Southwest*. Tucson: Cummings Publication Council, 1953.

———. *The Discovery of Rainbow Bridge: The Natural Bridges of Utah and the Discovery of Betatakin*, Cummings Publication Council Bulletin 1. Tucson: Cummings Publication Council, 1959.

Cutler, Hugh C. *Corn, Cucurbits and Cotton from Glen Canyon*, University of Utah Anthropological Paper No. 80. Salt Lake City: University of Utah Press, 1966.

Daniels, Helen Sloan. *Adventures with the Anasazi of Falls Creek*, Occasional Papers of the Center of Southwest Studies. Durango, Colo.: Center of Southwest Studies, 1976.

Darrah, William Culp. *Powell of the Colorado*. Princeton: Princeton University Press, 1951.

Dellenbaugh, Frederick S. *The Romance of the Colorado River*. New York: G. P. Putnam's Sons, 1902.

———. *A Canyon Voyage: A Narrative of the Second Powell Expedition*. New York: G. P. Putnam's Sons, 1908.

Dixon, Winifred Hawkridge. *Westward Hoboes: Ups and Downs of Frontier Motoring*. New York: Charles Scribner's Sons, 1924.

Eaton, Theodore H., Jr. *Prehistoric Man in the Navajo Country*. Berkeley: National Youth Administration, 1937.

———, D. Morris, and R. Morris. *Amphibians and Reptiles of the Navaho Country*. Berkeley: National Youth Administration, 1937.

———, Ruth N. Martins, and Agnes J. Walker. *Geology of the Navajo Country*. Berkeley: National Youth Administration, 1937.

———, and G. Smith. *Birds of the Navaho Country*. Berkeley: National Youth Administration, 1937.

Euler, Robert C. *Southern Paiute Ethnohistory*, University of Utah Anthropological Paper No. 78. Salt Lake City: University of Utah Press, 1966.

Faunce, Hilda. *Desert Wife*. Boston: Little, Brown & Co., 1934.

Ferris, Robert G., ed. *The American West: An Appraisal*. Santa Fe: Museum of New Mexico Press, 1963.

Fewkes, Jesse Walter. *Preliminary Report on a Visit to the Navaho National Monument, Arizona*, Bureau of American Ethnology Bulletin 50. Washington, D.C.: Government Printing Office, 1911.

Foster, Mike. *Strange Genius: The Life of Ferdinand Vandeveer Hayden*. Niwot, Colo.: Roberts Rinehart Publishers, 1994.

Fowler, Don D. *1961 Excavations, Harris Wash, Utah*, University of Utah Anthropological Paper No. 64. Salt Lake City: University of Utah Press, 1963.

Fowler, Don D. and C. Melvin Aikens. *1961 Excavations, Kaiparowits Plateau, Utah*, University of Utah Anthropological Paper No. 66. Salt Lake City: University of Utah Press, 1963.

———, et al. *The Glen Canyon Archeological Survey, Parts 1, 2, and 3*, University of Utah Anthropological Paper No. 39. Salt Lake City: University of Utah Press, 1959.

Fradkin, Phillip L. *A River No More: The Colorado River and the West*. New York: Alfred A. Knopf, 1981.

Freeman, Lewis R. *Down the Grand Canyon*. New York: Dodd, Mead and Co., 1924.

Frost, Kent. *My Canyonlands: I Had the Freedom of It*. London: Abelard-Schuman, 1971.

Gaines, Xerpha M. *An Annotated Catalogue of Glen Canyon Plants*, Museum of Northern Arizona Technical Series 4. Flagstaff: Northern Arizona Society of Science and Art, 1960.

Gillmor, Frances and Louisa Wade Wetherill. *Traders to the Navajos: The Story of the Wetherills of Kayenta*. Boston: Houghton Mifflin Co., 1934.

Goetzmann, William H. *Army Exploration in the American West, 1803–1863*. New Haven, Conn.: Yale University Press, 1959.

———. *Exploration and Empire: The Explorer and the Scientist in the Winning of the American West*. New York: Alfred A. Knopf, 1966.

Goldwater, Barry M. *Delightful Journey Down the Green & Colorado Rivers*. Tempe: Arizona Historical Foundation, 1970.

Goodman, James M. *The Navajo Atlas*. Norman: University of Oklahoma Press, 1982.

Gregory, Herbert E. *The Navajo Country: A Geographic and Hydrographic Reconnaissance of Parts of Arizona, New Mexico, and Utah*, USGS Water Supply Paper No. 380. Washington, D.C.: Government Printing Office, 1916.

———. *Geology of the Navajo Country: A Reconnaissance of Parts of Arizona, New Mexico, and Utah*, USGS Professional Paper No. 93. Washington, D.C.: Government Printing Office, 1917.

———. *The San Juan Country: A Geographic and Geologic Reconnaissance of Southeastern Utah*, USGS Professional Paper No. 188. Washington, D.C.: Government Printing Office, 1938.

———, and Raymond C. Moore. *The Kaiparowits Region: A Geographic Reconnaissance of Parts of Utah and Arizona*, USGS Professional Paper No. 164. Washington, D.C.: Government Printing Office, 1931.

Grey, Loren. *Zane Grey: A Photographic Odyssey*. Dallas: Taylor Publishing Co., 1985.

Grey, Zane. *Riders of the Purple Sage*. New York: Harper & Brothers, 1912.

————. *The Rainbow Trail*. New York: Harper & Brothers, 1915.

————. *Tales of Lonely Trails*. New York: Harper & Brothers, 1922.

————. *The Vanishing American*. New York: Harper & Brothers, 1925.

————, et al. *Zane Grey, the Man and His Work: An Autobiographical Sketch, Critical Appreciations, and Bibliography*. New York: Harper & Brothers, 1928.

Gruber, Frank. *Zane Grey: A Biography*. New York: World Publishing Co., 1970.

Guernsey, Samuel James. *Explorations in Northeastern Arizona: Report on the Archaeological Fieldwork of 1920–1923*, papers of the Peabody Museum of American Archaeology and Ethnology 12. Cambridge, Mass.: Peabody Museum, 1931.

————, and Alfred Vincent Kidder. *Basket-Maker Caves of Northeastern Arizona: Report on the Explorations, 1916–1917*, papers of the Peabody Museum of American Archaeology and Ethnology 8. Cambridge, Mass.: Peabody Museum, 1921.

Gunnerson, James H. *1957 Excavations, Glen Canyon Area*, University of Utah Anthropological Paper No. 42. Salt Lake City: University of Utah Press, 1959.

Hafen, LeRoy R. and Ann W. *Old Spanish Trail, Santa Fe to Los Angeles*. Glendale, Calif.: Arthur H. Clark Co., 1954.

Hall, Ansel Franklin. *General Report on the Rainbow Bridge–Monument Valley Expedition of 1933*. Berkeley: University of California Press, 1934.

Hargrave, Lyndon L. *Report on Archaeological Reconnaissance in the Rainbow Plateau Area of Northern Arizona and Southern Utah*. Berkeley: University of California Press, 1935.

Harris, W. R. *The Catholic Church in Utah*. Salt Lake City: Intermountain Catholic Press, 1909.

Harvey, Mark W. T. *A Symbol of Wilderness: Echo Park and the American Conservation Movement*. Albuquerque: University of New Mexico Press, 1994.

Hayden, F. V. *Ninth Annual Report of the United States Geological and Geographical Survey of the Territories for the Year 1877*. Washington, D.C.: Government Printing Office, 1877.

————. *Tenth Annual Report of the United States Geological and Geographical Survey of the Territories Embracing Colorado and Parts of Adjacent Territories, Being a Report of Progress of the Exploration for the Year 1876*. Washington, D.C.: Government Printing Office, 1878.

————. *Eleventh Annual Report of the U.S. Geological and Geographic Survey of the Territories for the Year 1877*. Washington, D.C.: Government Printing Office, 1879.

Hegemann, Elizabeth Compton. *Navaho Trading Days*. Albuquerque: University of New Mexico Press, 1963.

Henderson, Randall. *On Desert Trails, Today and Yesterday*. Los Angeles: Westernlore Press, 1961.

Hillers, Jack. *"Photographed All the Best Scenery": Jack Hillers's Diary of the Powell Expeditions, 1871–1875.* Don D. Fowler, ed. Salt Lake City: University of Utah Press, [1972].

Hunt, Charles B., Paul Averitt, and Ralph L. Miller. *Geology and Geography of the Henry Mountains Region, Utah,* USGS Professional Paper No. 228. Washington, D.C.: Government Printing Office, 1953.

Inskip, Eleanor. *The Colorado River Through Glen Canyon Before Lake Powell: Historic Photo Journal, 1872–1964.* Moab, Utah: Inskip Ink, 1995.

Iverson, Peter. *The Navajo Nation.* Albuquerque: University of New Mexico Press, 1981.

Jackson, William Henry. *Time Exposure.* New York: G. P. Putnam's Sons, 1940.

———. *The Diaries of William Henry Jackson.* LeRoy R. Hafen and Ann W. Hafen, eds. Glendale, Calif.: Arthur H. Clark, 1959.

Jennings, Jesse D. *Accidental Archaeologist: Memories of Jesse D. Jennings.* Salt Lake City: University of Utah Press, 1994.

———. *Glen Canyon: A Summary,* University of Utah Anthropological Paper No. 81. Salt Lake City: University of Utah Press, 1966.

John, Elizabeth A. H. *Storms Brewed in Other Men's Worlds: The Confrontation of Indians, Spanish, and French in the Southwest, 1540–1795.* College Station: Texas A&M University Press, 1975.

Jones, Stan. *Glen Canyon Dam and Steel-Arch Bridge.* Page, Ariz.: Sun Country Publications, 1984.

Judd, Neil M. *Men Met Along the Trail: Adventures in Archaeology.* Norman: University of Oklahoma Press, 1968.

Kelly, Isabel T. *Southern Paiute Ethnology,* University of Utah Anthropological Paper No. 69. Salt Lake City: University of Utah Press, 1964.

Klinck, Richard E. *Land of Room Enough and Time Enough.* Albuquerque: University of New Mexico Press, 1958.

Kluckhohn, Clyde. *To the Foot of the Rainbow.* New York: Century Co., 1927.

———. *Beyond the Rainbow.* Boston: Christopher Publishing House, 1933.

———, and Dorothea Leighton. *The Navaho.* Cambridge: Harvard University Press, 1946.

Kolb, Ellsworth L. *Through the Grand Canyon from Wyoming to Mexico.* New York: Macmillan, 1914.

LaRue, E. C. *Colorado River and Its Utilization,* USGS Water Supply Paper No. 395. Washington, D.C.: Government Printing Office, 1916.

———. *Water Power and Flood Control of the Colorado River Below Green River, Utah,* USGS Water Supply Paper No. 556. Washington, D.C.: Government Printing Office, 1925.

Lavender, David. *One Man's West.* Garden City, N. Y.: Doubleday, Doran & Co., 1944.

————. *Colorado River Country*. New York: E. P. Dutton, Inc., 1982.

————. *River Runners of the Grand Canyon*. Grand Canyon and Tucson: Grand Canyon Natural History Association and University of Arizona Press, 1985.

Leiby, Austin N. "Borderland Pathfinders: The 1765 Diaries of Juan Maria Antonio de Rivera." Ph.D. dissertation, Flagstaff: Northern Arizona University, 1984.

Lindsay, Alexander J., Jr., J. Richard Ambler, Mary Anne Stein, and Philip M. Hobler. *Survey and Excavations North and East of Navajo Mountain, Utah, 1959–1962*, Museum of Northern Arizona Bulletin 45. Flagstaff: Northern Arizona Society of Science and Art, 1969.

Lipe, William D. *1958 Excavations, Glen Canyon Area*, University of Utah Anthropological Paper No. 44. Salt Lake City: University of Utah Press, 1960.

————. *Anasazi Culture and Its Relationship to the Environment in the Red Rock Plateau Region, Southeastern Utah*. New Haven, Conn.: Yale University Press, 1967.

————. *Prehistoric Cultural Adaptation in the Cedar Mesa Area, Southeast Utah*. Flagstaff: Northern Arizona Society of Science and Art, 1974.

————, Floyd W. Sharrock, David S. Dibble, and Keith M. Anderson. *1959 Excavations, Glen Canyon Area*, University of Utah Anthropological Paper No. 49. Salt Lake City: University of Utah Press, 1960.

Lister, Florence C. *Kaiparowits Plateau and Glen Canyon Prehistory: An Interpretation Based on Ceramics*, University of Utah Anthropological Paper. No. 71. Salt Lake City: University of Utah Press, 1964.

————, and Robert H. Lister. *Earl Morris & Southwestern Archaeology*. Albuquerque: University of New Mexico Press, 1968.

Lister, Robert H. *The Glen Canyon Survey in 1957*, University of Utah Anthropological Paper No. 30. Salt Lake City: University of Utah Press, 1958.

————. *Those Who Came Before: Southwestern Archeology in the National Park System*. Tucson: Southwest Parks and Monuments Association, 1983 [revised 1993].

————, and Florence C. Lister. *Anasazi Pottery*. Albuquerque: University of New Mexico Press, 1978.

Locke, Raymond Friday. *The Book of the Navajo*. Los Angeles: Mankind Publishing Co., 1976 [4th ed., 1989].

Long, Paul V. *Archaeological Excavations in Lower Glen Canyon, Utah, 1959–1960*. Flagstaff: Northern Arizona Society of Science and Art, Inc., 1966.

Lyman, Albert R. *The Voice of the Intangible*. Salt Lake City: Deseret News Press, 1936.

————. *Indians and Outlaws: Settling the San Juan Frontier*. Salt Lake City: Bookcraft, Inc., 1962.

————. *The Outlaw of Navajo Mountain*. Salt Lake City: Deseret Book Co., 1963.

Lyman, Karl R. *The Old Settler: A Biography of Albert R. Lyman.* Salt Lake City: Publishers Press, 1980.

McNitt, Frank. *Richard Wetherill: Anasazi.* Albuquerque: University of New Mexico Press, 1957.

———. *The Indian Traders.* Norman, Oklahoma: University Press, 1962.

———, ed. *Navaho Expedition: Journal of a Military Reconnaissance from Santa Fe, New Mexico, to the Navaho Country, Made in 1849 by Lieutenant James H. Simpson.* Norman: University of Oklahoma Press, 1964.

———. *Navajo Wars.* Albuquerque: University of New Mexico Press, 1972.

McPherson, Robert S. *A History of San Juan County: In the Palm of Time.* Salt Lake City: San Juan County Commission, 1995.

———. *The Northern Navajo Frontier, 1860–1900: Expansion Through Adversity.* Albuquerque: University of New Mexico Press, 1988.

Martin, Russell. *A Story That Stands Like a Dam: Glen Canyon and the Struggle for the Soul of the West.* New York: Henry Holt, 1989.

Miller, David E. *Hole-in-the-Rock: An Epic in the Colonization of the Great American West.* Salt Lake City: University of Utah Press, 1959.

Miser, Hugh D. *Geologic Structure of San Juan Canyon and Adjacent Country, Utah,* USGS Bulletin 751-D. Washington, D.C.: Government Printing Office, 1924.

———. *The San Juan Canyon, Southeastern Utah: A Geographic and Hydrographic Reconnaissance,* USGS Water Supply Paper No. 538. Washington, D.C.: Government Printing Office, 1924.

Moon, Samuel. *Tall Sheep: Harry Goulding, Monument Valley Trader.* Norman: University of Oklahoma Press, 1992.

Morris, Ann Axtell. *Digging in the Southwest.* Garden City, N. Y.: Doubleday, Doran, 1933.

Nelson, Nancy. *Any Time, Any Place, Any River: The Nevills of Mexican Hat.* Flagstaff, Ariz.: Red Lake Books, 1991.

Ortiz, Alfonso, ed. *Southwest.* Vols. 9 & 10 of *Handbook of North American Indians.* Ed. by William C. Sturtevant. Washington, D.C.: Smithsonian Institution, 1979 & 1983.

Parkhill, Forbes. *The Last of the Indian Wars.* New York: Collier Books, 1961.

Perkins, Cornelia Adams, Marian Gardner Nielson, and Lenora Butt. *Saga of San Juan,* np: San Juan County Daughters of Utah Pioneers, 1957.

Porter, Eliot. *The Place No One Knew: Glen Canyon on the Colorado.* San Francisco: Sierra Club, 1963.

Potter, Loren D. and Charles L. Drake. *Lake Powell: Virgin Flow to Dynamo.* Albuquerque: University of New Mexico Press, 1989.

Powell, John Wesley. *The Exploration of the Colorado River and Its Canyons.* Washington, D.C.: Government Printing Office, 1875.

————. *The Exploration of the Colorado River and Its Canyons*. Meadsville, Pa.: Flood and Vincent, 1895.

Prudden, Lillian Y., ed. *Biographical Sketches and Letters of T. Mitchell Prudden, M.D.* New Haven, Conn.: Yale University Press, 1927.

Prudden, T. Mitchell. *On the Great American Plateau: Wandering Among Canyons and Buttes, in the Land of the Cliff-Dweller and the Indian of To-day*. New York: G. P. Putnam's Sons, 1907.

Pyle, Ernie. *Home Country, 1939*. New York: William Sloane Associates, 1947.

Pyne, Stephen J. *Grove Karl Gilbert: A Great Engine of Research*. Austin: University of Texas Press, 1980.

Reed, Erik K. and Dale S. King, eds. *For the Dean: Essays in Anthropology in Honor of Byron Cummings on His Eighty-ninth Birthday, Sept. 20, 1950*. Tucson/Santa Fe: Hohokam Museums Association and Southwestern Monuments Association, 1950.

[Rice, William E.]. *Hite, September 17, 1946*. Richfield, Utah: William E. Rice, 1946.

Richardson, Gladwell. *Navajo Trader*. Philip Reed Ruton, ed. Tucson: University of Arizona Press, 1986.

Roosevelt, Nicholas. *Theodore Roosevelt, The Man as I Knew Him*. New York: Dodd, Mead & Co., 1967.

Roosevelt, Theodore. *A Book-Lover's Holidays in the Open*. New York: Charles Scribner's Sons, 1916.

Rothman, Hal K. *Navajo National Monument: A Place and Its People, An Administrative History*. Santa Fe: Southwest Cultural Resources Center, 1991.

Ruess, Everett. *On Desert Trails with Everett Ruess*. El Centro, Calif.: Desert Magazine Press, 1940.

Rusho, W. L. *Everett Ruess: A Vagabond for Beauty*. Salt Lake City: Peregrine Smith, 1983.

Scorup, Stena. *J. A. Scorup: A Utah Cattleman*. Published by author, nd.

Scott, Hugh Lenox. *Some Memories of a Soldier*. New York: The Century Co., 1928.

Sharrock, Floyd W. *1962 Excavations, Glen Canyon Area*, University of Utah Anthropological Paper No. 73. Salt Lake City: University of Utah Press, 1964.

————, and Edward G. Keane. *Carnegie Museum Collection from Southeast Utah*, University of Utah Anthropological Paper No. 57. Salt Lake City: University of Utah Press, 1962.

————, Keith M. Anderson, Don D. Fowler, and David S. Dibble. *1960 Excavations, Glen Canyon Area*, University of Utah Anthropological Paper No. 52. Salt Lake City: University of Utah Press, 1961.

————, et al. *1961 Excavations, Glen Canyon Area*, University of Utah Anthropological Paper No. 63. Salt Lake City: University of Utah Press, 1963.

Shepardson, Mary and Blodwen Hammond. *The Navajo Mountain Community: Social Organization and Kinship Terminology.* Berkeley: University of California Press, 1970.

Spence, Clark C. *Mining Engineers and the American West.* New Haven, Conn.: Yale University Press, 1970.

Spicer, Edward H. *Cycles of Conquest: The Impact of Spain, Mexico, and the United States on the Indians of the Southwest, 1533–1960.* Tucson: University of Arizona Press, 1962.

Sprang, Elizabeth. *Good-bye River.* Reseda, Calif.: Mojave Books, 1979.

Stanton, Robert Brewster. *The Hoskaninni Papers: Mining in Glen Canyon, 1897–1902,* University of Utah Anthropological Paper No. 54. C. Gregory Crampton and Dwight L. Smith, eds. Salt Lake City: University of Utah Press, 1961.

———. *Down the Colorado.* Dwight L. Smith, ed. Norman: University of Oklahoma Press, 1965.

Stavely, Gaylord. *Broken Waters Sing.* Boston: Little, Brown, 1971.

Stegner, Wallace. *Beyond the Hundredth Meridian: John Wesley Powell and the Second Opening of the West.* Boston: Houghton Mifflin, 1954.

———. *Mormon Country.* New York: Duell, Sloan & Pearce, 1942.

———. *The Sound of Mountain Water.* Garden City, N. Y.: Doubleday & Co., 1969.

Steward, Julian H. *Archaeological Reconnaissance of Southern Utah,* Bureau of American Ethnology Anthropological Paper No. 18. Washington, D.C.: Government Printing Office, 1941.

Stone, Julius F. *Canyon Country: The Romance of a Drop of Water and a Grain of Sand.* New York: G. P. Putnam's Sons, 1932.

Trafzer, Clifford E. *The Kit Carson Campaign: The Last Great Navajo War.* Norman: University of Oklahoma Press, 1982.

Turner, Christy G. II. *A Summary of the Archeological Explorations of Dr. Byron Cummings in the Anasazi Culture Area.* Flagstaff: Northern Arizona Society of Science and Art, 1962.

———. *Petrographs of the Glen Canyon Region: Styles, Chronology, Distribution, and Relationships from Basketmaker to Navajo.* Flagstaff: Northern Arizona Society of Science and Art, 1963.

Van Valkenburgh, Richard F. *A Short History of the Navajo People.* Window Rock, Ariz.: Navajo Service, 1938.

———. *Dine Bikeyah.* Window Rock, Ariz.: Navajo Service, 1941.

Wade, Henry. *The Begay Story.* Atascadero, Calif.: Begay Story, 1978.

Walker, Henry P. and Don Bufkin. *Historical Atlas of Arizona.* Norman: University of Oklahoma Press, 1979.

Walker, J. G. and O. L. Shepherd. *The Navajo Reconnaissance: A Military Exploration of the Navajo Country in 1859.* Los Angeles: Westernlore Press, 1964.

Ward, Albert E. *Inscription House*. Flagstaff: Northern Arizona Society of Science and Art, 1975.

Webb, George Ernest. *Tree Rings and Telescopes: The Scientific Career of A. E. Douglass*. Tucson: University of Arizona Press, 1983.

Weber, David J. *The Spanish Frontier in North America*. New Haven, Conn.: Yale University Press, 1992.

Westwood, Richard E. *Rough-Water Man: Elwyn Blake's Colorado River Expeditions*. Reno: University of Nevada Press, 1992.

Wetherill, Benjamin Alfred. *The Wetherills of the Mesa Verde: Autobiography of Benjamin Alfred Wetherill*. Maurine S. Fletcher, ed. Rutherford, N. J.: Fairleigh Dickinson University Press, 1977.

Wheeler, George Montague. *Report Upon United States Surveys West of the One Hundredth Meridian Vols. 1–10*. Washington, D.C.: Government Printing Office, 1875.

Wilson, Carol Green. *Alice Eastwood's Wonderland*. San Francisco: California Academy of Sciences, 1955.

Woodbury, Angus M. *Preliminary Report on Biological Resources of the Glen Canyon Reservoir*, University of Utah Anthropological Paper No. 31. Salt Lake City: University of Utah Press, 1958.

———. *Notes on the Human Ecology of Glen Canyon*, University of Utah Anthropological Paper No. 74. Salt Lake City: University of Utah Press, 1965.

———, Stephen D. Durrant, and Seville Flowers. *A Survey of Vegetation in Glen Canyon Reservoir Basin*, University of Utah Anthropological Paper No. 36. Salt Lake City: University of Utah Press, 1959.

———, et al. *Ecological Studies of Flora and Fauna in Glen Canyon*, University of Utah Anthropological Paper No. 40. Salt Lake City: University of Utah Press, 1959.

Woodbury, Richard B. *Alfred V. Kidder*. New York: Columbia University Press, 1973.

Woolsey, Nethella Griffin. *The Escalante Story: A History of the Town of Escalante, and Description of the Surrounding Territory*. Springville, Utah: Art City Publishing Co., 1964.

Wyman, Leland C. and Stuart K. Harris. *The Ethnobotany of the Kayenta Navajo: An Analysis of the John and Louisa Wetherill Ethnobotanical Collection*. Albuquerque: University of New Mexico Press, 1951.

Yost, Billie Williams. *Bread Upon the Sands*. Caldwell, Idaho: Caxton Printers, 1958.

Young, Norma Perkins. *Anchored Lariats on the San Juan Frontier*. Provo, Utah: Community Press, 1985.

Zwinger, Ann. *Wind in the Rock*. New York: Harper & Row, 1978.

Index